BORROWED POWER

**Edited by Bruce Ziff
and Pratima V. Rao**

BORROWED
POWER

ESSAYS ON CULTURAL
APPROPRIATION

Rutgers University Press
New Brunswick, New Jersey

Contents

10419   P (ZIF)

v

Part 6   Appropriation and Tangible Cultural Property

Acknowledgments

We have been very fortunate to have had support and encouragement from a number of people throughout the course of this project. Thanks are due to Barb Strange, Janice Williamson, Merle Metke, Catherine Bell, Michael Asch, Raymond Morrow, and Rob Williams for their help. Jonathan Hart, one of the contributors to the collection, provided a number of useful suggestions, many of which were adopted. Pat Nugent helped with the proofreading, and Karen Gall prepared the index. A special debt of gratitude is owed to David Schneiderman, our colleague and friend, who helped us at every turn.

We also wish to thank Rutgers University Press; its production staff; Martha Heller, the acquiring editor at Rutgers, who thoughtfully guided us through the production process from start to finish; Jess Lionheart, our copyeditor; and the University of Alberta, which provided a special grant to defray the costs of production.

Several of the pieces in this volume have appeared elsewhere. Some of these were revised for this collection. We are grateful for the permissions granted by the copyright holders:

- Joane Cardinal-Schubert, "In the Red," which appeared in *Fuse Magazine* (Fall 1989): 20–28. Used with the permission of the author.

- Rosemary Coombe, "The Properties of Culture and the Politics of Identity: Native Claims in the Cultural Appropriation Controversy," which appeared in *Canadian Journal of Law and Jurisprudence* 6(2) (July 1993): 249–285. Used with permission of the author and the *Canadian Journal of Law and Jurisprudence.*
- Kwame Dawes, "Re-Appropriating Cultural Appropriation," which appeared in *Fuse Magazine* (Summer 1993): 7–15. Used with the permission of the author.
- Lenore Keeshig-Tobias, "Stop Stealing Native Stories," which appeared in the *Globe and Mail*, January 26, 1990, A-7. Used with the permission of the author.
- J. Jorge Klor de Alva, "Nahua Colonial Discourse and the Appropriation of the (European) Other," which appeared in *Archives de Sciences Sociales des Religions* 77 (January-March 1992): 15–35. Used with the permission of the author.
- Nell Jessup Newton, "Memory and Misrepresentation: Representing Crazy Horse," which appeared in *Connecticut Law Review* 27(1995): 1003–1054. Used with the permission of the author.
- M. Nourbese Philip, "The Disappearing Debate," which appeared in her book *Frontiers: Essays and Writings on Race and Culture, 1984–1992* (Stratford, Ont.: Mercury Press, 1992): 269–285. Used with the permission of the author.
- Anthony Seeger, "Ethnomusicology and the Law," which appeared in *Ethnomusicology* 36(3) (Fall 1992): 345–359, © 1992 by the Board of Trustees of the University of Illinois. Used with the permission of the author and of the University of Illinois Press.

Finally, we are grateful to Joane Cardinal-Schubert for permission to reproduce her painting *Borrowed Power*, and for allowing that title to serve as the title for this collection.

Bruce Ziff and Pratima V. Rao

BORROWED
POWER

Bruce Ziff and Pratima V. Rao

Introduction to Cultural Appropriation: A Framework for Analysis

The term *cultural appropriation* has been defined as "the taking—from a culture that is not one's own—of intellectual property, cultural expressions or artifacts, history and ways of knowledge."[1] This simple description bristles with uncertainty: What do we mean by "taking"? What values and concerns are implicated in the processes of appropriation? And how, if at all, should we respond? These are among the questions that are addressed in *Borrowed Power: Essays on Cultural Appropriation.*

A Point of Departure

This is a complex topic, owing partly to the fact that cultural appropriation is a multidimensional phenomenon. Consider the following illustrations (all of which are drawn from, or inspired by, the essays in this collection):

- *Example 1:* At the beginning of the nineteenth century, sculpted marble friezes were taken from the Parthenon on orders from Lord Elgin (at one time the British ambassador to the Ottoman Empire). These so-called Elgin Marbles were later sold to the British Museum in 1916, where they remain on display.

I

- *Example 2:* A folksinger from the United States recorded an ancient Senegalese folk song, the writer of which is unknown.
- *Example 3:* A muscle relaxant known as d-turbocurarine is patented by a pharmaceutical company. It was derived from an Amazonian arrow poison.[2]
- *Example 4:* A white writer published stories learned from members of a West Coast Native band. According to the customs and traditions of that band, the stories can be retold only by select elders.[3]
- *Example 5:* A nonaboriginal artist paints works based on images of Native cultures of North America. Patterns and symbols found on carpets, earthware, blankets, and clothing are used. Images of the peoples of the region, dressed in traditional attire, are also created.
- *Example 6:* The Nahua peoples of Mexico, under the hegemonic control of Spain, adopt the colonial discourses of this imperial presence, assimilating the cultural practices of this (European) Other.
- *Example 7:* W. P. Kinsella published a series of stories set on the Hobbema reserve in Alberta. The stories are all fictional, as are the characters, though some of those characters are given names of people living on the reserve.
- *Example 8:* Jazz, blues, soul, rap, and other musical forms emanating out of the Black musical experience in America are adopted by white musicians and audiences as part of a mainstream musical tradition.

If these are all instances of appropriation, then the range is broad; the net is cast widely. This is partly due to the fact that the idea of a "culture" is at the heart of the concept under study. That term is as indeterminate as any found within the social sciences.[4] It cannot, therefore, be relied upon to set clear limits as to where the concept of cultural appropriation begins and ends.

Consider the inherent ambiguity found in the convenient but intellectually austere definition quoted previously. It speaks of takings "from a *culture* that is not one's own." This merely begs the question of what counts as a culture for these purposes. Can a coherent conception of that term be developed? It might be taken to refer to the customs, values, and rule systems of a social group. When we hear people talk about social practices by asserting that "in our culture, we . . . ," they might be referring to values that they believe to be commonly held. But this prompts questions about what those values are and what we mean when we talk about a sense of sharedness. These problems are aggravated by the fact that analysis of cultural appropriation sometimes also emphasizes that what is being appropriated are cultural goods. Used in that way, "culture" connotes some type of creative product (whether tangible or otherwise): these are the *objects* of appropriation.

The meaning of "appropriation" is also open-ended. The examples bear this out. However, from among that array three general points emerge: (1) appropriation concerns relationships among people, (2) there is wide range of modes through which it occurs, and (3) it is widely practiced.

First, because appropriation connotes some form of taking, it contemplates a relationship between persons or groups. At the most mundane level, the breach of an author's copyright or the theft of an artist's canvas is an appropriative act. Here we seem to be able to define the relevant actors with ease. However, in doing so, we are making a statement about the rights of *individuals* based on views about authorship or creation that give credit (in various forms) to a given person. In other words, our definition of the actors in this little scenario is value-laden and is therefore contentious.

The eight illustrations show that a much different notion of stakeholders is contemplated in this book. Ongoing attempts by Greece to repatriate the Parthenon Marbles depend on notions of nationalism and national heritage, not individual entitlements. Indeed, most of the essays in this book conceive of relationships among communities. And in thinking about appropriation in this way, we can base the organizing elements in our relation-based analysis on ethnicity, race, nationality, class, gender, and so forth. Appropriated cultural groups abound. Hence, "real" cowboy poets lament the emergence of "wannabes" who endeavor to invade the genre.[5] Digital samplers borrow snippets of songs and tunes to create musical collages in ways that flirt with copyright laws. Similarly, Henry Jenkins has described a form of textual poaching in which fans of popular culture borrow freely: "Undaunted by traditional conceptions of literary and intellectual property, fans raid mass culture, claiming its materials for their own use, reworking them as the basis for their own cultural creations and social interactions."[6]

The need to describe a community of insiders and outsiders is implicit in most of what has been said about the practice of appropriation. Once we speak of a relational activity, a boundary line must be drawn, and problems of definition emerge. Sometimes the "in-ness" or "out-ness" of a particular individual will be reasonably incontestable. It is of course inevitable that certain divisions among cultural groups will be amorphous. Nevertheless, some test of group belonging seems required in discussions about cultural appropriation.

Just as defining the parameters of a cultural group is difficult, so, too, is establishing a theoretical basis for connecting a particular cultural practice to that group. If cultural practices develop from an amalgam of influences, it becomes difficult to assign these to one group over another. To do so would at least mean determining what degree of nexus is required between a cultural good and a given community. The existence of shared cultures and histories suggests that sometimes these entitlements might also be shared or sharable.

The difficulty of finding a connection between communities (or individuals) and certain cultural products is associated with the nature of commonly held notions of authorship—that is, the idea that we can locate the source of a given work in one person. One critique of authorship is based on the concept of intertextuality, a phenomenon that affects the processes of reading and writing texts. Intertextuality implies that each reading of a work is unique; this is a natural outflow of the reader's individuality. This view also recognizes that an author does not work tabula rasa but rather draws relentlessly on past creations. The result is that any given text is a "tissue of quotations drawn from innumerable centers of culture."[7] It is this latter element that is most salient here. It seems fair to question the validity of the conception of the author as creator when any given work of art is inevitably layered with the contributions of others. At the same time, and for the very same reason, it can be just as difficult to repose authorship in some cultural group.

Second, we can see from the eight examples that there are various possible *modes* of appropriation. Some forms are rather straightforward. The pilfering of the Parthenon Marbles was an act of appropriation (though views may differ on whether it was a *mis*appropriation). However, this description of appropriation will not do for the other listed examples; something more subtle is at play. The singer who performs a Senegalese folk song does not preclude others from doing the same. In other words, the taking of the song does not lead to a corresponding deprivation of the appropriated groups in the same way as it would if tangible objects were involved. Such is the nature of intellectual property interests: they give rise to what is sometimes referred to as nonrivalrous (i.e., nonexclusive) possession.

In addition, the remaining examples represent even more attenuated types of taking (at least if we view the Elgin Marbles example as the pure form). The borrowing of genres or the creation of stories *about* a culture is different again from the verbatim rendering of a song. But this is not to say that there is no appropriation in these instances. All of the examples reflect the central idea. The styles, forms, images, and topics were chosen by the various (appropriating) artists presumably because there is something evocative about them. Each such case is an instance of a current actor drawing on the creations of others.

Third, given the array of processes that can fall under the rubric of an appropriation, and the communities that it can affect, we can see that cultural appropriation is a pervasive phenomenon. If we conceive of the letters of the alphabet used in the English language as a cultural artifact belonging to the ancient Phoenicians (to whom its origins are attributed), we can appreciate how much latent traffic can occur in just this one cultural good. Acts of appropriation happen all around us in a vast number of creative domains as cultural influences blend, merge, and synthesize. The illustrations set out previously are about various creative realms (music, narrative, art, science), but many more domains exist (dance, philosophy, theology).

Moreover, appropriation can be viewed as a multidirectional phenomenon. Although it is perceived primarily as a taking from a subordinate into a dominant culture, this is not the only type of cultural borrowing that occurs. As example 6 illustrates, cultural appropriation can be construed to have a complementary opposite: cultural assimilation.

Given that appropriation is multidirectional, the issues could be conceived in purely acontextual terms. That is, we could raise questions about cultural takings of various kinds by members of culture A from culture B and vice versa, and through a type of "moral algebra," we could search for principles of universal fairness.[8] We could also tally up the benefits and detriments of all spheres of cross-cultural contact. Whether William Shakespeare appropriated Danish culture in *Hamlet* would be as worthwhile a question as any of those raised by the listed examples. Indeed, the discussion so far, which has been intentionally presented in a rather clinical way, invites that type of analysis.

However, to adopt this symmetrical approach would assume away, or at least downplay, an important part of the current debate. In particular, it would obscure the fact that the important questions about cultural appropriation are the political ones. When white writers appropriate the images of Blacks, a political event has occurred. The same is true when commercial interests exploit African folklore or indigenous knowledge from South America. These are events that teach us about power relationships and, in part, about how the law seeks to respond to appropriation.

It may be useful at this point to consider the ways in which power and the relationships of power can be construed as central to the concept of cultural appropriation. Figure 1 attempts to generate an understanding of cultural appropriation as just one form of cultural transmission (of which another is cultural assimilation).[9] This figure expresses the differential access to sources of power and the consequences for cultures and cultural forms that flow from this differential access to power. This model can be considered as a supplement (if not an alternative) to the general framework outlined in subsequent sections of this Introduction.

This figure is a structural representation of the social processes involved in cultural transmission. Although, admittedly, it is a highly simplified and abstract depiction, its purpose is to contrast the ways in which the transmission of culture can be construed and implicated differentially depending on whether the subjectivity of the receiver of culture is identified as being from a dominant or a subordinate group. Viewed in this light, cultural transmission can connote an *assimilative* practice—a process whereby cultural minorities often

Figure 1

A Structural Representation of Cultural Transmission: Appropriation or Assimilation?

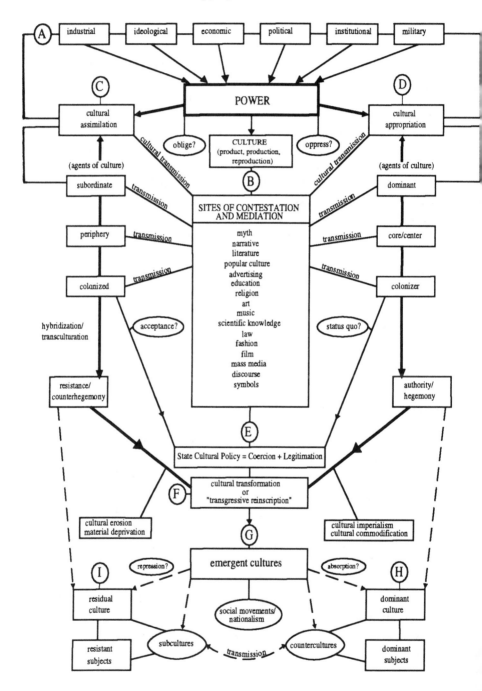

are encouraged, if not obliged, to adapt or assimilate the cultural forms and practices of the dominant group. Or cultural transmission can be seen as an *appropriative* practice—a process whereby dominant groups may be criticized and challenged when they borrow the cultural forms associated with subordinate groups. The analytical concept of power is situated as the focal point in this figure to indicate its centrality to questions of whether a particular cultural transmission should be read as appropriation or assimilation.

The specifics of the figure can be described in the following way. The boxes at A pointing toward "POWER" refer to the multiple sources of power. The box directly underneath "POWER" (at B) refers to the diverse and overlapping sociospatial networks and sites of power.[10] It is in these arenas that the production and reproduction of cultural products are contested and/or mediated.

Along the sidebars of the figure are C and D, under which are listed the various terms or labels used to describe the agents of culture occupying these spheres. (Note that the multiple identities of these agents of culture are informed by, among other things, gender, race, class, and status.) Depicted below are the antagonistic (and nonantagonistic) forms of responses that can flow from these agents of cultural transmission—namely, strategies of resistance to cultural assimilation/appropriation employed by subordinate groups that fear cultural erosion and may suffer material deprivation. Also found here are strategies of authority and legitimation exercised over the processes of cultural transmission by dominant groups that may practice cultural imperialism and engage in the commodification of cultural forms.

At E we see the cultural policies of the state. These policies might promote a "multicultural" (Canada) or a "melting pot" (United States) vision, but in either case these policies can give rise to institutionalized forms of both coercion and legitimation. It is through cultural policy (E) exercised by cultural agents (C and D) and made material in the sites of contestation and mediation (B) that may we witness cultural transformation (F).[11]

At G note the outflow of new emergent culture(s)—of which the principal offshoots are new legitimated forms of the dominant culture (H) espoused by the dominant subjects; the ancillary offshoots are the residual culture and practice (I) retained by subordinate and resistant subjects. In addition, note other extensions of the new emergent cultures—subcultures (linked to the residual culture) and countercultures (breaking from the dominant culture). What is reproduced or, conversely, what is repressed in the processes of cultural transmission (consisting of both appropriation and assimilation) results from the relative strengths and weaknesses of the cultural forces at play in a given time and place.

The figure emphasizes the place of politics within the cultural appropriation debate. Politics is generally about power: who gets to control the processes for allocating scarce resources. In the context of cultural appropriation, the resources at issue are the many and varied forms of cultural production, expression, and creation.

These elements have influenced heavily the selected coverage of this book. It is those aspects of cultural appropriation that we perceive as being an important part of the contemporary political landscape. Today's issues are about minority groups and subjects (the disempowered, colonized, peripheral, or subordinate) who are seeking to claim and protect rights to a cultural heritage. The reasons for this struggle—the values that are implicated in acts of cultural appropriation—are therefore rather central to this inquiry.

A Search for Values

There are those who view the recent attention paid to cultural appropriation with derision. Consider these stern rebukes:

> "Appropriation" is a key buzz-word in the bash-a-honky rhetoric now popular among "minorities" and others who have decided history has given them a raw deal.[12]

> The word "appropriation" . . . has lately become a rhetorical weapon in the hands of intellectuals claiming to speak for minority rights. Its power derives, oddly, from its very irrationality. In my experience, people hearing of it for the first time cannot believe that anyone would put forward so ludicrous an idea: even the most modest education in cultural history teaches us that art of all kinds has depended on the mixing of cultures.[13]

Importantly, both quotations reflect the idea that cultural appropriation is a political issue. These two critics see the controversy over appropriation as no more than an attempt by some to garner power. Equally, they both fail to consider the values that are implicated by acts of appropriation. What might these be?

When concerns about cultural appropriation arise within various domains, several claims tend to emerge. One is that cultural appropriation harms the appropriated community. This claim is therefore based on a concern for the integrity and identities of cultural groups. A second complaint focuses on the impact of appropriation on the cultural object itself. The concern is that appropriation can either damage or transform a given cultural good or practice. A third critique is that cultural appropriation wrongly allows some to benefit to the material (i.e., financial) detriment of others. A fourth argument is that current law fails to reflect alternative conceptions of what should be treated as property or ownership in cultural goods. This is a claim based on sovereignty.

The Prevention of Cultural Degradation

The first argument can be stated in capsule form: the cohesion of groups depends in part on the sharing of a common cultural heritage. In 1976, a UNESCO panel declared that "cultural property is a basic element of a people's identity."[14] The statement was made in support of the restitution of tangible cultural property, but it can perhaps be germane to all forms of appropriation. Such a claim focuses on the way in which cultural practices can enhance or diminish the vibrancy of certain groups.[15] Appropriation, the argument goes, can have corrosive effects on the integrity of an exploited culture because appropriative conduct can erroneously depict the heritage from which it is drawn. To the extent that the depiction is misleading, tears can appear in the fabric of a group's cultural identity.

The cogency of this claim depends on an understanding of both social policy and empirical evidence. The policy element focuses on the pursuit of cultural distinctiveness and multiculturalism and therefore on the question, Why should we be concerned about culture diversity? The empirical element involves an inquiry into how cultural appropriation produces harmful results.

Social Policy: The Worth of Difference

The policy questions relating to diversity have been examined by Jeremy Waldron. He has assessed the importance of cultural identity among marginalized groups by contrasting conceptions of cultural difference with a so-called cosmopolitan alternative.[16] Waldron considers and rejects the proposition that there exists a primary need that impels people to seek out cultural commonalities. For him, modern urban life in America involves a flourishing cosmopolitanism lived among a "kaleidoscope of cultures."[17] His thesis is that cosmopolitanism more realistically describes the modern world, with its myriad cultural, economic, moral, and political connections and interdependencies. This concept recognizes that cultures borrow from each other and that these transmissions occur in language, literature, culture, science, religion, and so forth. This leads Waldron to assert that a debt is owed to the world community and civilization, in addition to any comparable obligation that might be felt toward a particular cultural group.[18] It would be a short step for him to regard the practice of cultural appropriation as having positive consequences.

This analysis is highly revealing. Waldron rejects the preeminent importance of enhancing and protecting cultural difference, which is premised on an innate imperative to seek cultural identity. Nevertheless, he recognizes that diversity is a sine qua non to the existence of his cosmopolitan alternative;

without host cultures, the cosmopole cannot survive. At least for this limited purpose, difference is to be valued and sustained. Waldron also acknowledges that minority cultures are in a precarious position and that their continued existence is often threatened.[19] Perhaps most important, Waldron's entire approach assumes that our beliefs about pluralism are not products of nature but of politics. In other words, our respecting and encouraging difference or our stressing sameness is a policy decision.

As a matter of policy, a society might wish to promote homogeneity among its citizenry for any number of reasons—to quell dissent, to promote a particular vision of community, to give effect to principles of equality. The society might discount the importance of ethnic diversity on the belief that the interconnection of cultures is a normal process. Alternatively, liberal democracies may stress social variance, including cultural diversity, on the view that freedom involves individual quests for the good life. Both types of polity are built around notions of equality. The former promotes beliefs such as equality of opportunity; the latter, equal respect for difference. And within both, subordinate groups struggle. They may seek to achieve equality of condition; they may challenge the institutions that, by purporting to represent social neutrality, actually sanction a particular cultural baseline to which all are "allowed" to conform.[20]

Questions of cultural diversity can be based on public policy concerns. In a society in which diversity is the prized value, cultural appropriation may be of concern if it can be shown that appropriation erodes or degrades cultural identity and thereby threatens diversity. Moreover, even in a society in which diversity is *not* treated as a state goal, cultural cohesion may still be crucially important because cultural identity forms the basis of what is sometimes called the politics of difference or identity politics. We use these terms to mean the strategic mobilization of political power around a felt sense of common cause. In liberal democracies, oppressed groups vie for attention. For them, cultural connections can provide a cohesive force that allows for the development of identity, solidarity, and strength. To the extent that cultural appropriation can lead to cultural degradation, the ability to practice identity politics may be compromised.

Some of these ideas are reflected in Tony Kushner's play *Angels in America,* a poignant study of AIDS, homosexuality, and identity politics. The plot involves, among other things, a fictional account of the last days in the life of Roy Cohn, once a cohort of Senator Joseph McCarthy. When confronted by his doctor (Henry) with the news that he is dying of AIDS, Cohn's reply is sharp. He rejects the implication that he is gay because in the New York world of identity politics gay men are part of the disempowered and he, by contrast, is an influential political broker:

Your problem, Henry, is that you are hung up on words, on labels, that you believe they mean what they mean. AIDS. Homosexual. Gay. Lesbian. You think these are names that tell you who someone sleeps with, but they don't tell you that.

. . .

Like all labels they tell you one thing and one thing only; where does an individual so identified fit in the food chain, in the pecking order? Not ideology, or sexual taste, but something much simpler: clout. Not who I fuck or who fucks me, but who will pick up the phone when I call, who owes me favors. Now to someone who does not understand this, homosexual is what I am because I sleep with men. But really this is wrong. Homosexuals are not men who sleep with other men. Homosexuals are men who in fifteen years of trying cannot get a pissant anti-discrimination bill through City Council. Homosexuals are men who know nobody and who nobody knows.

. . .

Roy Cohn is not a homosexual man. Roy Cohn is a heterosexual man, Henry, who fucks around with guys.[21]

James Clifford has made a similar point. Reflecting on the discontinuity of cultures and traditions, and the fracturing of images of cultural purity in the modern world, he has suggested that "'cultural' difference is no longer a stable, exotic otherness; *self-other relations are matters of power and rhetoric rather than essence.*"[22]

If these assertions are right, then cultural appropriation is not only about the value of celebrating different cultural traditions; it is also about political praxis. This is true at least if the success of oppressed groups depends partly on the construction of a strong cultural identity. That identity becomes a glue that binds the movement. These images of culture allow for what bell hooks has called the "practice of self-love as a revolutionary intervention that undermines practices of domination" and that allows struggles of resistance to endure.[23]

Empiricism: Processes of Degradation

It is one thing to link culture to identity politics; it is another to connect this with cultural appropriation and degradation. Proving this connection is not an easy thing to do, but perhaps how the process might occur can be demonstrated. The first leg of the argument must focus on the role of representations of culture in the building of a collective image. Charles Taylor has maintained that our identity is shaped partially through recognition by others and partially through misrecognition and nonrecognition. The latter can produce palpable damage, particularly if demeaning images are mirrored back. On Taylor's view, "Nonrecognition or misrecognition can inflict harm, can be a form of oppression, imprisoning someone in a false, distorted, and reduced mode of being."[24]

The use of the swastika provides a helpful—if extreme—paradigm of the ways in which cultural symbols can be transformed through appropriation. It is well known that Adolf Hitler adopted the swastika symbol first to represent the Nazi Party and later to be part of the flag of the Third Reich. The ancient origins of that symbol are not as fully appreciated. The symbol is thought to be at least five thousand years old and prior to the Nazi appropriation was found among indigenous cultures all over the world, including several in North America. In China it has been used to represent the sun; it has been found on statues of the Buddha; it was central to the religious belief of the Jains. Among many cultures on different continents, it serves as a sign of good fortune.[25] Today the symbolic force of the swastika is marred for all of these cultures because of its close association with Nazi Germany. This appropriative act has all but destroyed the swastika, except perhaps for neofascists, who, during the Nazi swastika's half-life, continue to adopt it as an evocative symbol of hatred and intolerance.

However, it is not merely the appropriation of cognate symbols that matters. The potential infliction of cultural damage through the flawed rendering of the Other was explored by Edward Said in his influential work *Orientalism*.[26] Said attempted to demonstrate how Orientalist scholars, mainly from the West, devised a somewhat exotic, somewhat primitive, somewhat mysterious image of the Islamic Middle East; those images were perpetuated by succeeding generations of Orientalists, who built on and thereby validated these early conceptions. That process continued in the academic discipline of Orientalism without regard for the very different evidence that abounded. Stereotypes of Arabic life and custom are among the legacies of these depictions.

Said recognized that scholars impose structures upon the data they collect, transforming this material into units of knowledge.[27] But his description of Orientalism is of a far more pernicious force than even this suggests. He saw the study of the Middle East as both a premise and a preparation for colonial control. It created a dichotomy of East and West, essentializing the former, and described a social order susceptible to imperialism, facilitating a dominance of Occident over Orient. Concerns about the creation and perpetuation of stereotypes can be applied outside of the Orient as well.

The Preservation of Cultural Goods as Valuable Objects

The second complaint has two components. One is that cultural representations are best understood in their original setting; this is a claim based on aesthetics. Allied to this is a notion of stewardship. Here it is argued that we should protect cultural goods because they are a precious and finite resource.[28]

The aesthetic argument in relation to tangible artifacts stresses the importance of treating the work of art as intimately related to its setting. There can be no doubt that the experience of viewing the Parthenon Marbles in situ on the Acropolis would be different from seeing those works on display in the British Museum. Think of Marcel Duchamp's "Ready-mades": by taking ordinary objects (a shovel, a comb, a urinal) and placing them in a gallery, he forced a new reading of these items. Context counts.

When we turn to a consideration of intangibles, similar issues may arise. Dionne Brand's account of the curious treatment given Black blues singer Pinetop Perkins during an appearance at a workshop in Toronto in 1992 serves as illustration:

> Pinetop Perkins . . . is an old blues man and in a Black community of blues players and blues audiences his virtuosity would be accorded veneration and context as a kind of historic speech in a continuum. A language sent and understood and in action.
>
> At the blues workshop, Perkins is suspended in time, out of context, preserved as a museum piece, an icon no longer charged with readiness, place, dynamism, no longer seen as acting but inert, a remnant of a dead culture or rather a conquered culture.
>
> . . . At the blues workshop there were no contemporary Black blues pianists to spoil the mediation of Black culture as petrified in time, full of "ancient" sorrow but no present, disturbing anger and certainly no hostile intent.[29]

We can question whether anything wrong has happened here. Brand's complaint seems to be about how Pinetop Perkins was treated *and* about how poorly the musical genre was presented: as being "petrified in time." However, the danger of regarding a given performance context as proper is that this runs the risk of producing some of the very consequences seen by Dionne Brand—namely, freezing the growth of cultural expressions in time and place. The extraordinary feature of the incident involving Pinetop Perkins is that if any appropriation occurred at all, it was in relation to the setting in which he appeared—outside of the milieu of Black culture and beyond the reach of Black audiences.

Comparable issues emerge when the stewardship argument is applied to intangibles. In connection with tangible items, stewardship involves finding the means through which the survival and maintenance of culture can be assured or enhanced. Ukrainian art treasures can be ruined or destroyed. If left unattended, cultural practices can also be lost. In one sense, the same can be true of oral traditions and others based on performance, which can be lost through disuse. Moreover, the stewardship argument responds to concerns over the commodification and desecration of activities or objects such as sacred rituals or images.

By the same token, the concept of stewardship in the context of the cultural appropriation of intellectual property can imply the need for a level of purity of cultural expression that seems artificial. It is one thing to try to retain a faithful rendering of a practice, such as a traditional method of storytelling (if this is possible); it is another to try to preserve the practice forever *only* in its current form. This is where the analogy with tangible cultural property falters somewhat. The nonrivalrous nature of intellectual property allows some renderings to be protected—frozen in place like a museum diorama—while these very cultural traditions continue to evolve. Unless we claim that this evolution is an illegitimate part of the tradition, the stewardship rationale must allow this feature to endure. By doing so, the rationale recognizes the potential of appropriation to generate new artistic treasures. The only basis for preventing some forms of dissemination on stewardship grounds is if there is a danger that appropriative practices could undermine attempts at preservation. That might be true where, for instance, the prevalence of written texts eliminates the need for oral transmissions.

The Deprivation of Material Advantage

In the context of cultural appropriation, the crux of the third claim is that cultural products of the past are being wrongfully exploited for financial gain. As is well known, the law of intellectual property (including that regulating copyright, trademarks, and patents) is geared toward the same concern. These laws regulate the use of the works and creations of others. In the United States, the law has also developed protections against the imitation of celebrity images.

But the argument that cultural appropriation allows some to benefit from the contributions of others has another facet. It may be that those engaged in misappropriation are occupying the commerical field, thereby limiting the access of others. If we can assume that there is some notional finite space accorded in the marketplace of the creative arts for works of this nature, then it is possible that the work of one artist can foreclose opportunities for others. Now this argument is based partly on assertions about the market and so might yield to another view about how the market might react. It might be claimed, for example, that the success of those who appropriate the voice of Native writers has opened avenues for other writers. (At the same time, these spillover benefits are themselves potentially constricted by the fact that access to the market is unevenly available for minority and mainstream artists.)

The law of trademarks provides an analogue that is relevant to the appropriation of cultural products. A trademark functions to represent a product or business, to embody the goodwill that a commercial enterprise has established. Trademarks are regulated, in part, to preclude others from trading on that goodwill and deceiving customers. Trademark law recognizes the potency of symbols and therefore lends support to the argument based on cultural degradation. This body of law also tries to ensure that someone cannot free ride on the work of others. The rationale of the law is to ensure that financial benefits are not wrongly appropriated.

The Failure to Recognize Sovereign Claims

The following statements all contain the same idea: by the rules of the speakers and their cultures, cultural appropriation is wrong; it is theft. Put another way, though the American or Canadian law of property may fail to prevent certain forms of appropriation, other rule-based systems are possible and in some cases extant. Therefore, a clash of sovereign claims can emerge as to which rules about ownership should govern.

I have seen entire cycles of stories stolen right from the tongues of our storytellers and published only to the profit and the credit of the publisher and the typist.[30]

We say that it is our past, our culture and heritage, and forms part of our present life. As such, it is ours to control and it is ours to share on our terms.[31]

We are saying, "These stories, these customs are things we own, things that belong to us."[32]

In our culture, people *own* stories. Individuals own stories. Tribes own stories. Nations own stories. And there is a protocol if you want to tell those stories: you go to the storyteller. And if you don't and you start telling those stories, then you are *stealing.*[33]

The potential for a conflict of rules systems is reflected in a recent Australian judicial decision. In *Milpurrurru et al.* v. *Indofurn Pty. Ltd. et al.,* seven Aboriginal painters brought a copyright action against the manufacturers of certain patterned carpets.[34] The patterns were taken from the works of the plaintiffs. The claims succeeded. In the course of the judgment, the court described the traditional rules that govern the use of symbols among the Aboriginal community of which the plaintiffs were members. This is the account:

Painting techniques, and the use of totemic and other images and symbols are in many instances, and almost invariably in the case of important creation stories, strictly controlled by Aboriginal law and custom. Artworks are an important means of recording these stories, and for teaching future generations. Accuracy in the portrayal of the story is of great importance. Inaccuracy, or error in the faithful reproduction of an artwork can cause deep offence to those familiar with the dreaming.

The right to create paintings and other artworks depicting creation and dreaming stories, and to use pre-existing designs and well recognized totems of the clan, resides in the traditional owners (or custodians) of the stories or images. Usually that right will not be with only one person, but with a group of people who together have the authority to determine whether the story and images may be used in an artwork, by whom the artwork may be created, to whom it may be published, and the terms, if any, on which the artwork may be reproduced. . . .

If unauthorized reproduction of a story or imagery occurs, under Aboriginal law it is the responsibility of the traditional owners to take action to preserve the dreaming, and to punish those considered responsible for the breach. Notions of responsibility under Aboriginal law differ from those of the English common law. If permission has been given by the traditional owners to a particular artist to create a picture of the dreaming, and that artwork is later inappropriately used or reproduced by a third party the artist is held responsible for the breach which has occurred, even if the artist had no control over or knowledge of what occurred. The evidence . . . illustrates the severe consequences which may occur even in a case where plainly the misuse of the artwork was without permission, and contrary to Australian statute law. In times past the "offender" could be put to death. Now other forms of punishment are more likely such as preclusion from the right to participate in ceremonies, removal of the right to reproduce paintings of that or any other story of the clan, being outcast from the community, or being required to make a payment of money; but the possibility of spearing was mentioned by Mr. Wangurra as a continuing sanction in serious cases.[35]

These rules differ from those found under the Australian Copyright Act. In an important way this difference proved moot since the plaintiffs would have prevailed in either case. What is significant for the purposes of the present discussion is that the court acknowledged the Aboriginal rule system. At the same time, it is significant that the issue of whether that rule system should govern the action was not entertained.

Responding to Appropriation

Let us imagine a world in which we cared sufficiently about the harms of cultural appropriation to commit resources and take action. What forms should our response take? In what way should museums change their approach to curation? In what way should the work of writers and scholars change? Can the law play a role in responding to appropriative practices?

Answering these questions is complicated by the factors previously mentioned. How we treat this matter will depend on the domains and modes of appropriation and the values that are threatened by particular appropriative practices. Added to this is the problem of crafting an effective instrumental response, of doing something that will have consequences.

Consider, for example, how these issues might play out in the context of what might be termed *literary* or *voice appropriation*. Within the last five years or so, the debate about cultural appropriation in Canada has centered largely on this domain; several of the essays herein are drawn from the debate that ensued. The main concern has been whether white novelists were wrong in appropriating Native voices by writing about Native culture or by speaking through the intermediaries of Native characters. Broader questions of voice appropriation of minority cultures by mainstream artists developed quickly from this initial issue. Should would-be appropriators somehow be silenced? To do so raises some difficult questions: Are the central identifying variables based on ethnicity, gender, sexual orientation, or class? If our inventive domains are too constricted by this reasoning, are we thereby doomed to creative projects that cannot extend beyond the realm of autobiography?[36]

In *Orientalism,* Said identified the impact of Orientalism on Western attitudes toward Arabic culture. He was deeply troubled by the oppressive potential of Orientalist discourse. To return to our form of analysis, he was concerned with what we have termed *cultural degradation.* Let us assume that he is right. And for the sake of simplicity, let us assume that this is the only value offended by Orientalist conduct. We naturally search for ways to counteract those practices. Said resisted the conclusion that there was a real Orient that differed from the constructions of the Orientalists or that this dissonance in descriptions arose because most Orientalist scholars were from the West.[37] With equal emphasis he rejected "the limited proposition that only a black can write about blacks, a Muslim about muslims, and so forth."[38] However, in a world permeated by social constructions of reality there is something to be said about controlling the process of creating that world, of imposing some control over who can or should hold the pen.

One possible response is to assist minority voices in being heard, say, through the creation of funding opportunities. Within the context of the debate in Canada, some demands have been even more modest. For example, there are Native writers who have asked only that those engaging in cultural appropriation do so with "sensitivity and respect."[39] The Writers' Union of Canada, caught in the eye of the storm over voice appropriation, adopted a similar position. Its membership divided on the matter: concerns over appropriation were met with claims about free speech and artistic freedom. In response to the controversy, the governance of the union passed a resolution calling for "the responsibility and accountability that attend the freedom of imagination and the freedom of expression."[40]

The Writers' Union resolution reflects the difficulty of trying to construct an effective legislative response. Such an approach may well be futile. Nevertheless, a number of essays in this book consider whether the law—and the law of property in particular—can play an effective instrumental role.

There are a host problems associated with establishing a property law regime to regulate some facet of appropriation. First, in the fashioning of a conception of ownership, in whom should a property right be placed? And would that right be communal or individual? Within either of these categories an unlimited range of rights configurations exists. Second, it is necessary to balance concerns about cultural appropriation against other interests. So even though concerns about free speech do not trump all other values, freedom of expression nevertheless remains a matter that a law on cultural appropriation might logically address. Likewise, the natural process of cultural interaction produces new social goods of great value. The difficulty here lies in the law allowing creative processes to continue while responding to unacceptable appropriative practices, whatever these may be.

Third, even if a variety of different protections, whether communal, individual, or otherwise, were recognized, and even if within such a regime both the benefits and burdens of cultural appropriation were taken into account, there still remains a practical concern about whether the complexity of the phenomenon limits the efficacy of the law. The problems here take us back to the multifaceted nature of appropriation described earlier. When an instrumental solution is sought, each definitional obstacle must be confronted.

Within some appropriative domains, the idea of developing a legal regulatory structure is not novel. Generally, these issues have arisen in two contexts. One involves the attempts by nation-states to reclaim art and artifacts that are said to form part of a national heritage—the Parthenon Marbles controversy serves as the archetypal example. The other context involves efforts by indigenous peoples to reclaim sacred antiquities and other properties.

There is now a large body of law, at both the domestic and international levels, dealing with these types of tangible cultural property claims. For example, the UNESCO Convention on the Means of Prohibiting and Preventing the Illicit Import, Export, and Transfer of Ownership of Cultural Property (1970) is one international instrument designed to promote the repatriation of national cultural treasures to their countries of origin. On the domestic front, the Native American Graves Protection and Repatriation Act (1990) is designed to protect aboriginal sacred sites and to facilitate the restitution of artifacts and other objects. Importantly, these measures draw on the rationales of cultural integrity, aesthetics, and stewardship that have been briefly outlined earlier in this Introduction.

The adoption of a workable regime for *intellectual* property is perhaps more problematic. By and large, the present laws (in the United States and Canada) governing such matters as copyright, trademark, and patent are hopelessly inadequate to deal with the issues raised here. For example, a traditional folk song is considered by the law to be part of the public domain. Its antiquity, far from assuring its protection, sets it free. If not fixed, that is, recorded in some way, it is not amenable to protection. There must be a sufficient match between the traditional song and the putative copy before an infringement can be found. For this reason, styles, genres—let alone entire traditions—cannot be protected. And no claim of protection under the current law can be claimed unless its creator can be ascertained. Similar hurdles exist in relation to the claiming of protection for indigenous knowledge that forms the bases of modern science.

Some attempts have been made to reconfigure property law to expand the scope of the protection of indigenous cultures, and these may provide guidance as to how various issues might be resolved.[41] For example, the World Intellectual Property Organisation has undertaken an initiative that has yielded both a model act intended for incorporation into national laws and a draft treaty.[42]

Under the Model Act folklore is defined as the "totality of the traditional artistic heritage of the traditional heritage developed and maintained" by a community within a given nation-state.[43] What the act protects are *expressions of folklore*. These are defined as "creations consisting of characteristic elements of folklore," including,

(i)   verbal expressions, such as folk tales, folk poetry and riddles;
(ii) musical expressions, such as folk songs and instrumental music;
(iii) expressions by action, such as folk dances, plays and artistic forms of rituals; whether or not reduced to a material form; and
(iv) material expressions, such as
      (a) productions of folk art, in particular drawings, paintings, carvings, sculptures, pottery, terracotta, mosaic, woodwork, metalware, jewellery, basket weaving, needlework, textiles, carpets, costumes;
      (b) musical instruments;
      (c) architectural forms.[44]

The scheme of the Model Act is to regulate public performances or publications of expressions of folklore where they are made "with gainful intent" outside of their traditional or usual context.[45] In these instances the source of the folklore must be acknowledged, and approval for its use must be sought. The authorization is granted by a regulatory agency, which may levy a fee and set conditions for use. Folklore that is used for educational purposes or as part of original work is not regulated so long as this latter use is "compatible with fair practice."[46]

These measures resemble copyright protections. However, notice that the protections are perpetual so that creations that are treated as being within the public domain under current domestic laws would be covered. And there is no requirement that the creations be fixed. Nevertheless, the proposals are still rather limited. They exclude works that have an original element, even where these are highly derivative of an expression of folklore. By focusing on traditional elements of folklore, the act adopts a static, ancient, romantic conception of culture. The uses of folklore that trigger the regulatory mechanisms are, generally speaking, those made with a commercial aim.[47] The premise underlying the Model Act is that the applicant-user can exploit the folklore resource on the payment of a royalty fee. And although the act is concerned with the folklore of a community within a state, its use is controlled by a *state* authority.

Some have cast doubt on the utility of an instrumental response through the law (see the Coombe, Philip, and Newton essays). Others seem more sanguine. Patricia Williams has maintained that the deficiencies in rights discourse do not lie in the basic strategy of rights-seeking but rather in the narrow way in which rights have been defined. For her, "Rights are to the law what conscious commitments are to the psyche."[48] Put another way, her argument is that property rights, if effectively framed, can serve both as a countervail to oppression and as a source of empowerment. The right of exclusion, at the heart of the concept of property, is ultimately about power. Similarly, the discussion about cultural appropriation is about empowerment (and its converse).[49] It is therefore at least sensible to view the questions raised by this book through the optic of the law.

About *Borrowed Power: Essays on Cultural Appropriation*

This book is, in effect, a colloquium about the various facets of the appropriation of culture. Appropriative practices, as we have seen, can be found in a number of domains, and this, above all other considerations, has influenced the coverage and ordering of the collection. Because cultural appropriation may arise in so many realms, it has come under the scrutiny of scholars from a wide array of disciplines, including (but not limited to) anthropology, history (including art history), sociology, ethnomusicology, postmodern literary theory, political science, law, and (of course) cultural studies. In each of these realms a body of literature has developed. Yet until now there has been little interconnection among the various nodes of activity. Therefore, in this collection we have endeavored to bring together the work being undertaken in these various fields.

One of our aims in assembling this collection is to locate common themes. Another is to explore diversity. We want to reflect the ways in which differently situated thinkers explore the central questions. The result is an extraordinary sampling of discourses, a stunning array of styles. It is not just that, say, lawyers and anthropologists see issues differently and write from within different traditions; that is no doubt part of the explanation of the variety among the essays. It is also that some of the contributors write from their experiences within the appropriation controversy, whereas others do not. So several of the essays are personal, up-close accounts; other pieces adopt a different vantage point.

We have focused on the vast array of appropriative practices in search of those instances that have political significance in contemporary society. Hence, many of the contributions deal with issues that relate to the position of indigenous peoples; others focus on Black culture and its interrelationship with dominant white discourse. All of the contributions involve an examination of the dynamics of domination and subordination. And because these questions have formed part of an intense national debate in Canada for almost a decade, the collection has a substantial Canadian dimension. We feel that this debate deserves a wider audience.

The ordering of these pieces is based on the domains analysis. Six domain clusters are considered: (1) music and musical forms, (2) art and narrative, (3) colonial and postcolonial discourse, (4) popular culture, (5) science, and (6) tangible cultural property.

Part 1, which contains two pieces, deals with the appropriation of musical forms and works. In the first, "African-American Music: Dynamics of Appropriation and Innovation," Perry A. Hall discusses the appropriation of African-American music by the white-dominated wider culture. Hall's analysis is focused largely on the so-called modes of appropriation and their consequences. Hall notes that, ironically, although the dominant white culture may appropriate and absorb the aesthetic dimensions of Black culture, this is neither coupled with, nor does it lead to, an embrace of Black culture at the human level. Anthony Seeger's "Ethnomusicology and Music Law" takes up Hall's concerns over the need for a culturally sensitive treatment of musical works, though Seeger addresses the problem from a different context. He identifies the potential for conflict arising over such practices as collecting field recordings of indigenous music, reproducing ethnographic recordings on commercial record labels, and reproducing these recordings in supplements to textbooks. Elucidating the contentious ownership issues that arose as he tried to reconcile the various customary forms of ownership with American copyright law, Seeger demonstrates that a deeper understanding is needed of the various culturally specific regimes that protect musical forms of property.

Part 2 deals with appropriation in art and narrative. The essays contained here draw on the Canadian controversy about voice appropriation. In the first essay, "Stop Stealing Native Stories," Lenore Keeshig-Tobias writes of the cultural appropriation of Native stories by non-Native writers. She describes the process as one in which individuals associated with the Canadian cultural industry steal, commercialize, and then profit from the retelling of Native stories without necessarily seeking the permission or creative input of Native persons. Rosemary J. Coombe, in "The Properties of Culture and the Possession of Identity: Postcolonial Struggle and the Legal Imagination," endeavors to come to terms with the strains of discourse that have emerged in Canada. Arguing from the conflicting perspectives of both lawyer and anthropologist, she describes and analyzes the two dominant discourses in the debate, which she calls Romanticism and Orientalism. Coombe argues that from the postcolonial perspective, reliance on such categories of thought inherited from a colonial era and based in a philosophy of possessive individualism may not be the best way to confront the issues of cultural appropriation. In "The Disappearing Debate," M. Nourbese Philip examines the tensions that emerge when the critique over voice appropriation is met with claims of censorship. She argues that this shift is common in Western liberal democracies where censorship is the barometer used to compare the relative freedoms of societies and where the discourse of censorship has a tendency to become privileged over that of racism. Kwame Dawes's contribution, "Re-appropriating Cultural Appropriation," considers the provision of funding for minority artists as one response to problems of appropriation and examines the political dimension of this response. Dawes identifies that the arts and cultural world is inextricably linked to funding and that funding is a deeply political issue that requires highly politicized artists to challenge it. Noting the unprotected nature of Native and tribal copyright in the international marketplace, Joanne Cardinal-Schubert, in "In the Red," examines the appropriation, imitation, and commercialization of Native art and culture by the dominant white community. She discusses how this exploitative practice often incorporates a romanticized and distorted image of "the Indian."

Part 3 considers the appropriation of culture in colonial and postcolonial discourse. Jonathan Hart's "Translating and Resisting Empire: Cultural Appropriation and Postcolonial Studies" examines the exchange of cultures in a colonial and postcolonial context. Hart argues that by looking at the ways the colonial erupts in the postcolonial, we can begin to understand the complexities of identity, resistance, hybridity, and mediation in the cultural exchange and representations of the Europeans as well as in the other cultures they encountered during the course of empire. J. Jorge Klor de Alva's intricate "Nahua Colonial Discourse and the Appropriation of the (European) Other" investigates questions of cultural appropriation from the vantage point of the colonized and their strategies of resistance. He discusses the use of colonial discourse by the Nahuas of New Spain as a weapon for resisting Spanish domination and as a tool for adapting to the shifting social, cultural, and political conditions brought on by the colonizers.

Part 4 looks at appropriation in popular culture. Nell Jessup Newton's "Memory and Misrepresentation: Representing Crazy Horse in Tribal Court" addresses appropriation in the commercial realm. The focus of her discussion is a lawsuit brought by Seth Big Crow, descendant of the Lakota chief Tasunke Witko (Crazy Horse), against the distributors of a product called Crazy Horse Malt Liquor. Deborah Root, in "'White Indians': Appropriation and the Politics of Display," comments on what we may think is a seemingly innocuous practice: a white "hippie" of the counterculture generation (in her words, a Native "wannabe") dressed in the clothing of assorted ethnic (aboriginal, Afghani, and indigenous Latin American) groups. Root believes that such patterns of appropriation have developed and become normalized through the imperialist practices of Western culture, such as the depiction of Natives in popular culture as passive but heroic victims standing in the way of "progress."

Part 5 moves beyond appropriation in the arts to an examination of how the issues play out in relation to the appropriation of scientific knowledge and other forms of intellectual property. James D. Nason's "Native American Intellectual Property Rights: Issues in the Control of Esoteric Knowledge" maps out the central terrain. He looks at the new challenges posed by the appropriation of esoteric knowledge, such as sacred practices and scientific indigenous knowledge. Some of the challenges identified by James Nason are taken up by Naomi Roht-Arriaza in "Of Seeds and Shamans: The Appropriation of the Scientific and Technical Knowledge of Indigenous and Local Communities." She examines in detail the intellectual property issues that surround the appropriation of scientific and technical knowledge of indigenous communities and peoples, and she describes the many ways in which corporations in the business of biotechnology and genetic engineering have made billions of dollars by appropriating the knowledge of indigenous communities without providing any compensation.

Part 6 takes us from the realm of artistic and social practices and indigenous knowledge to issues surrounding tangible cultural property. James D. Nason's second contribution, "Beyond Repatriation: Cultural Policy and Practice for the Twenty-First Century," provides an analysis of issues concerning Native American cultural property, past, present, and future. Nason charts the developments that gave rise to the enactment of the Native American Graves Protection and Repatriation Act and the implications of the act. Against the background of Nason's discussion, the final essay can be seen as an important case study. In "A Coming Together: The Norton Allen Collection, Tohono O'odham Nation, and Arizona State Museum," Lynn S. Teague, Joseph T. Joaquin, and Hartman H. Lomawaima provide an account of the repatriation of cultural property once held in the private collection of Norton Allen. Their narrative describes how the donation of the Allen holdings led the way for an agreement between the O'odham Nation and the Museum. The agreement may well provide a model for other collaborative ventures.

What is cultural appropriation? Why should we care about it? How, if at all, should we respond? As the book progresses, the different modes of appropriation will become apparent; so, too, will the conceptions of community that the authors adopt. Our hope is that these values will shine through. Some of the contributors reflect concerns about *cultural degradation*. They claim that appropriators steal their cultural soul, misrepresent them, silence their voices, purport to speak for them. Because of this, important cultural goods may be weakened and destroyed. Some of the essays are based on *aesthetics and stewardship*. These claim that cultural treasures are sometimes diluted, altered, ruined, commodified; that sacred practices are trivialized; and that their sacredness is ignored or profaned. Other essays adopt a stance based on *material deprivation*. Appropriators abscond with the profits of someone else's intellectual property. They free ride on the property of others without proper compensation or recognition. Allied to this are claims of *sovereignty* in which these assertions are heard: We conceive of these cultural goods as ours and so have the right to control their use. Through appropriation, these sovereign claims are ignored.

In pursuing these themes, *Borrowed Power: Essays on Cultural Appropriation* purports to be neither comprehensive nor definitive. Instead, it endeavors to provide a forum for, and orchestrate a conversation about, the nature of a very complex subject. We hope this conversation is accomplished partially through this Introduction, partially through the Selected Bibliography, but principally through the essays that follow.

Notes

1. Resolution of the Writers' Union of Canada, approved June 1992. The union's definition continues "and profiting at the expense of the people of that culture." We

deal with the question of material gain separately (in Part 3) because we feel that appropriation can occur even in the absence of profit-taking.

2. See Steven R. King, "The Source of Our Cures," *Cultural Survival Quarterly* 15 (Summer 1991): 19.

3. This is a hypothetical inspired by the publication of *Daughters of Copper Woman* (Vancouver: Press Gang, 1981), by Anne Cameron. The book contains a collection of stories told to her by the Nuu-Chah-Nulth women of Vancouver Island. The book was published with their permission and with an acknowledgment, and the proceeds of sale were donated to a cause seeking to preserve Native lands from logging. See Julia V. Emberly, *Thresholds of Difference: Feminist Critique, Native Women's Writings, and Postcolonial Theory* (Toronto: University of Toronto Press, 1993), 94.

4. Eugene Halton, "The Cultic Roots of Culture," in *Theory of Culture*, ed. Richard Munch and Neil J. Smelser (Berkeley and Los Angeles: University of California Press, 1992), 29–63, at 30.

5. See Miro Cernetig, "Ode on the Range: Cowboy Poets Are Trying to Protect the Purity of Their Traditional Territory from 'Faux Cowpunchers,'" *Globe and Mail*, August 10, 1993, A1.

6. Henry Jenkins, *Textual Poachers: Television Fans and Participatory Culture* (New York: Routledge, Chapman and Hall, 1992), 18.

7. Roland Barthes, *Image, Music, Text* (1967), 146; quoted in Robert H. Rotstein, "Beyond Metaphor: Copyright Infringement and the Fiction of the Work," *Chicago-Kent Law Review* 68 (1993): 758.

8. Stanley Fish, *There's No Such Thing as Free Speech: And It's a Good Thing, Too* (New York: Oxford University Press, 1994), 4.

9. We wish to thank Jonathan Hart and Raymond Morrow for their useful suggestions in the preparation of this figure.

10. Michael Mann has suggested that "societies are constituted of multiple overlapping and intersecting sociospatial networks of power." See Michael Mann, *The Sources of Social Power* (Cambridge: Cambridge University Press, 1986), 1.

11. Peter Burke calls this "transgressive reinscriptions of culture." This term has been coined to emphasize the way in which one group adopts and "adapts, or converts, inverts and subverts the vocabulary [or in this case, culture] of another." (See Peter Burke, *History and Social Theory* (Ithaca, N.Y.: Cornell University Press, 1992), 98.

12. John B. Mays [visual arts critic for the *Globe and Mail*], "Squabble over Carr: The Woman Muddies Critique of Her Paintings," *Globe and Mail*, April 9, 1994, C5.

13. Robert Fulford, "The Trouble with Emily" *Canadian Art* 10 (Winter 1993): 38.

14. Richard Handler, "Who Owns the Past?" in *The Politics of Culture*, ed. Brett Williams (Washington, D.C.: Smithsonian Institution Press, 1991), 67. The Preamble of the UNESCO convention also provides that "cultural property constitutes one of the basic elements of civilization and national culture."

15. See generally Margaret Jane Radin, "Property and Personhood," *Stanford Law Review* 32 (1982): 957. In this context one might speak not of "personhood" but of "grouphood," a term coined by John Moustakas, "Group Rights in Cultural Property: Justifying Strict Inalienability," *Cornell Law Review* 74 (1989): 1179.

16. Jeremy Waldron, "Minority Cultures and the Cosmopolitan Alternative," *University of Michigan Journal of Law Reform* 25 (1992): 751.

17. Ibid., 762.

18. Ibid., 778.

19. Ibid., 761–762.

20. Charles Taylor, *Multiculturalism and "The Politics of Recognition"* (Princeton, N.J.: Princeton University Press, 1992), 25ff. See also, bell hooks, *Black Looks: Race and Representation* (Toronto: Between the Lines Press, 1992), 12–13.

21. Tony Kushner, *Angels in America, Part One: Millennium Approaches* (New York: Theatre Communication Group, 1993), 45–46 (emphasis added). Later in the play, Louis, the gay lover of a man dying of AIDS, makes the same point in the context of race: "Power is the object, not being tolerated. Fuck assimilation. . . . Ultimately what defines us isn't race, but politics" (90).

22. James Clifford, *The Predicament of Culture: Twentieth-Century Ethnography, Literature, and Art* (Cambridge, Mass.: Harvard University Press 1988), 14 (emphasis added).

23. hooks, *Black Looks*, 20.

24. Taylor, *Multiculturalism*, 25.

25. See further Thomas Wilson, *The Swastika: The Earliest Known Symbol and Its Migrations* (Washington, 1896); Will Hayes, *The Swastika: A Study in Comparative Religion* (Chatham, England: Order of the Great Companions, 1934).

26. Edward W. Said, *Orientalism* (New York: Vintage Books, 1979).

27. Ibid., 67.

28. This argument is explored in depth in John H. Merryman, "The Public Interest in Cultural Property," *California Law Review* 77 (1989): 339–364.

29. Dionne Brand, "Who Can Speak for Whom?" *Brick* 46 (Summer 1993): 14.

30. Lorne Simon, "Freedom of Expression? Are Native Voices Being Silenced in the Name of Artistic Freedom?" *Canadian Forum* 72 (July–August 1993): 46.

31. Ros Langford, "Our Heritage—Your Playground," *Australian Archaeology* 16 (1983): 6; quoted in Amanda Pask, "Cultural Appropriation and the Law: An Analysis of the Legal Regimes Concerning Culture," *Intellectual Property Journal* 8 (1993): 59.

32. Lynne Van Luven, "Borrowing the Stories of Others," *Edmonton Journal*, January 27, 1990, sec. E.

33. Lenore Keeshig-Tobias, "The Public Face of the Cultural Appropriation Debate: Who Speaks for Whom?" *Morningside (C.B.C. Radio),* April 1, 1992; transcribed in *Textual Studies in Canada* 2 (1992): 42.

34. Not yet reported, December 15, 1994 (Aus. Fed. Ct).

35. Ibid., 6–8 (per von Doussa, J.).

36. See also Joan Thomas, "Whose Freedom, Whose Voices?" *Winnipeg Free Press,* April 11, 1992, C36.

37. Said, *Orientalism*, 322.

38. Ibid.

39. *Morningside,* 47. See also Hartmut Lutz, *Contemporary Challenges: Conversations with Canadian Native Authors* (Saskatoon, Sask.: Fifth House Publishers, 1991), 6.

40. Resolution of Writers' Union of Canada, approved June 1992. Reacting to this measure, Tim Wynne-Jones, a member of the Writers' Union, commented: "This tokenism irks me but it is more sad than reprehensible", quoted in *Canadian Childrens' Literature* 68 (1992): 90.

41. See, e.g., Kamal Puri, "Cultural Ownership and Intellectual Property Rights Post *Mabo*: Putting Ideas into Action," *Intellectual Property Journal* 9(1) (1994): 91–103.

42. *Model Provisions for National Laws on the Protection of Expressions of Folklore;* reproduced as Annex 1 in "Working Group on the Intellectual Aspects of Folklore Protection," *Copyright* 17 (April 1981): 111; *Draft Treaty for the Protection of Expression of Folklore Against Illicit Exploitation and Other Prejudicial Actions;* reproduced in "Report: Group of Experts on the International Protection of Folklore by Intellectual Property," *Copyright* 21 (February 1985): 40.

43. Model Act, s. 2(1).

44. S. 2(2).

45. S. 3.

46. S. 4. Nor is permission required where the use is incidental. Additionally, section 14 provides that "the protection granted under this [law] shall in no way be interpreted in a manner which could hinder the normal use and development of expressions of folklore."

47. S. 3.

48. Patricia J. Williams, *The Alchemy of Race and Rights* (Cambridge, Mass.: Harvard University Press, 1991), 159.

49. See also Jane M. Gaines, *Contested Culture: The Image, the Voice, and the Law* (London: B.F.I. Publishing, 1991), 6–8; Pask, "Cultural Appropriation and the Law," 80–81.

Part I

The Appropriation
of Music and Musical
Forms

Perry A. Hall

African-American Music: Dynamics of Appropriation and Innovation

African-American musical sensibilities have profoundly affected mainstream popular culture over the years, appearances to the contrary notwithstanding. During the 1930s, for example, Benny Goodman became the "King of Swing" leading a mostly white band. It is true that in the course of his career Goodman, who was considered a progressive in racial matters, had the relatively good taste to feature several Black musicians and to eventually hire Fletcher Henderson as chief arranger.[1] (Of course, Goodman's rise to eventual coronation owed something to the twenty-four arrangements he had bought from Henderson earlier.)[2] Otherwise, with the exceptions of "Duke" (Edward Kennedy) Ellington and "Count" (William) Basie, among a few others, the era was dominated, in terms of both image and economics, by white bands and white musicians who were adapting, imitating, creating variations of, and in other ways "playing off" innovative sensibilities forged wholly within the crucible of African-American suffering, struggle, and triumph.

At this and similar points in the history of Black music, it becomes clear that a complex "love-hate" relationship connects mainstream society and African-American culture—in which white America seems to love the melody and rhythm of Black folks' souls while rejecting their despised Black faces. In no area is this complex relationship more evident than in musical tradition.[3] The pattern of separating the art from the people leads to an appropriation of aesthetic innovation that not only "exploits" Black cultural forms, commercially and otherwise, but also nullifies the cultural meaning those forms provide for African Americans. The appropriated forms become ineffective as expressions and affirmations of the unique cultural experiences from which they arise. Thus, at this and similar historical points new musical forms have emerged that seemed once again to establish the distinctiveness of Black music in a given sociohistorical context. This ironic process seems to reproduce itself perpetually as new forms are subjected to similar processes of cooptation and appropriation.

In this essay I explore the dynamics of diffusion and appropriation involved in this dialectic process in which certain patterns and formations recur. In this process fundamental African-American cultural sensibilities are continually reformed and co-opted, to be replenished and reformed again as a result of contact and interaction with the dominant Euro-American culture. This examination involves looking at the contexts and means by which innovation and appropriation tend to shape African-American popular music, the centrality of traditional "folk/popular" and African-derived aesthetic sensibilities in such innovations, and the manner and result of their exposure in and appropriation by the white-dominated wider culture. The essay's investigations suggest that mainstream absorption of aesthetic dimensions of Black culture does not lead to comparable embrace of Black culture at the human level.

There are few today who will argue with the premise that African America's contributions to American musical culture are foundational, definitional, and immense. Yet any more than surface examination of the process by which those contributions are realized reveals nefariously ambiguous dimensions in the cultural relationship of America to its (arguably) favorite sons and daughters in this regard. Emergent forms are initially ridiculed and subjected to attempted suppression. When, as is consistently the case, this resistance proves futile as musical forms are absorbed, they eventually become reshaped and redefined, subtly and otherwise, in ways that minimize their association with "Blackness." Award (recognition) and reward (compensation) structures often evolve that grossly enrich white appropriators, while only a few Black innovators have comparable levels of compensation.

Most poignantly, the Black human beings whose collective living experiences most consistently contribute innovative impulses to the music of the wider culture continue as despised, feared, rejected symbols of undesirability. This description does not refer specifically to individual performers and artists who bring innovation to the wider culture, though many of them have indeed suffered abuse of various kinds in this process. Rather, it suggests that, while the white-dominated wider culture absorbs aesthetic innovation, it continues to avoid engaging or embracing the human reality, the very humanity, of those whose shared living experiences collectively created the context in which such innovation is nurtured, maintained, and supported. In the course of this appropriative process, these people and their experiences, their connection to the aesthetics, have in essence become "invisible" as the forms purport to become "color-blind."

Looked at from this perspective, the process of cultural appropriation as it relates to Black music involves not so much a "borrowing" as a virtual "strip-mining" of Black musical genius and aesthetic innovation. Although this analogy may appear extreme, it accurately depicts a process in which the essential, social, aesthetic, and economic value of a form or instance of cultural innovation is fundamentally extracted and separated from the collective human host that cultivated it. And arguably this analogy exemplifies the more general manner in which people of color have given their lands, labor, culture, and much of their humanity to the enrichment of Western life.

Dynamics of Innovation

The processes involved in innovation in African musical culture invariably involve sentiments and sensibilities associated with the least assimilated sectors of the Black community. Contexts where dominant culture norms are absent or relatively inoperative, such as New Orleans's famous Congo Square (where enslaved Africans gathered by the hundreds outside the purview of any masters), a slave quarter, or a basement "rent party," often function as repositories for African-American cultural sensibilities in their most potent form. As Black culture has transformed throughout the decades, the least culturally assimilated sectors of the Black cultural landscape, where African orality and rhythmicity are strongest, have tended to generally coincide with the lower socioeconomic strata among African Americans.

It turns out, then, that sociostructural isolation leads not only to survival of these root sensibilities but also to cultural environments highly supportive of significant innovation that engages these sensibilities. In this context forms of Black music function to validate a distinctive sense of Black humanity in cultural spaces separated and differentiated from the dominant culture, spaces in which the dominant culture's scorn, devaluation, and rejection are replaced by affirmative expressions of self. This is an especially salient function of music, among other expressive forms, in the folk/popular reference frame of those relatively unassimilated segments of Black communities.

White Reaction: The Dynamics of Interaction

Assessment of the role of white attitudes toward expressions of African cultural sensibility in this process is confounded by several factors. White America has often become exposed to emerging forms of Black popular music, for example, as part of some more general confrontation of social mores and cultural sensibilities in which the source of these innovations is invariably dehumanized and devalued. Thus, although whites have consistently been attracted by Black rhythmic/muscial sensibilities, this attraction is often obscured or distorted by racist habits of thought and association that provoke suppression and denial, even while conjuring powerful attractions. Aesthetic attraction produces a dissonance that must be resolved through interpretation or incorporation of the attraction in ways consistent with the social construction of racial hierarchy.

Plantation diaries and antebellum travel reports consistently refer to whites' awareness of and interest in Blacks' rhythmic sense, along with other cultural traits whites found peculiar, yet fascinating, whether in the context of religious worship, work practices, or other observed activities. Typical is the observation of George W. Moore regarding the mistress of the Baring plantation: "I have often seen Mrs. Baring, when the Negroes were singing, catch the motion of their bodies and do just as they did."[4] Likewise, New Orleans's Congo Square attracted not only congregations of blacks who re-created aspects of the various African cultures from which they had come but also attracted interested white observers whose recorded fascination now forms part of our contemporary window to that time and place (throughout much of the antebellum period and into the 1880s) where African rhythms reverberated, possibly in their most potent form in North America.[5]

As innovations like ragtime and jazz emerge from such relatively unassimilated cultural spaces, they become visible to some whites, who view them initially from the safety of their own side of the cultural boundary. From this perspective, whites often describe their fascination, sometimes disguised as disgust or horror, in terms consistent with their own perceived cultural superiority. This framework is incompatible with recognition of innovation as genuine artistic or aesthetic achievement. Thus, initial reaction to new forms of musical expression is consistently negative and resistant, at least on the surface. Ragtime, for instance, came to general awareness initially as part of the "sporting life"—a euphemism usually associated with brothels, bars, gambling establishments, and other sites where sins of the spirit and flesh are partaken—and was therefore rejected by "polite" society. Commenting on what eventually turned out to be ragtime's redefinition of the American piano tradition in 1918, the New Orleans *Times-Picayune* instructed its readers that "rhythm, though often associated with melody and harmony, is not necessarily music." Indeed, rhythm was an "atrocity in polite society, and . . . we should make it a point of civic honor to suppress it. Its musical value is nil, and its possibilities of harm are great."[6] Eventually, however, ragtime revolutionized American popular music, in addition to influencing such "serious" European and American composers as Claude Debussy, Igor Stravinsky, and Charles Ives.[7]

Jazz was similarly associated with guilt in connection with the social environment of its formative period, which overlapped and paralleled that of ragtime, in the late nineteenth century. Indeed, during jazz's early formative period—from the mid-1890s until around 1905—the new sound was largely invisible to whites, indistinguishable from the "honky-tonk" and ragtime music associated with fast, sinful living. Charles "Buddy" Bolden—a musical ancestor claimed by virtually every one of the early New Orleans innovators—was trying his new sound as early as 1895. And though the eventual contribution of Creoles to the transformation was considerable, light-skinned Creoles initially scorned jazz as honky-tonk music, while "Papa" Jack Laine, considered a "white father" of New Orleans jazz, claimed he had never heard of Bolden at this point, although Laine apparently was familiar with some of the Creole players.[8]

Initially, then, the new sound remained unknown in the white community and was resisted by the established Black musical community. It was thus a phenomenon of the folk/popular masses, the least structurally and culturally assimilated sector of the community. By 1905, however, Black New Orleans was thoroughly in tune with the new music, and Creole musicians had been won over or had adapted by necessity. Over the next ten years the rest of the city followed suit.[9] Although (or, perhaps, because) the social activities associated with jazz were probably quite familiar to most residents, the established press's first nonderogatory mention of jazz did not occur until 1933, according to one source.[10]

Innovation: Western Form, African Essence

Ragtime and jazz also illustrate how the emergence of new forms involves the ascendance of or reemphasis on African-derived musical sensibilities that are retained in the folk, popular, or traditional African-American cultural reference frame and that contribute critically to the periodic reformation of distinctive musical forms. Piano ragtime was achieved from the imposition of African rhythmic patterns on piano playing styles—a syncopated attack on Western musicological sensibility that subordinated and extended Western harmonic concepts with the drive of African polyrhythms and in the process transformed the piano into a rhythm instrument. Similarly, jazz evolved from an original "New Orleans synthesis" involving aesthetic and social elements that met, merged, and mingled with the ancestral spirits of Congo Square in that city from the 1890s through the first two decades of the new century.

New Orleans's large Black population—especially large after hardening post-Reconstruction Jim Crow laws defined the numerous light-skinned Creoles as Black for segregation purposes—provided aesthetic elements, social context, and economic support for this musical transformation. The Creole tradition, forced by Jim Crow to socially redirect itself, brought band instruments and European training and performance styles. Creole bands (said to be adapted from the French tradition of military marching bands), string orchestras, and other musical ensemble forms contributed new instruments and instrumental arrangements that—like ragtime in relation to the piano—could be used to reexpress African-derived rhythmic, tonal, and improvisational senses, provided mostly by uptown Blacks.

The New Orleans tradition of brothels (as in the city's much-remembered Storyville red-light district), sporting establishments, and the like made it a significant center of ragtime piano music since such establishments were prime employers of its players.[11] Throughout jazz's developmental years, Mardi Gras, funeral and other parades, picnics, dances, private parties, and other mostly but not entirely Black affairs also provided an economy sufficiently organized to support jazz's innovators at the turn of the century.[12]

Blues, as a musical force and as a philosophy of life, came with the increasing numbers of residents from the delta areas in Mississippi and other rural enclaves who were finding their way to the city. In New Orleans and other Black urban environments, the equivalent of the field holler—described as the root from which rural blues grew in the late 1800s—was heard in the cries and chants of street hawkers, selling vegetables and other goods, each with a unique cry, sometimes accompanying themselves on harmonica, or homemade flute.[13]

Ragtime songs provided materials and concepts for adapting these instruments and arrangements to polyrhythmic and improvisational techniques in band performance. The multi-instrumental format—the fact that several musicians, instead of one piano player, were playing—allowed a geometrical increase of layers of rhythmic complexity and degrees of improvisational freedom.[14] Blues contributed an approach, a performance style, a body of melodies, a "vocal tonality" (techniques that shape the sound of instruments—especially in jazz horns—to imitate the human voice, recalling the rural cries, moans, and field hollers), and a pattern of improvisational interplay.

Thus, instruments designed in the European literate tradition of "reading" music fixed on paper were adapted to the African oral tradition of finding it "by ear." Led or directed by fluid, syncopated rhythmic patterns, this "aural" proficiency enabled melodic variation or improvisation. Ensembles composed of those instruments—which in the European tradition played fixed arrangements together—were redefined to accommodate fluid flights of polyphony in which the various instruments collectively improvised melodic variation on a polyrhythmic foundation. This saturation of a Western form with African music sensibility yielded the emotional directness—a unity between composition and performance—characteristic of Black performance styles. From this synthesis emerged a musical form that was unique and new, a form that involved Euro-American forms, instruments, and "influences" but was nonetheless wholly a product of Black experiences. As such, this form encompassed a reemphasis on "Black" aesthetic and cultural sensibilities in the form of African-derived orality and rhythmicity.

Black New Orleans around the turn of the century (when Crescent City had one of the largest urban concentrations of African Americans) was a crucible in which these sensibilities were forged and out of which boiled the major musical innovation in North American history. From these rich beginnings jazz innovators eventually moved up the Mississippi valley to Chicago (and places such as Kansas City, St. Louis, and Los Angeles), where jazz's potency spread into the consciousness of a broader world and became a social phenomenon.[15]

Diffusion, Appropriation, and All That Jazz

The fact that jazz, ragtime, rhythm and blues, and other forms have become firmly entrenched in American musical culture in spite of typical resistance and rejection affirms the premise stated earlier that, contrary appearances notwithstanding, white America has consistently been attracted by Black musical sensibilities. (During the twentieth century in particular, each generation has had a connection to an innovation in Black musical culture.) Black musical innovations eventually cross over into mainstream culture, and African-American cultural traits manage to penetrate social boundaries.

As new forms emerge to influence and even dominate mainstream musical culture, however, so also do events that lead to appropriation, on various levels, by the white-dominated wider culture of such aesthetic innovations. One aspect of this process is the tendency of the forms to become dissociated, in the discourse and perceptual framework of the white-dominated mainstream, from the African-American experiential context that created them. Actually, it seems more accurate to say that for the white-dominated mainstream the separation of the musical phenomenon from the people, and hence from previous negative associations with Black people and Black culture, is a necessary accommodation to the accomplished fact that such penetration has occurred in spite of previous criticism and rejection.

At the point at which ragtime's influence was expressed in the work of classical composers, the "influence" seemed to be far separated from the folk and the experience that had created it. As part of a "classical" composition, or a popular show tune, the rhythmic influence of ragtime (the name came from the fact that the syncopated rhythmic approach sounded like "ragged time" to Western ears attuned to conventional rhythm) had become diluted and was no longer connected to Blackness or to the stigmatized association with "low" life and culture.

In addition to separation of the aesthetic and experiential dimensions, the perception of economic value and the subsequent impact of market forces contribute to this dissociative tendency. In case of jazz, both aspects are evident. The process of obscuring the association between Black culture and jazz was evident before most New Orleans jazz players had even been heard by outsiders. Although riverboats and vaudeville tours had been spreading the new jazz sound over many regions in the early 1900s, what became widely accepted as jazz were derivations of the original New Orleans synthesis that came into wide popularity following the first release of a jazz record, made by a white—and inappropriately named "Original Dixieland Jazz Band"—in 1917.[16] In other words, by the early 1920s—when New Orleans originals such as King Oliver and his cornetist Louis Armstrong, pianist Ferdinand "Jelly Roll" Morton, and clarinetist Sidney Bechet had settled in Chicago to further develop and expose the new art form—jazz was already, in the minds of many, associated with white musicians.

Armstrong and Morton, pivotal figures linking New Orleans jazz with future forms, were in their most fertile, creative, and innovative periods during the 1920s.[17] Under the precepts of the recording industry's segmented marketing systems, however, recordings of their music were distributed on "race record" labels geared specifically to Blacks and remained invisible to most whites.[18] By that time music recorded by white dance bands, led by Paul Whiteman's, was being introduced to mainstream whites as "jazz" through record labels and performance venues specifically marketed to them.

The "symphonic jazz" of the 1920s was not particularly or closely associated with Blackness or with the "low-culture" contexts in which these forms had arisen. Whiteman ostensibly performed "symphonic" jazz by "taming" its "primitive rhythms" and making it more acceptable to white audiences.[19] The ironic result of this appropriation was that the music eventually lost much of the emotional directness and rhythmic vitality that had made it distinctive and provoked attraction in the first place.

In cultivating and exploiting this audience, Whiteman exemplifies one odious result of this pattern of appropriation: reaping value and economic profit from aesthetic innovations emerging from the tradition of cultural sensibility among ordinary Blacks, who remain mostly as disadvantaged and disenfranchised as ever. Whiteman became "King of Jazz" in this market, grossing $1 million in a single year during the 1920s.[20]

Among Armstrong's white fans during his early days in Chicago was a group of high school–age youths, several of whom later became important jazz figures. This group included Bix Beiderbecke, described in most sources as the best white jazzman of the latter 1920s.[21] From his apprenticeship in Chicago, Beiderbecke went on to facilitate the spread of jazz with the Wolverines, a young white band that played colleges, amusement parks, and resorts throughout the Midwest during the early 1920s.[22] Among the white dance bands he enlivened later in his career was the Whiteman band, where his presence no doubt constituted the closest that band came to jazz authenticity.

Meanwhile, Jelly Roll, along with several other original innovators, was to end his life in ignominious obscurity by the time band jazz became "swing" in the 1930s. Regarding Jelly Roll, who died in 1941, one writer observed, "In Morton's fifty-six years . . . are to be found the whole course of ragtime and jazz, their acceptance, their rejection, their triumphs, and their subtle spurious 'improvement' by the music business, the swift alternations of the true masters between comparative riches and fame, and complete oblivion."[23] Armstrong was more fortunate, although his earnings were less than one-tenth of Whiteman's.[24] Though many came to associate his popularity with "Uncle Tomism," his career and fame survived through the 1930s, in part because he *did* successfully appeal to whites as well as Blacks.

Systemic Issues

Even though some individuals, such as Whiteman, could be accused of crass commercial exploitation of aesthetic innovation, it would be inaccurate to say that *individuals* necessarily orchestrate the struggle that seems to ensue over definition and ownership once a form is absorbed or accepted into the broader cultural milieu. (This process of appropriation which often has indifferent or tragic results for Black innovators.) Attitudes and orientations among whites who are owners, producers, agents, or performers may range from cynically exploitive to wholly or at least relatively sympathetic, like those of Bix Beiderbecke, Benny Goodman, or Johnny Otis (a white rhythm-and-blues pioneer). As for the results, in which white participants are disproportionately recognized, rewarded, and compensated, it may be that the exploitive individuals are more numerous or more powerful. Or such results may simply illustrate that this struggle for cultural ownership is perhaps not especially a struggle of individuals—that systemic forces are prominent in this process.

The effects of racism, prejudice, and stereotypes, along with customs and habits of thought, on white-dominated mainstream social, institutional, and economic structures seem to move them inexorably, not needing any self-conscious conspiracy of individuals to reproduce patterns of racial inequality in matters of recognition and compensation. Indeed, the outcomes seem oblivious to the individual wills of the Bix Beiderbeckes, Benny Goodmans, Elvis Presleys, and John Lennons of the music world. Beiderbecke is often considered a sympathetic character in the story of jazz, and some even portray him as another victim of the process of appropriation.[25] Nevertheless, the market segregation practices of that time meant that the millions of people he may have played for never heard of Armstrong, much less appreciated and proportionately or appropriately rewarded his contributions to America's most original art form. In the instance of Beiderbecke, his presence in various white bands in the segregated music world of the 1920s helped spread the idea of jazz as a music not connected with the Black experience, no matter his will or intention.

As forms of jazz developed throughout the 1930s, the emergence of white swing bands and the Depression helped further legitimize this idea. The precise, arranged style of "swinging" that became a national phenomenon emerged among a group of Black bands (Fletcher Henderson, Don Redmon, Duke Ellington, Jimmie Lunceford, among others) that played regularly for predominantly white audiences.[26] In adapting a "hot" style of playing to appeal to these audiences, those Black "preswing" bands may have been guided by an optimistic sense that their merit as musicians and entertainers would be recognized, accepted, and fairly rewarded. Likely, however, the very popularity among white audiences of the arranged, "riffing" style that emerged between 1929 and 1935 contributed to its eventual appropriation and domination by whites. The combination of the effects of the Depression on recording, broadcast, and performance and the appropriation of the swing style by white bands, led by Goodman's but including Artie Shaw, Glenn Miller, the Dorsey brothers, and a host of others, severely limited Black exposure in this mainstream market and led to disproportionate distribution of the rewards and recognition of swing.

In the recording industry, session opportunities for Black band musicians became severely limited during the 1930s. Similarly, the lucrative big-band dance/concert circuit of the 1930s and early 1940s featured less than a handful of Blacks among the names associated with that storied era of swing. Moreover, so-called "jazz polls . . . began in the middle thirties wherein no Negro players won top positions, few Negroes even made the listings, and Harry James [Benny Goodman's trumpeter] invariably won top trumpet over Louis Armstrong."[27]

Fletcher Henderson's position as Goodman's chief arranger represented the prescribed pinnacle available to Black musicians in terms of mainstream recognition and compensation. Nor were economics and recognition the only, or necessarily the most important, terms in which losses are to be measured here. Not only did the industry built from the music called jazz—sprung from the very bosom of Black life—no longer support Black musicians economically; the music itself also was not even particularly associated with Blackness in the public mind. It could no longer function as a living definition and affirmation of what it meant to be Black in that time.

Appropriation and Cultural Meaning

Cooptation and expropriation of this kind tend to render such innovations in music, language, or other cultural traits ineffective in the key culture function—of marking and affirming Black ethnicity and identity.[28] Moreover, such episodes or tendencies are consistently accompanied and/or followed by some kind of reformation of indigenous African-American identity that clarifies and refocuses Black sensibilities and sets them off from those of whites. In the area of music this usually involves a reemphasis on rhythmic and polyrhythmic techniques and other aspects of the orality of Africa's heritage.

Like Congo Square—which allowed a maximum degree of coalescence and coherence among African slaves from many different cultures in an environment outside of the immediate purview of their dominators—each innovative period or context features increased cohesion among Blacks (including erstwhile disparate elements) as a community, the result of both external and internal factors. The New Orleans jazz synthesis occurred during a period in which cohesion had been largely imposed by Jim Crow definitions of social orientation after the failure of Reconstruction. During the 1930s, the sense of hopeful inclusion that had been evident in the "Jazz Age" of the 1920s was betrayed when economic depression forced many musicians out of the mainstream music economy.

Thus, in some ways this thrust toward new cohesion was imposed from without. Just as Jim Crow laws had forced uptown Blacks and downtown Creoles together in New Orleans, so did Depression economics force many who had thought in terms of an integrated musical universe to reconsider their options. Socially alienated and economically displaced, Black musical practitioners looked inward—in terms of community and perhaps also in terms of personal psychology—to find their aesthetic and economic constituency. And while the white icons of swing raked in the big bucks, Black bands played to, and were revitalized by, all-Black audiences on this "chitlin circuit."

In some ways this turning inward was an aesthetic choice. With swing, the rhythmic sense of jazz became watered down, and improvisation became limited and restrained. Before the crash "black musicians used more and more Western song forms, incorporated Western harmony, and played for increasingly integrated audiences."[29] All-Black bands on the chitlin circuit, however, especially the Southwest circuit that included Kansas City, St. Louis, and Oklahoma, had, according to LeRoi Jones (Imamu Amiri Baraka), "developed very much differently than the big Northeastern bands. . . . They had always remained much closer to the older, blues tradition, even after they began to master some of the instrumental techniques of the Eastern bands, they still . . . relied heavily on the blues."[30]

Popular on that circuit were bands led by Bennie Moten and by Count Basie, where many future innovators, including Lester Young and Charlie Parker, served apprenticeships.[31] In addition to theaters and other venues that catered to Blacks along this chitlin circuit, small clubs in city neighborhoods, southern rural roadhouses, and private house or rent parties—especially in the South, Southwest, and Midwest regions, where African-American folk masses have historically been concentrated—were settings for a revitalization, a reconnection to indigenous roots, to primordially African rhythms, residing, as they always have, in the cultural world of the folk masses.

Relieved, in a way, of the need, or stripped of the motivation, to alter expressive modes to appeal to white sensibilities, Black musicians found the space and the means to refresh their musical art by emphasizing those elements that made performance spaces distinctly African American, remaking Black identity in cultural terms, reforming the framework of ethnicity that defined Blackness and distinguished it from whiteness. Largely invisible to the swing mainstream, this flourishing Black "underground" moved contemporary Black expressive forms away from assimilationist pretensions and back toward the folk, popular, and African roots of core African-American culture.

The postwar era of the late 1940s and 1950s saw this underground culture emerge in two major innovative thrusts—the esoteric be-boppers and the raunchy, "jump-blues" band acts that became rhythm and blues. In both cases the reascendance of or reemphasis on African-derived rhythmicity was of central importance in reinforcing characteristics that most effectively distinguished the Black musical sensibility from that of the non-Black. The boppers brought a refocus on the primacy of syncopated polyrhythms, while engaging even more complex improvisational structures and extensions of European harmonic concepts. Jump-blues took its rhythmic pulse from the "boogie-woogie" sounds emerging from 1930s underground culture—a "fast shuffle" that anchored a pulsating dance rhythm at rent parties and juke joints—and came with an attitude that projected much more of what was considered unpretentious, down to earth, even raunchy and "gut-bucket," about Black life and much less of what was considered sophisticated and pretentious. It was as if Black musicians were deliberately making cultural space between themselves and perceived mainstream sensibilities, as if their wish was to make sure they were not mistaken for someone trying to appeal to "white" or otherwise highfalutin' tastes.

Postwar Popular Music

The role of these forms, especially rhythm and blues, in the subsequent lineage of American popular music reveals the recurrence of patterns applicable to the past. (Although bebop would require a somewhat different analysis, many of these patterns apply to it as well.) As was the case in New Orleans, some Blacks—in this case, middle-class, assimilation-minded, or ostensibly sophisticated ones—resisted the new "ethnicity" evident in the new rhythm and blues, characterizing it as "gut-bucket" and unrefined. And as was the case with the New Orleans synthesis, this "underground" was initially invisible to mainstream whites. Major record companies showed no initial interest in this "lower-class" Black music. The result was that a bevy of smaller, independent record companies, some which were Black owned, became important institutions in the "rhythm-and-blues world."[32] In 1949 when *Billboard* changed the name of its Black pop-music chart from "race" to "rhythm and blues," "it wasn't setting a trend, but responding to a phrase and a feeling the independent labels had already made part of the vocabulary."[33]

Conceivably, the perceived raw, raunchy attitude of early rhythm and blues made it unattractive to major companies, as it was for some middle-class Blacks. It is also conceivable that this very attitude, along with the pulsating rhythm, *did* help make it attractive to some young whites, progeny of the swing generation. With radio playing an important role (records and radio had been an important factor with jazz in the 1920s and 1930s), the sound of rhythm and blues drifted in and apparently was music to the ears of a generation of young whites in search of causes for which to rebel.[34] Eventually the rhythm-and-blues term *rock and roll* (which referred to having sex) came to serve as a label for a body of music that included some elements of rhythm and blues (for example, Bo Diddley, Chuck Berry, and Little Richard) and a lot of younger, mostly white, groups and musicians, Elvis Presley, Bill Haley, Buddy Holly, trying to move with the pulsating rhythmic sense that drove rhythm and blues.

As had been the case in previous instances of aesthetic appropriation, the evolution of rhythm and blues into rock and roll eventually overshadowed the connection of the Black music to Black humanity. The initial rock-and-roll explosion seemed to energize, even define, a new generation of white youth with electrifying dance rhythms. By 1960, however, it seems that "the state of [mainstream] popular music in America was a sorry one, with the initial wave of rock-and-roll having been replaced by the plastic posturings of the Fabians and Frankie Avalons."[35] Nearly to the extreme of Whiteman's "symphonic jazz," in the 1920s, this rock and roll came to represent a redefinition of Black music forms for non-Black uses. Little Richard clearly understood this, reminiscing on a Home Box Office television special about how a version of his rock anthem "Tutti Frutti" reached the number one spot on the pop charts: "By Pat Boone," Richard said, grimacing to the camera.

"Soul" music, which flowered in the 1960s, seemed in part a reaction to the rock-and-roll appropriation of earlier forms. Aesthetically, the evolution of rhythm and blues into soul music emerged from 1950s innovators such as Ray Charles and Sam Cooke, who obliterated tenuous barriers between sacred and secular worlds and brought gospel-inflected harmonies and gospel-style fervor (and call-response rhythmicity) to their decidedly secular performances.[36] Socially soul music functioned to reestablish a distinctive Black musical sound, an instrument of cultural cohesion in the context of the shared consciousness and heightened cohesion accruing from the social movements of that period.

Soul music's effectiveness as an instrument of cultural cohesion as well as of musical innovation was in part related to the mainstream music industry's inability to control it. Although many of the early companies specializing in rhythm and blues were no longer in business, independents were still controlling the market as soul music bloomed throughout the 1960s. The most important independent companies were New York–based Atlantic Records, Motown in Detroit, and Stax-Volt, out of Memphis, Tennessee.[37] With these legendary "indies" pumping out soulful sounds continually, the pale imitations offered by major companies in the late 1950s and early 1960s were of small effect.

Atlantic had survived from the early postwar era and remained an important rhythm-and-blues institution until the 1970s. White owned, Atlantic was Black oriented from the start and was where Ray Charles developed his pioneering "soul" sound. Motown rose in the late 1950s and established a dominant 1960s sound. Owned by a now-legendary black entrepreneur, Motown deliberately programmed some of its products for the white "crossover" market (Motown billed its products as "The Sound of Young America").[38] Although Motown's pursuit of the "legitimacy" and profits associated with white acceptance suggests a certain kind of assimilationism within the cultural context of soul music, that trend was counterbalanced during the mid- and late 1960s as a southern soul sound developed in Memphis (with Stax records), Muscle Shoals (Alabama), and other southern centers. And although this southern-based sound was aimed at the traditional, Black rhythm-and-blues market, white fans of 1960s soul also gravitated to this more "authentic" Black sound.[39] Eventually Motown counterbalanced itself, instituting its own version of this sound on a new label named "Soul," where Junior Walker and the All-Stars, Shorty Long, and Gladys Knight and the Pips were recorded.[40]

The 1960s and 1970s then, like the 1920s and 1930s, were a period when "the music of the black culture . . . became part of mainstream American expression."[41] And like the 1930s, the 1970s turned out to be an era when the potency of Black musical forms (1960s soul) merged with mainstream forms and sensibilities to create a "raceless" (disco) phenomenon that closed out that postmodern decade. Soul's success with crossover, like that of its popular culture predecessors, may have been a cause of its ultimate appropriation as disco.

Disco emerged in a period after the dominant Black or Black-oriented independent record companies had come under influence or control of major record companies and other large corporations, a process described in penetrating detail by Nelson George.[42] Once again, music forms that had come from African-American innovation and creativity were redefined, aesthetically and culturally, as a result of white participation. In the 1970s, after a furious evolution of media and communications technology, popular dance music could not be as completely divorced from Black culture as it had been in the 1920s or 1930s, when market channels were so separate that Blacks who were "lined up for Bessie [Smith] or Ma [Rainey], never heard of Paul Whiteman," and vice versa.[43] The channels of cultural separation were, by comparison, considerably more porous. Eventually, however, the notion that "raceless mainstream" meant white in the dominant reference frame became as clear as the image of actor John Travolta, whose "white-dancin'-fool" character in the movie *Saturday Night Fever* became, for the mainstream, the disco star of the 1970s. Moreover, the brazen attempt of MTV to take to the air with virtually no videos by Black musicians (rationalized again in terms of its projected "mainstream" or "classic rock" market) showed a still-enduring tendency to redefine Blackness out of mainstream conceptions of popular music.

However, even though images of disco pseudosophistication dominated the 1970s, the countercurrents of a "funk underground" can be found in that same period as well—an underground, or counterculture, that rejected pretentious sophistication in favor of the melodically stripped down, rhythmically souped up riffs of James Brown's "JBs," George Clinton's "P-Funk," and the music of other stars of 1970s funk. As had been the case in similar transformative moments in Black music history, the emergence of funk in the 1970s involved a new synthesis of mainstream form with essential Black rhythmic sense. In this case electrified instruments, instrumental techniques, and the form of the self-contained band were adapted from the "rock" music of that era. Like the previous underground, the funk sound was especially audible in the South and Midwest, where Black community concentrations abounded. It was heard less distinctly around the East and West Coasts, where disco chique was all the rage.[44] And like that previous counterculture, 1970s funk connected with elements that erupted in the 1980s as rap, hip-hop, and other "radicalized" forms of African-American musical culture, beginning once again the pattern of diffusing into and transforming mainstream culture itself.

The recent eruption of black urban youth culture as hip-hop and rap music illustrates the continuation of dynamics accompanying the emergence of previous forms. Just as early rhythm and blues expressed a rejection of attempted middle-class sophistication, rap music rejects pretentious sophistication in favor of knowing, in the starkest terms, "what time it is."[45] Like early rhythm and blues in the late 1940s, rap initially survived and grew largely on independent record labels, despite lack of interest, rejection, and even attempted suppression on the part of the mainstream record companies and radio stations.[46]

Rejection, criticism, and attempted censorship by mainstream whites and Blacks as well have not prevented large-scale identification among young Blacks with rap music and other hip-hop cultural symbols, such as language, dress, and "attitude." Moreover, the significant and growing attraction of rap for some white middle-class youths affirms the historical pattern of diffusion of indigenous cultural sensibilities into the wider culture. Although no especially dominant "white hip-hop" has yet emerged, the audience for this renegade sound has become dominated by yet another generation of middle-class white youths. This is one factor that may yet lead to a replay of musical changes in the familiar historical chord progression.

Appropriating the Meaning of Appropriation

Having examined the dynamics of aesthetic appropriation regarding African-American musical sensibilities, I wish to point to the role that scholars, analysts, and other formal observers may have in the process of separating aesthetic innovation from its experiential context. There is, for example, a tendency in jazz literature to pronounce that the opening of the Benny Goodman band at the Polomar in Los Angeles on August 21, 1935, "was the beginning of Swing as a mainstream development in popular music."[47] Such analyses may or may not also incorporate the broader perspective on swing's emergence such as is available in Thomas Hennessey's recently updated review of jazz's historical path into American mainstream culture.[48] (In considerable depth, Hennessey highlights the emergence during the late 1920s and early 1930s of the arranged "riffing" big-band style that became a national phenomenon and that was principally associated with black arrangers such as Fletcher Henderson, Don Redmon, Duke Ellington, and Benny Moten.) Regardless of whether jazz writers do incorporate this broader historiographic perspective, their assertions that Goodman's band marks "the beginning" help subtly shape discourse that diassociates aesthetic innovation from its experiential context. The language of the discourse has determined that "the Swing era was the era of Benny Goodman, of Artie Shaw, Glenn Miller, the Dorsey brothers, Charlie Barnet, Harry James, Woody Herman, Gene Krupa, and others."[49]

In the case of jazz, unfortunately, a significant amount of this kind of discourse comes from observers who undoubtedly consider themselves to be strong advocates and affiliates. For example, although most writers almost ritually acknowledge the African-American roots of jazz, James Collier, credited with among the most comprehensive of the jazz histories, proposes with remarkable alacrity that "it is therefore surprising—indeed astonishing—that the direct evidence for this belief is slim to nonexistent."[50] His logic for this somewhat startling assertion involves first minimizing the significance of figures such as Buddy Bolden and then arguing that other originators such as Jelly Roll Morton, Kid Orly, and Sidney Bechet were Creoles, "not 'blacks' in the ordinary sense of the word."[51]

His argument seems to miss what may be a subtle factor. When Creoles constituted a separate caste from Blacks in the Louisiana social hierarchy, they did not play jazz. In an otherwise illuminating summary of the Creole tradition in Louisiana history, Collier fails to note how Creole musicians, as a result of losing their "downtown" jobs, where they worked with and among whites, following the enforcement of local segregation legislation, had to redirect themselves aesthetically and economically toward the "uptown" Black community. At that time, Creole musicians did, in fact, become "blacks in the ordinary sense of the word," and it was in this specific context that they, incorporating techniques they had learned from uptown Blacks, participated in the creation of jazz. Indeed, it might be stated that Creole participation in jazz came directly as a result of the "discovery" by Creole musicians of their Blackness. In this context the answer to Collier's rhetorical question—"Is jazz actually 'expressive of and uniquely rooted in the experience of black Americans?'"—is simple.[52] Yes. Emphatically yes. It is.

Conclusion

In many ways it is certainly true, as Collier wants to argue regarding jazz, that popular music forms derived from Black innovation "surely . . . belong[s] to all of us."[53] As part of facilitating the evolution of popular culture from premodern folk cultural roots, demographics, modern technology, media, and various other factors have appeared to blur the distinction between what music or culture is or is not Black. It has become less accurate to speak of Black popular music than of the "Black influence on popular music."

However, the added complexity of modernity has not changed the basic dynamics of innovation, interaction, and diffusion with respect to African-American musical sensibility. Despite blurred or changing cultural boundaries, a discernible folk/popular strain of African-American culture remains the chief source of distinctiveness as well as the main source of innovation for those Black musical sensibilities that diffuse into and are appropriated by the white-dominated wider culture. The "mouth" or "source" of the historical stream of sensibilities connecting Black Americans with an African cultural heritage has always been located among the least assimilated sectors of the Black community. Historically this was the South. Today it also includes the least assimilated, structurally isolated urban areas.

As new aesthetic energies emerge from such sectors, diffusion into the white-dominated wider culture provides motivation for Black musicians to shape their products to cater especially to that interest, even while it also motivate whites to imitate or reproduce the new forms. In addition to profit as a motivation for appealing to white audiences, African American performers and innovators may be motivated by the possibility of being recognized and rewarded as artists rather than rejected and scorned as lowlifes, as Black entertainers in earlier periods were. (Scott Joplin and Jelly Roll both craved this recognition—even more, perhaps, than the financial reward—which tragically eluded both.)

In this process of interaction with mainstream culture, the new music form becomes a less authentic means of representing and expressing the peculiarities of Black "beingness." In effect, the now "integrated" phenomenon becomes redefined, and invariably the new concept is "white" for all practical purposes; it is no longer connected to blackness. Undoubtedly with the best of intentions, Collier, whose logic seeks to separate jazz from Black culture per se, illustrates how this happens almost better than I could: "Jazz has had a primarily white audience for perhaps seventy-five years. Jazz criticism was devised by whites and has been mainly in white hands ever since. Jazz education, since it began to have a real existence in the early 1950s, had been dominated by whites. And ever since jazz began to revive in the 1970s . . .

white players . . . have done as much to give the music direction as blacks have."[54]

Although some African-American artists have been able over the years to improve on the legacies of those earlier creative but tragic figures, the involvement of whites, as consumers, performers, and owners, with forms of Black music has the result of keeping that number low and of rewarding, in several senses of that term, white appropriation more than Black innovation. Moreover, as the innovations become dissociated from the experiential context from which they arise, they begin to lose their functions as statements of affirmation and humanity relative to those contexts. In the end the appropriative process accomplishes a destructive consumption of the dreams, the creative hearts, the very souls of Black folks. In some sense even the millions, really billions or trillions, of dollars reaped from "commercial exploitation" of African-American aesthetic genius cannot pay for that loss. It is perhaps some consolation that in spite of the continual siphoning of the creative impulses of African-American culture, its dynamism somehow allows it to go on re-creating, reshaping, and reaffirming Black humanity.

Notes

1. At various times and in various formats, pianist Teddy Wilson, vibraphonist Lionel Hampton, trumpeter Cootie Williams, and guitarist Charlie Christian were also featured.

2. Or he bought as many as thirty-six scores, depending on sources. See James Lincoln Collier, *The Making of Jazz: A Comprehensive History* (Boston: Houghton Mifflin, 1978), 261; Marshall Stearns, *The Story of Jazz* (New York: Oxford University Press, 1956), 200.

3. Ben Sidran, *Black Talk* (New York: De Capo Press, 1971), 32.

4. Quoted in William D. Pierson, *Black Legacy: America's Hidden Heritage* (Amherst: University of Massachusetts Press, 1993), 173.

5. Donald A. Donaldson, "A Window on Slave Culture: Dances at Congo Square in New Orleans, 1800–1862," *Journal of Negro Education* 69(1) (Spring 1984): 61–72.

6. *Times-Picayne,* June 20, 1918.

7. William J. Schafer and Johanes Riedel, *The Art of Ragtime* (New York: Da Capo Press, 1977; originally published in Baton Rouge: Louisiana State University Press, 1973), xi.

8. Donald M. Marquis, *In Search of Buddy Bolden: First Man of Jazz* (Baton Rouge: Louisiana State University Press, 1978), 43.

9. Ibid., 74.

10. E. Belfield Spriggins, "Excavating Local Jazz," *Louisiana Weekly,* April 22, 1933, 5; quoted in Marquis, *In Search of Buddy Bolden,* 2.

11. Rudi Blesh and Harriet Janis, *They All Played Ragtime* (New York: Oak Publications, 1971; originally published in New York: Knopf, 1950). "As early as elsewhere there was a school of piano ragtimers in New Orleans. Back so far indeed that

the black, itinerant John the Baptist of that city, who roamed the mid-American red-light districts from the late seventies into the nineties, is almost a legend. . . . Piano and band developed separately in New Orleans, but grew side by side into the same sort of music" (165).

12. Marquis, *In Search of Buddy Bolden,* 33.

13. Sidran, *Black Talk,* 37; Marquis, *In Search of Buddy Bolden,* 37.

14. Blesh and Janis, *They All Played Ragtime,* 168.

15. Martin W. Laforse and James A. Drake, *Popular Culture and American Life: Selected Topics in the Study of American Popular Culture* (Chicago: Nelson Hall, 1981), 75.

16. Ibid., 43.

17. Laforse and Drake, *Popular Culture and American Life,* 82; Blesh and Janis, *They All Played Ragtime,* 168.

18. Laforse and Drake, *Popular Culture and American Life,* 89.

19. Paul Goodman and Frank Otto Gatell, *America in the Twenties: The Beginnings of Contemporary America* (New York: Holt, Rinehart and Winston, 1972), 87.

20. Sidran, *Black Talk,* 68.

21. Laforse and Drake, *Popular Culture and American Life,* 89.

22. Ibid., 91.

23. Blesh and Janis, *They All Played Ragtime,* 176.

24. Laforse and Drake, *Popular Culture and American Life,* 45.

25. Beiderbecke certainly does share at least one fact in common with several important African-American innovators: a tragically short life. A familiar gang of suspects—alcohol, disaffection, alienation, and economic ruin—lurk suggestively around his death at age twenty-eight in 1931.

26. Thomas Hennessey, *From Jazz to Swing: African-American Jazz Musicians and Their Music, 1890–1935* (Detroit: Wayne State University Press, 1993), chaps. 5–7.

27. Sidran, *Black Talk,* 78.

28. Perry A. Hall, "Toward a Dramaturgical Analysis of Historical Transformation in African-American Musical Culture," *Word: A Black Culture Journal* 1(1) (Spring 1991): 29–38.

29. Sidran, *Black Talk,* 59.

30. LeRoi Jones, *Blues People: The Negro Experience in White America and the Music That Developed from It* (New York: Morrow, 1963), 167.

31. Ibid., 182.

32. Nelson George, *The Death of Rhythm and Blues* (New York: Dutton, 1988), 26.

33. Ibid.

34. Ibid., 61–69.

35. Ian Hoare, Tony Cummings, Clive Anderson, and Simon Frith, *The Soul Book* (New York: Dell, 1975), 25.

36. Peter Guralnick, *Sweet Soul Music: Rhythm and Blues and the Southern Dream of Freedom* (New York: Harper and Row, 1986), 50–66.

37. George, *The Death of Rhythm and Blues,* chap. 3.

38. Nelson George. *Where Did Our Love Go?: The Rise and Fall of the Motown Sound* (New York: St. Martin's Press, 1985), 103.

39. Hoare et al., *The Soul Book,* 55.

40. George, *Where Did Our Love Go?* 128.

41. Sidran, *Black Talk,* 53.

42. George, *The Death of Rhythm and Blues,* chaps. 5–6.

43. Sidran, *Black Talk,* 67.

44. George, *The Death of Rhythm and Blues,* 154.

45. Tommie Lee Lott, "Marooned in America: Black Urban Youth Culture and Social Pathology," (1990, unpublished ms), 19.

46. *Detroit Metro Times,* February 19, 1990.

47. Arnold Shaw, *Black Popular Music in America: From the Spirituals, Minstrels, and Ragtime to Soul, Disco, and Hip-Hop* (New York: Schirmer Books, 1986), 145.

48. Hennessey, *From Jazz to Swing.*

49. Shaw, *Black Popular Music in America,* 146.

50. James Lincoln Collier, *Jazz: The American Theme Song* (New York: Oxford University Press, 1993), 189. However, according to Collier, the generally accepted view is that, "though the genesis of jazz in the black subculture was widely accepted, by the middle of the 1920s it seemed clear to most people that it had washed through the society enough to have escaped the culture of its birth" (186).

51. Ibid., 189.

52. Ibid., 185.

53. Ibid., 224.

54. Ibid., 219.

Anthony Seeger

Ethnomusicology
and Music Law

Looking backward to the seminal thinkers in comparative musicology and forward to the global networks of electronic communications that will further dominate our artistic, scholarly, and communicatory processes, I think we should add a course on entertainment law to our ethnomusicology curricula.[1] The complexities of the relationships of melodic line and rhythm in Indian classical music, the poetic metaphors through which the Kaluli express their musical ideas,[2] and the reasons Suyá sing[3] have their counterpoint in the cultural elaboration of music-related law in the United States and other industrialized countries. Furthermore, the terms through which we will be able to experience and communicate about South Indian, Kaluli, or Suyá music are probably going to be established by the concepts of music of the industrialized countries, rather than the South Indians, the Kaluli, or the Suyá. Thus we must look at entertainment law not because it represents yet one more example of the ingenuity for complexification found in Homo sapiens, but because the daily exercise of our profession takes place within contexts partly defined by it.

Scholars, you may think, need not concern themselves with entertainment law because they are not in the entertainment business. Leaving aside the tendency of course evaluations to contradict that claim, how many ethnomusicologists collect field recordings? How many hold (or have ceded to a third party) copyrights on their publications? How many ethnomusicologists produce ethnographic recordings on commercial (albeit marginally so) record labels or as supplements to their textbooks? Most of us have done one or more of these things without much thought about the law that surrounds them. But there are possibly other reasons ethnomusicologists have not given much thought to entertainment law in their own countries. Among them are a theoretical predisposition to ignore judicial concepts related to music in our research, an uncritical (and perhaps unconscious) re-elaboration of the concepts of twentieth-century copyright law in our writings, and a lack of intellectual engagement with the globalization of the world's economy and its implications for the objects of our research.

Among the "founding fathers" of comparative musicology and ethnomusicology we find a predominance of psychologists and physicists, cultural anthropologists who tended to emphasize consensus over conflict, and historical and systematic musicologists, but few jurists. This contrasts with the situation in British social anthropology, where jurists abounded and Henry Maine's 1861 study of ancient law in Rome[4] had a profound influence on future approaches to social processes (including those of A. R. Radcliffe-Brown and E. E. Evans-Pritchard). The judicial tendency of social anthropology was further emphasized in the work of Max Gluckman and his followers, who argued that the best place to discover the structures of society was in areas of conflict—in arguments, court cases, rituals of rebellion, and so on. Of course, exclusive focus on conflict can lead to its own excesses. Social and musical processes proceed with a complex mix of consensus and conflict. The point, however, is that no major figure in the field of ethnomusicology ever defined the object of our study in terms of rights and obligations, conflict, or adjudication. The issues simply were not raised by our "ancestors" and have rarely been part of our theoretical reflections since.

Law is the codification of rights and obligations, but not all rights and obligations are laws. Some rights and obligations fall under the heading of custom (what people do); others may be called ethics (what people should do). Some of the rights and obligations related to music are very pertinent to an understanding of musical processes in any society, including that of the United States today; others are important for the practice of our profession, and yet others are barely generalizable beyond the society in which they are found.

How little we, as a group of professionals, seem to know about this subject was highlighted in responses to a questionnaire sent out by the ICTM in 1989. The International Council for Traditional Music's Copyright Committee sent a letter to ICTM members asking for information about music ownership in the countries in which they lived and in the communities in which they did their research. The form included questions about both formal copyright rules and traditional notions of ownership.[5] A relatively small percentage of those queried responded—although most of us recognize the issue to be an important one—and many of those who did respond appeared to know little about music ownership in either of their communities.

To show how complex the issue of music ownership can be I shall begin with the traditional set of concepts employed by the Suyá Indians of Brazil,[6] and then move through stages of research, publication, and dissemination of their music. This approach is meant to be cautionary as well as illustrative—I did not pay as much attention to these issues then as I would today, and there are no clear answers to some questions. Furthermore, many of these considerations apply to video and print media, as well as our own use of our colleagues' publications.

Ownership, Control, and Mastery in a Traditional Society

When talking about ownership of Suyá song, the best term to begin with is the concept *kandé*. *Kandé* translates roughly as "owner/controller," though it could also be glossed as "master of." Physical objects such as axes, stools, and cooking pots have *kandé*. Other people may use these items, but the *kandé* is the one who gives permission for their use, and the person to whom they are eventually returned. There is another sense in which people may be *kandé* of a physical object: they may be experts in manufacturing it. Thus the best pot-maker in the village might be called the pot-*kandé* because she knows best how to make them ("master potter" would be a reasonable gloss). The person for whom it was made would also be the pot-*kandé*. In this case one individual is a master of production; another is a controller of use. A single word refers to both.

Village leaders are also referred to as "owner/controllers." Historically, most villages have had two leaders. One of these is the village political leader, the *mẽro-pa-kandé* (*mẽ* = Suyá; *pa* = village; *kandé* = owner/controller/ master). The other major leader is the village ritual specialist, the *mẽro-kin-kandé* (*mẽ* = Suyá; *kin* = ceremonies; *kandé* = owner/controller/master). The two complement each other in that the political leader is rarely a specialist in rituals, but he is the leader of the strongest political faction. A ritual specialist is supposed to know more than anyone else about music and ceremony; he directs activities in a sphere that is supposed to be above factionalism. If political leadership is somewhat ascribed (a son of a strong faction leader is often also one), the position of ritual leader is achieved through learning and held because of knowledge rather than inheritance. In fact, the ritual specialist is often a relative of a strong faction leader.[7]

But the concept of "owning/controlling" song goes far beyond being the master of ritual knowledge. Since there are two major types of songs—individual (*akia*) and collective (*ngere*)—there are also two kinds of owner/controllers. As European law is based on the individual, I shall start with the individual.

Suyá men learn new individual shout-songs (*akia*) for each ceremony, and a man may learn dozens in a lifetime. He is taught these new songs by a "person-without-spirit" who in turn has walked in the forest and learned a song from some natural being (plants, fish, animals). The *originator* of the song is a specific plant, fish, or animal species. The *communicator* of the song (the person who most nearly fits the Western concept of "composer") is the person-without-spirit. The *owner/controller* (*kandê*) of the song is the person who learns it and sings it aloud for the first time. Thus the song I sang in the 1972 Mouse Ceremony was "my" song, although the ritual specialist taught it to me. The Suyá said I had become its "owner/controller" and if someone sang it badly, I could complain.[8]

The association of a person with his individual songs continues for a while after his death. After a man dies, he may be commemorated by a younger man (usually a relative) who will sing his shout-songs throughout an entire day. The young man's singing may provoke relatives of the deceased to tears, as they listen to the songs associated with their late kinsman's euphoria and participation in community life. The association doesn't often last beyond a single generation (I don't remember any Suyá singing a song of a person they had never seen alive), and I never heard of a spirit criticizing the performance of its songs.

Groups are owner/controllers of collective songs. These may be "very old," original to the ceremony, or historically composed unison songs. The "very old" songs come from a mythical past; the composed songs follow a similar process to that of the individual song. An animal's song is introduced to the group through a person-without-spirit, and then becomes associated with the group that sang it for the first time.

Virtually every Suyá group controls one or more songs. Each ceremonial moiety (literally one of a pair of groups) controls certain songs, and is identified with them. In some cases a moiety controls an entire ceremony. In that case the members of the opposite moiety formally ask the controlling moiety whether they may perform the ceremony. The controlling moiety is supposed to be stern, and ask if the supplicants are going to work hard and sing strongly, or are just wanting to fool around. They are assured that the affair will be serious, give their consent, and the ceremony is begun. Since the other moiety often controls a ceremony paired with the first one, the giving moiety often has to request permission shortly afterward. Ownership in these cases is more a right that one exercises in giving than in restricting. I did hear of one case in which a moiety did not give its permission.

There are other forms of intellectual property among the Suyá that are more individualized and more similar to our own concepts of creativity and control. Curing invocations (*sangere*) are different from songs. They are learned from other Suyá or made up, and are passed on by decision of their "owner/controller," who receives a gift in return. In the case of a very powerful invocation to remove the pain of scorpion and spider bites, the owner/controller thought it was so valuable that he didn't teach it to anyone, and died its sole possessor. In this case an individual may compose an invocation, perform it on sick people (who will give him or her a gift if they get better), and decide when and if they will teach it to someone else (also with the obligation for a return gift).[9]

Enter the Researcher with His Tape Recorder

My wife and I arrived among the Suyá as foreigners whose command of the language was that of an infant, and whose Suyá enculteration was less even than Indians they had captured in the past. The Suyá made considerable allowances for us, the extent of which I am still probably unaware. They knew about tape recorders, and had been recorded before I arrived. But since I had come specifically to study music, and since I stayed much longer than any previous visitor, I was a new element in the music control equation. The Suyá made no objection to my recording them, remarked that the tape recorder remembered things much better than I did, and even once asked me to play back a session where a man-without-spirit had taught them a song that subsequently no one could remember. Some of them also wanted to be sure the traditions that most of them valued would be preserved, and supported my systematic collecting. They didn't mind my taking the tapes back with me. What they didn't want was for me to play certain kinds of music for other nearby Indian communities. They didn't want the other Indians to "hear/know" the music. I think the real objection was that the other Indians might begin to sing certain of their songs, because once you hear/know it, you are able to sing it. Other songs, however, they had no objection to my playing to their neighbors on my way in or out of the field.

Suyá control went beyond asking me not to play certain recordings locally.

They wouldn't even record certain things. One song, whose performance was so powerful that it could bring down an enemy attack, was interrupted and left incomplete because they realized I would certainly play it sometime, and the location for playback had no effect on the power of the songs. They were always dangerous. With as little experience as they had with recordings, therefore, there were already some things the Suyá wanted to control. Because I stayed long enough to understand the subtlety with which they expressed these preferences, I have honored them. Most visitors would have not even known of their concerns, or cared much about them.

What were the rights and obligations in the recording encounter? Clearly, the Suyá thought they had rights over selecting the performances and controlling the playback. My obligations, I thought, required me to observe their desires. But how would future users know about our agreements—and would the Suyá in the future remember that they had given me permission to record these songs?

I thought I needed evidence of my right to make the recordings in the first place. I tried to have performers state their permission to record them at the start of every tape or every event (not being literate, it would have been absurd to ask them to sign a release they could not read in a language they did not understand). Who, though, was I asking? I may have been asking the wrong person. Or once asked, it may be difficult to say no, and possible only to say "Hmmmmm, what?"—easily misunderstood to be agreement in the heat of the event.[10] Whom should I have asked? The animal who originated the song?[11] The person who transmitted it? The person who was dead who had sung it? The person who was singing it? These issues were never clarified, partly because I wasn't very concerned with them myself, at the time.

Enter the Audio Archive

When I left the field, ownership presented new problems. Who controlled the recorded material? Was it "mine" because I recorded it during an individual investigation? This is certainly the feeling most field researchers have toward their recordings. But my research was done on a National Institutes of Health (NIH) research grant. Did the recordings belong to the NIH? Or did they belong to the University of Chicago because the NIH grant was given to the University, which subsequently awarded it to me? Or did they still belong to the Suyá who gave me the permission to record them, or to the specific groups that controlled them, or to the people-without-spirits who taught them, or to the animals that originally sang them? Or did they belong to the

Brazilian government that had given me permission to do the research and claimed to be the uniquely qualified agents of the Suyá?

I felt that the recordings were not mine, except in the sense that I had made them in the course of my research. The sounds belonged to the Suyá community and the tapes to some intermediary. Since some Suyá wanted the recordings preserved for their grandchildren, I deposited the tapes in the Indiana University Archives of Traditional Music. There were no suitable audio archives in Brazil at that time that would have preserved them.

The Archives of Traditional Music gave me a form to fill in and three degrees of restriction to choose among. Did I want free access for all purposes, free access for non-commercial purposes, or limited access requiring my authorization?

This raised some new issues. Who should decide about the restrictions? Who would guarantee that no one would make a copy of a ceremony, (inadvertently) take it to precisely the place the Suyá didn't want their music heard, and play it there? Once in the archives, who should be able to consult the recordings? I found out later that restrictions were such that in some cases members of the community recorded were prevented from listening to recordings of their own music because the depositor had restricted access, without exceptions. He/she had probably done so inadvertently, and then disappeared from the address list, so that the Archives could not request permission for others to use the material. Regardless of the motive, the enduring legacy was one of rights, and the collector had claimed them all.[12]

One of the things I subsequently did as Director of the Archives of Traditional Music was to revise the contracts to correct some of the inadequacies that stood out when I was trying to decide how to allocate rights to the sounds between the Suyá, myself, and the Archives. But it is difficult to predict future inadequacies. The point here is that although Western copyright law hasn't even been invoked yet, the networks of rights and obligations on these sounds are already very complex indeed. Each intermediary adds a level of overlapping rights.

Enter the Recording Company

The Suyá asked me why I hadn't issued a commercial recording of their music, as another community's anthropologist had already done. I took that as permission to negotiate to make one. But the issues of a commercial recording are distinct from field recordings. While I could be pretty sure my tapes wouldn't be played for nearby Indian communities, I could be virtually certain that some of the biggest fans of the future commercial recording would be those same nearby Indian communities. Nor could I or any of the other "owner/controllers" control where or how it would be played. Record companies are famous for making money, and artists are famous for complaining they aren't getting much of it. How would the non-literate Suyá and the innocent ethnomusicologist enter this complex domain?

We ended up co-producing the recording, the Suyá carefully selecting what should not be on the recording, I working on a sequence that would make sense to non-Suyá and writing the notes, and the Suyá receiving full royalties from the modest sales. In order to do so, I paid them in full in advance out of pocket, then reimbursed myself from the sales over time, paying income tax on those royalties (since the Suyá were considered minors, under the executorship of the Brazilian Government, there was no other way to get the royalties directly into their hands). Our recording was a somewhat costly endeavor for me, but very satisfying to the Suyá, who have also benefited from a Japanese CD reissue.

The basic issue in commercial recordings is trust. But not everyone carrying a tape recorder has proven to be trustworthy. Nor has every record company proven to be scrupulous. Nor have ethics about the recording and use of other people's music always been the same. Using the intellectual property of non-Western societies is still unregulated today, but our awareness is changing.[13]

Record companies and commercial recordings are the interface between communities like the Suyá and the multi-national recording industry. That industry operates according to a highly complex set of rules of its own that have nothing to do with the original animal composers, the people-without-spirits, the kandé who sang the song for the first time, the moiety that controls its performance, or even the ethnomusicologist who supplies them with a tape. Record companies usually copyright the recording and negotiate for its subleasing. Most record companies also have a publishing company, which may take out the copyright on any recently composed songs.

Copyright: Ownership and Control Become Business

Copyright law is complicated. Different countries have different laws. I will only deal with generalities here.[14] Like all laws, the codification of copyright law in the United States reflects a certain perspective (and certain powerful interest groups) within the music industry, and is the direct result of a particular set of historical processes in the United States.

Copyright is what it says: the right to make copies. Whether it is copies of sheet music or copies of a musical performance, the right to make copies can be claimed, registered, and negotiated. There are two aspects of music that may be separately copyrighted. One is the song, its melody and text. Thus Woody Guthrie can copyright "This Land Is Your Land," and certain uses of the song are controlled by the publishing company, which normally collects payment for commercial use. The second part is the singing itself. If I record the song "This Land Is Your Land" on a record, the company can copyright my singing, but it will have to pay a royalty to the publishing company for the song. But a company can own a song only for the life of the composer plus fifty years (current copyright length). After that, it is public domain. My grandchildren will be able to record "This Land Is Your Land" as often as they like without paying the publisher.

The copyright law in force today is based on a number of cultural presuppositions, four of which are central to issues faced by ethnomusicologists. First, the law is based on the concept of individual creativity—individuals copyright products of their own creation. Second, it is based on the idea that an individual should receive compensation for a limited period of time, after which the idea may be used by anyone without paying a royalty. After the expiration of a copyright, music enters "the public domain" and royalties may not be collected on it. Third, the law leaves somewhat unclear the status of arrangements of "traditional" songs. Fourth, the musical item copyrighted is item-title based. Let's look at the implications through three examples.

Copyright at Work

A composer once wrote a song to celebrate birthdays, and copyrighted it under the name of "Happy Birthday." Happily for him, the song became an integral part of rites of passage in the United States, and since a publishing company vigilantly administered the copyright, every concert performance, commercial recording, television performance, and film performance of that simple melody and repetitive text bring money to the composer and his publishing company—nearly $1 million a year in the 1980s (David Sengstack, former administrator of the copyright, conversation). Under existing copyright law a composer writes a song, copyrights it with a publishing company, and they both receive a considerable amount of money from the music industry, which is set up to allocate such royalties.

Copyright Unworkable

Compare "Happy Birthday" with a Suyá song called "Big Turtle Song" published on *A Arte Vocal dos Suyá*.[15] Sung during the dry season, its authorship in the distant past is attributed to a species of honeybee. Sharing its name ("Big Turtle Song") with dozens of other melodies and texts sung at the same time of year, "Big Turtle Song" doesn't fit the U.S. popular music–based model. It was originally composed over seventy-five years ago, and is "owned" by a community, not an individual. To complicate this, the Suyá are not considered fully "adult" in Brazilian law, and have neither corporate nor individual legal identity. Tacape Records and I may indicate our control of the use of the master tape on which that particular version of "Big Turtle Song" is recorded, but if someone else wants to use its musical ideas, there isn't much that I, the record company, or the Suyá can do about it. Even if we stretched some of the intentions of international copyright law and copyrighted the song as an arrangement of traditional material, we would not have the staff or expertise to ensure compliance.

Copyright Contested

Those are the pure cases. U.S. musical practice is filled with conflict and adjudication, as anyone who has spent much time with professional musicians or reads *Billboard* can attest. Whether the conflict is with management, boards of directors, recording companies, copyright infringement, or colleagues, it is clear that music is made in a social matrix as contentious as most of the rest of the society.

Consider "Home on the Range."[16] John A. Lomax collected the text in 1908, a schoolteacher set it to music, and Lomax published the song in his book of cowboy songs in 1910. A sheet music version followed in 1925, and the 1927 recording by Vernon Dalhart became popular.

In 1932, when Franklin D. Roosevelt was first elected president, the story quickly spread that "Home on the Range" was his favorite song. In concert halls, on records, and over the radio, the song spread throughout the world, but suddenly it was pulled from air play, off of record racks, and out of repertories. A couple in Arizona claimed to have written it and filed a half-million dollar lawsuit for infringement of copyright.

Music publishers [to contest the lawsuit] hired an attorney, Samuel Moanfeldt, to trace the song's heritage. He terminated the search in Kansas where he found the poem had been published as early as 1873 in the newspaper *Smith County Pioneer.* Further research revealed that it was written by Dr. Brewster Higley and set to music by Daniel E. Kelley, both early Kansas settlers.[17]

Some of the most in-depth research on western song seems to have been done under the sting of a lawsuit. It probably pays better than most research grants; the stakes are higher.

Not all of the copyright debate centers on who wrote a song. Some of it swirls around what the minimum definition of a musical idea is. What exactly is it that the copyright covers? This is the controversy about sampling, a widespread practice in contemporary popular music (but not restricted to popular music) in which a very short segment of a recorded performance is taken and used in a variety of ways in someone else's composition. As always, in popular music the stakes are high and the lawyers will be paid. The decision may not tell us much about music—though one could argue that the law courts are as good a place as a university classroom to determine the minimum definition of a musical theme. As with the search for the author of "Home on the Range," some very interesting research may result from conflict over this issue.

Steve Feld has observed that as American popular music adapts music from other parts of the world into hit-oriented recordings, the potential for exploitation increases. His presentation of the problem is metaphoric and powerful:

> Musical appropriation sings a double line with one voice. It is a melody of admiration, even homage and respect; a fundamental source of connectedness, creativity, and innovation. This we locate in a discourse of "roots," of reproducing and expanding "the tradition." Yet this voice is harmonized by a counter-melody of power, even control and domination; a fundamental source of maintaining asymmetries in ownership and commodification of musical works. This we locate in a discourse of "rip-offs," of reproducing "the hegemonic." Appropriation means that the issue of "whose music" is submerged, supplanted, and subverted by the assertion of "our music."[18]

An important form of exploitation is music copyright. If I take the melody of "Big Turtle Song" and set new words to it, I might copyright it "Words and Music by Anthony Seeger." Does this matter?

It only really matters when the song is a hit or is used in a film. The royalty payment for a copyrighted song on an album is about six cents per recording sold. If a company only sells 4,000 copies (about average for Smithsonian/Folkways releases today), a songwriter stands to gain $240 per cut (usually for a maximum of $2,400 if they composed all the songs on the album). If, however, the recording sells 7,000,000 copies (the case with the album *Graceland* by Paul Simon), the stakes are higher: a single song could yield $420,000 from that recording alone. If the Suyá "Big Turtle Song" could earn that much, or become the next "Happy Birthday" ritual music, the Suyá could manage very well on this interest from earnings from their cultural patrimony—something I think they could enjoy.[19] In fact, very little money is made on most research-based "ethnographic" recordings, which have generally sold relatively few copies and usually have to be subsidized to be published at all. Inflated expectations based on news items about the multimillion dollar contracts of Michael and Janet Jackson, however, can make even legitimate royalties seem like a deceit.

United States law favors song publishers over artists. In the United States, song publishers receive money from radio play of their music. Artists do not get paid when their recordings (as opposed to their compositions) get played on the radio. In other words, Woody Guthrie's estate gets paid when my version of "This Land Is Your Land" gets wide radio play, but I don't collect. This is not the case in Europe, where both artists and publishing companies collect payments. Of course, this may simply reduce airplay for new compositions. Some European radio stations are switching to old performances of music by dead composers because it is so much less expensive than paying royalties to performers and music copyright owners (this works better for European classical music than for popular music, of course).

U.S. copyright law has international implications, especially when the U.S. retaliates against publications it considers to be piracy. But in view of the shortcomings of U.S. copyright law, other countries are often suspicious of U.S. motives. Writing in *Music Business International* (1991) Dave Liang maintains that "nobody defends copyright infringements, but are the Americans attacking it in the right way?"[20] He suggests that some countries that do not rush to copyright reforms on the U.S. model are in fact trying to protect their local music industries from the transnational giants that dominate most of the globe.

In fact, the copyright law is far from equitable, and the U.S. is less generous than most to artists. The new GATT talks (the so-called Uruguay Round) may result in some changes of international copyright codes, however, and UNESCO has been working on statutes for controlling cultural property.[21] But there is a long way to go before "Big Turtle Song" is protected and the Suyá are collecting from public performances.

Six Perspectives on Music Ownership

I am concerned about musical rights from at least six slightly different perspectives—as a musician, as a researcher, as a co-producer with a tribal society of a commercial cultural product,[22] as a record company director who has to match costs to income within the entertainment industry business as it is set up today, as a member of the copyright committee of the International Council for Traditional Music (ICTM), and as an ethnomusicologist.

Each of my perspectives represents entire groups of people, and each views the implications of music ownership differently. Much of the conflict in the area can be explained by the fact that most actors have only a single perspective on the subject in which they have heavily invested, and don't really understand the concerns of other actors.

1. As a *musician,* I think we need to recognize that in many traditions musicians take existing musical ideas and transform them. Almost every performance is a creative event. In this area I am concerned about the effects of existing or intended laws that might inhibit live performances and restrict the exchange of musical ideas. There is a distinct possibility that future laws will further inhibit live, creative performances, although it is precisely the creative and performative nature of music that gives it much of its vitality.

2. As a *researcher,* I am concerned about the effect the perception that "someone is getting rich on our music" has had on music research. This is particularly important for ethnomusicologists today. It is sometimes very difficult to study a community's music because individuals and groups are suspicious of strangers carrying tape recorders. They may have some justification for their concern, since some "arrangements" of traditional music have reaped great financial rewards while the tradition-bearers themselves have never seen any money. Also, not everyone who proclaims him- or herself a researcher is in fact engaged in scholarly research—"research" covers a multitude of activities, some of which appear to be more like musical piracy. Yet some graduate students and many of my colleagues appear to be insufficiently aware of the ethical issues their apparently simply recordings may raise. As a result they are not obtaining the kinds of information about restrictions and the kinds of permissions while in the field that will enable their recordings to be appropriately used afterward.

3. As a *co-producer of a recording* with the Suyá Indians, I am concerned about the lack of protection provided by law against the improper appropriation of Suyá traditional music for other purposes—uses that would be rigorously policed if the music were performed by the Beatles, but which cannot be policed when it is "only" performed by the best living Suyá musicians.

4. As the *director of a small record company,* I am concerned about all of the ethical issues above, but I also have to produce recordings that can compete in price with other recordings in a given market. Small record companies go out of business all the time, or are absorbed by larger ones; there isn't much room for financial error. This means that I cannot allocate much more money to artists and songwriters than other companies do if I want to sell enough copies to make enough from one recording to pay for the production of the next one. It means I do not have time or staff to individually research the rights to every song on every recording but must rely on the opinions of the artist, compiler, or publishing companies. It means that whatever laws are put into effect must be reasonably simple for me to understand and concrete mechanisms provided to make it easy for me to obey them. Ideal laws will not

protect musicians, ensure compliance, or alter ethnomusicological practice. What we need is a new awareness of the issues of musical ownership and the ethics of inter-cultural music use—something akin to the ecological awareness that encourages individuals to change their individual attitudes and provides concrete means through which they can change their daily practices. Recycling, for example, works best where people are not only convinced it is a good idea but are also provided with convenient ways to recycle their waste. The same kind of awareness and convenience needs to be created for cultural property.

5. As a *member of the ICTM committee on musical copyright,* I hope that the United States and Europe will not impose their individualized, popular music–fuelled concepts of music ownership on the rest of the world through international conventions without some modification. I think we need to examine the shortcomings of existing systems, especially with respect to the rights of communities and vernacular artists to benefit from any commercial exploitation of their arts.

6. As an *ethnomusicologist,* I am concerned that this whole area of musical practice has been virtually ignored in ethnomusicological research and publications. There are dozens of fascinating topics to be thought through in this area, but few of us have made even a beginning on them. An ethnomusicology devoted entirely to the effects of the global economy on music would be limited indeed, but it certainly should not escape our attention altogether. Our discipline will be poorer for neglecting the rights and obligations associated with music, and we will have less and less to contribute to a dialogue about contemporary music, which is increasingly shaped by the very processes we appear to be ignoring.

Notes

1. I am indebted to Alan Jabbour, Krister Malm, Judith McColloh, and Steven Feld for sending me their publications (Joseph E. Hickerson, and Katherine W. Johnston, comps., "Copyright and Folksong [A Bibliography]." [Washington, D.C.: Library of Congress, Archive of Folk Culture, 1987]; Alan Jabbour, "Director's Column," *Folklife Center News* 5[2] [1982]: 2–4) and discussing this subject with me, and to Cultural Survival for giving me an opportunity to write some initial ideas about it. My research on the topic has been supported by the Center for Folklife Programs and Cultural History of the Smithsonian Institution. My research among the Suyá was funded by many different agencies over the years (see Anthony Seeger, *Why Suyá Sing: A Musical Anthropology of an Amazonian People* [Cambridge: Cambridge University Press, 1987], acknowledgments, for a complete list), to all of which I continue to be grateful.

2. Steven Feld, *Sound and Sentiment: Birds, Weeping, Poetics, and Song in Kaluli Expression* (Philadelphia: University of Pennsylvania Press, 1990).

3. Anthony Seeger, *Why Suyá Sing: A Musical Anthropology of an Amazonian People* (Cambridge: Cambridge University Press, 1987).

4. Henry S. Maine, *Ancient Law* (London: John Murray, 1906 [1861]).

5. For information on this, or a copy of the form, write to Krister Malm, ICTM Copyright Committee, Musikmuseet, Box 16236, S-103 26 Stockholm, Sweden.

6. Described in Anthony Seeger, *Nature and Society in Central Brazil: The Suyá of Mato Grosso* (Cambridge, Mass.: Harvard University Press, 1981), and *Why Suyá Sing: A Musical Anthropology of an Amazonian People.*

7. Seeger, *Nature and Society in Central Brazil,* 180–205.

8. Actually, they literally said that if someone sang it and fooled around singing it, I could, say "Hmmmmm, what?" I am not exactly sure what my rights might be beyond calling attention to the fact that I am the owner/controller and therefore the person in a position to say whether a performance is suitable or not.

9. Men-without-spirits who teach songs to their "owner/controllers" are not given any gifts, nor do they willfully withhold a song from people who ask for one.

10. Suyá etiquette demands that when you are asked for something you must give it, or at the most postpone giving it. Refusal to give something is a strong social act, and implies a severing of relationships. Thus it might be very difficult for the Suyá to respond to a direct question "May I record this?" with anything stronger than a "Hmmmmm, what? Later." This raises quite a few questions about the legitimacy of even formal contractual agreements between members of hierarchically ranged and culturally different communities.

11. When I was particularly insistent on knowing the meaning of a song text the ritual specialist couldn't understand, he said, "The only one who knows is the jaguar who taught us." The author seemed a bit beyond reach to me, and I dropped the question.

12. There are, of course, reasons that one might restrict members of the originating community from listening to tapes. For example, secret songs of one moiety or social group might need to be kept from another moiety or social group, or interviews about politics could be dangerous if they fell into the hands of the opposition.

13. See Cultural Survival, Inc., "Intellectual Property Rights: The Politics of Ownership," *Cultural Survival Quarterly* 15(1) (1991).

14. For more details consult E. P. Skone James and Peter Kleiner, "Copyright, United Kingdom and United States." ed. Stanley Sadie, *The New Grove Dictionary of Music and Musicians* (New York: Macmillian, 1981), 4:735–747, for general information; and S. Shemel, *This Business of Music* (New York: Billboard Books, 1990), for details about U.S. copyright practices in music. For criticism of current practices see R. Wallis and Kirster Malm, *Big Sounds from Small People: The Music Industry in Small Countries* (New York: Pendragon, 1984); and F. Dannen, *Hit Men: Power Brokers and Fast Money Inside the Music Business* (New York: Times Books, 1990).

15. Anthony Seeger e a Comunidade Suyá, *Música Indigena: A Arte Vocal dos Suyá* (recording) (Tacape 007, 1982).

16. Guy Logsdon, "Cowboy Songs on Folkways." Notes to recording *Cowboy Songs on Folkways,* Smithsonian/Folkways SF 40043 (1991): 4; John Lomax, "Half-Million Dollar Song," *Southwest Review* 32 (1945): 1–8; and John I. White, *Get Along Little Dogies: Songs and Songmakers of the American West* (Urbana: University of Illinois Press, 1975).

17. Logsdon, "Cowboy Songs on Folkways," 4.

18. Steven Feld, "Notes on the World Beat," *Public Culture Bulletin* 1(1) (1988): 31.

19. See Cultural Survival, Inc., "Intellectual Property Rights."

20. "Rights and Duties," *Music Business International* (June 1991).

21. Cultural Survival, Inc., "Intellectual Property Rights."

22. Seeger e a Comunidade Suyá, *Música Indigena*.

Part 2

Appropriation in Art
and Narrative

Lenore Keeshig-Tobias

Stop Stealing Native Stories

Aaa-Iii-Ee Y-aah! Clear the way. In a sacred manner I come. The stories
are mine!
—Ojibway war song

Critics of non-native writers who borrow from the native experience have
been dismissed as advocates of censorship and accused of trying to shackle
artistic imagination, but their objections are prompted by something much
more.

Where the Spirit Lives may be a bad film. *Bone Bird* by Calgary novelist
Darlene Barry Quaife may oversimplify native spirituality. W. P. Kinsella's
Hobbema stories may be insulting. But the real problem is that they amount
to culture theft, the theft of voice.

Canada's francophones have a strong and unique voice in North America.
Why? Because they have fought to ensure that their language remains intact.
Language is the conveyor of culture. It carries the ideas by which a nation
defines itself as a people. It gives voice to a nation's stories, its *mythos.*

How do Canadians feel about the U.S. mythos defining them and their
country? This is quickly becoming a reality, I fear, because Canadians have
been too quick to hand over their voice and their stories to Americans.

Stories, you see, are not just entertainment. Stories are power. They reflect
the deepest, the most intimate perceptions, relationships and attitudes of a
people. Stories show how a people, a culture, thinks. Such wonderful offer-
ings are seldom reproduced by outsiders.

This is the root of the problem with *Where the Spirit Lives,* which deals with the treatment of native students in government-sponsored residential schools during the 1930s. The film has been shown on the CBC and TV Ontario and as part of Canada Day at the recent festival in Palm Springs, California.

So what is it all about, anyway? In the end, a little Indian girl and her brother ride off into the vast, uninhabited wilderness (Anne Shirley goes west?). They ride right out of the sentimentalized Canadian consciousness—stoic child warriors noble in defeat, marching home with Bible in hand. (A book of truth, perhaps, but whose?)

Native people were not involved in any creative aspect of the film. Their voice was heard only through cultural consultants hired to provide the nuances and insights lacked by the movie's writer and producers.

Cultural insight, nuance and metaphor and symbols give a book or film the ring of truth, but their essence—the thing that gives stories universal appeal, that allows true empathy and shared emotion—is missing from *Where the Spirit Lives,* as it is from most "native" writing by non-natives.

Canadians all too often use native stories, symbols and history to sell things—cars, tobacco or movies. But why hasn't Basil Johnston's *Indian School Days* become a best-seller? Why hasn't *Half Breed* by Maria Campbell been reprinted? (Why, for that matter, has Ms. Campbell, as one of Canada's "celebrity" authors, never received a writer's grant?)

Where the Spirit Lives, after having squeezed out the native version of what happened in the residential schools, turns around and tells natives to make their own movies. How can we? Even if we had access to financial backers, they would say: "Residential schools? It's been done."

With native people struggling for justice with land claims and in education, what makes Canadians think they have equality in the film industry? In publishing? With agencies that make arts grants? In the arts themselves?

Instead, the Canadian cultural industry is stealing—unconsciously, perhaps, but with the same devastating results—native stories as surely as the missionaries stole our religion and the politicians stole our land and the residential schools stole our language. As Leslie Marmon Silko writes in *Ceremony,* stories "are all we have, you see—all we have to fight off illness and death." As a storyteller I was once advised by an elder that there is a season for storytelling—winter. "Blackflies, mosquitoes and other creatures like those stories," she cautioned.

How quaint, I thought. Nonetheless, I respected her advice and as time went on, I began to understand it. If storytellers sit around all summer telling stories, then surely they'll become the feast of blackflies and mosquitoes. My elder was telling me that these stories are meant for certain ears only—Native or non-Native.

So potent are stories that, in native culture, one storyteller cannot tell another's story without permission.

But why are Canadians so obsessed with native stories anyway? Why the urge to "write Indian"? Have Canadians run out of stories of their own? Or are their renderings just nostalgia for a simpler, more "at one with nature" stage of human development? There's a cliche for you.

Maybe Canadian stories about native people are some form of exorcism. Are they trying to atone for the horrible reality of native-Canadian relations? Or maybe they just know a good story when they find one and are willing to take it, without permission, just as archaeologists used to rob our graves for museums.

What about the quest for native spirituality? It is mostly escapist, and people such as Ms. Quaife would rather look to an ideal native living in never-never land than confront the reality of what being native means in Canadian society.

For example, residential-school survivors tell of children being forced to eat their own vomit when their stomachs could no longer hold down the sour porridge. They tell of broken knuckles from fingers being rapped. Some even tell of having pins stuck through their tongues as punishment for speaking their own language. (Now, that's censorship.)

And what about the teacher who was removed from one residential school for abusing children? He was simply sent to another, more remote school.

It's not that these stories have never been told; Canadians just haven't heard them. Nor does it mean our writers and storytellers are incompetent and inexperienced, as Mr. Kinsella seems to suggest.

It means our voices have been marginalized. Imagine, Canadians telling native stories because their government outlawed native languages, native culture.

However, as Ms. Campbell said on CBC Radio's *Morningside,* "If you want to write our stories, then be prepared to live with us." And not just for a few months.

Hear the voices of the wilderness. Be there with the Lubicon, the Innu. Be there with the Teme-Augama Anishnabai on the Red Squirrel Road. The Saugeen Ojibway. If you want these stories, fight for them. I dare you.

Rosemary J. Coombe

The Properties of Culture and the Possession of Identity: Postcolonial Struggle and the Legal Imagination

In 1992, a longstanding debate in Canadian arts communities erupted in the national public sphere. For three weeks that April, Canadians witnessed a remarkable exchange on the pages of the *Globe and Mail* as controversy raged about the propriety of writers depicting "cultures other than their own," when or if it was appropriate to "tell someone else's story," and whether it was possible to "steal the culture of another."[1] Although the issues addressed there continue to engage critical attention, the *Globe and Mail* debate was significant for it brought into sharp relief the limitations of addressing complex issues of culture and identity politics as a matter of "reading our rights." The positions emergent in this controversy serve to demonstrate how a liberal legal discourse of rights may fundamentally distort issues of cultural politics.

I was initially drawn to the debate because of its ironic implications for my own scholarly work. For too many years I have been working on a book, provisionally called *Cultural Appropriations;* my advance publishing contract specified that nomination.[2] I have been exploring the ways in which subaltern groups use mass media texts, celebrity images, trademarks, and other commodified cultural forms to forge identities and communities. I consider various subcultures that engage movie and TV stars to construct alternative gender identities, and the ways in which trademarks are invoked to challenge concepts of citizenship and reinscribe the space of the nation-state in minority struggles for political recognition.[3] By virtue of the fact that these texts are legally defined as private properties, to which intellectual property holders have rights of exclusivity, the proliferation of meaning in the public sphere is (once again) constrained by forces of capital. Laws that govern the relationship between those who claim a proprietary interest in a sign and those who seek to recode it grant enormous power to corporations to control the connotations of those signifiers that increasingly dominate the public sphere.[4]

In short, I have engaged in a consideration of cultural agency and subaltern struggle in consumer society, developing a concept of "cultural appropriation" as progressive cultural politics. Imagine my consternation, then, to find the term "officially defined" by the Advisory Committee for Racial Equality in the Arts (for no less august a body than the Canada Council). The term was deemed to mean "the depiction of minorities or cultures other than one's own, either in fiction or nonfiction"—and designated a serious issue to which the Council must attend.[5] The ironies of my response to this appropriation and definition of the phrase provoked me to reconsider the politics of certain knowledges, in this case, academic theory in law and anthropology. At first I was annoyed; a term I had used to connote progressive, subversive forms of cultural politics on behalf of subordinated social groups had been seized—exclusively to denote the invidious practice of white elites stealing the cultural forms of others for their own prestige and profit. I was uncomfortably aware that I had formed a rather proprietary attachment to the term; my own feelings of violation rather closely mirrored those voiced by corporations who were outraged when *their* trademarks were given unsanctioned meanings by others.

Exploring my responses to this debate about the "cultural appropriation" of others, I will suggest that my professional identities, both as lawyer and as anthropologist, situate me conflictually with respect to two dominant discourses and their deployment in postcolonial politics. The rhetorical positions of Romanticism and Orientalism, I suggest, function as dangerous supplements in contemporary struggles for political recognition. If my legal knowledge has made me suspicious of the former, my anthropological knowledge makes me uncomfortable with the latter. Struggling to establish positions on issues of cultural representation that avoid these seductive stances is virtually impossible within a discourse of rights and its juridical legacies.

The controversy over cultural appropriation is founded upon particular premises about authorship, culture, property, and identity that are products of a history of colonial appropriation and define the persistent parameters of a European legal imaginary. The limitations of these legal categories for postcolonial struggles, I will suggest, are apparent in responses to First Nations peoples' struggles for self determination. In addressing First Nations claims here, I seek to avoid speaking "on behalf of" Native peoples, but to speak alongside First Nations activists who have put this issue on the political agenda and to address the dangers of receiving these claims in traditional legal categories. Rather than solve the "problem" of cultural appropriation (which, in any case, is never singular, but specific to particular peoples with particular historical trajectories), I will suggest that we rethink the terms in which we address the question and the ethical responsibilities entailed in its consideration.

The *Globe and Mail* debate centered around a suggestion that government grants should not be made to writers who wrote about cultures other than their own, unless the writer "collaborated" with people of that culture before writing. Although the need to find a "collaborator" is a peculiar and perhaps telling choice of language, this is hardly a suggestion that most scholars, at any rate, were likely to reject. The public controversy evoked by this suggestion, however, was swift and furious, and it quickly polarized around two poles— Romanticism and Orientalism—that structure both our laws of property and increasingly configure many political claims for recognition, legitimacy, and self-determination.

In a series of letters to the editor, the tyranny of the state over the individual was invoked, and the transcendant genius of the Romantic author and his unfettered imagination was affirmed. Writers wasted no time evoking the totalitarian state, the memory of the Holocaust and the Gulag. As Timothy Findley forcefully interjected:

> Put it this way: I imagine—therefore I am. The rest—believe me—is silence. What has happened here? Does no one understand? In 1933 they burned 10,000 books at the gate of a German university because these books were written in unacceptable voices. German Jews, amongst others, had dared to speak for Germany in other than Aryan voices. Stop. Now. Before we do this again.[6]

Joy Anne Jacoby evoked Russian anti-Semitism to urge the Council "to rethink the implications of imposing any policy of 'voice appropriation' lest they find themselves imitating the Russian approach to cultural censorship";[7] one letter was addressed "A Letter to the Thought Police."[8]

Other critics proclaimed the absolute freedom of the author's imagination. Neil Bissoondath affirmed the autonomy of his ego in a quotation resplendent with the "I" of Romantic authorship:

> I reject the idea of cultural appropriation completely. . . . I reject anything that limits the imagination. No one has the right to tell me who I should or should not write about, and telling me what or how I do that amounts to censorship. . . . I am a man of East-Indian descent and I have written from the

viewpoint of women and black men, and I will continue to do so no matter who gets upset.[9]

One writer declared that for the past thirty-five years he had been appropriating the "voices of men, women, dogs, cats, rats, bats, angels, mermaids, elephants . . . [and] salamanders"[10] and that he had no intention of consulting with them or seeking their permission:

> In common with every writer worthy of his or her vocation, I refuse absolutely to entertain any argument demanding that I do so, or that I am to be in any way restricted in my choice of subject matter. I will not, in short, submit to such censorship.[11]

Another writer asserted that "appropriation of voice is what fiction is";[12] others lamented that "if cultural appropriation had never been permitted, Puccini could never have written *La Bohème*, Verdi's *Aida* would never have been performed, we would never have thrilled to Lawrence Olivier in *Hamlet* and we would have been denied the music of *Anna and the King of Siam*."[13]

In these constructions of authorship, the writer is represented in Romantic terms as an autonomous individual who creates fictions with an imagination free of all constraint. For such an author, everything in the world must be made available and accessible as an "idea" that can be transformed into his "expression," which thus becomes his "work." Through his labor, he makes these ideas his own; his possession of the work is justified by his expressive activity. As long as the author does not copy another's expression, he is free to find his themes, plots, ideas, and characters anywhere he pleases, and to make these his own. Any attempts to restrict his ability to do so are viewed as an unjustifiable restriction on freedom of expression. The dialectic of possessive individualism and liberal democracy is thereby affirmed. These are also the premises about authorship that govern contemporary intellectual property laws, particularly the law of copyright.

Critical legal scholars have written extensively about the inadequacies of Romantic individualism and its understanding of subjectivity, cultural agency, freedom of speech, and creativity. Often they have done no more than use fairly standard anthropological and poststructuralist insights into the cultural construction of self and discursive formations of subjectivity to counter the universalising rational individualism that dominates legal thought; it is not necessary to repeat those arguments here. The social experiences of authors inevitably shape their voices, and there is no doubt that the voices of people with remarkably similar social experiences continue to dominate the Canadian culture industries.[14] In a democratic society committed to multiculturalism and social equality, it is surely the work of a federal agency allocating public funds to support the work of marginalized minority writers and artists so that Canadian culture more fully represents national social diversity (and that's putting it in simple liberal terms).

The Romantic individualism expounded by writers in this debate determinedly ignores the balance of power in Canadian publishing. In the worldview presented, everyone is implicitly equal in their capacity to write or be written about—to speak or be spoken for. Such a position purports to be apolitical, but manages only to be ahistorical and blind to relations of power. It ignores the very real social lines along which representation has been structured and the very real difficulties faced by certain social groups to represent themselves and speak on their own behalf. Cultural representation and political representation are closely linked. It is, for example, inconceivable that a vehicle could be marketed as "a wandering Jew," but North Americans rarely bat an eyelash when a Jeep Cherokee® passes them on the road or an advertisement for a Pontiac® flashes across their television screens. More people may know Oneida® as a brand of silverware than as the name of a people and a nation.

For peoples in Canada experiencing discrimination and stereotyping, it must be insulting to have your identity analogized to that of mermaids and elephants, and cold comfort to know that an author has no intention of speaking to salamanders or angels before he writes about *them,* either. One can only assume that minority groups in Canada occupy the same mythical and inarticulate status in the writer's imagination. In such analogies, many Canadians are denied their humanity and deprived of any human knowledge from which others may learn. They are not seen as fellow members of a community whose historical experiences have shaped their current political struggles, but as archetypes and characters; not recognized as human beings to be engaged in dialogue, they are reduced to cultural fodder for the Romantic imagination.

Moreover, the very context in which the debate arose is conveniently elided. Puccini was not, after all, seeking funding from a government committed to multiculturalism when he wrote *La Bohème,* Warner Brothers would have "thrilled" us with Lawrence Olivier in *Hamlet* with or without the Canada Council, and if the Council were asked to fund a musical as blatantly imperialist and paternalistic as *Anna and the King of Siam,* we should indeed question the propriety of public funding.

But if the imperialist claims of the Romantic author colored one side of this debate, the essentializing voice of Orientalism crept into the other. The article that began the debate was titled "Whose Voice Is It Anyway?" The question presupposed that a "voice" was both unified and singular and could be possessed by an individual or by a collective imagined as having similar abilities to possess its own expressions. Proponents of the Canada Council suggestion defended their position on the grounds of the integrity of cultural identities, authentic traditions, and the need for authenticity in cultural life. In making these arguments, the tropes of possessive individualism become paramount; authors "have identities" which may or may not ensure "their own work's authenticity." The Canada Council director claimed that cultural appropriation was a serious issue, because "we have a need for authenticity. In our society today, there is a recognition that quality has to do with that authenticity of voice."[15] The chair of the Writers' Union of Canada declared that it was no different from a copyright claim in which any unlicensed use of an author's work is theft[16] (in fact there are major difficulties with the copyright analogy, which I will later address).

The *Globe and Mail* debate was soon related back to earlier discussions in which Native writers have appealed to white writers to refrain from telling stories involving Indians so as to enable Native peoples to tell their own stories and claim their own history. Questions of "Who's stealing whose stories and who's speaking with whose voice?"[17] have been posed by some Native cultural activists as "cases of cultural theft, the theft of voice."[18] Canadians were told that "stories show how a people, a culture, thinks"[19] and such stories could not be told by others without endangering the authenticity of cultural works. The Canadian culture industries were accused of stealing the stories of Native peoples. Native artists asked if "Canadians had run out of stories of their own"[20] and claimed that the telling of Native stories was theft, "as surely as the missionaries stole our religion, the politicians stole our land, and the residential schools stole our language."[21]

In many of the arguments used to support Native claims of cultural appropriation, Canada is either a country with its own culture or one in which there are multiple discrete cultures; one always has a singular culture of one's own, that has a history of its own, and one possesses an authentic identity that speaks in a univocal voice fully constituted by one's own cultural tradition. Most anthropologists and cultural studies theorists, I suspect, find themselves uneasy in the face of such arguments. It is possible to be simultaneously supportive of First Nations' struggles for self-representation and uncomfortable with the rhetorical strategies employed by many of those who are sympathetic to this end. For anthropologists today, such propositions about culture, authenticity, and identity are extremely contentious ones. Intellectually, we have been called upon to resist the siren call of authenticity, the reification of cultures, and the continuity of traditions.[22] It has become far more intellectually respectable and certainly more fashionable to focus upon improvisation, productive hybridity, the creative poetics of identity creation—cultural conjunctures rather than timeless essences, creolized intercultural processes rather than stable cultural traditions.

The culturally creative processes we celebrate, however, *are* fabrications, and the cultural resources with which emergent identities are fashioned may be tightly embraced by others in alternative systems of value. This is vividly illustrated in George Lipsitz's otherwise politically sensitive book *Time Passages,* discussing American popular culture and memory.[23] He waxes ecstatic about the emancipatory cultural creativity of the "Mardi Gras Indians"— black youths who dress and dance in Plains Indian costume during elaborately rehearsed street pageantry in New Orleans. Their "Indianness" is drawn from the Buffalo Bill imagery ingrained in American mass culture. They know that they are not "real Indians," but one gets little sense that they know there are any or if they believe, as a young child recently told me (as a mark of her worldly sophistication), that "there are no *real* Indians anymore than there are *real* trolls, witches, or fairies." In our constant utopian hope for reinventions of difference, I sometimes fear that we may simply reinscribe the authority of the Romantic author and his unfettered right to creativity. As Annie Coombes suggests, "hybridity" is no guarantee of postcolonial self-determination; it is as equally available to the colonizing practices of capital as it is to local strategies of resistance.[24]

Maintaining respect for cultural tradition, however, also risks reinscribing the authority of our own cultural categories, albeit in the guise of the liberal property holder. The concepts of culture, authenticity, and identity in the *Globe and Mail* debate were posed in *proprietary* terms, as debates about *propriety* so often are in contemporary politics. The argument was constructed upon the same philosophy of possessive individualism that grounds our legal categories and historically supported practices of colonial expropriation. The challenges that postcolonial struggles pose for Canadian society may not, however, best be met by reliance upon categories of thought inherited from a colonial era.

Although the term "postcolonial" has engendered controversy and criticism,[25] it is appropriate to the Canadian social and legal context I explore here. Unlike the liberal discourse of multiculturalism or cultural diversity, the term postcolonial and the language of struggle emphasize, rather than obscure, the very real histories of colonialism which we must confront and the relations of power inherited from our multiple colonial pasts that continue to shape social relations of difference. Debates about postcolonialism have particular relevance in a nation that still displays multiple manifestations of British Empire and embraces immigrants from the postcolonial Commonwealth. Furthermore, I think it is important to take up the implicit challenge posed by Linda Hutcheon when she suggests that when Canadian culture is called postcolonial today, the reference is very rarely to the Native culture, which might be the more accurate historical use of the term. . . . Native and Metis writers are today demanding a voice . . . and perhaps, given their articulations of the damage to Indian culture and people done by the colonizers (French and British) and the process of colonization, theirs should be considered the process of colonization, theirs should be considered the resisting, postcolonial voice of Canada.[26]

To demonstrate how legal rights discourse relies upon the colonial categories that shape its parameters, it is necessary to outline the conceptual logic that developed in the nineteenth century to categorize art, culture, and authorial identity—a logic that continues to mark the limits of the legal imagination. In *The Predicament of Culture,* Clifford describes the "art-culture system" that emerged from European imperialism as a means to categorize arts and cultural goods—categories that continue to inform our laws of property in a postcolonial age. We know that the concepts of art and culture are products of the European upheavals and expansions of the early nineteenth century, the ascendancy of bourgeois values, the specter of mass society, imperialist expansion, and colonial rule. Only in the early nineteenth century was art as an imaginative expression abstracted from industry as a utilitarian one. The emergence of an abstract, capitalized "Art," equated with individual creativity and expressive genius, was developed in the same period as the concept of capitalized culture, as a noun or the end product of an abstract process of civilization. It was possible by the end of the nineteenth century to speak of "Culture" with a capital C—representing the height of human development, the most elevated of human expression as epitomized in European art and literature—as well as plural "cultures" with a small c—imagined as coherent, authentic ways of life characterized by wholeness, continuity, and essence.

Clifford argues that two similar categories dominate our evaluation of expressive works. First, he defines the zone of "authentic masterpieces" created by individual geniuses, the category of "Art" properly speaking. Secondly, he designates the category of "authentic artifacts" created by cultures imagined as collectivities. Objects may, therefore, be exhibited in galleries as examples of a human creative ability that transcends the limitations of time and place to speak to us about the "human" condition; they are testaments to the greatness of their individual creators. The artistic imagination is universalized in the European image under the rubric of a universal "human" Culture. Alternatively, objects may be exhibited in museums as the authentic works of a distinct collectivity, integral to the harmonious life of a timeless community and incomprehensible outside of "cultural context"—the defining features of authentic artifacts. Objects may move between categories—occupying liminal zones. But when non-Western objects fully pass from the status of authentic artifact to the status of art, they also escape the ahistorical location of the "tribal," albeit to enter into a "universal" history, defined by the progression of works of great authors (the canon of civilization). They become part of a "human" cultural heritage—Culture capitalized—rather than objects properly belonging to "cultures" anthropologically defined.

These European cultural understandings are mirrored in our legal categories for the valuation and protection of expressive objects. Laws of intellectual property (copyright in particular) and laws of cultural property reflect and secure the logic of the European art/culture system that Clifford outlines. Laws of copyright, for example, developed to protect the expressive works of authors and artists—increasingly perceived in Romantic terms of individual genius and transcendent creativity—in the service of promoting universal progress in the arts and sciences. Copyright laws protect works, understood to embody the unique personality of their individual authors—the expressive component of the "original" is so venerated that even a reproduction or imitation of it is deemed a form of theft.

The idea of an author's rights to control his (the category of the author is a gendered one) expressive creations developed in a context that privileged a Lockean theory of the origin of property in labor in which expressive creation is deemed the author's "work." Intellectual work creates an "Original" arising spontaneously from the vital root of "Genius." Originality in mental labor (as opposed to manual labor) enables the author to claim not merely the physical object produced, but the literary or artistic expression itself—the "work" properly defined.

The literary work, for example, is neither the physical book, nor the ideas contained in it, but the form of the expression which the author gives to those ideas. Literary or artistic works were incorporeal entities that sprang from the "fruitful mind" of an author. The work carries the imprint of the author's personality and always embodies his persona, wherever it surfaces, however it is transmitted, and whatever the sources of its content or the ideas it expresses. He is entitled to exclusive possession of it, wherever it circulates.

If the original, expressive, and possessive individual dominates intellectual property laws, legitimizing personal control over the circulation of texts, laws of cultural property protect the material objects of culture. Culture may be defined here in either of the two ways established in the nineteenth century— as the universal heritage of humankind—Culture with a capital *C*—or in the plural anthropological sense, in which different cultures lay claim to different properties. These two positions on the nature of the "culture" that can rightfully possess the property at issue define the poles of an ongoing controversy in legal scholarship.

On the one hand, we have scholars of cultural property who expound a position of "cultural internationalism" which is nicely deemed a commitment to the cultural heritage of all mankind. On the other hand, we have scholars (and states) that espouse a position of "cultural nationalism" in which particular peoples have particular interest in particular properties, regardless of their current location and ownership. This is currently the position of over sixty nations who are party to a 1976 UNESCO agreement that prohibits importation of objects whose export is prohibited in the country of origin.

Cultural internationalists see the repatriation of cultural objects as "irrational" because in many of the signatory nations, the "supply" of cultural artifacts far exceeds the internal "demand"—"they are rich in cultural artefacts beyond any conceivable use."[27] As relatively poor nations, they would be better off exporting such objects to locations where they are valued. The popularity of cultural nationalism is deemed the result of symbolic values and "lack of ability to deal with cultural property as a resource like other resources to be exploited."[28] The possibility that other peoples may entertain other values is considered no more nor less likely than their sheer ignorance and ineptitude in recognizing cultural property as an exportable resource.

Cultural internationalists suggest that dealers, collectors, and museums should be entitled to participate in the decisions of nations to prohibit exports (after all it is "their" human heritage, too!). Other peoples may have other values, but the "universal human values" embodied in cultural objects are best evaluated by the one "universal" medium of exchange—money. It is suggested that a "cosmopolitan attitude" would situate objects where they could best be preserved, studied, and enjoyed. The market, of course, will move objects to their locus of highest probable protection—those who are prepared to pay most are most likely to preserve their investment. Nations that "hoard" "unused" objects are denigrated by cultural internationalists because they "fail to spread their culture, and thereby culturally impoverish other peoples in the world."[29] Cultural internationalists are easy to criticize from a cultural studies perspective. Their notions of value and rationality are decidedly Eurocentric; it seems to be beyond their comprehension that there are alternative modes of attachment to objects which do not involve their commodification, objectification, and reification for purposes of collection, observation, and display.

One suspects also that this purported universalism would not support the movement of Rembrandts from the Netherlands to Lagos, despite the fact that Rembrandt's paintings might be "over-represented" in their country of origin, that the Dutch "fail to spread their culture" to the Third World, and that they thereby contribute to the "cultural impoverishment" of Africa's peoples. The existence of vast "underused" holdings in European museums does not appear to have led to movements to establish better museums in

Niamey, Lima, or Nanjing despite the vastly larger numbers of people whose "cultural impoverishment" might thereby be alleviated. The "cosmopolitan" attitude espoused appears more Eurocentric than worldly, more monocultural than respectful of cultural difference, and less concerned with the purported "interests of all mankind" than with the interests of maintaining Western hegemony. Culture with a capital *C* serves very particular cultural interests.

The case for "cultural nationalism," on the other hand, is made on behalf of a people's or nation's patrimony in the name of maintaining and preserving cultural identity. These arguments are bound to find more sympathy with those sympathetic to progressive cultural politics, because they presuppose that values are salient only within local cultural contexts that cannot be reduced to a purported "common" denominator by market principles. Indeed, some cultural objects are seen as so integrally related to cultural identity that they should be deemed inalienable—as essential to the preservation of group identity and self-esteem. The realm of culture with a small *c*—in the anthropological sense of particular bounded forms of life is enshrined here.

"Cultural nationalism," however pluralistic in intent, employs a European logic of possessive individualism when it claims objects as essential to identities and elements of authentic traditions. Possessive individualism—the relationship that links the individual to property as formulated in Locke's labor theory of value —increasingly dominates the language and logic of political claims to cultural autonomy. Focusing upon developments in Quebec's cultural heritage laws, anthropologist Richard Handler shows how national culture is envisioned as a kind of property and the nation is imagined as a property-owning "collective individual."[30] The modern individual is the self-contained human monad, one that is completely oneself. "We conceive of this individual as having, as we say, 'an identity.' Identity means 'oneness,' though it is oneness of a special sort . . . sameness in all that constitutes the objective reality of a thing."[31] This modern individual is also defined by the property she possesses. Modernity has extended these qualities to nation-states and ethnic groups, who are imagined on the world stage and in political arenas as "collective individuals." Like other individuals, these collective individuals are imagined to be territorially and historically bounded, distinctive, internally homogeneous, and complete unto themselves. In this worldview, each nation or group possesses a unique identity and culture that are constituted by its undisputed possession of property. Within cultural nationalism, a group's survival, its identity or objective oneness over time, depends upon the secure possession of a culture embodied in objects of property.

The UNESCO principle that "cultural property is a basic element of a people's identity" thus begins to look less like respect for cultural diversity and more like another form of Western cultural imperialism. Being is equated with having (and excluding and controlling). What identifies a nation or culture are the traits that distinguish it from other cultures—what it has and they don't. Moreover, those properties that define a nation's culture in a cultural nationalist worldview are characterized by their "originality" or "authenticity." Cultural traits that come from elsewhere are, at best, borrowed and at worst, polluting; by contrast, those aspects of national culture that come from within the nation, that are original to it, are "authentic." Again, contemporary anthropology challenges such claims. The notion that only pristine objects untouched by the forces of modernization bespeak cultural identities has long been discounted as a form of imperialist nostalgia. The capacity of peoples to live in history, and to creatively interpret and expressively engage historical circumstances using their cultural traditions to do so, is now recognized as the very life and being of culture, rather than evidence of its death or decline.

The rhetoric of cultural nationalism that informs cultural property rights bears traces of the same logic that defines copyright. Each nation is perceived as an author who originates a culture from resources that come from within and can thus lay claim to exclusive possession of the expressive works that embody its personality. There is, however, a significant difference in the scope of the claims that can be made on behalf of a culture and those that can be made on behalf of an individual author. Copyright laws enable individual authors not only to claim possession of their original works as discrete objects, but to claim possession and control over any reproductions of those works (or any substantial part thereof) in any medium. Cultural property rights, however, enable proprietary claims to be made *only* to original objects or authentic artifacts. The Western extension of "Culture" to cultural Others was limited to objects of property, not to forms of expression. The full authority of authorship was thereby confined to the Western world.

To make this concrete, consider the Picasso paintings that figure so prominently in Clifford's discussion of Primitivism. When an African "statue," produced in a collectivity for social reasons, makes its way into a Picasso painting, the statue itself may still embody the identity of the culture from which it sprang, but any later reproduction of it that alludes back to the Picasso work may be legally recognized as the embodiment of Picasso's authorial personality. The possession of a culture is profoundly limited, whereas the possession of an author extends through time and space as his work is reproduced through mass communications systems. Royalties flow, not to the object's society of origin, but to the estate of the Western author, where the fruits of his originality are realized for fifty years after his death. (We see the same process at work in the expropriation of textile patterns, recipes, and design motifs from Asia and Africa.)

Native peoples' claims of cultural appropriation cannot be legally resolved as a matter of property rights without doing immense violence to the character of these claims themselves. Native peoples face a legal system that divides the world up in a fashion foreign to their sense of felt need. The law offers two possibilities of property that reflect two visions of culture. Intellectual property laws enable individual artists imagined as acultural Romantic authors to collect royalties for the reproduction of their personal expressions as reward for their contribution to a "human" cultural heritage. Cultural property laws enable collectivities to physically control objects that can be shown to embody the essential identity of a "culture" statically conceived.

These categories, I would argue, serve only to culturally impoverish the self while they Orientalize the Other. By deeming expressive creations the private properties of individuals, who can then control circulations of signification, we deprive ourselves of immense opportunities for creative worldmaking and invest the author with censorial powers. By representing cultures in the image of possessive individuals, we obscure people's histories, their interpretive differences, their ongoing transformations, and the cultural dimensions of their political struggles. The Romantic author and authentic artifacts are both, perhaps, fictions of a world best forgone.

Harvard law professor Martha Minow has suggested that most legal treatments of identity questions fail to acknowledge that the cultural, gender, racial, and ethnic identities of a person are not simply intrinsic to that person, but emerge from relationships between people in negotiations and interactions with others. "The relative power enjoyed by some people compared with others is partly manifested through the ability to name oneself and others and to influence the process of negotiation over questions of identity."[32]

> Lawyers and judges who address legal questions of identity should keep in mind its kaleidoscopic nature. They should examine the multiple contributions given to any definition of identity. They ought to examine the pattern of power relationships within which an identity is forged. And they need to explore the pattern of power relationships within which a question of identity is framed . . . who picks an identity and who is consigned to it?[33]

It is precisely the inability to name themselves and a continuous history of having their identities defined by others that First Nations peoples foreground when they oppose practices of cultural appropriation.

In an effort to create a critical consciousness of racism and its eradication, cultural critic bell hooks also adopts a pragmatic approach to questions of identity.[34] She asserts that cultural critics must confront the power and control over representations in the public sphere, because social identity is a process of identifying and constructing oneself as a social being through the mediation of images.[35] Hence subaltern peoples need to critically engage questions of their representation and its influence on questions of identity formation. Native peoples are legitimately concerned with the ahistorical representations of "Indianness" that circulate in the public sphere and the manner in which such imagery mediates the capacities of others to recognize their contemporary identities as peoples with specific needs in the late twentieth century.

Hooks asserts that an identity politics, however necessary as a stage in the liberation of subordinated peoples, must "eschew essentialist notions of identity and fashion selves that emerge from the meeting of diverse epistemologies, habits of being, concrete class locations, and radical political commitments."[36] A return to "identity" and "culture" is necessary more as a means of locating oneself in a political practice than in the embrace of the positivism projected by cultural nationalism. Hooks links this political project to a feminist anti-essentialism which also links identity to a history and a politics rather than an essence:

> Identity politics provides a decisive rejoinder to the generic human thesis, and the mainstream methodology of Western political theory. . . . If we combine the concept of identity politics with a conception of the subject as positionality, we can conceive of the subject as non-essentialized and emergent from historical experience.[37]

In the face of continuing racisms and ethnocentrism, assertions of identity and culture should not be dismissed and critiques of essentialism must recognize the very different positions occupied by subaltern groups. Abstract and universalizing criticisms of essentialism may appear to oppressed peoples as threatening—once again preventing

> those who have suffered the crippling effects of colonization or domination to gain or regain a hearing. . . . It never surprises me when black folks respond to the critique of essentialism, especially when I denied the validity of identity politics, by saying, "Yeah, it is easy to give up identity, when you've got one."[38]

Critiques of essentialism are useful, however, suggests hooks, when they enable African Americans to examine differences within black culture—for example the impact that class and gender have on the experience of racism. They are also necessary to condemn notions of "natural" and "authentic" expressions of black culture which perpetuate static, ahistorical, and stereotyped images of black people's lives and possibilities.[39] As long as the specific history and experience of African Americans and the cultural sensibilities that emerge from that experience are kept in view, essentialism may be fruitfully criticized. "There is a radical difference between repudiation of the idea that there is a black 'essence' and recognition of the way that black identity has been specifically constituted in the experience of exile and struggle."[40]

First Nations peoples have very different histories and very different contemporary needs, but face similar dilemmas in their representations of identity in contemporary Canadian society. When they specify their unique histories, they are often accused of essentialism, but when they write or paint, their work is often criticized for not being "authentic" or sufficiently "Indian."[41] When First Nations peoples make claims to their own images, stories, and cultural themes, however, they do not do so as Romantic authors nor as timeless homogeneous cultures insisting upon the maintenance of a vanishing authenticity. They do not lay claim to expressive works as possessive individuals, insisting upon permissions and royalties for the circulation of authorial personas in the public realm.[42] The appeals made here cannot be reduced to a purely monetary claim for the royalties due to individuals, because they encompass an insistence upon the respect due to peoples, their histories, and their collective self-determination. Nor is the assertion of cultural presence made in the name of an ahistorical collective essence, but in the name of living, changing, creative peoples engaged in very concrete contemporary political struggles.[43] Our liberal discourses of rights, however, afford them little space to make these kinds of claims.

Native peoples discuss the issue of cultural appropriation in a manner that links issues of cultural representation with a history of political powerlessness; a history of having Indian identity continually defined and determined by forces committed to its eradication. Alienated from their own historical traditions, first by government and now by commerce, they find their "culture" valued while their peoples and their political struggles continue to be ignored. The experience of everywhere being seen, but never being heard, of constantly being represented, but never listened to, of being treated like artifacts rather than as peoples, is central to the issue of cultural appropriation. The Canadian public seems intensely interested in things Indian but seem to have less interest in hearing Native peoples speak on their own behalf. When Native writers assert that they are better situated to tell the stories of their experiences, they are accused of curtailing artistic imagination. Such critics reinscribe Native peoples as objects of human culture, rather than authorial subjects in their own right—once again they are "ideas" and themes for the expressive works and proprietary claims of others. Like angels and mermaids, they are imagined, rather than engaged, in dialogue.

Despite the immense limitations of the metaphors of possessive individualism, they *have* become dominant in world political culture. Subaltern groups and less powerful nations must, unfortunately, articulate their political claims in "a language that power understands,"[44] and the language that power understands is increasingly that of possessive and expressive individualism. There are many reasons to be pessimistic about its possibilities. Certainly the perils of making claims in the language of possessive individualism are real ones, as Native peoples in Canada have discovered. For instance, in a presentation on Native cultural autonomy and the appropriation of aboriginal imagery at a meeting of independent filmmakers, Métis videomaker Loretta Todd quoted Walter Benjamin; she was promptly accused of appropriating Western culture![45] She responded that she *was* part of Western culture—as a product of colonization, how could she be otherwise?—and Benjamin was part of that culture. Her interlocutors informed her that white use of Native imagery was equivalent to her use of Benjamin, because Native imagery was now simply a part of contemporary culture.[46]

Other white Toronto artists—self-proclaimed "environmentalist tribesmen" who call themselves Fastwurms—responded to questions about the propriety of their employment of Native ritual themes by slandering their aboriginal critic as "a self-appointed spokesperson for Native artists."[47] In speaking for a culture to which one makes a proprietary claim, one always risks allegations that the identity one must possess to make such claims is not the undivided one demanded of the property-holding possessive individual. One sees continuous attempts to silence Native people's interventions in the debate by questioning their authenticity and representativeness.

This tactic of deeming some people of aboriginal ancestry to be "real Indians" while denying the ability of others to speak on behalf of Native concerns is reminiscent of the historical policies of colonial authorities who arbitrarily conferred and withheld Indian status on spurious grounds that failed to recognize indigenous practices defining community membership. There is also embedded in this argument the notion that all Native peoples must agree for them to have a position that can be recognized as "Native," but as Paul Smith reminds us, "We have differences in political opinion. After all, we come from hundreds of nations and histories."[48]

Curiously, however, there is a constant insistence that aboriginal peoples must represent a fully coherent position that expresses an authentic identity forged from an uncomplicated past that bespeaks a pristine cultural tradition before their voice will be recognized as Native. No one, of course, asks white authors what gives them the authority to speak on behalf of artistic license or what criteria of representativeness they fulfill in order to make claims in the name of the authorial imagination. Nor do we expect uniform positions on the parameters of freedom of speech. The ability to speak on behalf of "universal" values is assumed, even as we argue what their contents might be, whereas people of aboriginal ancestry are often challenged when they name themselves and their experiences. In many ways, this logic mirrors that of the law and its categorizations. In dividing intellectual property and cultural property, authors with intellect are distinguished from cultures with property. Those who have intellect are entitled to speak on behalf of universal principles of reason, whereas those who have culture speak only on behalf of a cultural tradition that must be unified and homogeneous before we will accord it any respect. Such arguments are generally used, moreover, to silence and delegitimate particularly unwelcome Native voices, rather than to invite more indigenous participants to contribute their viewpoints and join the debate.

The Fastwurms, for example, denounced their aboriginal critic by claiming that they consider themselves "intrinsically to be a non-western culture."[49] Situating themselves outside of any cultural history, they attempted to escape inclusion within the history of the Western art world. Richard Hill, however, suggests that it is impossible to entertain any such "escapist fantasy":

> Unless whites can acknowledge and respond to their histories of power and racism as it effects all areas of culture, as it inscribes itself in their own minds, an equal and meaningful dialogue is impossible.[50]

Artists have recently demonstrated more concern with issues of cultural appropriation, and the colonial histories that inform their work, but they have done so in a manner that focuses more attention on the cultural influences upon individual imaginations than upon the lives and contemporary circumstances of Native peoples. When Toronto artist Andy Fabo was chastised for his use of the symbolism of the sweat-lodge ceremony, he defended his work against Cardinal-Shubert's accusation of "cultural plagiarism" on personal grounds:

> The first art museum that I ever visited was The Museum of The Plains Indians in Browning, Montana. I was eight years old at the time and for better or worse, the experience had an incredible impact on me.[51]

The museum figures here less as an edifice of imperialism than as the mysterious origin of a personal fetish—as indeed an artist might personally experience it. For a gay artist concerned with questions of AIDS, healing, and otherness, the sweat-lodge might indeed constitute a powerful symbolic image, but Fabo's use of it illustrated no reflexive consideration of the legacy of power that enabled him to exploit its symbolic excess.

Liz Magore, another artist whose work has figured prominently in debates about appropriation, foregrounded the issue in her photography. As Richard Hill describes her show:

> I notice the photographs on the nearby wall in black and white that depicted a man paddling a canoe, a blond hippie-looking woman in a headband, people

camping on the beach, etc. . . . The title of the photo of the blonde woman was called "Cheyenne type." . . . This must be done ironically but how can I say for sure whether Magore's work was ironic? Maybe she was trying to point out the overlap of cultures, or the richness of First Nations culture as a resource for white artists. I left the work not knowing quite what was going on. . . . Perhaps it was merely another case of white people talking about themselves using First Nations culture as their medium? Sometime later I read a statement by Magore about the photographs mentioned above. She said that she wanted to deal with her personal history of appropriating from First Nations cultures "slowly and gently," and indeed she does. So slowly and gently, in fact, that the work loses any serious claim to criticality. In effect, it seems to do more to prop up old stereotypes than to aggressively call them into question. This is especially true when the work is shot in the context of a national gallery which inevitably lends its authority to the piece. . . . She defends her project on the grounds that although the photos are embarrassing, "a disavowal of my own history is equally uncomfortable."[52]

Artists who address such issues seem more concerned with delineating the influence of Native images in their own personal histories and in the dominant culture from which they draw their artistic inspiration than in acknowledging the actual histories of colonization in which those images came to figure as part of a consciousness. When non-Native artists claim that Native images are a part of their cultural heritage, they are not wrong, but they are incredibly selective. To claim Native spiritual practices and traditions of motif and design as part of one's contemporary culture or in the name of one's personal cultural mediation,—while bypassing the history of racism, institutional abuse, poverty, and alienation that so incorporated it—is simply to contribute to the process by which the painful realities of contemporary Native life are continually ignored by those who feel more comfortable claiming the artifacts they have left behind. Once again the Romantic author claims the expressive power to represent cultural others in the name of a universalized cultural heritage.

First Nations peoples may well be compelled to articulate their claims "in a language that power understands," but in the *substance* of their claims they contest the logic of possessive individualism, even as they give voice to its metaphors. Engaging in "double-voiced rhetoric," they appropriate and subvert these metaphors through the character of the claims they make. First Nations peoples make it clear that issues of culture and the proper place of texts cannot be separated from spirituality, political determination, and title to traditional lands. This nexus of ecological, spiritual, social, and territorial concerns is central to any understanding of cultural appropriation.

Self-determination and sovereignty include human, political, land, religious, artistic and moral rights. Taking ownership of these stories involves a claim to Aboriginal title over images, culture and stories.[53]

In discussions of cultural appropriation, First Nations peoples strive to assert that the relationships that stories, images, motifs, and designs have to their communities cannot be subsumed under traditional European categories of art and culture and the possessive individualism that informs them. It is difficult for Native peoples to even speak about "rights"[54] to cultural expressions or creative skills that may be passed generationally through matrilineal inheritance.[55] Some stories are considered so powerful that one storyteller seeks permission before repeating a tale told by another.[56] To equate the need for such permissions to a copyright license is to reduce the social relationship between Native storytellers to one of contract and the alienation of market exchange relationships. These relationships, however, are ongoing ones which bind generations in a spiritual relationship with land, customs, and ancestors based upon traditions of respect, not the values of commodity exchange.

When Loretta Todd discusses First Nations ideas about ownership in the context of cultural appropriation, she discusses property in terms of relationships that are far wider than the exclusivity of possession and rights to alienate that dominate European concepts:

> Without the sense of private property that ascended with European culture, we evolved concepts of property that recognized the interdependence of communities, families and nations and favoured the guardianship of the earth as opposed to its conquest. There was a sense of ownership, but not one that preempted the rights and privileges of others or the rights of the earth and the life it sustained. . . . Ownership was bound up with history. . . . Communities, families, individuals, and nations created songs, dances, rituals, objects, and stories that were considered to be property, but not property as understood by the Europeans. Material wealth was re-distributed, but history and stories belonged to the originator and could be given or shared with others as a way of preserving, extending and witnessing history and expressing one's worldview.[57]

First Nations peoples are engaged in an ongoing struggle to articulate, define, exercise, and assert aboriginal title, not only in terms of a relationship to territory, but in a relationship to the cultural forms that express the historical meaning of that relationship in specific communities.

For Native peoples in Canada, culture is not a fixed and frozen entity that can be objectified in reified forms that express its identity, but an ongoing living process that cannot be severed from the ecological relationships in which it lives and grows. By dividing ideas and expressions, oral traditions and written forms, intangible works and cultural objects, the law rips asunder what many First Nations people view as integrally related—freezing into categories what Native peoples find flowing in relationships. For those sympathetic to their ends to attempt to reduce these claims to assertions of intellectual property rights is simultaneously to neglect significant dimensions of Native aspiration and impose colonial juridical categories on postcolonial struggles in a fashion that reenacts the cultural violence of colonization. Colonial categories of art, culture, and authorial identity are deeply embedded in our legal categories of property, but the claims of others to objects and representations may well force these Western categories under new forms of scrutiny. As new subjects engaged in postcolonial struggles occupy the categories bestowed upon us by a colonial past, they may well transform the weakening colonial edifice upon which these categories are founded. New agents with new agendas may articulate old categories in new ways; the concept of aboriginal title promises to transform prevailing relations between politics, property, and propriety.

Ultimately the questions of "whose voice it is," who speaks on behalf of whom, and whether one can "steal the culture of another" are not *legal* questions to be addressed in terms of asserting rights, but *ethical* ones to be addressed in terms of moral and political commitments. To come back to the politics of knowledge and its deployment, I would suggest that in contexts of postcolonial struggle, the postmodern claim that cultures are constructed, emergent, mobile, and contested may seem somewhat empty. Such universalizing anti-essentialisms only beg questions of perspective—for whom is culture emergent and contested and in what circumstances? How does this claim sound in the struggles of those for whom "culture" may be the last legitimate ground for political autonomy and self-determination? From what position can one confidently make such a claim? Ultimately, questions of culture and its appropriation are political, rather than ontological, ones that demand empathetic identifications rather than formal resolutions—a situational ethics to which we must always attend.

Notes

1. Although the controversy died down in the national press, references and allusions back to it can be found throughout 1992, as, for example, in a books column by Philip Marchand titled "When Appropriation Becomes Inappropriate," *Toronto Star,* November 23, 1992, B5. I have not pursued the debates in the Canadian press since then.

2. See Rosemary J. Coombe, *Cultural Appropriations: Authorship, Alterity, and the Law* (New York: Routledge, Chapman and Hall, forthcoming).

3. See Rosemary J. Coombe, "The Celebrity Image and Cultural Identity: Publicity Rights and the Subaltern Politics of Gender," *Discourse* 14 (3) (1991): 59–88,

and "Tactics of Appropriation and the Politics of Recognition in Late Modern Democracies," *Political Theory* 21 (1993): 411–433.

4. For a discussion of the importance of media in the constitution of contemporary public spheres, see Michael Warner, "The Mass Public and the Mass Subject," in *The Phantom Public Sphere,* ed. Bruce Robbins (Minneapolis: University of Minnesota Press, 1993); and Nicholas Garnham, "The Mass Media, Cultural Identity, and the Public Sphere in the Modern World," *Public Culture* 5 (1993): 251–266. I discuss the importance of intellectual properties in "Authorship and Alterity: Democracy in Postmodern Spheres," in *Authorial Imperium: The Politics and Poetics of Intellectual Properties in a Postcolonial Era,* ed. Peter Jaszi and Martha Woodmansee (Durham, N.C.: Duke University Press, forthcoming).

5. S. Godfrey, "Canada Council Asks Whose Voice Is It Anyway?" *Globe and Mail,* March 21, 1992, C1, 15.

6. "Letter to the Editor," *Globe and Mail,* March 28, 1992, D7.

7. "Letter to the Editor," *Globe and Mail,* March 28, 1992, D7.

8. *Globe and Mail,* March 31, 1992, A16.

9. Godfrey, "Canada Council Asks Whose Voice Is It Anyway?" C15.

10. Richard Outram, "Letter to the Editor," *Globe and Mail,* March 28, 1992, D7.

11. Ibid.

12. Russell Smith, "Letter to the Editor," *Globe and Mail,* April 3, 1992, A3.

13. Bill Driedger, "Letter to the Editor," *Globe and Mail,* March 28, 1992, D7.

14. This point was made by Alan Hutchinson, "Giving Smaller Voices a Chance to Be Heard," *Globe and Mail,* April 14, 1992, A16.

15. Godfrey, "Canada Council Asks Whose Voice Is It Anyway?" C1.

16. Godfrey, "Canada Council Asks Whose Voice Is It Anyway?" C15.

17. Lenore Keeshig-Tobias, "Stop Stealing Native Stories," *Globe and Mail,* January 26, 1990, A7.

18. Ibid.

19. Ibid.

20. Ibid.

21. Ibid.

22. See, for example, James Clifford, *The Predicament of Culture: Twentieth-Century Ethnography, Literature, and Art* (Cambridge, Mass.: Harvard University Press, 1988); and Renato Rosaldo, *Culture and Truth: Remaking Social Analysis* (Boston: Beacon Press, 1989).

23. (Minneapolis: University of Minnesota Press, 1991).

24. Annie Coombes, "Inventing the 'Postcolonial': Hybridity and Constituency in Contemporary Curating," *New Formations* 18 (1992): 39–52.

25. See Arun O. Mukherjee, "Whose Postcolonialism and Whose Postmodernism?" *World Literature Written in English* 30(2) (1990): 1; Ella Shohat, "Notes on the Postcolonial," *Social Text* 32 (1992): 99; and Ruth Frankenburg and Lata Mani, "Crosscurrents, Crosstalk: Race, Postcoloniality, and the Politics of Location," in *Displacement, Diaspora, and Geographies of Identity,* ed. Smadar Lavie and Ted Swedenburg (Durham, N.C.: Duke University Press, 1996).

26. "Circling the Downspout of Empire: Post-Colonialism and Postmodernism," *Ariel* 20(4) (1989): 149, 156.

27. John Henry Merryman, "Two Ways of Thinking About Cultural Property," *American Journal of International Law* 80 (1986): 831, 832.

28. Ibid., 832 n 5.

29. Ibid., 847.

30. "Who Owns the Past?" in *The Politics of Culture*, ed. Brett Williams (Washington, D.C.: Smithsonian Institution, 1991): 63–74; and "On Having a Culture," in *Objects and Others*, ed. George Stocking (Madison: University of Wisconsin Press, 1985), 192–217.

31. Handler, "Who Owns the Past?" 64.

32. "Identities," *Yale Journal of Law and the Humanities* 3 (1991): 97, 98–99, citing Angela Harris, "Race and Essentialism in Feminist Legal Theory," *Standford Law Review* 42 (1990): 584.

33. Ibid., 112.

34. bell hooks, *Yearning: Race, Gender, and Cultural Politics* (Toronto: Between the Lines Press, 1990).

35. Ibid., 5.

36. Ibid., 19.

37. Ibid., 20, citing Linda Alcoff, "Cultural Feminism vs. Poststructuralism: The Identity Crisis in Feminist Theory," *Signs* 13 (1988): 405, 433.

38. Ibid., 28.

39. Ibid.

40. Ibid., 29.

41. On accusations of essentialism see Loretta Todd, "What More Do They Want?" in *Indigena: Contemporary Native Perspectives*, ed. Gerald McMaster and Lee-Ann Martin (Vancouver/Toronto: Douglas and McIntyre, 1992), 71–79. Lee Maracle notes that publishers are absolved of charges of censorship when they choose not to publish Native works (often returning works to writers with "Too Indian" or "Not Indian enough" written on them by non-Native editors who presume the authority to judge the works' authenticity), while she is accused of "being a fascist censor" for objecting to non-Native use of Native themes and stories. See Lee Maracle, "Native Myths: Trickster Alive and Crowing," *Fuse Magazine* (Fall 1989): 29.

42. I do not wish to suggest here that artists and authors of First Nations ancestry never wish to have their works valued on the market, or that they would eschew royalties for works produced as commodities for an exchange value on the market. That would be essentialist indeed! Instead, I am suggesting that in the debates surrounding cultural appropriation, Native peoples often assert that there are other value systems than those of the market in which their images, themes, practices, and stories figure and that these modes of appreciation and valuation are embedded in specific histories and relationships that should be accorded respect. Copyright laws, of course, only protect individual authors against the copying of their individual expressions, and do not protect ideas, or cultural themes, practices, and historical experiences from expropriation by cultural others.

43. The best demonstrations of this are found in Native art and literature where issues of identity are engaged in innovative fashions that often appropriate and transform European cultural forms to examine the specificity of First Nations history as it figures in contemporary political struggles and the need to forge alliances with other subordinated groups. The Romantic notion of art for art's sake is often challenged, as is the art/culture system that relegates Native expressive forms to an ethnographic realm, or, alternatively, claims them as Art, only to deny their claims to cultural specificity or political statement. For examples see the various artists whose work is fea-

tured in McMaster and Martin, especially the essay by Cree art instructor Alfred Young Man, "The Metaphysics of North American Art," in *Indigena,* ed. McMaster and Martin, 81–89.

44. Handler, "Who Owns the Past?" 71.

45. Loretta Todd, "Notes on Appropriation," *Parallelogramme* 16 (1990): 24.

46. Ibid.

47. Dai Skuse, Kim Kozzi, and Napoleon Brousseau, "Letter to the Editor," *Parallelogramme* 13 (1989–1990): 2.

48. Paul Smith, "Lost in American," *Borderlines* 23 (1991–1992): 17–18, 18.

49. Skuse, Kozzi, and Brousseau, "Letter to the Editor," 4.

50. Richard Hill, "One Part per Million," *Fuse Magazine* (Winter 1992): 12–22, 14.

51. Andy Fabo, "Letter to the Editor," *Parallelogramme* 13 (1989–1990): 4.

52. Hill, "One Part per Million," 20.

53. McMaster and Martin, "Introduction," in *Indigena,* ed. McMaster and Martin, 17.

54. David Alexis writes that rights are a further imposition upon Native peoples. "Indian people do not think in terms of rights but in terms of responsibility. Whatever flows from the fulfilment of those responsibilities are the gifts in life. The demanding of status from one's mere existence is ludicrous. The so-called fishing rights won by Indian people are not a gift bestowed by white people because of recognition by the white people of those rights. Those so-called 'rights' are the result of traditional people fulfilling responsibilities to fisheries through traditional ceremony and lifestyle . . . a gift from the creation [that results from] a fulfilment of responsibility through Indian belief." From "Obscurity as a Lifestyle," *Borderlines* 23 (1991–1992): 15.

55. Joane Cardinal-Shubert, "In the Red," *Fuse Magazine* (Fall 1989): 20–28, 20.

56. Keeshig-Tobias, "Stop Stealing Native Stories," 7.

57. Todd, "Notes on Appropriation," 26.

M. Nourbese Philip

The Disappearing Debate; or, How the Discussion of Racism Has Been Taken Over by the Censorship Issue

Argument by the white middle class, for the white middle class, about the white middle class. Such was the long-winded, rather tedious debate that took place in last winter's newsletters of the Writers' Union, relating to issues of censorship and the writer and voice. This debate had been sparked by the rejection of three short stories by The Women's Press for an anthology of short fiction, *Imagining Women,* on the grounds that the writers in question, all white, had drawn on and used the voices of characters from cultures and races other than their own. The Press also took issue with the use, by one of the writers, of magic realism, a style pioneered in Latin America. According to the Press, these practices constituted racism. To buttress this position, the Press issued policy guidelines stating that it would "avoid publishing manuscripts in which the protagonist's experience in the world, by virtue of race or ethnicity, is substantially removed from that of the writer."

As often happens around issues such as these, the debate quickly assumed a dichotomous nature, with the pro-censorship forces arrayed against the anti-censorship hordes. Racism was the issue that detonated the explosion at The Women's Press; to the exclusion of any other, censorship became the issue that has monopolized the media's attention. Censorship of white writers; censorship of the imagination; censorship by publishers. Censorship in all its myriad forms became, in fact, the privileged discourse.

The quantum leap from racism to censorship is neither random nor unexpected, since the issue of censorship is central to the dominant cultures of liberal democracies like Canada. In these cultures, censorship becomes a significant and talismanic cultural icon around which all debates about the "individual freedom of man" swirl. It is the cultural and political barometer which these societies use to measure their freedoms. Censorship is as important to the state intent on imposing it as it is to those who are equally committed to opposing it.

Since writers and artists are, by and large, the ones who express the cultural ideas of their age, their individual and collective roles are crucial to the process that assigns significance to ideas such as censorship. Western liberal democracies, in fact, usually grade their relative freedoms and those of other countries according to the freedoms allowed these self-appointed purveyors of cultural representation. In turn, the latter come to share, in no small way, in the rewards of the system.

Historically, racism has never been assigned a central place in the West. As an issue it has remained remarkably absent from debates on the economy, society or polity; racism, in fact, has never been as privileged a discourse as censorship. In more recent years, however, we have seen the privileging of certain types of racism—such as anti-Semitism—over others: one can easily gauge the degree of privileging by the nature and frequency of media attention, or by government activity on the matter. Racism against Africans, however, remains a relatively unimportant issue, except in those instances when the latter are perceived as potential or real disruptors of the social fabric. One very effective way of ensuring that this type of racism remains marginal to the dominant culture is to have another issue that is more privileged, such as censorship or freedom of speech. Two recent examples of the privileging of censorship and freedom of speech over issues of race arose from the public lecture at the University of Toronto in 1987 by Glen Babb, the South African consul, and the much-publicized theories of racial superiority by University of Western Ontario professor Philippe Rushton.

In the latter case, despite public outcry and opposition from students, despite widespread reports of his shoddy scholarship, and despite his recommendations that governments act on his findings, Rushton has been allowed to keep his position at the university and to continue teaching. All in the name of freedom of speech.

Furthermore, on those occasions when racism against Blacks does assume a more public profile, as happened in the last few months in Toronto after the shooting of a Black adolescent, it usually occurs in an aberrational context. Racism is thereby reduced to the level of the personal, and presented as a rare form of disease which, if treated appropriately—usually with a task force—

will quickly disappear. There is a profound failure, if not a refusal, to understand how thoroughly racism informs all aspects of society.

At the heart of this attitude lies a paradox: the ideology and practice of racism have as old a tradition as that of the "rights of man." While John Locke argued for the freedom of man, he had no intellectual difficulty accepting that these freedoms could not and should not extend to African slaves. The ideological framework of Western democracies, erected upon the belief in freedom of the individual, is supported as much by this ideology (and its offshoots), as by that of racism. However, one discourse, censorship, becomes privileged; the other, racism, is silenced. To insist on its lesser status, thereby excluding it from the dominant forms and fora of discussion, becomes one of the most effective ways of perpetuating racism. To do so is, in fact, profoundly racist.

Woman as Other constitutes one of the building blocks of the patriarchy; Black as Other one of the building blocks of white supremacist ideologies. The white, male author has never flinched from representing women or Blacks in his writing, misogynist and/or racist point of view and all. While many of the classified "great works of literature" have been novelistic studies of women by men—*Anna Karenina, Madame Bovary* and *Tess of the D'Urbervilles,* to name but three—and while there have always been significant literary sorties into "exotic" cultures by writers—Kipling, Conrad and Forster come to mind—a quick survey of English literature reveals that works written from the point of view of the Other, Black, female or even working class have not comprised a major part of that literature. In that respect, contemporary literature differs not at all.

The vociferousness, therefore, of the defense of this right—to write from the point of view of the Other—as we have witnessed it recently, is clearly disproportionate to the actual exercise of that right. Is it merely that this right is all of a piece with the rights accruing to a writer living and writing in a liberal democracy? Or does the impulse for the unquestioning defense of this right lie elsewhere?

Sara Maitland, the English novelist, writes that "whether men can do women's stories is another question, one that feminist literary discourse asks often; but it is certain that the oppressed develop insights about their oppressors to a greater degree than the other way about because they need them in order to survive."[1] In virtually every sphere of life, women have had to learn what men want and don't want; what turns them on and what doesn't. Black people, in the course of their individual and collective history of labor, have been privy to what no outsider ought to be in another's life. As cleaners, servants, and domestics, Blacks have known when or whether the white master was or wasn't fucking his wife, or anyone else for that matter. Black women have suckled their whites' charges and, in many instances, provided the latter with emotional nourishment that, through exploitative economic practices, they have been unable to provide their own children. Consider, for example, the many foreign nannies caring for the children of white Canadians, while their own children remain at home in the Caribbean or the Philippines. As in the case of women, which Maitland so well identifies, to ensure their survival, Blacks have had to know what angry white people look like, and how to recognize when the latter were happy and when not. And today the media, for the most part in flagrant contempt for all but the dominant culture, continue to teach Blacks how their erstwhile masters look as they go about their lives.

It borders on the trite and hackneyed to say that writers tend to draw on what they know best as raw material for their work. "Write what you know" is one of the most consistent pieces of advice given to young writers. One would, therefore, assume that when writers from traditionally oppressed groups begin to come to voice publicly, knowing almost as much about their oppressors as they do about their own lives, they would write about their oppressors—at least as much as they write about themselves. Blacks about whites; the working class about the middle and upper classes; women about men. They have good reason to do so: they have, by their labor, earned the vision of the insider.

The paradox, however, is that once an oppressed group is finally able to attain the means of making its voice heard—voicing its many silences—it is far less concerned in rendering audible the voice of its oppressors, and infinitely more interested in (and committed to) making public their own reality and their own lives. The explosion in feminist publishing, for instance, has resulted in women writing and publishing their own stories, *about* themselves and *for* themselves. Men have not been entirely absent from these works, but neither has there been a demonstrated eagerness to write from the point of view of men. And so too for Blacks. What Black writers have wanted to voice is not the voice and experiences of the white person, but the reality of Black people, *from the point of view* of Black people. Given the ubiquitous nature of racism, whites or their systems of domination must perforce figure, to a lesser or greater degree, in these works: their point of view will, however, not be privileged.

This paradox ought to give us pause, if nothing else, to wonder why the *ability* to use the voice of the Other, as we have come to know it in literature and art, has for the most part realized itself in the oppressor using the voice of the oppressed, and not the other way around. It is an ability that is first engendered, then supported by the interlocking and exploitative practices of capitalism, racism, and sexism. And, linked as it is to privilege of one sort or another—race, gender, or class, or all three—it is an ability which serves that privilege. It is, in fact, that very privilege that is the enabling factor in the transformation of what is essentially an exercise of power into a right. That right in turn becomes enshrined and privileged in the ideology servicing the society in general.

The "right" to use the voice of the Other has, however, been bought at great price—the silencing of the Other; it is, in fact, neatly posited on that very silence. It is also a right that exists without an accompanying obligation, and as such, can only lead to abuse.

The ability to use the voice of the Other; the "right" to use the voice of the Other. In the trite words of the popular song about love and marriage: "You can't have one without the other." To those who would argue that in a democracy everyone has the right to write from any point of view, I would contend that for far too long certain groups have not had access to any of the resources which enable writing of *any* sort to take place, let alone writing from a particular point of view. Education, financial resources, belief in the validity of one's experiences and reality, whether working class, female, or Black: these are all necessary to the production of writing. They are also essential factors in the expression of one's ability to write. The exploitative practices of capitalist economies have, in fact, deprived these groups of the ability to express themselves through writing and publishing. Without that ability, the right to write from *any* point of view is meaningless. It goes without saying that the ability to write without the right is equally meaningless.

All of this appears more than reason enough to prohibit white writers writing from the point of view of persons from other cultures or races. The emotion—anger at the injustices that flow from racism—is entirely understandable. However, despite the reckless exercise of privilege on the part of white writers, I believe such a proscription to be very flawed and entirely ill-advised. My reasons for this position are as follows: first, such a rule or proscription is essentially unenforceable (unless, of course, one is the late Ayatollah) and for that reason should never be made. Secondly, prohibiting such activity alters not one iota of that invisible and sticky web of systemic or structural racism. If all the white writers interested in this type of writing were voluntarily to swear off writing from the point of view of persons from other races and/or cultures, it would not ensure that writers from those cultures or races would get published any more easily, or at all. For that to happen, changes have to be made at other levels and in other areas such as publishing, reviewing, distribution, library acquisitions, and educational curricula. Thirdly, and, to my mind, most importantly, for those who unquestioningly clasp the rights of the individual writer most clearly to their breasts, such a proscription provides a ready-made issue to sink their anti-censorship teeth into. Such a proscription becomes, in fact, a giant red herring dragged across the brutally cut path of racism.

As the fallout from The Women's Press debacle so clearly showed, all available energy in the writing community went into discussing, arguing and debating whether white women writers, or white writers in general, ought or ought not to be using the voice of the Other. There was no discussion about how to enable more Black women to get into print, or how to help those small publishing houses committed to publishing work by Black authors, or any attention paid to the many tasks that must be undertaken to make the writing and publishing world truly non-racist.

Funding, publishing, distribution, critical reception—racism manifests itself in all these areas. For the Black writer the problem is hydra-headed; its effect as multi-faceted as profound. If, as the late critic Raymond Williams argued, "no work is in any full practical sense produced until it is also received," then much of the writing by Black writers in Canada fails to be fully produced.[2] "Burning books," the late Russian poet Joseph Brodsky writes, is "after all . . . just a gesture; not publishing them is a falsification of time . . . precisely the goal of the system," intent on issuing "its own version of the future."[3] This "falsification of time" which results from the failure to publish writers is as characteristic of the dominant culture in Canada as in the Soviet Union. In both cases, the state's intention is to "issue its own version of the future." And the Canadian version will, if possible, omit the contributions of Blacks and other non-dominant groups.

It is not that the question of the individual privilege of the white writer is entirely unimportant. That privilege is heavily implicated in the ideology of racism, white supremacy and their practices. The weight of racism in the writing world, however, does not reside with the individual white writer, but in the network of institutions and organizations that reinforce each other in the articulation of systemic racism. The writer is but a cog in that system. It is, perhaps, typical of a liberal democracy that racism in the writing and publishing world would be reduced to the individual writer sitting before her word processor, with only the imagination for company.

The imagination is free! Long live the imagination! One could hear the cry echoing around Canada as the controversy concerning the writer and voice rippled out across the country. Many writers saw the suggestion that they merely consider their social and political responsibility in selecting subject matter as an attempt to control that great storehouse of the writer: the imagination. One writer argued publicly that when she sat at her desk, her imagination took over and she had no choice but to go with it. Are we to conclude, therefore, that there are no mediating actions between what the writer imagines and what eventually appears on the printed page? Are we, as writers, all engaged in some form of literary automatism? While acknowledging that surrealist writers have indulged in automatic writing, the product of their writing was not intended to be realist fiction. The mandate of surrealism, if writing can ever be said to have a mandate, was to challenge what had, until then, been the art traditions of the Western world.

The imagination, I maintain, is both free and unfree. Free in that it can wander wheresoever it wishes; unfree in that it is profoundly affected and shaped by the societies in which we live. Traditionally, the unfettered nature of the imagination has done very little to affect the essentially negative portrayal of women by men in the arts. By and large, this portrayal has conformed closely to patriarchal visions of women. It required, in fact, a feminist reform movement to ensure the more realistic and positive images of women with which we are becoming increasingly familiar.

To state the obvious, in a racist, sexist and classist society, the imagination, if left unexamined, can and does serve the ruling ideas of the time. Only when we understand how belief in the untrammeled nature of the imagination is a part of the dominant culture can we, as Elizam Escobar[4] suggests, begin to use the imagination as a weapon. The danger with writers carrying their unfettered imaginations into another culture—particularly one like the Native Canadian culture which theirs has oppressed and exploited—is that without careful thought, they are likely to perpetuate stereotypical and one-dimensional views of this culture.

Regarding the issue of whether a white writer should use a style pioneered in a Third World country, there is again the problem of unenforceability. There is, however, a more serious error in this approach. The assumption behind the proscription is that because the style in question—magic realism—was pioneered in Latin America, it must, therefore, be entirely a product of that part of the world. Yet much of Latin American culture, particularly that of the middle and upper classes, has traditionally drawn heavily on European culture; the main articulators and purveyors of this style within Latin America—white males for the most part—are products of European learning and tradition. One could further argue that magic realism is as much an heir to European traditions of surrealism, for instance, as to the Latin American sensibility and mindscape. Does that make it a Third World or First World style? Would it be acceptable, then, to use a European style, but not a European style one step removed?

All of this is not to deny that magic realism, as we have come to know it, is inextricably bound up with Latin America and its unique realities. But the proscription and its underlying (and unarticulated) assumptions reveal how little understanding there truly is of the complex nature of these societies and their histories. Latin America plays the exotic, kinky Other to the straight, realist realities of the affluent West.

A proscription such as this, or the position of The Women's Press that they will only look at manuscripts where the protagonist's experience is one with that of the author, raises more questions than it answers. What does the latter policy mean for the Black writer using the novel form—a form developed by the white, European bourgeoisie? And does the Press' position mean automatic exclusion of a manuscript by a Black writer who, in order to explore racism, develops a white character? If we accept the argument that the oppressed know more about their oppressors than the latter about them, and if we accept the fact that groups like Blacks or Natives are, in the West, essentially living in a white world, how can we argue that a Black writer's experience is substantially removed from that of a white character? Surely, as the Kenyan writer Ngugi Wa Thiong'o argues, the issue is what the Black writer does with the form, and not merely the origin of the form. But note here how the debate about these issues once again fails to address the issues and concerns of Black writers, how the controversy is continually presented in terms of issues for white writers—a trap the Press neither challenged nor managed to avoid itself.

This rather tiresomely limited approach, albeit rooted in a recognition of the appropriation of non-European cultures by Europeans and North Americans, takes us into very murky waters and distorts the issue: how to ensure that *all* writers in Canada have equal access to funding, to publication, and to full reception. What Black writers can benefit from, in my opinion, is not proscription, such as we have to date, but equal access to *all* the resources this society has to offer.

If, however, the debate in the Writers' Union newsletter[5] is evidence of where writers in Canada are in their thinking on racism in writing and publishing, then there is every reason to be pessimistic about the potential for change. With very few exceptions—all the more noteworthy and noticeable for their rarity—writers defended their rights and freedoms to use whatever voice they chose to use. I would have hoped that along with that defense would have been *some* acknowledgment of the racism endemic to this society, and to the literary arena. It would have been reassuring if the debate had revealed a wider acknowledgment and understanding of The Women's Press' attempt, flawed as it was, to do something about racism as publishers. The issues of racism, personal, systemic or cosmic, has, however, been notably absent from this debate.

Some months later, in the spring of 1989, when presented with the issue, the Writers' Union failed to endorse the setting up of a task force looking into issues of racism in writing and publishing in Canada. This despite significant attempts by a female and feminist minority. The Union *did,* however, pass a motion condemning "the failure of the law of Canada to protect freedom of expression and to prevent far-reaching intrusions into the essential privacy of the writing process." If any proof were needed of my earlier arguments, this tawdry display of white, male privilege provided it; it also confirmed how little interest the Union had in even acknowledging the existence of racism.

The Writers' Union has, to my mind, entirely abdicated its position as an organization that claims to be concerned about the rights of all writers in this country. It is primarily concerned about the rights of white, male writers, and certainly not about Black writers. The Old Boys' Network of Writers would be a far more suitable appellation.

"All art," critic Terry Eagleton writes, "has its roots in social barbarism. Art survives by repressing the historical toil which went into its making, oblivious of its own sordid preconditions. . . . We only know art because we can identify its opposite: labour."[6] There is an evident and appalling failure on the part of white writers to grasp the fact that, despite their relatively low incomes, as a group they are extremely privileged and powerful. There is an accompanying failure to understand how the silencing of the many enables the few to become the articulators and disseminators of knowledge and culture. This is the social barbarism to which Eagleton refers, and it continues today in the erasure of the presence of those others who, by their labor and toil, still help to create art today.

Furthermore, how can white writers insist on their right to use any voice they may choose, and not insist on the equally valid right of African or Native writers to write and to have their word adequately received? How can white writers insist on this right without acknowledging that, on the extremely unlevel playing field that racism creates, the exercise of this right could, in all likelihood, mean that work by a white writer about Natives, for instance, would be more readily received than similar work by a Native writer? To insist on one's right in a political vacuum, as so many writers have, while remaining silent on the equal rights of other writers to be heard, is fundamentally undemocratic and unfair.

The corresponding obligation to the right of these writers to use any voice they may choose to is first to understand the privilege that has generated the idea that free choice of voice is a right. Second, but more importantly, these writers ought to begin to work to expand the area of that right to include those who, in theory, also have a right to write from any point of view but who, through the practice of racism, have been unable to exercise that right, thereby making it meaningless. Ngugi writes that "the writer as a human being is, himself, a product of history, of time and place."[7] This is what many writers in Canada today have forgotten: that—to continue in the words of Ngugi—they "belong to a certain class" and they are "inevitably . . . participant[s] in the class struggles of [their] times." I would add to that, the race struggles of their times. These writers have refused even to acknowledge their privilege vis-à-vis their own white working class, let alone Blacks or Natives.

Writers are no more or less racist, classist, or sexist than other individuals. Neither are they any less sensitive to the issue of racism than the average Canadian—which is probably not saying much. Writers ought, however, to recognize and acknowledge that along with their privilege comes a social responsibility. Essentially, the individual writer will decide how to exercise that social responsibility. Writers may, of their own accord, decide not to use the voice of a group their culture has traditionally oppressed. Others may decide that their responsibility impels them to do something else; but they ought to be impelled to do something.

Writers coming from a culture that has a history of oppressing the one they wish to write about would do well to examine their motives. Is their interest a continuance of the tradition of oppression, if only in seeing these cultures as different or exotic, as Other? Does their interest come out of the belief that their own cultural material is exhausted, and that just about anything having to do with Africans, Asians and Natives is bound to garner more attention? Is it, perhaps, the outcome of guilt and a desire to make recompense? Such writers have to examine whether they can write without perpetuating stereotypes.

Many readers must be aware of the debacle the English feminist publishing house Virago faced when it found that one of its published titles—a collection of short stories about Asians in England—was, in fact, written pseudonymously by a white male—a Church of England minister. It is interesting to note that one of the readers of the manuscript prior to publication, an Asian woman, had drawn attention to the fact that all the girls in the collection of short stories were drawn very passively; the boys, on the other hand, were portrayed as being very aggressive. She actually questioned the authorship of the work, but her suspicions were overridden. We cannot conclude from this that writers from a particular culture would be above pandering to stereotypes about their own culture. For instance, the upper class writer from any culture runs the risk of stereotyping the working class of that culture; however, the chance of stereotypes being portrayed is, in my opinion, far greater with a writer who is, essentially, a stranger to the culture as a whole.

White writers must ask themselves hard questions about these issues; they must understand how their privilege *as white people,* writing *about* another culture, rather than *out of* it, virtually guarantees that their work will, in a racist society, be received more readily than the work of *writers* coming from that very culture. Many of these questions are applicable to all writers: for instance, the Black middle class writer writing about the Black working class; or the upper class Asian writing about the Asian peasant. If, after these questions are asked—and I believe responsible writers must ask them if they wish to be responsible to themselves, their gifts and the larger community— writers still feel impelled to write that story or that novel, then let us hope they are able to "describe a situation so truthfully . . . that the reader can no longer evade it."[8] Margaret Laurence accomplished this ideal in her collection of short stories *The Tomorrow Tamer;* the secret of her accomplishment lies, I believe, in the sense of humility—not traditionally the hallmark of the white person approaching an African, Asian or Native culture—that writers need to bring to the culture to which they are strangers. Writers must be willing to learn; they must be open to having certainties shifted, perhaps permanently. They cannot enter as oppressors, or even as members of the dominant culture. That sense of humility is what has been sorely lacking in the deluge of justifications that have poured forth in support of the "right" of the white writer to use any voice.

While Canadian writers find it very easy to defend the rights of Chinese writers who have been silenced by the state, there is general apathy to the silencing of writers here in Canada through the workings of racism, both within the marketplace and through funding agencies. In an essay titled "The Writer and Responsibility,"[9] South African writer Nadine Gordimer argues that artistic freedom cannot exist without its wider context. She identifies two presences within the writer: creative self-absorption and conscionable awareness. The writer, she says, must resolve "whether these are locked in a death-struggle, or are really foetuses in a twinship of fecundity." For some, artistic freedom appears to be alive and well in Canada; these writers, however, pay not the slightest heed to the fact that the wider context includes many who, because of racism, cannot fully exercise that artistic freedom. In Canada, that wider context is, in fact, very narrowly drawn around the artistic freedom of white writers.

As for the twin presences of creative self-absorption and conscionable awareness which Gordimer identifies, conscionable awareness on any issue but censorship has been disturbingly absent from the debate on the writer and voice. Creative self-absorption, or literary navel-gazing, is what rules the day in Canada.

Notes

1. Sara Maitland, "Triptych," in *A Book of Spells* (London: Joseph, 1987).
2. Raymond Williams, *Marx: The First 100 Years* (London: Fontana, 1983).

3. Joseph Brodsky, *Less Than One* (New York: Farrar, Straus and Giroux, 1986).

4. Escobar is a Puerto Rican painter who is serving a sixty-eight-year sentence in state and federal prisons in the United States for seditious conspiracy arising out of his involvement in Puerto Rican liberation struggles.

5. In 1988, the Writers' Union ran a series of letters in its newsletter on the issues of cultural appropriation and the writer and voice.

6. Terry Eagleton, "How Do We Feed the Pagodas?" *New Statesman,* March 20, 1987.

7. Ngugi Wa Thiong'o, "Kenyan Culture: The National Struggle for Survival," in *Writers in Politics: Essays* (London: Heinemann, 1981).

8. Anton Chekhov, quoted in Isaiah Berlin, *Russian Thinkers* (London: Hogarth Press, 1978).

9. Nadine Gordimer, *The Essential Gesture: Writing, Politics, and Places* (London: J. Cape, 1988).

Kwame Dawes

Re-appropriating Cultural Appropriation

Definitions are exclusionary in their nature. I consider, for political purposes, people of the Nations that existed in North America prior to the arrival of Columbus and his people "people of color." At the same time, it is important to declare that the term "people of color" is a euphemism for people who are not white European types. This label may appear to exclude some who share the sentiments and experiences of the people I am writing about. To these people I say, be assured that if you share the experiences described in this article, consider yourself a member of this political unit—this artificial construct.

I am acutely aware of the incredible differences within these groups. I am aware that many members of what I have come to term "people of color" would rather not be identified as such. All I can say is that the people I speak of share the experience of oppression and disenfranchisement at the hands of white society. Rather than fall into the trap of accepting the divisive game of comparing exploitation scars like locker-room denizens, we are better off consolidating our shared experience as we fight the common foe—oppression, which is spoken and acted out in the idiom of racism.

Finally, in explanation for why I persist throughout this essay to refer to both "people of color" and "First Nations people," I should state this strategy is purely one of political expediency. By drawing attention to the distinctions between these two groupings, I am foregrounding the especially relevant and pressing nature of oppression and abuse that is distinctly and undeniably Canadian—that of its relationship with the First Nations of this geographical area. I do so, also, to counteract the tendency of many Canadians (white, of color, of First Nations) to divide (so as to weaken) the constituents of the racial struggle along very specific lines. I am asserting that we all—First Nations people, and so-called "people of color"—share a common struggle. By doing this I seek to preempt any attempt to exclude First Nations people from the discussion, which is often the tactical wont of many white debaters.

Artists who fall under the typically problematic rubric "people of color and First Nations peoples" in Canada have learned that it is virtually impossible to conceive of an existence free of politics. This is especially evident among artists who seek to assert an independence of artistic vision within a largely white-dominated and white-funded mainstream.

It becomes important for such artists to negotiate their way into funding for their projects from a wide variety of organizations which have in common the harrowing concept of jury selection. There are several breeds of this creature (juries), each with its own peculiar foibles and pitfalls for the artist. The first entails the easily identified white-dominated and white-peopled juries that seek to uphold the tenets of quality and excellence in their own limited and archaic terms. The second is a peculiar creature, for it includes in its composition the carefully selected "minority" figure (read someone non-white) who is expected to validate the ethical practices of the institution that has selected him/her, especially in the area of racial issues. They become hired race-relations officers whose dependence on these organizations for a salary places incredible pressures on them to conform to and support the status quo. This individual, more often than not, is pulled away from the pool of artists and is then expected to make sound judgment on the works of his/her peers and fellow warriors/workers from the position of adversary (other/them/ those people/etc.).

It is these bureaucratic structures that generally determine the fate of so many projects embarked upon, or dreamed up by non-white artists. Their actions within the past few years indicate that while there is a level of tokenism and apparent concern for racial questions with regard to funding in this country, the artistic community (including both the artists themselves and the administrators) has failed significantly to address the very real expectations of the non-white population. This mainstream network of funding agencies persists with a conservatism that shies from any fundamental philosophical or structural change, opting instead for a mechanism that is able to absorb new ideas and new ways of approaching certain issues within the already existing structure. And herein lies the reality that non-white peoples are in no way gaining a significant power base in these organizations. The fact is that the hierarchical structure continues to produce and implement policies that suit its own interests while using tried and proven strategies of divide and conquer to disarm the call for fundamental change that is coming from non-white groups all over the country, and from the non-white individuals who are coopted into the system.

There seems to be a pressing desire among many non-white artists and producers to bring about a shift in philosophy within these structures that will ensure that the work of such "minority" artists is treated with intelligence, sensitivity and respect by those who control the funding. It is also important to these artists that the structures which undergird these funding organizations augment this respect and intelligence with a clear acknowledgment, through the implementation of new policy, that racism is a reality in the society and that such racism can occur within these very organizations. It is obvious to many that such respect and intelligence are not inherent in the current systems and so there is a pressing need for action to change this. The current debate surrounding the question of cultural appropriation, for instance, has provided the typically unimaginative instincts of top-heavy bureaucratic structures that participate in the funding business with another tool of exclusion and ghettoization which appears to wear the face of cultural tolerance and sensitivity. In fact, without an understanding of the role of power and its history in the context of colonialism and imperialism in determining what constitutes cultural appropriation, one is left with what can easily be another tool of fascist cultural exclusivity. Is Bob Marley's lyric "War" cultural appropriation because the text of the song is taken from a speech by Haile Selassie, an Ethiopian emperor? Is Marley, a Jamaican of Scottish and Jamaican descent, appropriating the culture of Ethiopia, and, if so, is this a bad thing? Is it the same as racist renditions of Native American culture or African culture seen in many Hollywood films? How is such difference defined and legislated without creating a situation in which simplistic criteria like "it's about Black people and he is white, thus we throw it out" become the operating rationale for funding policies?

Quite naturally, the greatest cry against cultural appropriation has come from people who are railing against the actions of exploitative white artists. Thus, it appears that support for legislation that seeks to end cultural appropriation would come from this group of individuals as well. And in many instances this is the case. However, it is also quite clear that the people who are designing and implementing policy to respond to these cries for change are not usually people of color or people of First Nations descent. Instead, white bureaucrats are formulating these policies and in many ways are merely replicating old racist and divisive models of government through an appropriation and misinterpretation of progressive political ideology. If legislation continues in the direction that it threatens to go, what will happen is that only Blacks will be able to write about Black experience, and only whites will be able to write about their experience. Cree people will not write about the Mohawk, nor will the Iroquois write about the Inuit. A straight woman will never include in her work a lesbian character, nor will a Mayan write about a Spanish-Mexican homosexual. The only artists who will be able to produce work of rich variety are those who have incredibly complex and mixed heritages, who are bisexual, who are androgynous, or those who don't need funding.

Can an Other person, a person different from myself because of sex, race, sexual orientation or history, effectively write about my experience in a way that I can connect with? As an artist, an avid reader and a viewer of films I must conclude that this is possible. It has to be. This does not mean that the picture will be perfect. But, by the same token, I would never presume to think that because someone is Black like myself, and male and heterosexual, that he automatically has the capacity and skill to represent my experience. However, I make a distinction between exploitative readings of my experience and readings that emerge out of dialogue and honest interaction founded on common humanity. To deny the possibility of art emerging out of such a context is to deny art its power—it is, in fact, to deny the very concept of learning.

But the issue is far more complex than that. One could quite easily declare on the basis of the above statements that legislation that seeks to uproot cultural appropriation is inherently absurd and unprogressive. Cultural appropriation—the argument goes—is not a bad thing all the time, and world cultures are already too intertwined to do anything about changing them. However, such thinking assumes that we are playing on an even playing field. This is not the case. Our society is marred by significant inequities which have, for years, led to the exclusion of "minorities" and communities not regarded as belonging to the "mainstream" of the society from telling their own stories. Riding on the back of a carefully designed and efficiently implemented system of the cultural oppression of colonialism and imperialism, much of Canada's cultural behavior merely reflects a privileging of white Eurocentric values. In this context, minorities have often been excluded from funding which would allow them to tell their stories—instead, white artists have had greater access to the money available, even when they are telling stories that have been taken from the cultures of the "minority" people. In light of this inequity, there is a strong and compelling case that can be made for a reassessment of the philosophical foundation upon which funding decisions are made. Such a reevaluation would be founded on the argument that since so many whites have told, for years, the stories of non-whites, and have, in the process, brutally misinterpreted them and established a discourse of inferiority in such portrayals, it is time to shift the emphasis and favor, instead, the non-white artists who are willing and able to tell their own story and to tell it well. This is not to dismiss the noble and sincere sentiment that may have gone into the hundreds and thousands of pseudo-anthropological folk song and tale collections that have been produced by white writers over the past five hundred years, beginning in America with Columbus' quasi-anthropological evaluation of the Arawak people. However, as has been demonstrated in countless instances, many of these works are flawed by the heavy-handed application of Western values, prejudices and belief systems to the interpretation of the folkways of non-white people. This, coupled with exploitive absence of accountability to the people being written about, and the related lack of respect for their values, has generated work that is at best of poor and unreliable quality and at worst simply offensive and totally destructive.

In order to favor the non-white artist on the basis of this argument, certain assumptions about art have to be made. The first and most important is that art is essentially a commodity that exists within a political and ideological landscape. We must dismiss the notion that art exists outside of culture, or the idea that art somehow transcends culture and politics. It does not. This is the reality regardless of whether we like the idea or not. Art is money, art is power, art defines effectively. Art may be seen as a means by which we interpret and represent society in a fashion that is dictated by our discourse—our history, our culture, our social realities and our politics. If we grant, then, that white artists have essentially dominated the highest echelons of art for too long, and if we further accept that this is a product, not of artistic ability, but of political and cultural will, then there is a place for the redressing of what is essentially an injustice. There is a place for suggesting that non-white artists be allowed to tell their own story. In fact it must go further than that—non-white artists should be encouraged, aided, supported and funded such that they can tell their own stories. At the same time, white artists should be heavily scrutinized such that they can be discouraged from embarking on projects that essentially perpetuate the negative stereotyping of non-white cultures. For those who are quick to scream censorship, let it be understood that this has less to do with censorship than it has to do with copyright questions. As simplistic as this may seem, the rationale for such action is founded on the belief that white artists have been stealing from and misinterpreting non-white artists for too long. Now non-white artists are seeking to get back what is rightfully theirs.

The funding agencies and policy making structures should, as a consequence, so restructure themselves to allow non-white artists to feel and be included in the artistic mainstream. This means a redefinition of what constitutes mainstream—moving away from the notion that anything mainstream must be either white or acceptable to whites. These are political considerations and require political measures. But despite the compelling nature of the argument presented here, it is necessary to continue to bear in mind that political policy on such matters can easily shift from the liberal to the fascist. One must be wary, for instance, of the fact that legislation in such areas is often being carried out by individuals who are not necessarily sympathetic to the philosophy of change. In the context of this issue, this is a significant danger, for policies may be implemented in such a way as to aggravate the situation and perpetuate the ghettoization of non-white communities in the society. What I refer to here is the perpetuation of the concept of the existence of homogeneous and pure races and cultures and the hierarchical values that many racists over the years have attached to them. Instance: Hitler's attitude to jazz and Black culture in Nazi Germany, for instance. Would we applaud his passionate plea for his pure white people to not "appropriate" the music of Black America?

The fact is that we are dealing with a society that has still not fully internalized the need for systematic change when it comes to racism. Consequently, action that seeks to redress racist tendencies is being implemented by people who have not fully accepted the negative reality of racism. There are still many instances of racist policy of which the administrators who carry out legislation are blissfully unaware. They have not yet understood the pervasiveness and Hydra-like nature of racism. They just don't get it.

It is easy, then, for such ideological constructs to be redefined and misappropriated to suit the interests of a ruling class. The truth is that if, in fact, the legislation took the form of what I describe above, then we would have a situation that would simply ghettoize all communities, thus consolidating the domination of a "pure" white society and culture. Such politically rooted criteria would assume great importance so that questions of artistic quality would become redefined. This in itself may not be a bad thing except that this redefinition would be premised on the understanding that works produced by non-whites are defined and recommended purely on the basis of their politics and race-centeredness rather than on their vision and artistic credibility. Such thinking already exists today in the attitude that many Canadians have toward notions of affirmative action and employment equity. Here, the non-white worker, it is assumed, is inherently weaker in skill and intelligence than the white worker but has managed to progress simply on the basis of his/her skin color. Translated into the art business, white artists are now dismissing the credibility of the work of non-white artists on the assumption that the only reason that such non-whites have been published, produced or displayed is that their works are a part of the privileged "minority backlash." So a white male academic is able to say to me, without the slightest acknowledgment of his racism and dismissal of my abilities, "You are lucky being Black—you will get a job easily. Now if you were a woman and maybe gay . . ." This is the kind of self-pitying cynicism that comes from people who have had it too easy in the past and who are now lamenting their loss of power without realizing that the power they once held was wrongly and unjustly acquired. They fail to recognize as well that their movement to positions of power at the time was not based on merit, but facilitated by their skin color. Such attitudes as de- scribed above are also becoming basic to the cultural arena, and it stems from the basic philosophy that is ingrained in the psyche of many white Canadians.

It is evident that Canada's dealings with institutionalized racism are as var- ied and regionally defined as is the landscape of this country. There are parts of Canada where the pressure to recognize diversity is having virtually no impact. The reasons vary. On the one hand, one may cite the reality of num- bers. Some areas of Canada are so effectively white that they manage to create an invisible under-class that does not in any way have power or recognition. The second has to do with the attempt by many communities to deny their diversity in a futile but dangerous quest to present a face of whiteness in a diverse community. Here little acknowledgment is given to the presence of racism. The non-whites remain marginalized or are sucked into white society, where they must conform to white values and standards and where they learn quickly how to adapt, knowing, in the process, where familiarity and affinity with whites end. Here, there is no compulsion or pressure to recognize the presence or the needs of the non-white community. Think of how comforta- bly many regional theater companies and art centers in this country design their seasons with the least regard for the question of cultural diversity. They grant themselves the pretended luxury of choosing on the basis of artistic taste and merit, when in fact all they are doing is consolidating the culture and values of the white community while denying the non-white community. The third paradigm entails the diverse community that seeks to celebrate its diversity through a process of denial. They deny repeatedly that there exists any racist sentiment or behavior in the community. They augment this position by resisting any calls to put in place mechanisms of complaint and protest against racist behavior. They are adamant about not accepting policies like affirmative action or employment equity, for such policies simply acknowledge something that they are not willing to accept—that there is racism in their communities. These are happy communities with a smug sense of self-righteousness who exist in denial mode until the keg blows.

Is it any wonder, then, that so many non-white political groups and artists are now advocating a hardline legislative practice which is often akin to a quota system? Hardly, because this is often the only way that many artistic centers and government funding agencies will be forced to be accountable not only to the wealthier whites who are filling the theaters, bringing in the money to see themselves on stage, on screen and on the tube, but to the less powerfully positioned non-white disenfranchised minority that such organizations are constitutionally bound to serve as well.

The struggles at Oka, the Meech Lake détente in Manitoba, the race disturbances in Halifax and Toronto and the wide-reaching aftershocks of the explosion in Los Angeles have all in some way contributed to the forcing of the issue in Canada today. Things are now at a political level as Canada searches for its sense of identity and a way to construct and understand itself in the context of today's realities. Native Canadian Nations are especially well-positioned at the moment to bring about systematic change to Canadian policy toward them, and they are acting. It is hoped that their gains will be understood by themselves, and by all society as models for the re-evaluation of the values and systems of governing that have existed in this country for a very long time. It is hoped that other non-white groups who have participated in the fight for fundamental change will be able to participate in the reorganization of the society's attitude to race relations during this period. The schizophrenic history of exploitation and guilt that has characterized the relationship of white society to the Native Americans is unique and brings with it a compelling case for change which white Canada is beginning to listen to. Sadly, Canada is less inclined, at the moment, to listen to non-white and non-Native groups. However, the evolving demographics of Canadian society present a compelling case for dialogue. It is in the context of such dialogue that we can then turn our minds to resolving the troubling question of cultural appropriation, for it is when the society begins to deal with this issue that we will start to see changes in the infrastructures that support the artists in this country.

When cultural appropriation is counteracted by the qualities of respect, sensitivity and equal opportunity, the result is work that is wonderfully developed and filled with the richness of cultural interaction and dialogue. It is the difference between stealing and getting permission to take, borrow or share.

The cry for measures against cultural appropriation emerged out of a sense of abuse and exploitation felt by disenfranchised minorities which characterized the work of many white artists dealing with subject matter that they did not respect or understand. It also involved the question of money. Many artists have stolen from other cultures without giving acknowledgment; they have misrepresented cultures and values with complete disdain and disregard for the values of the people that they have exploited, and, in the process, they have made significant amounts of money from such efforts. In many instances, our understanding of ourselves has been determined by the language and ideology of these exploitive artists whose sense of accountability is minimal largely because it is they who have the funding and power.

Thus it is possible for white documentary filmmakers to shoot Aztec people and yet state in the overdub that they are Mayans without these filmmakers feeling the least bit of anxiety about their credibility as cultural documenters. Quite simply, the audience they feel accountable to would not know the difference. It is this disrespect, this constant "dissing" of other cultures through exploitive artistic tendencies, that has driven many non-white artists to call for action against cultural appropriation. The truth is, what we are looking for, as non-white artists, is a chance to be able to determine how our stories are going to be told, and a chance to ensure that our values and culture are respected by those who seek to describe them. We, quite understandably, sometimes feel, in light of past practices of whites, that we are the only ones who can fairly treat our own experience. We are suspicious of the motives and practices of those who do not share our history of pain and abuse. Some of us take this thinking even further, suggesting that white artists do not have the capacity to tell our stories because they speak from a "comparatively superficial perspective," which does not allow them to share the pain and suffering that we have felt under their rule.[1] It is an understandable instinct, but it must be tempered by the awareness that it is an instinct born out of the demand for respect, accountability and dialogue.

For we concede, as well we must, that there are very few existing cultures that can be described as completely void of influence from other cultures. This may be, for many, a lamentable fact of imperialism and colonialism, but for me it is a compelling fact of industrialization and the instinct to explore and learn about other people. I suspect that this is a fact of the human condition. We are social creatures who have consistently shown a propensity to adapt our values, our sense of beauty and art, and our concepts of identity and place according to the cultures and civilizations that we encounter. This kind of interaction and sharing of culture—whether it be exploitive or that of mutual respect and sharing—is something that is arguably inherent in human behavior. To deny this, therefore, is to deny a fundamental human trait. Thus, any attempt to formulate policy that seeks to uphold a concept of culture as a homogeneous entity that is static and not subject to change through interaction and dialogue is bound to lead to the adoption of totalitarian and inhuman practices. More importantly, it entails the denial of the commonality of human experience. Interaction is inevitable; influences must occur. What need not be inevitable are exploitation and the movement toward a denial of one's own identity. As well, the kind of hierarchical structures that establish "superior" cultures as the ultimate goal of "inferior" cultures through the processes of so-called influence and change must be completely rejected as manifestations of genocidal tendencies. Cultural appropriation, understood in its most negative of manifestations, amounts to robbery. Coping with robbery and thievery is something that all societies have somehow had to do, and the principles inherent in such coping mechanisms could be applied to cultural appropriation. We abhor robbery. We resent when our things are taken from us without our permission and flaunted by the thief as trophies and as things that belong to that person. We resent it because in the process our achievements are denied and our enemy has managed to ride toward success on our backs. We also resent it when we give people permission to do something on our behalf and they completely misrepresent us. They make a mockery of our message and shamefully betray the trust that we had in them. Our instinct is to try and retrieve what was taken from us—the actual item that we gave in good faith to the bad messenger—and to reassert who we are and what is ours so that generations can see the truth and appreciate it. If we do not do this, our children's inheritance, that which was given to us, will no longer be there for them, and they will be very poor indeed.

It is time to ensure that such exploitation be arrested. More crucially, it is time to ensure that when our gift of culture is being displayed by those with whom we have been willing to share it, that it is presented in a manner that indicates that the artist feels accountable not only to one's financiers, but to us, the part-suppliers of this person's content.

Ultimately, then, it is possible to conceive of a situation in which artistic value operates side by side with cultural and political awareness in the judging and funding of projects within this society. We must accept that the criteria for what constitutes artistic quality are not only personally determined, but further determined by the cultural legacy of each of us, and that such legacies cannot be valued in terms of "good, better, best." While the pervasiveness of Western culture has supplied most cultural communities with shared criteria for artistic value, the same can be said about the impact of Eastern and Southern—that is, the Asian continent and the combined "Southern" worlds of

Africa, Australia and South America[2]—values on what we understand to be modern universal artistic tastes. It is incumbent on the individual who seeks to value work to have a broad conception of what is of quality and value in a Canadian society, which is becoming increasingly complex in its cultural makeup. This is a wonderful challenge facing artists and art administrators across the country, and it must be seen as an opportunity for the enrichment of art within the country. To shy away from it through the protectionism of exclusionary and divisive legislative practices would be to deny this country of one of its greatest assets, the diversity of its cultural heritages. Further, to reinforce the division through ghettoized policies of funding and support will only deprive the community of a chance to enrich its cultural infrastructure through an equitable process of cross-fertilization.[3] Finally, to privilege one culture over another will simply ensure that a dominant and unequal trend of exploitation will continue denying the identity and existence of a large segment of the population.

These were my contemplations after spending four days with a dynamic and motivated group of artists and facilitators at the "About Frame About Face" meeting of the Independent Film and Video Alliance in Banff, Alberta, in June 1992. Many of these artists have found themselves sometimes sacrificing time they would rather spend doing their own creative work, struggling to see that the systems that operate around the industry are so ameliorated to ensure that there exists a freedom to create in a climate of something that transcends mere tolerance[4]—one of deep interest and pride. Many are highly positioned in the structures-that-be and may function, through the alliance of ideas, visions, and strategies for change, and, importantly, through the support from fellow strugglers, as catalysts for fundamental change in a manner that will encourage a change in the system. At the end of the conference there was a sense of community, a shared vision about art and its incredible dynamic with society. Most significantly, there emerged a commitment to uphold and promote the values of respect, responsibility, accountability and equal opportunity in efforts that entailed the crossing of cultural lines and the sharing of multiple heritages. In this environment of trust and shared values, there was a kind of liberation from the prison of marginalization within marginalized and ghettoized communities, through a determination to work against the patterns of exploitation inherent in the many centuries of abusive cultural appropriation. Here, those who had felt what it meant to be robbed resisted the human urge to simply rob the next potential victim who seemed weaker (perpetuating the pattern of the colonizer), by seeking to assert a desire, instead, to share, to dialogue, and to work together in celebrating each other's culture. Each artist of color, each First Nations artist has the responsibility to

act and speak out in defense of such liberating ideology. Non-white communities should force funding institutions and art centers to look at their policies
and their track record over the past few years from the perspective of those
who are most significantly affected. This examination will reveal the flaws in
the systems and will then force the various agencies to listen to the directives
given by these communities as to what must happen next.

Excitingly, the vision is founded upon the knowledge that there remain
thousands of incredibly dynamic and appealing stories to be told by First
Nations people and people of color and the country can only be enriched by
the telling of these stories. These artists realize that they still have to sacrifice a
great deal, but feel that things could be made better for those who are now
emerging as film- and videomakers, poets, playwrights, artists, musicians,
dancers and producers. The artists at this conference demonstrated what is
becoming increasingly clear in the arts and cultural world of Canada, that art
is inextricably linked to funding, and that funding is a deeply political issue
which requires highly politicized artists to challenge it. One day we may be
able to leave the artists to do their art, but this is not the day. Today we must
define the parameters of our oppression and in doing so, evolve the mechanism of our liberation. It is we who must define what cultural appropriation
really means and not allow it to be coopted into the strategies of exploitation
and subjugation that mainstream society is so expert at creating and implementing. We must be watchful of those who, through what can only be
described as cynical and twisted irony, choose to appropriate even the very
weapons of our liberation. This is the challenge facing First Nations artists and
artists of color today. Let us not be deceived: if we do not acknowledge our
shared histories of oppression and instead choose to wage our wars in isolation, we will all lose. My language is, admittedly, adversarial, but this kind of
rhetoric is sometimes necessary when we speak of something as critical as the
fate of our cultures and heritages. The prospects are exciting and promise
intriguing developments in the future.

Notes

1. Janisse Browning, "Self-Determination and Cultural Appropriation," *Fuse
Magazine* 15 (Spring 1992): 33.
2. By using these terms, I am merely completing the global circuit in the illogical
and geographically questionable Western political terms "East and West/North and
South." In actuality, I am suggesting that the process of cultural influence is fairly
universal and is usually reciprocal. What is often varied are the terms upon which such
influence takes place.
3. I am acutely aware of the fact that I speak idealistically here and that the world
I envisage is utopian. However, there is a lot that can be said about utopias which exist

in our collective imaginations, as they provide us with useful paradigms: ideals upon which to test our actions and to base our interactions.

4. When my mother said she wouldn't tolerate my behavior any longer, she meant that all this time she had hated my behavior and this would be the last straw. I don't understand how we have come to apply the term "tolerance" as a positive value in society. Tolerance is applicable only when two parties are so much against each other that grudging compromise is necessary. Tolerance is the last recourse before full-out war. Tolerance is not to be seen as the ideal. I hate to be tolerated: I would rather be accepted. If, of course, you really hate my guts, then please, by all means, tolerate me, but at least we will know exactly where we stand.

Joane Cardinal-Schubert

In the Red

Understanding is a consumer product in your society; you can buy some for the price of a magazine. Like the TV ad says, "*Time* puts it all right in your hands." Once you've bought some understanding, it's only natural to you to turn it around and make a profit from it—psychological, economic, or both. Then you'd get even fatter, more powerful. And where would I be?
—**Jimmie Durham**

The opposite condition to poverty is to have money.

Money, that is what appropriating is about. Whether the issue is land or art or iconography or ceremonial reliquiae, the focus of the deprivation is money. Something to be gained by imitation, copying, stealing. Where do ethics enter this issue; where does the law intervene?

The rights to cultural practices and creativity among Native people are tribal or are passed on from one individual to another in each generation through matrilineal inheritance.[1] Even craft skills are often passed generation to generation.

The alleged pirating and $250 million sale in the Asia Pacific Rim of a traditional design used in hand-knitted Kwagiutl sweaters by the Japanese demonstrates the unprotected nature of Native and tribal copyright in the international marketplace."[2] Beaded key rings, earrings and comb cases are all being produced in the international marketplace.

> **re•lin•quish** (rilinkwiʃ) v.t. to give up, renounce, *to relinquish a right* ‖ to let go of, cease to hold in the hand **re•lin•quish•ment** n. [fr. O.F. *relinquir (relinquiss-)*]

In the 1960s, there was a rush on the Northwest Coast culture, and black shoe–polished totems could be found in every souvenir shop across the nation. Now there is a rousing business in sweatshops. Native artists are being exploited in the "limited edition print market," the T-shirt market, the publishing business, the doll market, and by the dominant society's artists, curators, writers, and granting institutions. This does not occur as readily in western Canada because the culture base is stronger and the cultural information, having been passed down from generation to generation, is held by the Native people.

In the West, where contact time is less than 150 years, we experienced a cutoff from our culture by the residential school program begun in the 1870s by the church and the government. This, along with the introduction of an agricultural work program for adults, almost removed Native people from their cultural base. Herding people, displacing many onto the reserves after the treaties were signed, however, proved to be more of a boon culturally for Native people as they were in a position of gathering and sharing knowledge.

On the Northwest Coast, the Potlatch was outlawed until the late 1950s. On the Plains, the Sweatlodge ceremony and the Sundance ceremonies were not allowed as late as 1960. These ceremonies parallel the Christian church in terms of gathering and unifying people. It is very effective to outlaw strengthening, spiritual practices. Natives had to pay for permits to leave the reservations—small tracts of fenced land mirroring concentration camps. Indian agents often pocketed money made from selling meat rations, and the Native people had either no meat, or rotten meat, to eat. A sense of aimlessness prevailed. These were people forced into a dominant society soap playing 24 hours with the same script. Native people could not vote until 1962.

Native languages were not allowed in the school, children were beaten and punished for speaking "Indian." With the outlawing of the customs, the ceremonies, and by forbidding people the use of their own language, much of the culture was interrupted for generations. If a Native woman married a white man, she lost her status, and so did her children. If a Native man married a white woman, he kept his status, as did his children—this was government-imposed intervention in traditional cultural practices. As a result, for 100 years a growing population of non-status Indians moved to the cities and small urban areas, taking with them the knowledge of their elders. Now with the introduction of Bill C-31, government intervention is trying to restore the lost status to two and three generations of people.

As well as the displacement of ceremonies and language, Native people suffered the loss of their cultural icons, their reliquiae. Ceremonial objects were taken from them and systematically collected by museums and collectors throughout the world as evidence of a dying culture. Some of the more numerous pieces collected reside in collections in the former U.S.S.R., Germany and Sweden. These ceremonial objects are an important link in the cultural practice of most ceremonial rituals. Without them, life was meaning-less—they were the cultural videos and bibles of the time. If someone were to remove the chalice from the tabernacle in the Catholic ritual, the ceremony could not continue. There would be no meaning without the symbolic ritual that goes along with that particular reliquiae, and the participants would have to deal with the horror of its loss as an icon. This is our heritage!

Because Native peoples were in a position of stress and closeness, they behaved like any people who are held in terrorist captivity; they examined their strengths and unified. Enough information was passed from generation to generation so that the language was retained, as was the ritual of the cere-monial culture, which probably accounted for the enormous resurgence of the culture in the 1960s.

This was partially due to the education of the non-status Indian in the white world. Many were educated in professions; many went back to their people to share their knowledge. On the Northwest Coast, Bill Reid, a Haida artist, was one of the major influences in the renaissance of the Northwest Coast carving; Mungo Martin (Tony Hunt's grandfather, a Kwakuitl chief) also contributed greatly to the revival of ceremonial dance.

On the Plains in the early 1960s, Cree Chief Robert Smallboy from Hob-bema, Alberta, took a small band of followers, including his 89-year-old mother, from the liquor-ridden reserve west to their traditional lands on the Kootenai Plains. There they lived in tipis and learned about their ancient traditions. This led to the return of the Sweatlodge and the Sundance Cere-mony and further unified the Native people of the Plains. The Smallboy dance troupe toured extensively, reviving an interest in dance for the genera-tions to come.

At the same time, Alex Janvier was making quite a name for himself as a contemporary Native artist after graduating from the four-year art program at the Alberta College of Art in 1960. He began to show his work extensively both nationally and internationally. In the East, Norval Morrisseau—an Ojibwa who had raised his family living near the garbage dump on the re-serve—contracted tuberculosis. While in the sanatorium he began to paint his life history, and the father of Contemporary Canadian Indian Art was born. Seeing his success, a number of young Natives, some of them pushed by their agents and patrons, began to imitate his style; curators and critics began to write about them, and the Woodland school of painting was penned. Artists like Benjamin Chee Chee and Daphne Odjig became gross national products (GNPs) of Canada.

In the early 1960s, there was an explosion of Native art. As a result of this success by Native artists, white artists began to paint Native children with teardrops in their eyes; there was an attempt to romanticize the Indian; they were curiosities. Tourist shops abounded with fake artifacts and jewellery. Fringed coats and moccasins were the rage; the general public loved the idea of the Indian. This attitude, it seems, continues.

This year an exhibition was organized by Tom Hill and Deborah Doxtater at the Woodland Cultural Center in Brantford, Ontario, entitled "Fluff and Feathers." Its aim was to point out to the public that Indians had been created out of Hollywood stereotypes, comic books, toys and folk artists' depictions. The exhibition pointed out that Indianness has been used to sell tobacco, oranges, medicines, motor oil, environmental conservation, and escape-fantasy recreation for adults and children; it showed that Plains' tipis, dress, tomahawks, totem poles, and beaded moccasins are all symbols of Indianness easily recognizable in Canadian popular culture.

> **ap•pro•pri•ate** (əpróupri:eit), I. v.t. pres. part.
> **ap•pro•pri•at•ting** *past* and *past part.* **ap•pro•pri•at•ed** to take for one's own property, *the régime appropriated foreign industrial undertakings* || to steal || to set aside for a special purpose, *to appropriate profits to a reserve fund* 2. *adj.* (əpróupri:it) suitable [fr. L. *appropriare* (*appropriatus*), to annex]

This exhibition allowed people to put on Native symbols such as headdresses, buckskin, feathers and blankets. But as curator Deborah Doxtater commented, "They will do this, however, within the context of an exhibition that shows how distorted images of Indianness have been generated for centuries. This fantasy behaviour will be recorded for them by mirrors and video cameras so they can view themselves as unreal images too. This hopefully will stimulate visitors to think about how they are not accurate depictions of how Indian people are."[3]

An exhibition of artifacts at the Glenbow Museum in Calgary, summarized as the "artistic traditions of Canada's Native Peoples," pushed the false assumption that these objects were created for art's sake. Although the works were aesthetically pleasing, they were frozen in time—objects lifeless without their function. Native people have always embellished functional objects, but Native languages, like Inui, have no word for art. Ceremonial reliquiae are objects of beauty, but the dominant culture has no business transplanting their cultural ethic as if to sanction that beauty or aesthetic which acts as an extra function only.

The exhibition was called "The Spirit Sings," but it pushed the notion that Native culture was dead, wrapped up, over and collected. A number of Native artists—Jane Ash Poitras, Daphne Odjig, Alfred YoungMan, Alex Janvier, myself and others—held a protest exhibition at the Wallace Galleries in Calgary. We protested the fact that Native culture was being used by the Olympics to foster a worldview that Native culture was dead, all over, collected; and that what was still practiced was frozen in the 18th century. We believe that the Olympics should have held exhibitions featuring contemporary Native art as it is now.

In these changing times when the world has grown so much smaller through travel and communication, we cannot stay nailed to the past. As in all aspects of life, we push ahead to have the latest in technology and knowledge.

We move ahead in art as well as trying to become mainstream artists. We have, however, achieved a greater role in the art world by accident of birth. We are more visible, we are different, we have a sign on our foreheads INDIAN/PRIMITIVE. This stereotype is aided by exhibitions like "The Spirit Sings." Many Native artists are educated in schools and universities alongside our white peers. We have access to all the latest information and modern technology. Many of us speak many languages, we have become professionals, critics, curators, administrators and artists, and yet we still have an adjective in front of our name or our profession: Indian/Native Architect, Indian/Native doctor, Indian/Native lawyer, Indian/Native artists.

> **pos•ses•sion** (pezéʃən) a possessing or being possessed ‖ that which is possessed ‖ (*pl.*) property ‖ a territory under the political and economic control of another country ‖ (*law*) actual enjoyment of property not founded on any title of ownership to take possession of to begin to occupy as owner ‖ to affect so as to dominate [O.F.]

We are in the position of producing "art on the edge," which is the current trend every self-respecting curator in Canada is looking for to make their career. We have become part of the GNP of Canada. The Canadian Government is pushing our work in international exhibitions, but they are still not inviting any of us to the openings.

When the exhibition "In the Shadow of the Sun," which is the signature exhibition of the Museum of Civilization, opened in Dortmund, West Germany, in December of 1988, none of the artists in the exhibition was informed as to when the exhibition opened, nor were any artists sent an invitation. No artists fees have been paid, and, although the exhibition opened in Ottawa in late June, only minimal information was provided to the artists about arrangements for press coverage, lectures or travel plans, or their part in the opening ceremonies. "It seems that we have to even combat the romanticization of the Indian past as well as fight off the imposed purism of many non-Indian anthropologists who are unable to accept innovation in Indian art. They don't seem to understand that environment changes; culture and Indians too have changed in the last century."⁴ "Edward Curtis did not record a vanishing race," says Jaune Quick-To-See-Smith. "Dying cultures do not make art; cultures that do not change with the times will die."⁵

In historical terms we have evidence, in both the U.S. and Canada, that Native peoples have been on this land base for thousands of years. Across this country we have several historic sites that teach of our culture's focus.

Head Smashed In Buffalo Jump, near Fort McLeod, Alberta, is a World Heritage Site. It was in use over 6,000 years ago, about the same time the pyramids were being built. On this land base we harvested medicines, we had acetylsalicylic acid from the red willow, we had natural dyes, fibers, fruits and vegetables. The buffalo was a complete survival package. We were the first campers on the land. Our travois were our trailers and RVs. We were the first astronomers and environmentalists. We used pigment that has survived on rock faces for thousands of years and had our own stone tablets—the mountains and cliff faces—where we recorded our history. We made ceramics. Our installation sculptures of Sweatlodges and Sundances stood for many years before they went back into the earth after their use. Our rock rings and medicine wheels are every bit as remarkable as Stonehenge or the Pyramids. We were the first performance artists and maintain that dance tradition. We have evolved into the 20th century as a people with our culture intact, and it is our reference to these traditional ways that continues to teach us and strengthen us. We have only been exposed to the Western world for little over 100 years. In this short period of time, we have come out of our beginning to the space age, and, while we were in this state of transition, we had to negotiate with the dominant society, which has had thousands of years to evolve.

We have had our language and much of our ceremonial life—put on hold for much of that time—replaced with transplanted cultural traditions which, happily, did not take. It has taken us this long to say this doesn't work, and we have begun to return to our customs, beliefs and methods as they relate to the land base that we come from. We will teach the world, as one of the aboriginal peoples, how to again live in harmony—to create a balance. We can do this as a people because we have not lost our connection with the earth and the position we occupy as one of the components of the whole.

As artists, our work points out in ironic terms what has happened. We are creating works of art that are cultural signposts that we have to put up. Now, even though our artists have degrees from Ivy League universities and colleges, we are still Native/Indian artists—a category somewhat like the category of women artists or folk artists—not to be taken seriously. In Canada one of our best known artists, Alex Janvier, applied to the Canada Council (our national funding body for artists) and had his proposal/application marked "Indianne," and cast aside.

Recently, in conversation with a Canada Council employee, Janvier was asked to re-submit with the promise that it would be taken care of. He declined, saying he had gone on this long without them.[6] After 20 years working as an artist, I cannot get a grant from them, two of the excuses being, "Oh, we don't know who you are," and once, when I applied to use Emily Carr as my mentor, they remarked, "We're afraid if you go to B.C., you may start painting totems." This kind of patronizing attitude is more than annoying; it is incredible, outrageous, and racist—especially since I have been in more than five exhibitions that used my slides to gain funding from the Canada Council for exhibitions proposed by white curators. To one government body I am a gross national product, but to another I am a Native artist, not really an artist. How then, I wonder, did I manage three years of art college and achieve a BFA at a bona fide university? How did I end up graduating with credentials and become a non-artist because of my Native heritage?

In our world of Euro-Canadian and Euro-American dictums, it is interesting to see the influence our culture has on mainstream art. As art that is viewed as primitive, we are dead art makers of a dead art. As such, we are vulnerable to appropriation and vast pillaging by the dominant culture. Just as Picasso pillaged African art, and Max Ernst, and Paul Klee took much from Indian Pitograph/Petroglyphs, white mainstream artists today feel quite justified in creating works rampant with misused symbolism and visual cultural language. Why else would Toronto artist Andy Fabo think that he could appropriate the imagery of the Sweatlodge ceremony and incorporate it in his steamroller rip-off of cultural icons, which seem of late to focus on the "mining" of art by Natives.

In her review of the exhibition (at Toronto gallery Garnet Press) published in *Vanguard,* Linda Genereux tries to legitimize Fabo's imagery by saying that he had seen a Northwest Coast mask.[7] The Northwest Coast people do not practice the Sweatlodge Ceremony.

It is a Plains' tradition, newly revived and a subject that is fundamental to the work of an internationally known artist of Native heritage. This is uninformed, irresponsible editing by *Vanguard,* a Vancouver-based art magazine, now defunct. Genereux goes on, assuring the reader that the artist is "choosing images which have been carried into the modern era." Fabo seems to regard other artists' work as giant "Art K-Marts."

Money. It does strange things to people. Not only are our cultural icons being played with, but ancient ceremonies and sacred rituals are being mimicked by artists who insist that their philosophies come from communing with nature. Blatant copies of the Sundance Ceremonies and evidences of rites are piggy-backed by so-called environmental artists/tribesmen like Fast Wurms, a Toronto group that applies for individual grants as a group and gets them on an ongoing basis. Is it because they are white that their interpretation of Native culture is suddenly a valid art form, and are their hikes from the grey-scapes of the big city into the woodland valid forages into a ceremonial time?

There are positive aspects to being a Native artist. Three years ago the National Gallery of Canada bought a work by Manitoulin Island artist Carl Beam, called *Northern American Iceberg*. It was large and its images were frozen in time. Photographic references to chiefs of the past were juxtaposed with a self-portrait of the artist. Diane Nemiroff, Acting Curator of Contemporary Art at the National Gallery, put together an exhibition called "Cross Cultural Views" International artists Jenny Holzer, Hans Haacke and John Scott were included. My work, the work of other Native artists Jane Ash Poitras, Robert Houle and Bob Boyer were borrowed from collections and presented in the same exhibition. No catalogue was produced, and the artists were not notified of the exhibition. However, this was the first time in its more than 90-year history that the National Gallery had bought the work of a Native artist.

One would tend to think that the cross-Canada sad exclusion of artists of Native heritage from the current contemporary art exhibitions would require innovation, and some groups and individuals have risen to this challenge, such as the Canadian Native Arts Foundation. But the question arises, "Why should we become exclusive because we have been excluded?" Will we set up our own foundation for every discipline?

I believe it is time for this art racism to stop. It is up to the curators and administrators in this country to remain informed. Let them be the innovators. We have been the innovators all through historic times. I submit that the needed innovation in Native arts is for artists of Native heritage to demand their rights as citizens of this country and to expect those with influence to cut out their racist policies and attitudes.

In 1983, the Society of Canadian Native Artists (SCANA) held a conference in Hazelton, B.C. Surrounded by some of the oldest totems of the Northwest peoples, they pledged to become an information and lobby group for artists of Native ancestry networking with government and people in the arts. In 1985, Robert Houle, former curator of the Museum of Civilization, organized the Native Business Summit in Toronto, which introduced Native businesses to each other and the public. In 1987, in Lethbridge, Alberta, Alfred Youngman at the Department of Native American Studies at the University of Lethbridge organized "Networking: Swimming in Mainstream." Featured at the conference were Edward Poitras, Bob Boyer, Pierre Sioui, Jane Ash Poitras, Carl Beam and myself. As well, the exhibition "Stardusters" was at the Southern Alberta Art Gallery. Curators, critics and historians along with anthropologists, archaeologists, and gallery dealers arrived from all points. Representatives from colleges and universities in New Mexico and California were in attendance. Museum representatives from New York, Ottawa, Toronto, Calgary, Los Angeles and Phoenix were there to hear what these upstart contemporary Native artists had to say. We were all there for each other, and a lot of positive exchanges resulted: a video and publication are available from the University of Lethbridge, Native American Studies.

The exhibition "Revisions" opened at the Walter Phillips Gallery in Banff during the 1988 Winter Olympics. Curated by Helga Pakasaar, and including artists of Native heritage, the exhibition aimed at counterpointing the Glenbow exhibition "The Spirit Sings." Pakasaar is quoted in *Vanguard* explaining the meaning of "Revisions." The title "alludes to the process of amending and correcting history, specifically that of Native culture, as well as suggesting the necessity for new visions from a Native perspective."[8]

> **pov•er•ty** (póvərti:) n. the condition or quality of being poor ‖ (of soil) unproductiveness‖ deficiency in or inadequate supply of something, *poverty of ideas* ‖ monastic renunciation of the right to own, *a vow of poverty* [O.F. *pouerte, poverté*]

This is the only way to counteract the indiscriminate appropriations and plagiarism that are going on. Only by publishing imagery will it become apparent to these rip-off artists that Native people deserve the same professional respect given to the artists in the mainstream who have lawyers lurking in the background protecting copyright.

In Canada, copyright is protected unless signed away. No one may copy the work of a living artist, and, far from being upset by Arlene Stamp's reworking the Gladys Johnston paintings, I am touched by the fact that she included a bibliography with the work. Indeed there was no plagiarism there. However, when a friend of artist Miyuki Tanobe saw what she assumed to be Tanobe's work on a card offered as a gift on an Air Canada flight, she was surprised on inspection to see the name of Alberta DeCastro, a Toronto artist. Tanobe filed suit in Federal Court in Toronto earlier this year.[9]

"Since the 20s, composers, lyricists, writers and authors have had the right to their intellectual property. In 1988, an amendment to the Copyright Act extended it to visual artists."[10] Because of this amendment to the Copyright Act, it is only reasonable to expect that both arts and crafts organizations should set up stricter guidelines. Perhaps they should require artists to sign a waiver if they want to avoid being implicated in future art suits.

Intellectual property law will become even more focused when provincial laws are created to further protect the artist. But the most critical change has to come in the educational institutions and in the home. Copying is stealing. We need to return to personal ethics. So I have an announcement to make to all you artists out there with no ideas. Since you can no longer steal images from Native artists, forget about the Aborigines and the Maoris—we are in contact with them too.

> **mon•ey** (mΛni) pl. **mon•eys, mon•ies** n. anything that serves as a medium of exchange for goods and services in the form of tokens which have a value established by a commonly recognized authority, e.g. the government of a country, or by custom. The tokens are usually minted mental pieces (coinage), or promises to pay, recorded on paper (bank notes etc.) but may be whatever is locally accepted (beads, shells, cattle etc.) ‖ personal wealth, *his money is all in hotels* ‖ (*pl., esp. law*) sums of money.

In 1987, the aboriginal peoples of the world held a conference in Vancouver, and one of the important issues discussed was the protection of traditional ceremonial practices and cultural icons. These issues will be covered under the General Agreement on Tariffs and Trade (GATT) and are being re-negotiated as an important aspect of the free trade agreement between Canada and the United States. At the Montevideo Round of GATT negotiations, it was noted that "failure to enforce intellectual property rights is a barrier to trade because that which is stolen is not sold."[11]

This brings us back to *Money.* The critical reason behind artists ripping off other cultures is based on money and achieved by access to information available through technology. "This access to fashion and historic periods has produced what Thomas Shales has called 'The ReDecade,' a decade without a distinctive style of its own; a decade characterized by the pervasive stylistic presence of all previous periods of history."[12] It is Native culture, which retains a distinctive style of its own, that is so attractive to the public. Collectors are willing to pay "big bucks" for this originality, which, in the case of Canada, may be the only true Canadian art. Artists who have hooked themselves into the dictums of Toronto/New York/Europe are quick to recognize that here is a unique form of expression coming out of a distinct cultural ethic. They want a piece of the action—hence the imitation, plagiarism, copying and stealing. The fact that "Native art" is not included in generic exhibitions by the National Gallery and that Native artists are not the recipients of grants from the Canada Council sets the tone for how these artists are treated by other public galleries in Canada. It also determines that we are non-artists and makes our work susceptible to pillaging because it is not published. The saving grace for Native artists is the commercial galleries that carry their work, and whose patrons are willing to put out hard-earned money for art that has, as the late Illingworth Kerr described a good piece of art, "a punch to it." Money again!

As money is the scourge responsible for the land grabbing and the misuse of the earth, so will it be the saving grace. When focus is placed on the amount of money lost by the breakdown of the systems of control, it will be corrected. In the art world it will be shown that to allow the plagiarism of the artists' intellectual property (their art) will hurt the country financially. If Native artists are to continue to be part of the GNP of Canada, we cannot allow cheap imitations to exist, and we cannot continue to finance their production with grants and the machinery of public relations. Similarly, we do not need anthropologists, archaeologists and government bodies going around anointing some of our first people with "Indian holy water" and supplying them with a number. It is not the number that people look for when they label one "Native" or "Indian" by their prejudice. If you look like a Native, you are treated like one, and that is many things to many people. We all get the 100 percent expression of racism; there is no 25 percent or 50 percent amount of prejudicial treatment.

The Canada Council's recent decision to follow the ethnological dictums of the Heard Museum in Phoenix as to the nature of Native art is a big mistake. Native people know who they are, and there is no need for a registry or sanction by an institution of a people. This is a self-conscious move on the part of people in power who obviously lack knowledge and, therefore, are operating from a position of fear. Art is art, and is determined by aesthetic. Aesthetic is determined by patronage; patronage comes from responses to art and reflects an appreciation by the individual. Great art occurs when individuals in numbers both support and appreciate the work of an artist. Government bodies should not be in the position of determining who is an artist and who is not. Their function should be to aid the artist in the buying of materials and providing money for travel to necessary venues. Instead it has become an insular group of self-serving artists and in many places across the country, particularly the West, the laughingstock of Canada. Does the fact that someone doesn't know you mean that you don't need the money to carry out an installation for a major museum? When I was unable to receive funding to make work for an exhibition, I went ahead anyway.

With a sense of irony, I dedicated my sculpture installation *Preservation of a Species: Deep Freeze* for the exhibition "Beyond History" at the Vancouver Art Gallery, May 31–July 15, 1989, to the Canada Council. Constructed of newspaper, masking tape and black paint along with elements found in my studio, I privately called it *In the Red*.

Notes

This manuscript was written in 1989 after many years of frustration with the status quo. It was previously published in *Fuse Magazine* (Toronto) from a lecture presented at the Ontario College of Art, 1989, and also was presented at the San Francisco Art Institute, 1989. I am pleased to say that many changes have occurred in the last 6 years—in government agencies, in educational institutions, and in the home.

1. Harry Hillman Chartrand, *The Crafts in Post-Modern Economy: The Pattern Which Sells the Things* (Ottawa: Canadian Council, 1988), 22.

2. Ibid.

3. Deborah Doxtator, "Fluffs and Feathers," *Artscraft Quarterly* (Winter 1989): 26.

4. Lucy Lippard, in *Women of the Sweetgrass, Cedar, and Sage* (New York: Gallery of the American Indian House, June 1–29, 1985).

5. Jaune Quick-to-See Smith, in *Women of the Sweetgrass, Cedar, and Sage,* (New York: Gallery of the American Indian House, June 1–29, 1985).

6. Conversation with Alex Janvier, March 1989.

7. Linda Genereux, "Review of Andy Fabo's Exhibition," *Vanguard* 15 (December-January 1986–1987): 40.

8. Marie Morgan, "Il Revisions," *Vanguard* 12 (April-May 1983): 16.

9. Ingrid Abramovitch, "Artist Influence or Copying?" *Ottawa Citizen*, January 2, 1989.

10. Ibid.

11. Chartrand, *The Crafts in Post-Modern Economy*, 24.

12. Ibid., 20.

Part 3

Appropriation in Colonial and Postcolonial Discourse

Jonathan Hart

Translating and Resisting Empire: Cultural Appropriation and Postcolonial Studies

The debate over cultural appropriation is about whether speaking for others or representing them in fictional as well as legal, social, artistic, and political work is appropriate or proper, especially when individuals or groups with more social, economic, and political power perform this role for others without invitation. The appropriation of culture probably occurred before human records, but it has also been a function of "tribal," national, and imperial expansion.

Thus, the purpose of this essay is to set out what cultural appropriation is and to articulate its role in imperialism, colonialism, and postcolonialism. This essay also looks at how the history of colonialism bears significantly on the making of someone else's culture into property in a world that calls itself postcolonial and how that practice is resisted.

Imperialism is about the expansion of political property through the acquisition of colonies. That colonization involves setting up the cultural example of the imperial center, while that center also appropriates aspects of the colonized cultures officially and unofficially. In the wake of empire and the migration of peoples, especially in this century in the postcolonial period, the debate over what constitutes cultural appropriation by the dominant culture has become a important concern in multicultural societies.

Cultural appropriation becomes a question of cultural rights and difference and enriches or makes problematic, depending on the view, the possibility of community. Can all the claims of different cultures find expression in a community or nation? Perhaps the postmodern and postcolonial nation finds its greatest hope in such expression. Nonetheless, there is anxiety that the controversy over cultural appropriation reflects fault lines in contemporary multicultural societies that will lead to ethnic conflicts like those in the former Soviet Union and Yugoslavia. Rather than take sides in the debate, I am more interested in providing some historical and cultural background to it.

General Remarks on Cultural Appropriation

Something, then, about cultural appropriation raises anxiety. This upset can take the form of worry over cultural negotiations, wanted and unwanted, over general issues of race and gender or specific examples such as arts funding and music. Consider controversy over rap music in the United States, where the record companies, the artists, and groups calling for censorship have collided. Should white American record executives profit from a music that exploits tensions and violence in the Black community, or are they giving Black artists a vehicle for wealth and free expression? The anxiety in debates over culture and who owns it, who gets to speak and who gets to listen, is frequently political in nature; the people involved in the debate often take the matter personally.

Indeed, "culture" and "appropriation" are notoriously complex terms. As a working definition, however, culture is the material, spiritual, and artistic expression of a group that defines itself or that others define as a culture, both according to daily lived experience and according to practice and theory. Culture is and is not self-conscious; some group must identify it. Appropriation is the making of what belongs to one individual or group into the property of another individual or group. That something can be tangible or intangible property. The appropriating can be achieved through ventriloquy, translation, or dispossession of lands and other property.[1] It can be figurative or literal. Cultural appropriation occurs when a member of one culture takes a cultural practice or theory of a member of another culture as if it were his or her own or as if the right of possession should not be questioned or contested. This same appropriation can happen between groups as groups. One issue in the debate over cultural appropriation is whether the term describes anything that exists or, if it does exist, whether it is harmful.

Two opposing voices should help focus the debate. A recent exchange provides a good summary of the issues involved in appropriation. At the heart of the discussion are artistic and intellectual freedom in relation to cultural integrity and who obtains what funding or other resources in the production of art, thought, and culture. James O. Young outlines three arguments against voice appropriation. First, members of one cultural group misrepresent other members of another cultural group and thereby harm them. Second, when a majority culture misrepresents a minority culture, it limits the audience the minority can reach in representing itself. Third, when other cultural groups misrepresent cultures, they steal the religious and cultural meaning of those cultures' stories and pictures. Young sets out to refute all three arguments, even the first, which he claims is the strongest, by means of exceptions or counterarguments.

Rather than rehearse Young's counterarguments, I wish to stress only that he maintains that the representations by outsiders are not all harmful distortions. Taking up R. G. Collingwood's view in *The Principles of Art,* Young thinks that the artist should steal with both hands (similar to T. S. Eliot's view of great artists). Young argues that artists should take care in representing other cultures but should not give up artistic freedom. Artists should aim for aesthetic success, which precludes insensitive representations of minority cultures.

John Rowell opposes Young's views and says that he would wish Eric Clapton well commercially if he were singing the blues but would not fund him if he applied for a government grant. In a rebuttal to Young, Rowell says that Young obscures the real issue, which is the use of material of a minority culture by a member of the dominant culture, who even sometimes pretends to be from that group. Rowell does not see transcultural borrowing as the actual subject of the controversy, however. He argues that funding agencies should adopt a relativism that recognizes cultural difference. Moral grounds take precedence over aesthetic grounds in Rowell's counterscheme. More minority voices, he concludes, are needed in the debate on cultural appropriation.

Young and Rowell do agree on the necessity of understanding and carefully considering minority cultures. This view which comes from members of the dominant cultural group, reflects a desire to be sensitive to different cultures in a multicultural and postcolonial society. Whether it is possible to prevent one culture from assimilating ideas and culture from its own interpretations of another culture, rather than from representations of minority cultures by members of those cultures, is an open question. Who can represent whom is an intricate epistemological and ontological problem. In part, it hinges on experience.

To clarify the mutuality, and mutual suspicion, of cultural exchange, I wish to take a brief look at appropriation in and of Shakespeare. Could William Shakespeare alone represent himself? What would that do to the Shakespeare industry around the world in various cultures and languages? Should other cultures be allowed to represent him? Certainly, in the early phases of post-colonial writing and critique people of many linguistic, racial, and ethnic groups adapted Shakespeare to write back against the European empires that had, until so recently, governed them. The Japanese have built a reproduction of Shakespeare's Globe Theatre before the "English" have. Can the English today, who are culturally different from their ancestors, bridge the difference of time and interpret Shakespeare? What is the difference among the inter-pretations that go into writing, reading, and critique? Should Shakespeare have tried to represent ancient Greeks, Egyptians, and Romans or, in later history, French, Italians, British, Moors, and others, or should he have limited himself to stories about his boyhood in Stratford? Perhaps Shakespeare's time bounds his potential cultural appropriations: he did live at a time before his-torical difference had taken hold or copyright law prevailed. Through histori-cal imagination, it is possible to see that the postmodern period will possess certain concerns over the debate on representation (or *mimesis*) and that sub-sequent ages will take different views of the question.

The debate on cultural appropriation needs to be encouraged as a sign of freedom rather than as a screaming across the abyss. It would be hypocritical of the dominant culture to cry Stalin while shutting down debate over the issue. In the debate over the appropriation of the Other, even the putatively trans-verbal world of music is now debated. Sally Kilmister, for instance, discusses music in terms of its relation to translation, gender, and androgyny. She picks up on Carl Dahlhaus's topos of unsayability (related to the classical topos, or rhetorical strategy, of inexpressibility) and its link with Theodor Adorno's view of music as a fetish and of listening as regression. Kilmister also connects unsayability (that which is unutterable) with Virginia Woolf's "Impressions of Bayreuth," an ambivalent critique of this unsayable nineteenth-century music because this essay examines "the difficulties inherent in either an appropria-tion or a repudiation of music's seductive lure."[2] This political debate over appropriation tries to implicate even the putatively apolitical spheres of instru-mental music and lyric poetry. The drama of Shakespeare, the symphonic music of Ludwig von Beethoven, and the lyric-driven rhythms of rap all turn into points of friction in multicultural societies. If an Asian American is a great pianist, does she avoid Beethoven because of his European origins and because she does not want to appropriate European culture, or for historical and political reasons, is it necessary to redress the inequities of cultural ex-change in the past? The difficulty here is that Chinese culture is ancient and complex and does not need to be patronized and that Chinese and European cultures meet in the Americas partly through this musician. Is culture more sacred than cars and other European and Euro-American inventions now used throughout the world, so that its globalization should be watched even more warily than multinational corporations? Will Australians refuse to drive Japanese cars because their improved design was produced in another culture? Is it possible that cultural appropriation occurs within countries where dominant cultures must be aware of their impact on minority cultures but that the model is problematic among countries? Each situation seems to be different, and any notion of First, Second, Third, and Fourth Worlds is problematic. It is doubtful that any global and universal theory of cultural appropriation will be satisfactory. Part of the definition may hinge on technical development, which might be inversely proportionate to cultural development. Some of the most complex cultures have only recently began industrial and technological development. In speaking of cultural appropriation, we must complicate the debate with specific examples and with history and then proceed with some caution. This is a world where each country contains uneven "development," so to talk about "post" this and that is only one part of the story.

Postmodernism, Law, and the Commodification of Culture

The politics of postmodernism and postcolonialism has uncertain and multiple valences. Similar techniques and forms in theory and practice can be used for opposite political ends. "Postmodernism" assumes the recycling of writing and history; "postcolonialism" assumes a movement, at least politically, beyond the colony as the empire's property. If utopian vision beyond the old properties of politics and history resides in these two "post" terms, a presumption and a triumphalism that characterized imperial narratives and themes might also threaten to make problematic these after-discourses. Before suggesting that the ancient question of property underwrites the rhetoric of cultural appropriation, I want to use cross-cultural terms and images to unsettle the relation between colonizer and colonized that is often represented in colonial and postcolonial studies.

In a time when the prefix *post* is everywhere, as if our period were epochal or apocalyptic, it is important in the arts, humanities, and social sciences to examine self-consciously this urge to be beyond or after in technique or time and to analyze and complicate the intellectual property of terms such as postcolonialism. There are days when I think that postmodernism is not just another aftermath and that postcolonialism is as intricate as quipu. In speaking about cultural appropriation, I use "aftermath" and "quipu" as a means of showing the stress between the nostalgic essentialism of identity politics and the displaced hybridity, if not hybrid displacement, of words and art. "Aftermath" is literally grass growing after the harvest, and I use this agrarian image in counterpoint to emphasize the urbanity of this age after the modern.

Quipu (ke-poo), which is an image from the ancient history of the "New World" and involves a metonymy for writing, should represent something from the past that complicates the already complex world of postcolonial studies. The ancient Peruvians used quipu as a substitute for writing/recording by variously knotting threads of different colors.[3] As etymology shows, English is a language built on cultural appropriation. To use this language, like so many others, especially in this age of rapid travel and information exchange, is to bear witness, consciously or not, to culture as a commodity to be traded, fairly and freely or not. Words and names become a form of displacement. Place-names are especially revealing in this regard. In this so-called New World, or the Americas, the descendants of Europeans often use aboriginal names such as Mexico and Canada for the places they live in while obliterating others. It is difficult to know whether such investment and divestment of indigenous names are systematic or situational. It is possible that the theft or borrowing returns as a reminder of what has been stolen from the other culture. There is a history that returns with lands, names, images, and ideas. The quipu can and cannot be appropriated in the alphabetic world of English.

The borrowings, lendings, and enforcement of property may be an idea that owes too much to the development of Western law, whether through the biblical tradition of the Jews, the laws of Greek and Roman lawgivers such as Solon and Justinian, or more vernacular and national versions that King John or Napoleon may have devised. Thou shalt not steal. Let the peers decide. Guilty before proven innocent. From property the idea of cultural property develops, although the distinction was never so clear. In English-speaking countries the copyright law of 1709 leaves its traces in squabbles over photocopying and the protection of individual, if not group, intellectual property.[4]

Cultural appropriation has complex legal dimensions. Property can be intellectual, cultural, and physical ("tangible"). The debate over voice or cultural appropriation in which Young and Rowell participated has implications for other related controversies. For obvious reasons, in a situation where intellectual property has become associated with cultural appropriation, legal judgments, scholarship, and theory have made and will make contributions to what we can say about, and do with, culture. Rosemary J. Coombe argues that the models of authorship that dominate Anglo-American laws of copyright are those that incorporate possessive individualism, which is recognized in 1814 under the influence of Romanticism—authors can find plots, characters and themes from others as long as they do not copy another's expression.[5] For Coombe, the cultural essentialism and possessive individualism (the latter being a central concern for C. B. Macpherson) of this tradition, which define legal categories of property, do not account for the forms the Natives in

Canada employ to seek recognition.[6] Western histories of colonialism and imperialism do not consider Native ideas of identity, authenticity, and culture, and in this view societies, such as Canada, need new conceptual and legal tools to accommodate the needs of Natives in a postcolonial and postmodern world.[7] Cultural borrowing, then, needs to be understood in its historical context. For Natives, ecology, spirit, and territory are part of the culture in cultural appropriation.[8] Loretta Todd contends that aboriginal title represents "the term under which we negotiate with the colonizers . . . which asserts a reality that existed before Native peoples were positioned as Other."[9] In response to Todd, Coombe says that non-Natives should comprehend the contingency and historical specificity of their laws, especially their implication in colonialism and imperialism. Essentialism and individualism are not the only properties of culture, so aboriginal title presents a new possibility.[10]

In a discussion of cultural appropriation and the law, Amanda Pask outlines how the structure of the law precludes the recognition of claims based in culture. She argues that the law must not continue to wish for the disappearance of cultural difference but should respond to those, like the Natives, who are culturally different. For Pask, the ultimate problem of cultural appropriation arises from a failure to acknowledge other ways of doing things.[11] The law is another systematic textual, epistemological, conceptual, and material means of perpetuating stereotypes and of continuing to colonize those who would refuse colonization. A postcolonial law would attempt to find other ways and incorporate alternate cultural traditions.

In my view, there might be an excavation of legal history to understand the religious and secular reasons given to the settlement of the New World. The papal bulls and the treaties between the Portuguese and the Spanish dividing up the colonial world in the fifteenth and sixteenth centuries and the subsequent French, English and Dutch challenges to them, especially the notion of *terra nullius,* or "unoccupied lands," might provide ways in which to include alternative laws from other traditions. The specific historical intentions of the European popes, monarchs, advisers, and colonizers will show dissention from within nations and rivalries between them.[12] The famous debate, for the benefit of the Spanish king, between Brother Bartolomé de Las Casas and theologian Juan Ginés de Sepúlveda over whether Aristotle's concept of natural slavery applied to the aboriginal inhabitants of the New World demonstrates the dissension from within. The creation of the Black Legend, which the French, English, and Dutch based in large part on Las Casas's denunciation of Spanish treatment of the Natives after Columbus, illustrates the rivalry between European nations and still has resonances in our culture through Michel de Montaigne, Jean-Jacques Rousseau, and others. Later treaties and laws in Spanish, Portuguese, British, and French America, especially in the new nations in the Western Hemisphere from the late eighteenth century onward, will probably receive increasing legal scrutiny.

In Canada, as in Australia, this reassessment has taken and will take the form of land claims.[13] A culture has to have a home and some resources and property to protect itself. The reparations of war and invasion have occurred in international law, but where do we stop going back in history? In terms of cultural appropriation, can we connect the Norman invasion of England, the spread of Islam into northern Africa and southern Europe, the European invasion of the New World, and the Chinese invasion of Tibet? What time limitations and doctrine of reparations and natural justice could the law develop in these clash of cultures? The law bears some relation to the society it represents, so how can we expect an international law to take into account all these cultures? The notion of what is legal and what is just is something discussed in Western philosophy since Plato, but these ideas change over time. Aristotle's notion of natural slavery is a kind of natural justice that no one in Western culture, let alone other cultures, would endorse in the late twentieth century. In the multicultural nation new systems of law might supplement the dominant legal system, but not without difficulty. Given the stakes, however, such an attempt is worthwhile.

Cultural appropriation through law is only one aspect of culture as property. Culture has long been a commodity. Traditionally, cultural exchange has followed trade routes. But the weight of culture is more than simply the balance or imbalance of trade. In practical arts, such as pottery, where yesterday's urn is today's art, this commodification has long been the case, but in more abstract matters of the mind or spirit, the division between use and ornament is less clear. Techniques and ideas have crossed borders and followed trade routes for thousands of years. When anyone confronts European colonizers with the metaphor or political argument of cultural appropriation, is he or she using European concepts to criticize European colonial practices, or have Europeans obscured various traditions of intellectual or cultural property or of property law? Is it possible that the colonized are appropriating European culture to criticize it? Perhaps European intellectuals are taking up alternative or oppositional techniques from within their tradition to oppose European or Western imperialism past and present. Quite possibly, they are also ventriloquizing indigenous peoples and other colonized groups as a means of activating change now.

The mixing of cultures has always brought about such forms of resistance and ventriloquy, but whether cultural appropriation might also enact mediation and understanding is a problem worth considering in the context of postcolonialism and postmodernism. A typology of cultural appropriation, as opposed to the ethical wish of its utopian form, might be suggestive of the possibility of dialogue and mediation between various groups, but without denying the presence of resistance and repression.

In exploring cultural appropriation, we can easily devise a nostalgia or be sublimated in a utopia, forgetting in an imagined past and future what is difficult here and now. Who gets to say who owns what and for how long is a sobering question beside the human yearnings for the golden age and the promised land, the union of individual and community, unity without uniformity. For whatever reason, the mirages vanish, and others take their place. Somehow the teleological urgings of Christianity and Marxism sometimes become circular; the future becomes the past and the past the future in a present that is never quite present. It is as if Giambattista Vico or Friedrich Nietzsche got a hold of typology or dialectic and twisted its tail. The protean beast, which turns out to be time, is not really the eternal recurrence but something linear, perhaps like a maze and without a plan. Time just goes on and on. And, almost helplessly, we cut out shapes to make it our own or to dispossess others of the time in which they lived or live. In this new mirage, or allegory, still not far from being shadows on the cave wall, possession, dispossession, and repossession become territorial rites that make space for time. History, modernism, and colonialism are mapped into patterns in which hopes of liberation are made in a time that comes after, a kind of hope amid the anguish. The more one enters into the postmodern and the postcolonial, the more one looks at the wall, into the abyss, not sure what it is, not sure whether writing will do anything but throw up more patterns in the rush hour. And there are voices jostling, and a great deal of pain, in crossing fictional and actual boundaries as they knot as though they were translated in the many colors of a quipu. Self-conscious examination and problematization are two strategies in facing these terms and the debates they represent.[14] The problems I am about to examine arise in postcolonial studies in two contexts, first, in the colonial and postcolonial and, second, in European history and its representations of the translation of empire.

Cultural Appropriation and Colonialism

In discussing the background to the appropriation of culture and to colonization, I consider one aspect particularly important: *translatio imperii*, or the "translation of empire." This classical myth of the Western movement of empire from Greece involves later European appropriations of the myth of empire and the "civilization" of the barbarian. As I think that colonialism has to be understood before postcolonialism can be fully apprehended, I wish to turn to a few classical, medieval, and early modern instances of the trope of *translatio imperii*. I further wish to appeal to the ancient and early modern as a means of seeing where the rapture might happen in the colonial moment that allows ways of thinking toward a postcolonial state, even in the midst of empire, and therefore represents a prolepsis to postcolonialism.

One of the main recurrent imperial themes is the ways in which colonizers, regardless of whether they have been the colonized, identify with earlier empires and create a myth of continuity. The colonized justify their transformation into colonizers by appropriating the political and military culture of earlier regimes.

The Athenians were not interested in empire in the sense that Alexander the Great was and the Romans later were. Greece was a loosely related group of city-states, and the Greek world was in many ways a commercial "empire." Anthony Pagden's discussion of barbarism is instructive here. Aristotle discussed the term *barbarian,* as would Thomas Aquinas and the neo-Aristotelian commentators. The word is, as Pagden notes, unstable because it was applied over time to the Berbers, Turks, Sythians, Ethiopians, Irish, and Normans. Nevertheless, these uses had one thing in common: "implication of inferiority."[15] The word "barbarian," which was coined in the seventh and sixth centuries B.C., meant "foreigner," including the Egyptians, whom the Greeks respected. By the fourth century B.C., however, the word had come to mean, and still means, someone of cultural and mental inferiority. The *barbaros,* for the Hellenistic Greeks, meant a babbler who could not speak Greek, someone devoid of the logos, of speech and reason. Barbarians lacked *civis* and polis, the civil society of the Greek family of humankind, the *oikumene.* The Greeks' failure to admit the *barbaroi* into the Hellenistic community was "a denial of their humanity."[16] Aristotle thought that the birds watching over the temple at Dimedia were able to differentiate between the Greeks and *barbaroi* because the one group has access to the mysteries through the logos, whereas the other does not.[17]

Although Aristotle considered the barbarians to be human, he thought that they behaved like beasts, so that the Achaeans and the Heniochi, tribes of the Black Sea, had gone savage and enjoyed human flesh.[18] Cruelty and ferocity, as Pagden says, are the marks of barbarism, and behavior is the key difference between the civilized and the barbarous. The word *civilized* should also provide a clue to the importance of the civic and civil life of the city to the Greeks. When the barbarians lived in cities, they did so under tyrannous conditions and devoid of freedom. The idea of the barbarian, as Pagden recognizes, is crucial for an understanding of xenophobia, of projections onto others, and of imperialism. It is also important for the problematic of translation of empire. Pagden is explicit about this link: "The definition of the word 'barbarian' in terms that were primarily cultural rather than racial made its translation to the largely non-Greek speaking Christian world a relatively easy business."[19] Here, the narrative of conversion or of spreading Christian civilization began. To pursue the translation of empire, there had to be a sense of the civilized world and those barbarians beyond it.

Although each subsequent empire expressed some anxiety over the influence of the earlier empire, the Romans borrowed from the Greeks and emergent "empires," and European and American nations from the Middle Ages and Renaissance onward have incorporated this myth of the translation of empire. Humanism and classicism are partly built on that foundation. There are hundreds of individual examples of rulers in the West picking up on this trope.

European contact with America soon revealed that this translation of empire and this assimilation of new peoples into a successor to the Greek and Roman Empires would be a difficult, if not new, balancing act. The Amerindians represented new peoples whom Europeans knew nothing about. Even though the American experience was novel, many Europeans tried, for obvious reasons, to fit the Amerindians and their lands into the framework of European experience.

In 1519 Charles of Spain became Emperor Charles V of the Holy Roman Empire. In 1521 Ferdinand Magellan's voyage around the globe uncovered a world of diverse peoples that the classical chronicler Eusebius and his successors had not known. Nevertheless, the idea of a universal Spanish monarchy persisted into the 1700s, a rule in which universal meant European. But universality of the past was not the same as the universality of the future, and this was a problem that the Spanish and Europeans generally had a hard time facing. Peter Martyr, an Italian humanist, wondered whether the Amerindians were inhabitants of the Golden Age who had escaped corruption as their land had long ago been severed from Europe. Gonzalo Fernández de Oviedo wrote his universal history with an understanding of empire in its traditional Mediterranean and Western European meaning and spoke of Charles as being part of a direct line of emperors from Caesar.

But Oviedo and colonial administrators and missionaries came to see that the Amerindians had their own traditions. The debate between Las Casas and Sepúlveda over the treatment of the Amerindians represented two ways at incorporating America into European history. Las Casas saw the contact as fulfilling Christian universal history in the conversion of the Indians, who were human and had souls to be saved. Sepúlveda argued for the growth of the Spanish monarchy and empire and did not consider important the conversion of the Indians, whom he thought were not completely human.[20]

Here begins European migration on a scale not yet seen. What is remarkable is that Europeans could not shake the incommensurability of their representations of the "New World" with what they experienced. Although experience and observation modified the image of the Indians of America as being in a state of nature as opposed to civilization, it was hard to give up old ways entirely. There might be understanding and misunderstanding now, but incomprehension persisted in new forms. Europeans experienced what Pagden has called the problem of recognition.[21] Europeans of each age brought with them a set of expectations. Many of the fantastic natural phenomena, such as fauna and satyrs, pygmies, cannibals, and Amazons, that Europeans expected to see in America during the late fifteenth and early sixteenth centuries came from popular oral tradition that travel writers and scientists from Pliny to John de Mandeville used. The specter of a new barbarian raised itself repeatedly in the colonial world.

It is the image of the barbarian projected and the empire translated that postcolonial theorists see in the world then and now. These notions of barbarism met with resistance within European culture from the earliest times and continue to be resisted into the present. Vico's cycles moved toward a new barbarism in a *corso* that would be followed a few hundred years later by a *ricorso,* but he thought certain cultures escaped this cycle by experiencing a stop in its development, like the Carthaginians whom the Romans destroyed and the American Indians with the coming of the Europeans. Anne-Robert-Jacques Turgot, the philosophe, did not care about the coming and going of empires because that pattern did not alter the progress of reason and knowledge.

A large number of myths of imperial translation came into being after the Enlightenment as European imperialism expanded at an unprecedented rate. The growth of Russian, German, and American power also complicated this expansion of empire. The discussion of cultural appropriation arises mainly from the wake of these European empires. Because cultural appropriation is tied to empire, are discussions of it as vulnerable as those about empire? In *History of England from the Accession of James II* (1849–1861), Thomas Macaulay said something that is a warning to all who write about empire: those who neglect the art of narration should remember "that histories of great empires, written by men of great ability, lie unread on the shelves of ostentatious libraries."[22] If discourse might have once been underestimated in a Western philosophy dominated by notions of mimesis and reality, as Jacques Derrida, Michel Foucault, and other poststructural theorists assert, it is possible that it is now overestimated as a force in the world. This observation also applies to what might become an increasing gap between the theory and the practice of cultural appropriation. To be moral critics, like Noam Chomsky and Edward Said, is an important but difficult task. The problem for all of us writing on cultural appropriation, colonization, postcolonialism, and imperialism is, How do we advocate historical change that recognizes the difference between then and now, the very historicity of experience, and maintain a moral view that has a transhistorical standard that allows such ethical judgment? If we allow for moral progress in history, will our blindnesses not seem foolish to those who come after?

In this debate on cultural appropriation and colonialism, the very nature of syntax, grammar, and rhetoric is called into question. Are Portuguese, Spanish, French, and English by their very nature agents of appropriation because they are languages of empire (often cannibalizing Latin and Greek as well as, for English, early Germanic) and have absorbed words from conquered cultures? English is an amalgam of the languages of Roman, Germanic, and Norman conquerors but also an absorption of the languages of the peoples of the British Empire. The cultural property of English involves traces of the colonizer and colonized. From the beginning cultural appropriation seems to be a matter of ambivalence and instability. Language is at the heart of cultural appropriation. Who is speaking and from where? Trinh T. Minh-ha criticizes anthropology as a conversation about us—white men—and them—speechless subjects that the "us" group invites to speak about their context.[23] This concern seems legitimate, especially politically, because the balance of power between the colonized and colonizer, particularly when they are from very different cultures and have disparate technologies, has been pronounced since the Industrial and Technical Revolutions.

Although my focus is not on the relations between Native Americans and Europeans, I use this relation as a background to what is often seen more conventionally as postcolonialism—that is, the aftermath of the French and British Empires. My rationale is that both empires owed debts to those of Portugal and Spain (not to mention the classical antecedents of Greece and Rome) and that these precedents helped build much of the imperial strategy in their early relations with the Natives. All the countries of the Americas have a postcolonial dimension that is often denied, particularly in the United States. Although more and more indigenous sources are coming to light, the Native side of the story has largely been silent or left to European representations. It is important to shed light on the Native part of the archive to achieve a greater understanding of the history of the European contact and settlement of the Americas.

There will be certain problems. The texts often derive from Native texts worked out in a Europeanized grammar of the original language, and Europeans discuss these texts in European languages. Many Native groups have lost their languages and use English, French, Spanish, and Portuguese or new dialects that mix European and indigenous languages. Europeans transported African slaves to the New World, and they took the place of American Indians as a source of wealth through enforced labor. American history, which involves Native decimation by European disease and cruelty, affects the language of the Americas. So language fails us: the American Indian Nations did not think of their lands as new; nor did they decide to name them after Amerigo Vespucci—that was up to a German printer who later retracted the honor, but to no avail. But even though there is considerable political wisdom in members of a dominant group not speaking for others from less dominant groups, the desire for responsible political action is also with "us" (I use "us" and "them" to demonstrate how language fails us and them). If the rich leave the poor to speak for themselves, will anyone hear them? Or will the rich use only their own language to represent the poor?

There is in European thought a radical and liberal tradition that has argued for the abolition of slavery, for the rights of women, and for the end of empire. Perhaps the political, economic, and social structures demanded the change, and words were rationalizations of those forces or were irrelevant wishes. But perhaps they had some effect. In the history of Spanish colonization, Sepúlveda and Oviedo argued against the humanity of the American Indian, whereas Las Casas defended them. The synopsis of *A Short Account of the Destruction of the Indies* (1542, pub. 1552) says Las Casas spoke for Natives thus:

> Everything that has happened since the marvellous discovery of the Americas—from the short-lived initial attempts of the Spanish to settle there, right down to the present day—has been so extraordinary that the whole story remains quite incredible to anyone who has not experienced it at first hand. It seems, indeed, to overshadow all the deeds of famous men of the past, no matter how heroic, and to silence talk of other wonders of the world. Prominent amid the aspects of this story which have caught the imagination are the massacres of innocent peoples, the atrocities committed against them and, among other horrific excesses, the ways in which towns, provinces, and the whole kingdoms have been entirely cleared of their native inhabitants. Brother Bartolomé de Las Casas, or Casuas, came to the Spanish court after he entered the Order, to give our Lord, the Emperor, an eye-witness account of these enormities, not a whisper of which had at that time reached the ears of people here. He also related these same events to several people he met during his visit and they were deeply shocked by what he had to say and listened open-mouthed to his every word; they later begged him and pressed him to set down in writing a short account of some of them, and this he did.[24]

Here, once again, is the contradictory voice of cultural appropriation. The Americas are a marvelous discovery, which is quite different from any Native perspective. This "discovery" of Otherness is a matter of heroism and wonder, which evoke the traditions of natural history (Pliny), history (Herodotus), epic (Homer, Virgil), and travel literature (Marco Polo). But beside this is Las Casas's outrage at genocide and his defense of the humanity of the Natives, which defies Sepúlveda's application of Aristotle's theory of natural slavery and which draws on a radical New Testament distrust of class and race that institutional Christianity sometimes perverted. Here is opposition from within us to stand up for them. Las Casas did not have enough of an effect on Spanish policy to save the Indians, however. The mediation between us and them is also a possibility; for some a crossing of cultures is a sellout, whereas for others it is the only hope any of us has.[25] Here is the tradition of the Other from within.

Montaigne took up opposition to Europeans' abuses against the peoples they were subjecting. On Christopher Columbus's first voyage, he had divided the Natives into good and bad, depending on how pliable they seemed and how pro-Spanish they were. He had subdivided the bad Natives into Amazons and Cannibals.[26] When Montaigne asked the Natives who were in Rouen when Charles IX was visiting there what they found most remarkable,

> they mentioned three things, of which I am sorry to say I have forgotten the third. But I still remember the other two. They said that in the first place they found it very strange that so many tall, bearded men, all strong and well armed, who were around the King—they probably meant the Swiss of his guard—should be willing to obey a child, rather than choose one of their own number to command them. Secondly—they have a way in their language of speaking of men as halves of one another—that they had noticed among us some men gorged to the full with things of every sort while their other halves were beggars at their doors, emaciated with hunger and poverty. They found it strange that these poverty-stricken halves should suffer such injustice, and that they did not take the others by the throat or set fire to their houses.[27]

The Other becomes a way of criticizing the injustice in European politics and economics. The colonized becomes, as Minh-ha and Said suggest, a medium for a discussion between Europeans, but, unlike later anthropologists, who are said to have valued scientific objectivity, Montaigne revealed his own awareness of the subjectivity and imperfection of his knowledge and his situation.[28] He admitted to forgetting the third remarkable thing the Natives observed in Europe and later complained about how bad his interpreter had been. Montaigne's anthropology turned the lens on Europe, but did he do so through cultural appropriation, or did he avoid ventriloquy to counterbalance European prejudice?

Some of the debate on cultural appropriation arises from this critical, alternative, or oppositional tradition within European and Western culture, but in postcolonial, multicultural societies a new questioning of that tradition has recently occurred. Perhaps Montaigne foreshadowed the new movement in anthropology to use its own methods to look at European culture as an Other. Jonathan Swift had the king of Brobdingnag complain about European ethnocentricism, which is something that Las Casas and Montaigne also criticized, even though they were, by definition, very European in their cultural training.[29] Earlier in the essay on cannibals, Montaigne alluded to the old debate on barbarism and spoke about a new spirit that might escape ethnocentrism, perhaps the ideal of a scientific anthropology even if the practice must fall short: "I do not believe, from what I have been told of this people, that there is anything barbarous or savage about them, except that we all call barbarous anything that is contrary to our own habits. Indeed we seem to have no other criterion of truth and reason than the type and kind of opinions and customs current in the land where we live."[30] Is this cultural appropriation or the distance of criticism saying that we cannot get outside our cultures and times in matters as important as truth and reason?

The other group that shakes up the us and them are the mediators or go-betweens.[31] Mediation between European and Native in this early colonial period, which involved intermarriage, translation, interpretation, and diplomacy, has left traces today. Mediators cross cultures in different ways, and they confuse the us/them split of colonizer and colonized that lies at the heart of empire and that has sometimes had too tight a grip on postcolonial studies. La Malinche was Hernán Cortés's mistress during his campaign to conquer the Nahua (or Aztec).[32] The Broken Spears, which is a collection of Angel María Garibay K's translations into Spanish of Nahuatl oral accounts of this conquest, says La Malinche translated from Nahuatl into Mayan. Then Jeronimo de Aguilar, a Spaniard who lived among the Mayas for eight years and one of the two captives Cortés had wanted to ransom, translated the Mayan into Spanish for Cortés.[33] Native and European cross each other's cultural boundaries even if precariously and controversially. De Aguilar gladly came back to Spanish culture when Cortés ransomed him, whereas Gonzalo Guerrero wanted to remain a cacique with fine children rather than return to a life as a solitary Spanish pauper.

In Samuel de Champlain's narrative about New France, Etienne Brulé is either a French hero or a traitor. At the end of this account, the boy whom Champlain had taught to be a mediator has betrayed him. In Of Plymouth Plantation: 1620–1647 (pub. 1856), William Bradford told the story of another mediator—Squanto. In Bradford's narrative, the tale is one of reconciliation, friendship, love, and redemption. Through Bradford's mediation, we hear of Squanto's mediation; through the governor's culture, we witness Squanto's acculturation. Whether Squanto is a hero or a turncoat depends on which Native or English view the reader chooses to accept. Mediators are controversial.[34]

Mediation, which may allow for hope and possibility in colonization and its wake, also encounters problems of textual provenance, transmission, and reception. Cultural mediation and interpretation surround the text from the beginning. Even though this situation is true of texts generally, in texts that involve the crossing of cultures and cultural appropriation the problem becomes even more acute. The European representation of the Native (or any Other) also relates to the Native account of the European. Even the most informative among pre-Conquest Native documents were mostly redone under Spanish influence during the 1540s. Europeans developed a myth that American Indians had no writing because these records threatened the scriptures and European authority and tradition. From 1492 to 1519, there was no Native chronicler of the exchange—Las Casas was the principal defender of Native rights.[35]

The focus on the European use of language and symbolic systems in the exchange with American Indians and other indigenous peoples, although important, is only part of the story of appropriation and adaptation.[36] Increasingly, collections of Native representations of the contact or exchange with Europeans, like *The Broken Spears,* and scholarly studies are beginning to provide a balance in the debate. Two examples of this movement to analyze the roles of colonial discourse as a means of resisting the European colonization of local populations or of adaptation through their own ideas to shifting cultural, social, political, and economic conditions are Vincente L. Raphael's study of Tagalog society under early Spanish rule and J. Jorge Klor de Alva's essay on Nahua colonial discourse. Klor de Alva's work emphasizes the Nahua appropriation of the European Other and of the Other's voices by way of the adaptation of the alphabet to Nahuatl as tactics by the Nahuas to accommodate themselves to Spanish initiatives and to their own visions of truth and reality.[37] The European first-encounter narratives, according to Klor de Alva, are discontinuous because they move from the unexpected to novelty, then to discovery, and finally to justification of the imposition of modes of behaviors on the Other. These discontinuities are "cracks between an 'us' and a 'them' that needed to be filled with the mortar of Christian faith and set in the mould of the Spanish polity."[38] De Alva concludes that the Nahuas represented themselves as the only ones who could know what Natives said so that they could control Spanish translation of their intentions, language, and customs and that if disease had not struck, they might have survived into the twentieth century as a dominant bicultural and bilingual community. Instead, incorporation yielded to exclusion, and the Nahuas were decimated.[39]

The relation between appropriation and mediation applies as much to people in a postcolonial world as it does to those in a colonial one. Mediation becomes as ambivalent for postcolonial subjects as for European and Native in the early modern period. Indeed, Ross Chambers, a theorist of mediation, builds his theory on Gérard de Nerval and other nineteenth-century writers but applies his model to modernist and postmodernist texts from Australia, Quebec, Argentina, and elsewhere. Between seduction and irony he sees a mediation, and mediation in reading creates a conversion of a subject (a shifting), a room to maneuver between desire and power, a crossing over between them.[40] Like Chambers, I see a connection between textual or semiotic appropriation and political appropriation. Columbus's diaries and Las Casas's editing of that text are just as indicative of cultural appropriation as are the postmodern texts Chambers discusses.[41] The point cannot, however, be made enough about the link between semiotic (textual and visual signs) and political appropriation. Chambers sees the intricacy of the relation:

> But mediation is the necessary precondition and ally of appropriative practices. Unmeditated discourse, if such a thing could exist, would be perfectly literal and so absolutely dictatorial; it is the fact of mediation that introduces into any discursive situation the element of distance and otherness that splits what is said into "what is said" and "what is understood," and it is this possibility of understanding *otherwise* that makes appropriative (re-)interpretations possible.[42]

The connection between speaker or writer and audience is never literal and unmeditated culturally. The discourse has a cultural context in which it is framed and received. Interpretation, which occupies the heart of the human sciences, is a form of mediation. The oppositional, alternative, or critical tradition I have been outlining in European culture is predicated on this Otherness from within, what Chambers calls "understanding *otherwise*." Appropriation is available to all people and groups on the political spectrum. Chambers sees openness, provisionality, and instability of outcome in appropriation and reappropriation. He cites this example: the civil rights movement appropriated TV, and the antiabortionists have reappropriated these tactics, the going limp and being dragged off to police vans before the cameras, and who knows what groups will make such actions their property next? Thus, appropriation threatens those who seek stable and definitive meanings.[43]

For some, however, resistance and counter hegemonic theory and practice are alternatives. Their objective is to restore the colonized as subject rather than deconstruct the opposition of colonizer and colonized as a means of avoiding a simple inversion or reversal of this imperial cultural trap. The argument is, then, that the postcolonial critique that refuses and displaces European claims to constructing the colonized can deprive those who were colonized of their identities as autonomous individuals who have agency. Benita Parry looks at Frantz Fanon, who lived through the decolonization after World War II, and sees within his work a tension between Nativism and an incipient postcolonial turning away from Europe as a source of ideas and models. For Fanon, Europe had not produced the whole person, who across the world had experienced an oppositional and emancipated humanism. Parry asks a question that resonates in our age, which is still caught between colonialism and postcolonialism: "What is less certain is whether the time for transnational politics had come when Fanon was writing, whether it has now, and whether the prospect of his post-nativist 'whole man' is one that wholly delights."[44]

In the establishment of, and resistance to, empire, a movement of appropriation and reappropriation is expressed. The forms may remain the same, but the content can be opposite. The desire for mediation in postcolonial studies may also be implicated in appropriation, but it, too, represents a hope that in the wake of empire people do not get caught up in the fight of oppositions. Whether this hope is pious or the basis for practical action is for each reader to decide.

Appropriation and Postcolonialism

The debate over the crisis of representation involves a doubt over whether it is legitimate or just to describe or speak for others. But representation has always been in crisis. The Platonic Socrates, himself in the liminal region between fiction and dialectic called the "dialogue," thought that representation that sings the literal praises of the state is good, whereas fictional representation is bad because it creates shadows, a copy of a copy of a copy, and thereby deflects people away from the good and just. Aristotle opposed his teacher by making *mimesis,* or the representation of reality, the foundation of poetry, so that poets describe the real. Both Plato and Aristotle thought philosophy to be greatest, the one because it guaranteed an understanding of essential ideas and the other because it expressed universals in human experience.

Great metanarratives and systems, essential truths and universals, are all under attack in our postmodern age. There is a new crisis in representation: unstable meanings are part of a postmodernist and poststructural perspective. Owing to the mediated nature of representation, some critics have suggested on political and epistemological grounds that mimesis is a dangerous or bad thing; by extension representative government is equally offensive.[45] Gayatri Chakravorty Spivak's exploration of whether the subaltern can speak mediates between the retreat of the intellectual from speaking for others and those who are dangerous and careless in speaking for others. Spivak prefers a speaking *to* others in which intellectuals neither deny speaking nor affirm the authenticity of the oppressed but are open to a new "countersentence" or history that the oppressed can produce and to which intellectuals should listen.[46] This dialogue allows for the possibility of alternative critique. Linda Alcoff attempts to extend Spivak's analysis by saying that people must be more aware of the dangers of speaking for others in the following four ways: (1) the impetus or motive for speaking, (2) the bearing of our location and context on what we are saying, (3) accountability and responsibility for speaking, and (4) the effects of the words in discursive and material contexts.[47]

Location is a central idea in a postwar world in which there has been a great movement of peoples. The language of exile and the shifting nature of place characterize the postcolonial world. Location ranges from the institutional to the geopolitical. In thinking beyond narratives of initial or originary subjectivities, Homi K. Bhabha argues for innovative theory and a crucial politics through a focus on processes or moments produced in the articulation of cultural differences. He explores these spaces in between, especially those who live on the boundaries, and hopes for a radical revision of the idea of the human community.[48] Salman Rushdie speaks of "hybridity, impurity, intermingling, the transformation that comes of new and unexpected combinations of human beings, cultures, ideas, politics, movies, songs."[49] Cultural hybridity and mediation, which involve an in-between identity (not an essential one), oppose an essential view of cultures that are opposed in old oppositions and that appropriate and are appropriated.

Annie E. Coombes examines hybridity in regard to the difficulties arising from the curatorial strategy of presenting exhibitions that produce an exchange of cultures by claiming to radically disrupt the boundaries of the West and Other. In this analysis she assumes the recognition of hybridity as a significant cultural strategy for the politics of decolonization. Coombes advocates, as Benita Parry and Stuart Hall have, strategic essentialism.[50] Power and transgression lie at the heart of this question. For Coombes, one of the troubles with appropriating "hybridity" as a sign of postcolonial self-determination is that it is a term from art history and anthropology used to describe a cultural concept and the cultural object. Museums of fine art and ethnographic museums, both implicated in capitalism and colonialism, are homes to exhibitions. To relocate with success the cultural sign of cultural assimilation, appropriation, and transformation demands a self-consciousness in which cultural objects assigned to the Other are, at any particular moment, already circumvented.[51] Coombes thinks that an exploration of the hybridity of all cultures should allow for an examination of its specific conditions rather than a monolithic repetition of hybridity as an encounter between the West and the Other.[52]

Appropriation has an intricate relation to colonialism and postcolonialism. One view of the shift from colonialism to postcolonialism is that the first group of writers imitates texts from the imperial center, the second group abrogates them, and the third appropriates them. In discussing nineteenth-century "postcolonial" writers, Gareth Griffiths uses this successive model to show how for postcolonial authors, at least in the present sense, to go beyond abrogation, they must appropriate imperial texts for their own uses.[53] Another kind of appropriation is Shakespeare's *The Tempest,* which has been used as a source for a pamphlet on Bermuda and for Montaigne's *On Cannibals.* In turn, Shakespeare's play became a trumpet for empire and the white man's burden and then was adapted by postcolonial writers in several languages to write back against the empire. Caliban was appropriated as a tragic hero of the triumph of European colonialism.[54]

In the French-speaking world, postcolonialism has not caught on as a term, but that is not to say that interesting new work on hybridity in culture, such as studies of Creole, is not being done.[55] Françoise Lionnet calls attention to the work of writers in Francophone countries who have represented displace-ment, exile, and intercultural exchanges, and she observes more generally, "The global mongrelization or *métissage* of cultural forms creates hybrid iden-tities, and interrelated, if not overlapping, spaces."[56] Lionnet draws on ex-amples from contemporary postcolonial Francophone women who have perspectives on multiculturalism different from those in the United States. Cultural appropriation in the Francophone world is not simply a matter of assimilation of the Francophonie to France, of mimicking or imitating the colonizer.[57] The local and the global are interrelated, and the old opposition of center and margin is no longer tenable.[58]

Because Europe and the cultures it came into contact with were changed by colonization, indigenous traditions must be acknowledged and understood so that postcolonialism does not become a property, a kind of front, for neo-colonialism. But these traditions have also changed over time, before and after contact with Europeans. To talk of an essential tradition, then, is problematic. Change has also occurred in European culture, which is also not an essence. There are differences between Europeans and indigenous cultures, which are sometimes erased more for ideological than for historical reasons. On both sides the notions of culture and property have altered so that cultural appropriation has changed in history.[59] The present can also appropriate the past. The best way to look at cultural appropriation is as an interaction between changing cultures over time and not simply as a static transaction between two sides.

Postcolonialism and Postmodernism

It is difficult to address postcolonialism without saying a few words, no matter how inadequate, about postmodernism. Both terms are slippery and do not define adequately what they stand for. In my view, postmodernism involves a coming after and then a recycling of techniques. The coming after is a subsequence to all periods but bears a more direct relation to modernism, which, as an avant-garde, postmodernism must criticize. The recycling is usually of techniques that are premodern and, more often than not, early modern. Sometimes even the Enlightenment is recycled against the heirs to the Enlightenment. Laurence Sterne is refitted to trim James Joyce's sails just as Miguel de Cervantes is recalled to show that the Victorian novel was not the culmination of the tradition of the novel. Postmodernism is heir to modern technological developments so that it revolves around instant communication, which differentiates us from previous ages, though again not entirely from our Victorian and modernist parents and grandparents who gave us the telegraph and telephone. But this is a world of uneven developments, even within countries, so that to speak of one unified postmodern world would be misleading. Instead, we need to recognize what I have elsewhere called our living archaeology and what I might call here our simultaneous worlds. So many of us and our societies are primitive, modern, and postmodern at once.[60] It is also true that in repressing modernism, postmodernism has gone too far in equating modernization with modernism, in stressing the nationalist, organicist, or fascist aspects of modernism and not its experimental, fragmentary, and alienated elements.

It is a current interest to relate postmodernism to postcolonialism. A commonplace too often forgotten is that the beginnings of the term *postmodernism* are in architecture—that is, in a critique of high modernism as a celebration of advanced technology and the affluence of capitalism.[61] Postmodernism, in which Jürgen Habermas's pursuit of truth and Jean-François Lyotard's questioning of the grand narratives contend, has affinities with postcolonialism.[62] Postmodernism can be appropriated to be used against new radical movements, just as postcolonialism is in danger of being packed in the belly of the Trojan horse of neocolonialism. Some voices oppose relating the postcolonial to postmodernism. Arun P. Mukherjee argues against grouping postcolonial texts under "postmodernism" because of this term's genesis from white European males; Mukherjee thinks that this classification will not do for nonwhite writing.[63]

Postcolonialism can be ironic and may not use postmodern deconstruction to go beyond existing orthodoxies into areas of social and political action. One danger is that postcolonialism can be appropriated, consciously or not, by those of us who write about it in the institution as part of a paradigm shift that becomes domesticated among granting agencies, institutes, publishers, journals, museums, galleries, and universities. Voice appropriation becomes a question of mobile maneuvers as institutional identities threaten to ossify antiessentialist or strategic essentialist tactics of postmodern postcolonialism. Irony and ambivalence, whether adopted from Friedrich Schlegel, Walter Benjamin, or William Empson, are Socratic or German romantic tools negotiated through modernism and displaced into the repertoire of postcolonialism and postmodernism. The rhetoric of temporality occupies postcolonialism as much as it does history and the philosophy of history. If Lyotard questions the grand narratives of the European Enlightenment, Said looks at how postcolonial strategies question the nature of representation, cultural property, and property itself, whereas Spivak and Bhabha discuss agency and the interruption of the narration and reading of nation and empire. Young considers postcolonialism's critique of European historiography and of Otherness to be subsumed under postmodernism, as in Bhabha's work, but Henry Louis Gates thinks that Western academic interest in making colonialism a field of all writing may yet be another project of European universalism. Literary criticism and theory have appropriated the form and content of rhetoric, philosophy, history, and literature itself. Postcolonialism, which is a kind of cultural critique or cultural studies, is cross-disciplinary theory and practical criticism. It appropriates from these traditional sources.

A key question is whether postcolonial theory, which is centered in the Western university, has appropriated postcolonial fiction. Is this another case of the critic feeding off the artist? Or do we need cultural mediators to create an audience or to go between writers/artists and readers/viewers? Spivak has wrestled with this difficult question with sensitivity. Nonetheless, it is hard to know whether any form of irony or ambivalence is subversive or evasive or both. Do postcolonial critics provide models in countries subject to economic colonialism, or is their discourse an institutional and professional discourse of privileged Western universities? As I have argued, from the first contacts between Europeans and Native Americans, to use just one example of "first encounters," the role of mediators has been important but precarious. By attempting to unmask, contain, and circumvent ethnic and racial suspicion and hatred, postcolonial theorists are attempting something significant and problematic. To cross boundaries and to understand those translations are the tasks of postcolonialism. In postcolonial studies, theorists use subaltern voices, European high theory, the fiction of the former colonies and European fiction, so that cultural appropriation is fine if it criticizes empire and essentialism in race, nation, and religion.

No one has done more to establish postcolonial studies than Edward Said, a mediator who has crossed many boundaries.[64] What distinguishes postcolonialism most is its focus on empire and its attempt to see beyond empire or read the wake of empire even while new forms of empire may be in the making. Edward Said's landmark *Orientalism* (1978) and *Culture and Imperialism* (1993) mark the take-off and the power and velocity of postcolonialism.[65] Although imperialism has, thanks largely to Said, recently become a central concern of literary studies, he reminds us of the early critical work by historians and others in the field, such as J. A. Hobson's *Imperialism: A Study* (1902); Said also expands on Raymond Schwab's *La Renaissance Orientale* (1950).[66] Nor does Said think that empires began with the British and French Empires, but he is particularly interested in those as an imperial kind whose vastness and whose dominion over so many different peoples had never occurred in the world. But it is Said's work that has helped inspire a generation of English-speaking students to look into imperialism in literary texts. He has brought Joseph Conrad, Aimé Césaire, and Frantz Fanon into classroom and critical discourse in North America and beyond.

In the Introduction to *Culture and Imperialism,* Said indicates that he wants to emphasize the resistance to empire that he did not address in *Orientalism,* the mutual relation and response to imperialism of the heirs to colonizer and colonized, and the new ways of seeing texts like Charles Dickens's *Great Expectations* (1861) and Joseph Conrad's *Nostromo* (1904) (the former as a tale of banishment, alienation, and the experience of living through empire and the latter as a critique and celebration of empire). Said is interested in moral criticism, as evidenced by this moment in the Introduction: "To the extent that we see Conrad both criticizing and reproducing the imperial ideology of his time, to that extent we can characterize our own present attitudes: the projection, or the refusal, of the wish to dominate, the capacity to damn, or the energy to comprehend and engage with other societies, traditions, histories."[67] Here is a call for an understanding of historical difference between Conrad and us in conjunction with an assumption that a kind of transhistorical ethic can be taken in this comparison of then and now. Imperialism mutates but remains the same. But Said is too subtle to make such a bald statement. The world has changed, he says, because for some time globalization has brought nonwhite immigrants into the heart of the metropolitan centers of Europe and the United States. Therefore, Said asserts, "for the first time, the history of imperialism and its culture can now be studied as neither monolithic nor reductively compartmentalized, separate, distinct."[68] The implied question becomes, Whose place is this anyway? The division of territory and culture as the property of the colonizer in opposition to the colonized is no longer the case.

Said's quest is to map the relation between narrative and empire, especially as they appear in his life—that is, the British, French, and American imperiums. He focuses on their shared idea of overseas rule. More than in previous work, Said looks at American imperialism. He also celebrates the new work in Middle Eastern and Indian studies by women and makes the apt point that narratives of emancipation have been about excluded groups fighting for integration. With a humanistic view of the university as a utopian space in which to explore possibilities, which is not too different from Northrop Frye's, Said also alludes to New York, the city of his exile, as a state for his meditation that he offers to the reader as a possible "salutary alternative to the normal sense of belonging to only one culture and feeling a sense of loyalty to only one nation."[69] Said writes from the utopian space of the university that is and is not of the world and in the putative dimension between his "Oriental" and "Western" selves and experiences. Connected hybridity and hybrid connection are Said's ideals for facing the new reality of the global village. It is, as he notes, empire that has brought us together to study about empire.[70]

Postcolonial Irresolution, Indigenous Identity, and the Hybrid

It may be possible to see more clearly several key relations in the connection between cultural appropriation and postcolonialism: the colonial and postcolonial, Native rights and the postcolonial, identity and hybridity, mediation and resistance, to name a few. Has the postcolonial escaped the dilemmas of the colonial? Simon During sees the emptiness of postcolonial culture and the tendency of postcolonial identity toward irresolution and paradox: as Northrop Frye asked of Canadian culture so many years ago—is there any here here?[71] Poststructuralist and postmodernist notions of self or subject reveal a discomfort with Renaissance or modern claims for identity and individualism. But this is a European view that is not accepted by all, let alone all Europeans, not even by those who work in the rarefied world of critical theory. There are levels of qualification in views of the person and the state. For instance, Tom King is an aboriginal novelist who lived in Alberta and moved to Minnesota. He does not like the term *postcolonial* because it assumes that in relation to Native culture the time to begin is with the arrival of Europeans in North America.[72] King also eschews the term because it implies that Natives now forget their own traditions and write entirely about their struggle as "wards" of their "guardians." Thus, postcolonialism neglects Native traditions that have survived colonization. For King, Native writing is an alternative, not a construct of oppression, so that it should not be held hostage to the nationalism that postcolonialism suggests for it. King sees Native writing as a counternarrative or counterclassification.

Perhaps, then, it is not necessary to have an either/or between traditional nationalism in which people die in the streets because they are supposed to have a certain identity and postmodern/postcolonial self-invention and hybridity. But I think the crossing of boundaries and the flexibility of mediation can suggest one way to live in the world and to respond to movements and mixing of culture in the global village. By way of illustration, I wish to turn to Louis Riel, a mythical and controversial figure in Canadian culture who led the Northwest rebellions of 1869–1870 and 1885. In 1869 the federal government, in preparation for the 1870 transfer of land from the Hudson's Bay Company (which had controlled the Northwest since 1670 when Charles II gave Prince Rupert his charter) to Canada, sent out a surveying team. The Métis feared that this meant that the Canadian government would threaten their livelihood, mainly as fur traders, by encouraging Protestant farmers from Ontario. The Métis, still suffering from the grasshopper plague of 1867–1868, chose Riel as secretary of their National Committee, which halted the surveys and prevented William MacDougall from entering the new territory as lieutenant governor. On November 2, 1869, the Métis seized Fort Garry (today Winnipeg); Hudson's Bay Company officials offered no resistance.

The committee invited the French and English settlers of Red River to send delegates to Fort Garry. While they were discussing Riel's List of Rights, some Canadians took up arms against the committee. Riel imprisoned the Canadians, issued the Declaration of the People of Rupert's Land and the Northwest, and, on December 23, became head of the provisional government. The Canadian government sent goodwill commissioners, and Riel was convinced to hold a convention of forty representatives, equally divided between French and English. They first met on January 26, 1870, and they debated and endorsed the List of Rights and agreed to release the Canadian prisoners. They also resolved to send three representatives to negotiate admission into the Canadian Confederation. Some of the Canadians who had escaped appeared as an armed force, and their leaders were court-martialed. Donald A. Smith, chief representative of Hudson's Bay Company in Canada, convinced Ambrose Lépine, Riel's associate, to pardon Charles Boulton, but Smith could not prevail on Riel to do the same for Thomas Scott, who was executed by a firing squad on March 4, 1870. Bishop Taché of St. Boniface in the Northwest, summoned from an ecumenical council in Rome, arrived four days after the death of Scott and brought a federal proclamation of amnesty. Taché convinced Riel's council to free prisoners and send delegates to Ottawa, where they negotiated articles that were to appear in the Manitoba Act passed on May 12, 1870. The transfer of power was to occur on July 15.

The federal government agreed to give the Métis 1.4 million acres and guaranteed bilingual services for the new province. The federal government also sent A. G. Archibald and a military force to maintain peace in the area. Riel fled to the United States but then returned when the province was threatened by a Fenian raid from the United States in autumn 1871. He offered Métis cavalry to Archibald. Riel was elected to the federal parliament in 1873 but was expelled as a result of a motion by the Orange leader. Riel was reelected in 1874 but did not try to take up his seat. Riel and Lépine were given a five-year exile in February 1875.

Just after the motion of exile, Riel had a nervous breakdown and was admitted to a hospital in Montreal as Louis R. David and was later transferred to a mental asylum as Louis la Rochelle. Riel thought he would establish a new North American Catholicism and make Bishop Bourget of Montreal pope of the New World. After being released in January 1878, Riel went to New York State and then to Montana territory, where he joined the Republican Party, became an American citizen, and married Marguerite Monet, a Métis. In 1883 he became a schoolteacher.

In June 1884 a group of Canadian Métis asked him to help them gain their legal rights in the Saskatchewan area of the Northwest. Early in July Riel and his family reached Batoche. Riel was convinced that he was a prophet of the New World. Riel and his men seized the parish church on March 19, 1885, but he surrendered about two months later. On July 6, he was charged with treason, and on July 20, his trial began in Regina. The jury found him guilty but recommended clemency. The verdict was twice appealed and dismissed. Three physicians examined Riel. One found him insane, but the official report was a whitewash and did not reflect any dissension. The federal cabinet decided to hang him. He was executed in Regina on November 16, 1885, and his body was removed to a place in front of the Catholic cathedral in St Boniface. Quebec did not vote for the Conservatives federally for about another hundred years, and to this day there are calls for a retroactive pardon. Riel is controversial even still.[73]

The very ambivalence of Riel makes him problematic. He combines progressive aspects such as a politics of liberation and nostalgic and conservative religious elements. The images of Catholicism and France coexist with his declaration of rights and his vision of independence for the Métis and the Northwest. He is rebel and mystic, prophet of a new age and throwback to a religious past, French and Amerindian. As Thomas Flanagan says, Riel listened to his mother's stories about his descent from the French nobility, but in his "later life, compassion for the Irish as fellow unfortunates alongside the French Canadians within the British empire was to be a hallmark of his thinking."[74] He was hanged as a rogue in the view of Orangemen from Ontario and died as a martyr for the Catholics of Quebec. For many of the Métis, he was the last chance at the dream of being heard as the European settlers moved West.

Riel is a figure who disturbs the opposition of colonizer and colonized, the simple division between European and Indian that could be an excuse for conscious or unconscious racism, exploitation, and even genocide, because he was a Métis, part French and part Indian in a country that was supposed to have two founding nations and languages and that was supposed to be making treaties with the Indians, nation to nation. Here was a man who was and was not European, was and was not Indian. He was part of a group that confounded the oppositions that built Canada and put its indigenous peoples on reserves. In the history of colonization there are many figures like Riel. He questions the category of race, the destiny of Europe, and the "purity" of culture. As a figure Riel unsettles the demands of imperialists and nationalists, of too many traditional cultures, European and other, to set up a situation of either/or and we/they, to build an ideological wall around a nation, cast out those who have not been allowed into the definition, and pretend, sometimes in a ghastly fantasy with the grossest consequences, that culture is not oblique, complex, and ambivalent.

Riel, then, becomes like the figure of the hybrid. Hybrid languages break down the opposition between a European and an indigenous language.[75] The potential of hybrid or Métis discourse is to mix European and other cultures; the difficulty, as in Riel's case, is that the European cultural element is given too great a sway. But as times have changed since Riel, it is possible to look to analogous figures and writers today, when there can be more exchange between the cultures because the British and American Empires are traces. Only the influence of American political power, something Riel does not seem to have concentrated on (Britain was the world power then), affects the Creole and Métis. The danger and liberation may now lie in American popular culture, which has made such inroads into Native households, as everywhere else.

In Riel there was a narrative of liberation but also an eruption of the colonial and the feudal. There have been narratives of resistance to empire and narratives of imperial celebration for three thousand years or more in Western culture. To come after empire and to get beyond it may be far more difficult than we recognize. In the meantime even though postcolonial seems an inadequate term because the colonial has not entirely left us, neocolonialism may still be with us, and strange manifestations of premodern and modern identities may remain with us like an archaeology. The translation of empire and the resistance to it should be studied, even if that study is marked with a disjunction between ethics and history, because no matter how short we fall of the mark, it is too important an area to let alone. Cultural appropriation is at the heart of debates on postcolonialism and neocolonialism. Who speaks for whom? Can we get past old ways of exchanging culture? Our futures depend on this debate, but they have to come to terms with our pasts. The postcolonial has to see through itself in the colonial. Quite possibly, the appropriation of the past is at the center of human cultures as they meet.

Notes

My thanks to the editors of this collection, Bruce Ziff and Pratima V. Rao, for their help and encouragement. I also thank Jane Moore, Catherine Belsey, Christopher Norris, Terence Hawkes, and others at the Centre for Critical and Cultural Theory (Cardiff) for their invitation and comments on my talk "Some Theoretical Difficulties in Postcolonial Studies" (January 1994) and Ken Ruthven and his colleagues at Melbourne (July 1994) for their invitation to give the paper "Colonialism and Postcolonialism" and for their questions. These two talks contained different versions of earlier material on the topic, some of which appears in a revised form in this essay.

1. "Ventriloquy" is speaking for others, often while being unaware of doing so or pretending not to. It can also be a displacement of one voice onto another. Ventriloquy occurs as much in writing as in political speech. I had used this term for well over a decade before I began to think in the specific terms of cultural appropriation. I came to realize that voice appropriation was a kind of ventriloquy.

2. Sally Kilmister, "Aesthetic and Music: The Appropriation of the Other," *Women: A Cultural Review* 3(1) 1992: 31.

3. *The Compact Oxford English Dictionary,* 2d ed. (Oxford: Clarendon Press, 1991), 1493.

4. Harold G. Fox, *The Canadian Law of Copyright and Industrial Designs,* 2d ed. (Toronto: Carswell Company, 1967), 18.

5. Rosemary J. Coombe, "The Properties of Culture and the Politics of Possessing Identity: Native Claims in the Cultural Appropriation Controversy," *Canadian Journal of Law and Jurisprudence* 6(2) (1993): 251–252, 259.

6. Ibid., 253.

7. Ibid., 254–255.

8. Ibid., 270–272.

9. Loretta Todd, "Notes on Appropriation," *Parallelogramme* 16 (Summer 1990): 32; quoted in Coombe, "The Properties of Culture," 285.

10. Ibid.

11. Amanda Pask, "Cultural Appropriation and the Law: An Analysis of the Legal Regime Concerning Culture," *Intellectual Property Journal* 8 (1993): 86.

12. See Leslie C. Green and Olive Dickason, *The Law of Nations and the New World* (Edmonton: University of Alberta Press, 1989).

13. See Tim Rowse, *After Mabo: Interpreting Indigenous Traditions* (Melbourne: Melbourne University Press, 1993).

14. See Janice Hladki, "Problematizing the Issue of Cultural Appropriation," *Alternate Routes* 11 (1994): 95–119, esp. 95–96; and Francis Barker, Peter Hulme, and Margaret Iversen, eds., *Colonial Discourse/Postcolonial Theory* (Manchester: Manchester University Press, 1994), 4.

15. Anthony Pagden, *The Fall of Natural Man: The American Indian and the Origins of Comparative Ethnography,* rev. ed. (Cambridge: Cambridge University Press, 1986), 15. The following discussion draws on 15–26.

16. Ibid., 16.

17. Aristotle, *De mirabilibus auscultationibus* 836a: 10–15; cited in ibid., 16.

18. Aristotle, *Politics* 1338b: 19, and *Nichomachean Ethics* 1148b: 19ff, cited in ibid., 18.

19. Ibid., 19.

20. Ernst Breisach, *Historiography: Ancient, Medieval, and Modern* (Chicago: University of Chicago Press, 1983), 178–79. Breisach's various references to examples of *translatio imperii* have been important for my framing of this myth.

21. Pagden, *The Fall of Natural Man,* 10.

22. Thomas B. Macaulay, "History of England from the Accession of James II," in *The Complete Writings* (Boston: 1901), 1:276; quoted in Breisach, *Historiography, 251.* See also *213, 243, 245.*

23. Trinh T. Minh-ha, *Woman, Native, Other: Writing Postcoloniality and Feminism* (Bloomington: Indiana University Press, 1988), 63–65.

24. Bartolomé de Las Casas, "Synopsis," in *A Short Account of the Destruction of the Indies,* trans. Nigel Griffin, intro. Anthony Pagden (London: Penguin, 1992), 3.

25. Jonathan Hart, "Images of the Native in Renaissance Encounter Narratives," *ARIEL* 25 (October 1994): 55–76; Jonathan Hart, "Mediation in the Exchange Between Europeans and Native Americans in the Early Modern Period," *Canadian Review of Comparative Literature* 22 (1995): 319–343; Anthony Pagden, *European Encounters in the New World* (New Haven, Conn.: Yale University Press, 1993), 1–15; Ross Chambers, "No Montagues Without Capulets: Some Thoughts on 'Cultural Identity,'" in *Explorations in Difference: Law, Culture, and Politics,* ed. Jonathan Hart and Richard W. Bauman (Toronto: University of Toronto Press, 1995), 25–66.

26. See Hart, "Images of the Native," 55–76.

27. Michel de Montaigne, *On Cannibals,* trans. and ed. J. M. Cohen (Harmondsworth: Penguin, 1963), 119.

28. See Minha-ha, *Woman, Native, Other;* Edward Said, "Representing the Colonized: Anthropology's Interlocutors," *Critical Inquiry* 15 (Winter 1989): 205–225.

29. Hart, "Images of the Native," " 55–76.

30. Montaigne, *On Cannibals,* 108–109.

31. See Ross Chambers, *Room for Manoeuvre: Reading (the) Oppositional (in) Narrative* (Chicago: University of Chicago Press, 1991); Chambers, "No Montagues Without Capulets"; Stephen Greenblatt, *Marvellous Possessions: The Wonder of the New World* (Chicago: University of Chicago Press, 1991), 119–51.

32. See Ramón A. Gutiérrez, *When Jesus Came, the Corn Mothers Went Away: Marriage, Sexuality, and Power in New Mexico* (Stanford, Calif.: Stanford University Press, 1991), 48.

33. Miguel Leon-Portilla, ed. *The Broken Spears: The Aztec Account of the Conquest of Mexico* (Boston: Beacon Press, 1993), 3; Bernal Díaz, *The Conquest of New Spain,* ed. and trans. J. M. Cohen, rpt. (Harmondsworth: Penguin, 1983), 86–87.

34. See Hart, "Mediation," 319–343.

35. Vine Deloria Jr., "Afterword," in *America in 1492: The World of the Indian Peoples Before the Arrival of Columbus,* ed. Alvin M. Joseph Jr. (New York: Random House, 1993) 429–430; Gordon Brotherston, *Image of the New World: The American*

Continent Portrayed in Native Texts (London: Thames/Hudson, 1979), 15, 21; Hart, "Mediation."

36. See Tzvetan Todorov, *La Conquête de l'Amérique* (Paris: Seuil, 1982); Johannes Fabian, *Language and Colonial Power: The Appropriation of Swahili in the Former Belgian Congo, 1880–1938* (New York: Cambridge University Press, 1986).

37. J. Jorge Klor de Alva, "Nahua Colonial Discourse and the Appropriation of the (European) Other," *Archives de Science Sociales des Religion* 77 (1992): 16.

38. Ibid., 17.

39. Ibid., 32.

40. Chambers, *Room for Manoeuvre*, 245.

41. Hart, "Images of the Native," 55–76.

42. Chambers, *Room for Manoeuvre*, 219.

43. Chambers, "No Montagues Without Capulets," 25–66.

44. Benita Parry, "Resistance Theory/Theorising Resistance or Two Cheers for Nativism," in *Colonial Discourse/Postcolonial Theory*, ed. Barker, Hulme, and Iversen, 193; see also 172–173.

45. Linda Alcoff, "The Problem of Speaking for Others," *Cultural Critique* 19–20 (Winter 1991–1992): 5–32.

46. Ibid., 22–23.

47. Ibid., 24–27.

48. Homi Bhabha, *The Location of Culture* (London: Routledge, 1994), 1–6, 207–209. See also Homi Bhabha, ed., *Nation and Narration* (London: Routledge, 1990), 4.

49. Quoted in Peter Wollen, "Tourism, Language, and Art," *New Formations* 12 (1990):57.

50. Annie E. Coombes, "The Recalcitrant Object: Cultural Contact and the Question of Hybridity," in *Colonial Discourse/Postcolonial Theory*, ed. Barker, Hulme, and Iversen, 89–90. See also Parry, "Resistance Theory," 172–196; Stuart Hall, "Cultural Identity and Diaspora," in *Identity, Community, Culture, Difference*, ed. Johnathan Rutherford (London: Lawrence and Wishart, 1990), 222–224.

51. Coombes, "The Recalcitrant Object," 90.

52. Ibid., 111.

53. Gareth Griffiths, "Imitation, Abrogation, and Appropriation: The Production of the Post-Colonial Text," *Kunapipi* 9 (1987): 20.

54. See Jonathan Hart, "Traces, Resistances, and Contradictions: Canadian and International Perspectives on Postcolonial Theories," *Arachne* 1 (1994): 68–93.

55. Ibid., 84–87; Patrick Chamoiseau and Raphael Confiant, *Lettres créoles: Traces antillaises et continentales de la littérature: Haiti, Guadeloupe, Martinique, Guyane, 1635–1975* (Paris: Hatier, 1991); George Lang, "Kribich, 'Cribiche,' ou ecrevisse: L'avenir de l'eloge de la Creolite," in *Convergences et divergences dans les littératures francophones*, ed. Danielle Deltel (Paris: L'Harmattan, 1992), 170–181.

56. Françoise Lionnet, "'Logiques Métisses': Cultural Appropriation and Postcolonial Representations," *College Literature* (10) (1992): 101.

57. See Aimé Césaire, *Une Tempête: D'apres la Tempête de Shakespeare—Adaptation pour un théâtre nègre* (Paris: Seuil, 1961); Frantz Fanon, *Peau noire, masques blancs* (Paris: Seuil, 1952); Édouard Glissant, *Le Disours antillais* (Paris: Seuil, 1981).

58. Lionnet, "'Logiques Métisses,'" 105, 116.

59. See Hart, "Traces, Resistances, and Contradictions," 86–87.

60. See ibid., 68–93.

61. See Linda Hutcheon, "Circling the Downspout of Empire," *ARIEL* 20 (1989), 150; Simon During, "Waiting for the Post: Some Relations Between Modernity, Colonization, and Writing," in *Past the Last Post: Theorizing Colonialism and Post-Modernism,* ed. Ian Adam and Helen Tiffin (Calgary: University of Calgary Press, 1990), 23–45; Hart, "Traces, Resistances, and Contradictions," 83–84, 87–88.

62. Hart and Bauman, eds., *Explorations in Difference.*

63. Arun P. Mukherjee, "Whose Postcolonialism and Whose Postmodernism?" *WLWE* 30 (1990): 1–9.

64. See Jonathan Hart, "The Book of Judges: Views Among the Critics," *Canadian Review of Comparative Literature* 17 (1990): 115.

65. Edward W. Said, *Orientalism* (New York: Vintage Books, 1978); Edward Said, *Culture and Imperialism* (London: Vintage Books, 1993).

66. John A. Hobson, *Imperialism: A Study,* rev. ed., (London: Constable, 1905); Raymond Schwab, *La Renaissance Orientale* (Paris: Payot, 1950). Said also cites William H. McNeill, *The Pursuit of Power: Technology, Armed Forces, and Society Since 1000 a.d.* (Chicago: University of Chicago Press, 1983).

67. Said, *Culture and Imperialism,* xxii.

68. Ibid., xxiii.

69. Ibid., xxxi; Jonathan Hart, *Northrop Frye: The Theoretical Imagination* (London: Routledge, 1994), 164–190; Northrop Frye, *On Education* (Don Mills, Ont.: Fitzhenry and Whiteside, 1988).

70. Said, *Culture and Imperialism,* xxviii. See also Pagden, *The Fall of Natural Man,* 14–26.

71. Simon During, "Postmodernism or Postcolonialism?" *Landfall* 39 (1985): 366–80; Simon During, "Postmodernism or Postcolonialism To-day," *Textual Practice* 1 (1987): 32–47; During, "Waiting for the Post," 23–45. See also Northrop Frye, *The Bush Garden: Essays on the Canadian Imagination* (Toronto: Anansi, 1971).

72. Thomas King, "Godzilla vs. Postcolonial," *World Literature Written in English* 30 (1990): 10–16.

73. My summary is indebted to George F.G. Stanley, "Riel, Louis," *The Canadian Encyclopedia* (Edmonton: Hurtig, 1985), 1584–1585. For a discussion of Riel's religion, see Thomas Flanagan, *Louis "David" Riel: Prophet of the New World* (Toronto: University of Toronto Press, 1979).

74. Flanagan, *Louis "David" Riel,* 8, 5–6.

75. Chamoiseau and Confiant, *Lettres créoles;* Lang, "Kribich, 'Cribiche,' ou ecrevisse.

J. Jorge Klor de Alva

Nahua Colonial Discourse and the Appropriation of the (European) Other

Introduction: What Is Colonial Discourse?

By "colonial discourse" I mean the ways of talking, writing, painting, and communicating that permitted ideas to pass from one discourse (or bounded register of signs, codes, and meanings) to another in order to authorize and make possible the ends of colonial control *and* the strategies of resistance and accommodation to it.[1]

As in any colonial or hierarchized multiethnic situation, in New Spain all social encounters between ethnic groups had the potential of being politicized, and ignorance of the appropriate rules of engagement invited confusion or threatened disaster. Consequently, an awareness of the formulas needed to translate the other's desires or commands was critical to survival. As subjects shaping their destiny under colonial rule, the Nahuas devised sociopolitical maneuvers that were embedded in native ideational systems that served, for better and for worse, to reinterpret colonial society in ways familiar to them. These systems were expressed not only in the straightforward presentation of interests, as found in the relevant documents, but also in the criteria, implicit in their discursive practices, that enforced rules for ordering reality and assessing truth claims. These discursive constituents of Nahua consciousness are everywhere in evidence: in their translations of Spanish demands, in the ploys with which they fended off the threatening effects of the linguistic hierarchy that resulted from the colonial experience, in their self-serving expressions of submission, in their guarded assertions of claims, and in their imaging of the European Other.

Although much attention has recently been paid to "colonial discourse," it is overwhelmingly focused on the Europeans' use of language and other symbolic systems to further their domination of non-whites,[2] while relatively little is being said about the roles of colonial discourse as a weapon to resist that domination or as a tool by which the victims of colonization could adapt themselves, *through their own conceptualizations,* to the shifting social, cultural, and political conditions.[3] This brief essay, part of a longer study on the subject, is meant to be a contribution to the examination of these latter roles by focusing on the Nahuas' appropriation of the European Other (in the course of "first" encounter narratives) and of the Other's voice (through the adaptation of alphabetic literacy to Nahuatl) as tactics useful in their efforts to accommodate themselves to the initiatives of the Spaniards and as vehicles for affirming their vision of truth and sociopolitical reality.

Nahua Moral and Political Discourses

In the fifteenth century, European stories about first encounters between distinct cultures were either imaginary or referred to events known only textually, primarily in the works of Classical authors. In the wake of the voyages of Columbus the tales underwent substantial modifications as soldiers, sailors, missionaries, and colonists began to describe actual and imagined meetings with the natives of the Americas. Though these early observers rarely read each other's works,[4] the accounts that were widely disseminated ultimately renovated the (obsolete) canon of first encounter discourse. The new standards included a constant characterization of the unexpected as novel, the highlighting of novelty as a discovery, and the converting of discovery into a justification for the imposition of modes of behavior and belief.[5] As a consequence, the narratives of this form of colonial discourse were ultimately about discontinuities: cracks between an "us" and a "them" that needed to be filled with the mortar of Christian faith and set in the mold of Spanish polity.

Parallel to this rhetorical tactic, aimed at delegitimizing Indian ways and beliefs in favor of European social and ideological control, the Nahua communities articulated a counternarrative of continuity. I suggest that this discursive maneuver had as its goal (in fact, even if not always consciously) the domestication of European objects, acts, and ideas by hitching them to indigenous ends, practices, and institutions. I also claim that although this discursive strategy afforded many local and short term advantages, in the long run it proved to be counterproductive for the native communities as a whole. Its weakness was due, in part, to the asymmetrical sociopolitical and cultural effects that followed for each side from their respective discourses on ethics and politics, and from their differential conceptualizations of the Other. I make this observation while taking as my point of departure some basic empirical facts, like widespread depopulation through plagues; novel military and political tactics; gunpowder and horses; the utility of many European technical, political, social, religious, and administrative practices; and the advantages recognized by the Nahuas of numerous Spanish crafts, agricultural practices, and tools.

In general, I believe Spanish moral and political discourses were characterized by (1) a moral absolutism, permitting an unequivocal attack against whatever could be defined as deviant; (2) with minor exceptions, a determination to exclude the Other, making it possible for the Europeans to respond in common to real or imagined native opposition or mere differences through a common assumption that the integrity of one culture was founded on the negation of all others; and (3) a belief that Spaniards held the dominant cultural and political position worldwide, giving them a sociocultural and political edge over both the more narrowly drawn indigenous outlines of ethnic boundaries and their more local assertions of hegemony or privilege.

Nahua discourses on ethics and politics stood in sharp relief to this aggressive stance. First, much to the chagrin of the missionaries,[6] the Nahuas had more tolerant and flexible rules of conduct and approached religious beliefs less dogmatically.[7] Logically, this led to a marked tendency toward moral ambiguity in the face of a new ethical system and to a search for a politics of accommodation in contrast to the Spaniards' more single-minded sense of righteousness and exclusion.[8] Furthermore, to the extent a precontact fusion of ethics and supernatural cosmology remained in force, Nahua narratives exhibited a commitment to situational ethics over subjective intentionality founded on the normative assessment of the relation between human acts and the empirical categories, like time (calendric dates), space (ritually charged locations), and direction, within which they took place.[9] In addition, from a Western perspective Nahua behavior can be represented[10] and generally was interpreted as being too rooted in a pragmatic and this-worldly morality, making it nearly impossible for it to respond collectively and forcefully out of broadly held, translocal principles. For example, a complaint heard among the missionaries was that the Nahuas, whatever their public claims, were unwilling to die for the new faith—unlike the then recently baptized Japanese[11]—seeking instead only the immediate rewards of local interest and temporal gain,[12] and not believing in punishment in the afterlife.[13] These characteristics left native moral behavior open to dogmatic challenges that could combine references to ideal universal codes with appeals to very real authorities able to impose them.[14]

Second, native social and political discourses generally exhibited a seamless vision of reality that left little epistemic space for the conceptualization of an Other that genuinely broke away from known categories. For instance, as is evident in the story of the first Tlaxcalan-Spanish contacts[15] or the tale of the conquest of México-Tenochtitlán,[16] they wrote about themselves as a people who initially had difficulty clearly outlining the nature and significance of a fundamentally novel intruder. A sixteenth-century Tlaxcalan historian, Diego Muñoz Camargo, gives us excellent insights into the muddle resulting from the complex criteria used by the Nahuas to determine the distinction between gods (hierophanies) and humans, and points to the political consequences of this seeming confusion by summarizing, as follows, the arguments employed by the Tlaxcalans when they initially attempted to make sense of the first non-American Others in their midst:

And finally, on this argument on whether they were gods or men, they could not resolve [it], because if they were gods . . . they would not cast down our oracles, nor . . . harm our gods, because these would be their brothers, and thus since they harm and cast them down they ought not to be gods, but rather bestial and barbarous people. . . . On the other hand, they believed they were gods because they came in very strange animals, never seen or heard in the world . . . , [but when the spies reached Mexico they knew] that in the end they are men because they become sick, eat, drink, and sleep, and do other things men do. But they were very astonished that [the Spaniards] had brought no women except that Marina [Malintzin, Cortés' native interpreter], and that could not be except by the art and command of the gods. Otherwise how could she know their language? . . . And the crossbow and sword, they asked themselves, how could it be possible that human forces could employ them? And thus left with such confusion, they decided to await what their design would be. And seeing how few they were, [Motecuhzoma] paid no attention nor imagined his perdition, but rather understanding that if they were gods he would placate them with sacrifices and prayers . . . , and if they were men, their power would be insignificant.[17]

Third, as this quote helps to make evident, Nahua political discourse was ultimately so centered on its local truths that even its limited capacity to conceptualize the macrohistorical configurations did not permit it to transcend its limited geographic and sociopolitical perspectives. The result of this cognitive parochialism is that over time the political and moral ideologies did not provide the effective ideational, political, or socioeconomic contestation that would have stimulated a unified and competitive response at levels beyond the individual town or hamlet. Nonetheless, at the local level their assimilationist mode of interpretation, particularly of the Spanish and their world, permitted them to add many of the newly introduced practices to the Nahuas' long repertoire of survival tactics.

The Other as a Familiar Tale

Nahua colonial narratives about first (and subsequent) encounters with the Other were an important part of this repertoire even if, as already noted, the moral and political discourses that informed them and the too familiar conceptions of the Other they articulated led to serious negative results. More precisely, the relevant problems can be traced to the differential effects produced in the colonial situation by the contrasts between (our understanding of) the Nahuas' historical consciousness and that of Spaniards. Without disregarding the (very limited) role of prophecy in colonial Spanish thought,[18] it is fair to say that the Europeans celebrated first encounter narratives as founding charters that clearly marked both the break between the powerful We and the weak They, and the boundary between Spanish Christians and Nahua sinners. In doing so, these founding charters were meant to legitimate a new (and genuinely unexpected) order based on the need to maintain the former distinction as a necessary prerequisite for overcoming the Christian sinful pagan division. On the other hand, cognate Nahua texts served a very different purpose. By being rooted in a fundamentally prophetic sense of history flowing from a cyclical perception of time, instead of legitimating the establishment of a new order, first encounter narratives represented the fulfillment of historical predictions that justified the continuation of past sociopolitical trajectories. In effect, with positive and negative results, these first encounter discourses both represented and contributed to the encoding of the colonial situation into native registers.

An analysis of the Nahua strategy used to employ the archetypal story of "the first encounter" suggests, as Muñoz Camargo made evident, that the Other is always latent in the We, revealing itself as something already known and expected, predicted by the forefathers, former rulers, or contemporary diviners. The arrival of the Other is always a political act: a response to an imminent threat to the social whole. By affirming that continuity is in order, it signals a way out of the immediate danger and thereby guarantees that local historical developments will continue to unfold without interruption. This semiotic move, which seeks to restrict the signification of the Other by inscribing it within familiar signs, is part of a much broader discursive strategy used by precontact local and regional Nahua leaders to legitimate their authority, claimed to derive ultimately from the gods. The precontact discourse within which the appearance of the Other is embedded is composed of the many creation and regeneration myths, whose vestiges can be found today in numerous texts.[19] In these narratives man-cum-gods build and destroy, but most important of all, they hold out the promise that the inevitable cycle of time, wherein one age, one people, or one ruling dynasty is succeeded by another, will be delayed as long as possible if the proper rituals are performed.[20]

It follows, therefore, that the accounts of the Cortés-Quetzalcoatl identification, by Muñoz Camargo and others, imagined the Other in the role of a supplement. I use the term in a Derridian sense[21] to mean an addition which, rather than evoking (Spanish-style) separations between a We and a They, completed the signification of the Nahuas' otherwise incomplete image of their corporate selves by making possible the fulfillment of the prophecy of the Eternal Return.[22] For example, in the well-known apocryphal story of the conquest described by the informants of the missionary-ethnographer Fray Bernardino de Sahaggún, one finds the Nahuas arguing that when Motecuhzoma heard of the arrival of the Spaniards,

> he thought . . . this was Topiltzin Quetzalcoatl who had come . . . For it was in their hearts that he would come . . . to find [his rule]. For [it was said Quetzalcoatl] had travelled [eastward] when he departed [in the ancient part].[23]

Later the text adds that when Motecuhzoma met Cortés he told him:

> O our lord . . . You have come to govern your city of Mexico; . . . which for a moment I have . . . guarded for you. . . . The [past] rulers departed maintaining that you would come to visit your city. . . . And now it has been fulfilled.[24]

These quotes also point to a common characteristic of historical hermeneutics that reaches an unexpected extreme with the Nahuas: no matter how transcendent a natural or social event may be, its interpretation falls within the framework of local knowledge of sociocultural reality.[25] Less epic but more relevant cases of the appearance of the Other, which point to this restricted exegesis and the problems it raised for the natives who sought to maintain a boundary between what was and was not Spanish, are found in the archives of the Mexican Inquisition.

In the 1536 trial record of a popular Nahua prophet and cult leader, Martín Ocelotl, a witness accuses him of having told the following to a group of natives secretly gathered "in a house below the ground":

> "I have had everyone from this region called [together] . . . [to tell them] to hurry up and plant all the fruit trees they can . . . because, due to a lack of water, great hunger will come and the corn will not grow. . . ." . . . And [Martin] also told him to tell his lord that two apostles, with very long teeth and nails, and other frightening insignia, had come down from heaven and that

the friars would become Chichimictli [i.e., *tzitzimime*]. And that from then forward when this witness and those of his town wanted something, that they should go to that [underground] house, *because from there everyone in the region had sprung.*[26]

It is unlikely that we will ever understand the full sense these accusations had for the Nahuas, but the following is evident. Polygenesis must have been a credible belief during the early colonial period, when corporate communities at the *altepetl* (city) or, better, the *calpulli/tecpan* (limited territorial/social unit) level could still have claimed to have local origins. Other Inquisition transcripts second this observation, as can be seen in the example of 1539 when don Andrés, a native leader from Culhuacan, stated that "there is a kind of cave . . . from where his grandparents were born, and that some gods also came out from that cave."[27] The assumption that different peoples had distinct origins would have had the paradoxical effect of oversimplifying the formation of ideas about the Other. For one thing, as in the Cortés-Quetzalcoatl identification or (better) in the case of don Andrés' grandparents, the origins of supernatural entities and humans could be of the same sort. It follows that polygenesis helped to sustain the idea that however alien others may seem, their behavior, appearance, and being should be understood as foreign versions of familiar categories. This mixing of classes of beings was common among the Nahuas, as the widespread belief in nagualism, whereby shamans magically transformed themselves into animals or objects, affirms.[28]

Against this epistemic background the sociopolitical events that followed the appearance of the Europeans could be reconstructed along a historical or cultural continuum that blurred (to us) the historical distinctions between an Indian past and a colonial present. This is evident in the quote above, where, although as a prophet of the collapse of Spanish rule Ocelotl sought to underline the distinctions between the European and indigenous worlds, he nonetheless predicted the transformation of the friars into "Chichimictli," or *tzitzimime,* the precontact demonic creatures who would descend on the earth and devour everyone at the conclusion of the present epoch. This same crossing of cultural/ontological categories (not to be confused with the Spanish identification of the native gods with devils—considered to be different aspects of the same supernatural creatures) took place even where, to a greater degree than with Ocelotl, a very conscious effort was made to avoid doing so.

For instance, as late as 1558 another native cult leader named Juan Teton was recorded by an Indian chronicler, Juan Bautista, to have gone about preaching how necessary it was for the natives to return to the ancient faith. He demanded that they renounce their baptism by washing their heads and announced to them, in the style of his predecessor, that the time to do this was short. For Teton the end of the world was imminent because the "binding of the years," the completion of a fifty-two-year cycle in the precontact calendric chronology, which always threatened the violent expiration of the historical era, coincided precisely with 1558. According to Bautista's *Diario*, the Nahua prophet is said to have done and uttered the following:

Juan Tetón . . . tricked and fooled those of Coahuatépec and . . . Atlapolco, he mocked their baptism. And the way in which [he] tricked . . . them to wash their head was the following. . . .

First he tells . . . those of Coahuatépec: "Listen. . . . Do you know what our grandparents are saying? When it is our binding of years there will be complete darkness, the *tzitzimime* will descend, they will devour us and there will be a transformation. Those who received baptism, . . . who believed in God, will be changed into something else. He who eats the meat of the cow, will turn into that; he who eats pork . . . , will turn into that; he who eats . . . sheep, will turn into that and will go about dressed in their skin; he who eats rooster meat, will turn into that. Everyone, in that which is their food . . . , in the [beasts] they eat, . . . will be transformed, . . . will perish, . . . because their life, . . . their count of years [will end]. . . .

"Look at those from Xalatlauhco . . . who first believed, don Alonso: three capes and three hats their children and the [leaders] had made. All transformed themselves into something else, all went about grazing. They no longer appear in the town where they were, but rather in the plains, in the forests they are on their feet: they are cows.

"Now I have done my duty by you [I count on you]; it will not be long before the marvel takes place: if you do not believe what I tell you, together with them you will be transformed. . . . I will mock you, because you received baptism. [Otherwise,] I will forgive you, so that you will not die. . . . Also there will be hunger: [so] guard your . . . squashes and . . . maize ears. . . .

"When they shout at you in Chapultepec, you will go marching on your belly on the sand; then the Old Woman with hard teeth will see you and with this she will be afraid of you, with this she will not eat you, instead she will leave you. . . . And it will happen that only there the Possessor of the Earth will cause our sustenance to grow. Everywhere [else] in the world everything that is edible will dry up."[29]

Indeed, all the narratives quoted above reflect the Nahua epistemic matrix, where order is conceptualized as the balanced replacement of one thing (be it a ritual, leader, deity, or cosmos) by another in regular rotation.[30] The cultural assumption that order was less the result of an imposition than the product of a taking of turns made it logical to categorize colonial hegemonic moves as being of the same sort as any others previously encountered. On the one hand, this facilitated the Nahuas' efficient reorganization of their local polities along new lines founded on traditional principles.[31] On the other, the rotational ordering scheme left the Nahuas with too little surplus meaning to collectively assess, *from the perspective of the Europeans,* the socio-economic significance of much that took place during the early decades of the colonial period. By being able to account for all things and by expecting power to be shared, they greatly reduced the possibility of making their way around those ideological and colonial strategies of domination founded on clear differences between peoples, practices, and faiths. In effect, these native beliefs generated local truths about the Spaniards that made them and their colonial constructions more familiar and intelligible and less threatening and enigmatic than they should have been, thus depriving the Nahuas of the arms needed to fight successfully for any but the most local forms of hegemony.

First Encounters and the Counternarrative of Continuity

The least self-conscious examples of initial culture-contact narratives can be found in the official documentation of Nahua bureaucratic and judicial life. This corpus, penned by native scribes, is the least mediated record we have of the conflicts and accommodations that occurred during the myriad of mundane exchanges that took place between the Indian and European worlds. In some of the official documents that are narrativized, dramas of everyday life encounters between the two peoples are captured using descriptions of imaginary events couched in traditional rhetoric and resolved by employing the topos of the European-is-indigenous transfiguration. This latter strategy of continuity served some native communities to advance a stated position by delegitimizing the claims put forward as novel by those who wielded (more) power; others, who enjoyed status or wealth, employed this tactic to justify their own claims as logical conclusions that followed from the (newly) established order.[32]

A pertinent example of this last point, which can shed new light on the Spanish image in colonial Nahua thought, is found in a type of land title called *títulos primordiales* ("primordial titles"), used in late seventeenth- and eighteenth-century cases where proper possession was in question. The particular manuscript[33] is part of a set of documents employed by the residents of Santiago Sula ("Zolan," place of the quail), a native community southeast of Mexico City, to challenge the assertions of the owners of a nearby hacienda who sought to expand its boundaries at the expense of the Nahuas. The record only survives in a very Nahuatlized Spanish, and its revealing narrative is rare for being so explicitly un-European. But it is precisely this charged combination—of conflicting linguistic codes struggling to represent a native claim in a native style in an official colonial document—that makes the narrative so exemplary. Indeed, for all its fantastic episodes it is more suggestive of the real life engagement of cross-cultural encounters than the various politically or nationalistically motivated Nahuatl texts that lament, in elevated prose, the conquest of Tenochtitlan and its aftermath.

While these primordial titles were usually fraudulent, the political position maintained by the Nahuas in this text is typical of that found in the genre. The people of Sula are neither overtly nor consciously opposed to the overall colonial administration or the local Spanish secular and religious officials. Instead, the protagonists maintain that the community's peaceful possession of the land is guaranteed to them precisely by the fact that (precontact) initiatives to deprive them of their property had failed when they were undertaken by the Mexica/Tenochca (the so-called "Aztecs" who founded México-Tenochtitlán in the middle of a lake). And, consequently, they rightfully received confirmation of their title from the Spanish officials shortly after the early postconquest surveys of land ownership began.

The relevant part of the story comes after the acts of possession and precedes a description of the border markers. Therefore, it is a bracketed narrative wherein native discourse (though it survives only in an indigenous translation) is permitted full expression, surrounded by the chronicling of Spanish legal rituals on one side, and the exigencies of empirical description on the other. The tale unfolds as follows:

Here will be . . . declared how the Mexica, before they settled the site of Mexico City, came to Sula, [but were] not permitted . . . to [stay]. They were walking along . . . the road with trumpet and banner, and the people of Sula came [out] to meet them so that they would not take away their rule. . . .

Then the one called Aza Persia come shouting saying, "My lords, you here of Sula, let us [stop] here, for we are very tired and have come walking a very long way."

And then Martin Molcatzin, the Zolteuctli ["Quail-lord"], [and] Martin Huitzcol answered and said . . . , ". . . All those who are here are dwellers of this town. . . . so you can go ahead, for you cannot halt here."

These two . . . brothers . . . said, "Lady Ana Garcia, we are from here and we are sons of the ancients; we were born in this valley and our grandfathers and grandmothers are from here; . . . they are those of the ancient time [i.e., pagans]. And you, where do you come from? Perhaps you have been exiled from somewhere. Go on with you, we have our questionnaires. Just go ahead and take the road which begins at our border [short recital of borders and measurements]. . . . And know and understand that it is not far to where you are to go; you come from a lake, and now you are very close to another lake [up] ahead. It could be that there [is] a place for you there. . . . And so have a good trip, you are very close to a town where they might admit you and give you some place."

And when they heard what they told them, they all went away, and Ana Maria [sic] and her daughter called Juana Garcia began to shout, saying, "Señor, señor, you have these lands, señor Zolteuctli, we have heard what you said."

Well, my very beloved sons, I will now tell you and declare that God our lord saw fit to create him whom they call Zolteuctli, who is Martín Molcatzin, who turned himself into a serpent in the manner of a quail. The Mexica, whom they call the people of inside the water, were leaving, and got to the borders of Sula, and just where the border . . . is, they found a very large and frightful serpent in the fashion of a quail . . . , and for this reason they called it Zolcoatl [Quail-serpent], and it was all spread out there and frightful. And the Mexica were greatly taken aback, for never had they seen a serpent like that, so they were very frightened, and they went away and the people of Sula were left very content. Because if the Mexica had stayed, they would have ruled the land which the People of Sula possessed, which their ancestors and grandparents left them and which they are still possessing now.

My beloved sons, what we say here occurred this way, and understand it very well. This Martín Huitzcol wanted to feed them. . . . But the older brother, who is Martín Molcatzin, did not want it to be; if they had fed them there, they would have stayed there and not gone away. God our lord orders everything, and so all the food was left behind.[34]

Without any sense of contradiction, in another part the Sula document describes the arrival of the first Spaniards by noting that

when the señor Marqués brought the Catholic faith, the fathers of the order of . . . St. Francis came carrying a Holy Christ . . . and the Spaniards, those with the white hides and with tubs on their heads, carrying their swords under their armpits, said they were called Spaniards and that they had been given license to establish all the towns formally and [the Sula people] should think what saint they wanted to be their patron, because the Catholic faith was in Mexico City already.[35]

The Indo-Christian order that was established, the only one known to the protagonists, is even more strongly affirmed by being contrasted with the missionary inspired vision of a liminal and chaotic world previously inhabited by the ancestors:

In the old days they did not yet know God, but worshipped whatever they felt like . . . and they went about in the wilds, hiding among the crags and in the grasslands, before they were baptized in the year of 1532.[36]

Before one is tempted to see in this historically precise date the Western use of temporality to emplot the narrative, we must turn to other parts of the text where the Spaniards are said to have entered Sula in 1607 *and* 1609. These are not mere errors; instead, they suggest the extent to which a Christian chronology is not informing the essentially mythical narrative.

Now, what are we to make of all this?

At the most superficial level we note, in keeping with the observations made earlier, that the references to pre- and postcontact elements are so mixed as to suggest that distinctions between things European and things indigenous were neither systematically nor routinely made by Nahuas who grew up generations after the first contact with the Spaniards. This is borne out in the long colonial record, where natives discriminate primarily along local politico-ethnic lines and only very rarely between macrocultural categories like "Spanish" or "Indian." As could be expected, almost everything European tended to lose its pedigree to the extent it became assimilated into native life. Thus, before the Spanish arrived, Mexica ("Aztec") leaders could be imagined as having been named Aza Persia, Ana, María, or Juana García, and Spanish-style written questionnaires could be exhibited in defense of one's claim to peaceful possession.

At a more analytical level, first encounters—with Mexicas, Spaniards, or any outsiders—are not seen as ruptures. Rather, they are special ("sacred") moments charged with precisely the kind of energy that fuses the social whole into a unit by successfully testing its capacity for solidarity, for common identity, and for shared purpose. For instance, the Mexica threat to the cultural integrity of Sula was answered by the fantastic transformation of Zolteuctli (Martín Molcatzin), and with him the whole community, into avatars of Quetzalcoatl, the well-known Plumed Serpent. This communal mustering of magical forces is narrated as a charter myth of evil defeated, trials overcome, and stability established. Thus, the plot is narrativized as an epic, the perfect genre for a founding myth.

It is worth noting that here it is the Indians rather than the intruders, as in the case of Cortés and the Spaniards, who were ironically identified with the deity. This suggests once more that the popular Quetzalcoatl-Cortés tale was less a story of foreigners misidentified than one of foreigners appropriated. In fact, in the context of the whole document this fantastic legend, fuses three temporally distinct first encounters into one redemptive narrative: the meeting with the Mexica, the arrival of the Spaniards, and the confrontation with the hacienda owners. Although each represents a distinct kind of turning point requiring a different response, all are resolved by answering a threatened imposition with an incorporating solution.

First, the Mexica are resisted by being encouraged to settle in the nearby lake or town. That is, they are called on to be neighbors, not intruders. After all, it is not until the Mexica have decided to leave the people of Sula alone that the latter are said to assault them with their frightful transformation. This ambiguity toward the Mexica is reiterated by Martin Huitzcol's invitation to them to share a meal that would seal the Mexicas' right to live as one with the people of Sula. The behavior of the two brothers, then, demonstrates the tension between the desire to include and the need to exclude that characterizes Nahua encounters with other ethnic groups.

Second, the episode of the entrance of Cortés and the friars is recounted as proof of the legitimacy of the protagonists' civic integrity and landholding rights. Therefore, in an ironic reversal, the acceptance by the villagers of the early Spanish claims to authority and the townfolks' willingness to carry out the demands made on them by the Europeans are used in the narrative to show their right to the land, which they assert had always been theirs. In effect, the first Spaniards encountered are described as having come to confirm native ways against future intruders, Spanish or otherwise. Accordingly, the attempt to defeat the hacienda owners makes use of the native recitation of their dual founding myth—pragmatically supplemented by a liberal sprinkling of disjointed allusions to Christian, juridical, and cultural motifs—in order to argue that the *hacendados* belong precisely to the category of intruders already deemed subdued in the past and so noted in the historical record.

Now, although I have claimed that cognate counternarratives of continuity were ultimately a weak defense against Spanish narratives of rupture and imposition, the logic in the Sula case makes us think the Nahuas may have been successful in more instances than most historians believe. Nevertheless, the native assimilation of the colonial European world, even if done selectively so as to better defend themselves against specific acts of aggression, was a dangerous tactic. It was an early form of pluralism, the kind that came easily to polygenists, polytheists, former residents of independent city-states, and those who were quick to find similarities between the ways of strangers and themselves. But most Europeans were not pluralists, and in Sula as elsewhere, other times, other intruders, and other legal demands came until the narrative of inclusion was muted by the rising cry of exclusion. This latter voice became more audible as the demographic collapse of the plague-ridden native communities made space for the growing demands of the colonists. In turn, the Spaniards' resulting successes confirmed in their minds the veracity of the early tales of discovery, conquest, Hispanization, and Christianization. Yet the Nahuas, by incorporating the European world into their own, managed to defend their localized interests to a surprising degree throughout the duration of the colonial period. And one of the central ploys that made this possible was their appropriation of the Other's system of communication through the impressment of alphabetic literacy on behalf of the native communities.

Nahua Words in Foreign Letters

Although the diffusion of European-style literacy in the Americas was meant to facilitate the sociocultural, political, and economic ends of the colonists—a topic I have discussed elsewhere[37]—the Nahuas made much use of the alphabetization of Nahuatl to express their side of colonial discourse. The existence of a writing system before contact and the relative ease with which the Nahuas employed Spanish cultural forms, both to affirm themselves as corporate groups and to accommodate their needs to the changing colonial circumstances, made it possible for them to turn this important tool to their advantage in a relatively short time.

In the Castilians' efforts to bring all of the Iberian Peninsula and the New World under the dominion of the monarchs, one of the most important tactics was to take control of the local languages and to impose their own.[38] However, Spanish language policy in New Spain was always subject to contradictions and dissensions. On the one hand, although they were unsuccessful during most of the colonial era, some officials of the Crown repeatedly attempted to force the inhabitants to speak Spanish. On the other, many of the missionaries who manned the language frontiers sought to protect the natives from secularizing influence and extreme forms of exploitation by isolating them linguistically from the Spaniards. And the settlers, whose primary interest was to wrest a living, especially from the Indians, and who generally made up a minority in the non-urban areas, either learned enough Nahuatl to attend to their affairs or negotiated their contacts through bilingual intermediaries. Furthermore, because the demographic ratios began by overwhelmingly favoring the natives, and a multiplicity of languages confronted the Europeans' limited number of colonial agents, the officials were ultimately forced to establish effective communication primarily by disregarding some languages and teaching a few natives to read and write the one they spoke.

To facilitate the exchange of information, Nahuatl was foisted on a number of native communities throughout Mexico, particularly those who had limited demographic and economic resources, were in possession of marginal lands, or lived a non-sedentary existence. This policy followed a well-established practice of the Mexica ("Aztecs"), who in the course of their own precontact, nation-building efforts forced a number of non-Nahua groups to learn their language. While the transformation of Nahuatl into an official language of colonization (a lingua franca) maximized the political usefulness of the native leaders, the training of a cadre of literate noblemen to mediate between Spanish officials and other native rulers and laborers[39] put in indigenous hands much of the power both to determine how orders would be implemented and to interpret for the colonial officials the ways in which these were carried out. In addition, the introduction of European-style literacy among the Nahuas, while helping the Spanish to establish political control over the newly developed sectors of native colonial leaders and intellectuals, also contributed to the native stockpile of survival mechanisms by adding a key tool with which to advocate for pro-Indian concerns.

Although relatively little is known about everyday language instruction outside the schools for Indians, the colonial records suggest that the missionary grammars and vocabularies were not closely followed by the literate Nahuas, especially the local notaries. The literary or "vehicular" language (more precisely "code") of formal instruction, Christianization, and ritualized communication made use of Classical Nahuatl, which was based on the *pillahtolli,* the elegant, affected speech of the *pipiltin,* or "nobles." However, the notaries used primarily a vernacular Nahuatl that evolved out of the so-called *macehuallahtolli,* or "rustic, common speech," spoken by the *macheualtin* ("commoners"). This straightforward prose, which closely adhered to the everyday language of the people, was used throughout the colonial period for writing testaments and petitions and for recording land, census, and tribute data as well as for keeping municipal council minutes.

The fact that most colonial documents are written in the vernacular points to both the colonists' incomplete control over the development of the literacy they introduced and the failure of the missionary schools either to inculcate fully their version of "correct" Nahuatl or to monopolize the instruction of native literacy. Furthermore, the speed and thoroughness with which the natives appropriated the European form of literacy to serve local political and sociocultural ends, as is evident in the relevant documents we have today,[40] coupled with their general disregard of Classical Nahuatl as the vehicle of communication, even before the native nobility began its precipitous decline in the late sixteenth century, underline the limited capacity missionaries and colonial officials had to monitor the inscription of local bureaucratic and administrative data. Nonetheless, Classical Nahuatl, the language modeled after the one used by those who controlled the ideological machinery of precontact central México and which represented the purest ritual speech of the indigenous secular and religious leaders, functioned within the colony as a critical vehicle for the missionary ethnographies that exposed to the Spaniards the ways of the Nahuas.

However, the vernacular Nahuatl of the notaries enhanced the capacity of the native communities to pursue their independent interests in the new sociopolitical order because it was more intelligible (when read) to more people than was Classical Nahuatl and, consequently, a greater number could participate in the assessment, formation, and censoring of the official writings. Likewise, as a consequence of the relegation of record keeping to notaries whose interests were local and generally in keeping with the needs of the community, the employment of the vernacular both reflected and facilitated censorial maneuvers favorable to the corporate group.

As might be expected, the notaries were ordinarily the only literate Nahuas in the villages and small towns. They worked primarily on the official communications and records of the native rulers, particularly in their capacity as municipal council members. However, they also served the individual legal and bureaucratic needs, very rarely personal ones, of anyone who could pay their fee. The pragmatic texts they wrote in the service of private and official clients facilitated the structural linking of the peripheries to the center, thereby contributing to the adoption by the Nahua communities of Spanish-style bureaucratic processes as a supplement to the traditional administrative practices that had remained in place.[41] These additions made it easier for the indigenous leaders to manipulate Spanish methods of resource and personnel management on behalf of the Nahua community (even if at times their initiatives were detrimental to particular individuals).[42] At the same time, the European procedures contributed to the replacement of various record keeping and administrative practices whose precontact utility was rendered inefficient in the colonial context.[43] Lastly, literacy in the towns promoted the implementation of Spanish-style tactics and documentary forms (e.g., testamentary, juridical, tributary, notarial) that could help protect the integrity of the corporate communities by opening up for their use the colonial institutions able to promote their interests and redress their grievances.[44]

Although the mundane prose of the notaries generally served the everyday needs of the Nahuas better than the trope-laden language of the elite, Classical Nahuatl rhetoric was also manipulated by the literate natives to make their voices heard, to advocate for their constituencies, and to paint a more favorable picture of themselves before their Spanish detractors. The following text, drawn from a lengthy 1560 letter by the native council of Huejotzingo to Philip II and written in Classical Nahuatl, is a superb example of the employment of these self-serving moves within a counternarrative of continuity. Because the authors were cosmopolitan second- and third-generation (bilingual?) leaders in close contact with the Spaniards, their representations are more historically accurate than those found in the previously cited narratives; however, theirs is an equally biased picture of the initial encounters.

> Our lord sovereign . . . with our words we . . . stand before you, we of Huejotzingo who guard for you your city. . . . Very humbly we implore you: Oh unfortunate are we, very great and heavy sadness and affliction lie upon us, nowhere do your pity and compassion extend over us and reach us, we do not deserve, we do not attain your rulership. And all the while since your subjects

the Spaniards arrived among us . . . we have been looking toward you, we have been confidently expecting that sometime your pity would reach us. . . .

Our lord sovereign, before anyone . . . made us acquainted with your fame . . . and before we were taught the glory and name of our Lord God, before the faith reached us, and before we were Christians, when your servants the Spaniards reached us and your captain general don Hemando Cortés arrived, although we were not yet acquainted with the omnipotent, very compassionate holy Trinity, our Lord God the ruler of heaven and possessor of earth . . . enlightened us so that we took you as our king to belong to you and become your people and your subjects; not a single town surpassed us here in New Spain in that first and earliest. . . . We gave ourselves to you. . . . No one intimidated us, no one forced us into it, but truly God caused us to . . . gladly receive the newly arrived Spaniards. . . . We . . . embraced them, we saluted them with many tears, though we were not acquainted with them, and our fathers and grandfathers also did not now them. . . . Since they are our neighbours, therefore we loved them; nowhere did we attack them. Truly we fed them and served them. . . . Although the people who are called and named Tlaxcalans indeed helped, yet we strongly pressed them to give aid, and we admonished them not to make war; but though we so admonished them, they made war and fought for fifteen days.

And when they began their conquest . . . we helped not only in warfare, but also we gave them everything they needed. . . . And when they conquered the Mexica and all belonging to them, we never abandoned them or left them behind in it. And when they went to conquer Michoacan, Jalisco and Colhuacan, and . . . Pànuco . . . Oaxaca and Tehuantepec and Guatemala, [we were] the only ones who went along. . . . We did our duty very well. But as to those Tlaxcalans, several of their nobles were hanged for making war poorly; in many places they ran away, and often did badly in war.

Our lord sovereign, we also . . . declare before you that [when] your fathers the twelve sons of St. Francis reached us . . . they came to teach us the . . . holy Catholic faith and belief. . . . We gladly received them. When they entered the city of Huejotzingo, of our own free will we honored them. . . . When they embraced us so that we would abandon the wicked belief in many gods, we forthwith voluntarily left it; likewise they did us the good deed [of telling us] to destroy and burn the stones and wood that we worshipped as gods, and we did it; very willingly we destroyed, demolished, and burned the temples. Also when they gave us the holy gospel . . . with very good will and desire we received and grasped it. . . . No one forced us. . . . No one . . . was ever tortured or burned for this, as was done on every hand here in New Spain. [The people of] many towns were forced and tortured, were hanged or burned because they did not want to leave idolatry, and unwillingly they received the gospel and faith. Especially, those Tlaxcalans pushed out and rejected the fathers, and would not receive the faith, for many of the high nobles were burned, and some hanged, for combating the advocacy and service of our Lord

God. But we of Huejotzingo . . . always we served you. . . . Therefore now, in and through God, may you hear these our words so that you will take pity on us . . . and aid us in [this trouble] with which daily we weep and are sad. We are afflicted and . . . your . . . city of Huejotzingo is as if it is about to disappear and be destroyed. Here is what is being done to us: now your stewards and royal officials and the prosecuting attorney Dr. Maldonado are assessing us a very great tribute. . . . The tribute we are to give is 14,800 pesos in money, and also all the bushels of maize.

Our lord sovereign, never has such happened to us in all the time since . . . the Spaniards came to us, for your servant don Hernando Cortés . . . in all the time he lived here with us, always greatly cherished us and kept us happy; he never disturbed nor agitated us. Although we gave him tribute, he assigned it to us only with moderation; even though we gave him gold, it was only very little; no matter how much, no matter in what way, or if not very pure, he just received it gladly . . . because it was evident to him and he understood well how very greatly we served and aided him. Also he told us many times that he would speak in our favor before you. . . . But perhaps before you he forgot us. . . . Therefore now we place ourselves before you. . . . [W]hen Licentiate Salmerón came to us . . . he saw how troubled the town was with our tribute in gold . . . [and] set our tribute in money at 2,050 pesos. . . . We never neglected it. . . . But now we are . . . very afraid and we ask, have we done something wrong, have we somehow behaved badly or ill toward you . . . or committed some sin against almighty God? Perhaps you have heard something of our wickedness and for that reason now this very great tribute has fallen upon us, seven times exceeding all we had paid before."[45]

In keeping with (a far less transparent version of) my thesis, the image of the Other in the thought of these official Nahua leaders cannot escape being assimilated into their local historical project. Although the commonly heard assertion of loyal cooperation with the contact-period conquerors and missionaries is obviously a calculated response by Nahuas who are fully conscious of their dependent status, a cunning manipulation of ideology and rhetoric permits them to translate their discourse of subordination into a historically grounded claim not only to relief but to specific rights. Thus, the Christian discourse preached by the friars and the political one taught by the Spanish military and Crown officials are appropriated and reencoded to fit within the registers that affirm local sovereignty and promote the favorable accommodation of local socio-economic interests with those of the colony.

These same discursive maneuvers can be found in the work of those indigenous scribes who worked under Sahagún or the other missionary-ethnographers.[46] While ostensibly (and perhaps genuinely) in the service of Christianity, they made possible the inscription of Nahua histories, myths, legends, didactic dialogues (huehuehtlahtolli), and poetry, along with many of the unacceptable precontact practices and beliefs. In doing so they guaranteed their survival despite the break in the collective memory precipitated by the arrival of the Spaniards.[47] And while the ethnographic works of the missionaries may not have contributed as much to the dissemination of the ancient customs as some priests and colonial officials thought,[48] their mention by the priests during confessional interrogations[49] or in the course of their preaching[50] and proselytizing[51] helped to keep before the Nahua listeners a list of cultural and sociopolitical options that differed from or directly opposed Spanish polity and Christian ideology. These counternarratives embedded in the religious literature were complemented by the Nahuatl and Spanish texts that resulted from the early ethnographic efforts, like the *Historia de los Mexicanos por sus pinturas* and the *Histoire du Mechique*[52] or the *Anales de Cuauhtitlan* and the *Leyenda de los soles.*[53] These were further supplemented by the histories, chronicles, poetry, and mythical tales inscribed by the few literate Nahuas writing independently of the missionaries.[54] These authors were not only capable of appropriating the voice of the others for their own purposes, but, as we have seen, also their words.

Alphabetization had other significant political effects stemming from the breakdown of the precontact Nahua writing system. As a complex form of writing composed of a combination of ideograms, pictograms, (a few) syllabic glyphs, color codes, and the symbolic use of pictorial space and image orientation, literacy in this register required that the narratives associated with the pictorial books, whose hieroglyphs served as mnemonic devices, be taught in the schools or the urban centers or handed down across the generations and social sectors via groups of ritual specialists and creative artists.[55] However, with the independence of writing from orality made possible by alphabetization, the link between literacy and the authority of the traditional native leaders (the keepers of the correct "reading" of the hieroglyphs) was weakened, and both missionaries and newly emergent local leaders quickly rushed into the space created by this rupture. Thus alphabetization helped to replace the authority of the traditional native priests and teachers by that of the generally pro-Indianist missionaries and the newly formed native *cabildos,* or "town councils."

In addition, although the standardization of the language imposed a canon that sought to delegitimize regional dialects, the dialectical variability of the extant documents suggests this effort had limited effect. Indeed, while the attempt to homogenize the population contributed to colonial control by promoting the breakdown of regional differences (linguistic, cultural, and social), these managed to continue well into the colonial period due to the surviving forms of ethnic regionalism and local autonomy and the failure on the part of Spaniards to impose a pan-Indian consciousness. In fact, the centralizing forces of colonial organization were met quite ably by the fragmenting influences of provincial Spanish and Nahua leaders, both of whom sought to put obstacles before those who wished to allocate labor and resources independently of local concerns. Their efforts made proselytization, acculturation, and control more difficult for the government officials and the missionaries. And while the implanting of linguistic uniformity slowed the creation of parochial indigenous writings that reflected local speech patterns, interests, and demands, these are nonetheless evident in the testamentary, juridical, and administrative records penned by native notaries.

Lastly, along with assimilating otherness as a standard sociocultural practice, the Nahuas were frequently accused by the missionaries[56] of deliberately constituting themselves as the Other of the Spaniards by magical and linguistic maneuvers aimed at distancing the effects of the Europeans and thwarting their intentions. For instance, it was well known in the sixteenth and seventeenth centuries that Nahuas who engaged in the prohibited religious, curing, and divinatory practices shared an esoteric language, *nahuallahtolli,* that was ostensively used to communicate with supernatural beings. The opaqueness of this language had at least three practical functions, all of which contributed to the local community's cultural and social integrity. First, it constituted a magical discourse whose power and danger were controlled by using complex tropes to confine its circulation so that witchcraft and unintended effects could be minimized. Second, the restrictions placed on the communication of this discourse contributed to maintaining the boundary between the professionals who used it and the uninitiated who were the recipients of its effects. Thus, like the jargons of professionals anywhere, which by restricting the dissemination and intelligibility of a code keep the initiated in power and in possession of prestige or wealth, *nahuallahtolli* and cognate discourses helped to keep the native specialists employed and the social and ethnic boundaries firm. Third, the tropological richness of this cabalistic language served as a discursive form of resistance to the advances of colonial and Christianizing forces. As was well known by local priests, it made possible a secret communication system whose proper use distinguished the conspirators who employed it from the collaborators who denounced it.

In effect, there were many reasons for the Nahuas to conspire with the missionaries in promoting the latter's claim that only the indigenous could understand the occult code. Sahagún summarized the situation best when he stated:

> Our adversary the Devil . . . planted in this land a forest or mountainous thicket full of scrubby undergrowth in order to perform his business from it

and to hide in it as the wild beasts do. . . . This forest or thicket are the chants that in this land he plotted to have sung in his service . . . without their being able to be understood except by those . . . who are native and fluent in the language.[57]

If only natives could know what natives said, Nahuas could maintain in their power the keys to the Spanish translation of their language, customs, and intentions. This technique of control contributed to their marginalization and fit well within the Spanish imaging of the Nahuas as the Other, but it also made space for the Nahuas to give indigenous solutions to their colonial conditions. By way of conclusion I suggest that, with the appropriation of the European Other, as expressed in their counternarrative of continuity, and the appropriation of the voice of the Other, the Nahuas accommodated and affirmed themselves in dangerous but functional ways. Had there been no plagues followed by widespread depopulation, these tactics may have permitted them to survive into the twentieth century as a dominant bilingual and bicultural community. Still, disease took its toll, and in the end colonial practices of exclusion won out over a strategy of incorporation.

Notes

1. I first discussed some of the ideas explored in this essay in "Language, Politics, and Translation: Colonial Discourse and Classical Nahuatl in New Spain," in *The Art of Translation: Voices from the Field,* ed. Rosanna Warren (Boston: Northeastern University Press, 1989); and "El discurso nahua y la apropiación de lo europeo," in *Imágenes interétnicas en el Nuevo Mundo: Intepretationes contemporáneas,* ed. Manuel Gutiérrez Estévez, J. Jorge Klor de Alva et al. (Madrid: Ediciones Siglo XXI, 1992).

2. See, for example, Johannes Fabian, *Language and Colonial Power: The Appropriation of Swahili in the Former Belgian Congo, 1880–1938* (New York: Cambridge University Press, 1986).

3. Vicente L. Rafael, *Contracting Colonialism: Translation and Christian Conversion in Tagalog Society Under Early Spanish Rule* (Ithaca, N.Y.: Cornell University Press, 1988).

4. See Antonello Gerbi, *La naturaleza de las Indias Nuevas: De Cristóbal Colón a Gonzalo Fernández de Oviedo* (Mexico: Fondo de Cultura Economica, 1978).

5. See, for example, Hernán Cortés, *Cartas y documentos,* intro. Mario Hernandez Sánchez-Barba (Mexico: Editorial Porrúa, 1963), 3–328.

6. Bernadino de Sahagún, *Florentine Codex: General History of the Things of New Spain,* trans. and ed. Arthur J.O. Anderson and Charles E. Dibble, 12 vols. (Santa Fe and Salt Lake City: School of American Research and the University of Utah, 1950–1982), introductory volume, 74–76.

7. See, for example, Diego Durán *Historia de las Indias de Nueva España e Islas de la Tierra Firme,* ed. Angel Marie Garibay K., 2 vols. (Mexico: Porrua Hnos., 1967), 237.

8. See Louise M. Burkhart, *The Slippery Earth: Nahua-Christian Moral Dialogue in Sixteenth-Century Mexico* (Tucson: University of Arizona Press, 1989).

9. See, for example, Alfredo Lopez Austin, *Cuerpo humano e ideologia: Las concepciones de los antiguos nahuas,* 2 vols. (Mexico: Instituo de Investigaciones Antropológicas, Universidad Nacional Autonoma de México [UNAM], 1980); Hernando Ruiz de Alarcón, *Aztec Sorcerers in Seventeenth-Century Mexico: The Treatise on Superstitions by Hernando Ruiz de Alarcón,* ed. and trans. Michael D. Coe and Gordon Whittaker, Monograph Series 7 (Albany and Austin: Institute for Mesoamerican Studies [SUNY-Albany] and University of Texas, 1982); and Burkhart, *The Slippery Earth.*

10. See Frances Karttunen and James Lockhart, eds. and trans., *The Art of Nahuatl Speech: The Bancroft Dialogues,* Nahuatl Studies Series 2 (Los Angeles: UCLA Latin American Center Publications, 1987); and Juan Baptista, *Libro de los huehuehtlahtolli: testimonios de la antigua palabra,* ed. Miguel León-Portilla and trans. Librado Silva Galeana, facsimile of 1600 original (Mexico: Comisión Nacional Conmemorativa del V Centenario del Encuentro de los Dos Mundos, 1988).

11. Bartholome de Alva, *Confessionario mayor y menor en lengua mexicana* (Mexico: Francisco Salbago, 1634), 11v–12v.

12. Gerónimo de Mendieta, *Historia eclesiástica indiana,* ed. Joaquín García Icazbalceta, 2d ed. (Mexico: Editorial Porrúa, 1971), 99, 513.

13. Juan Baptista, *Advertencias para los confessores de los naturales* (Mexico: M. Ocharte, 1600), 54v.

14. J. Jorge Klor de Alva, ed. and trans., "The Aztec-Spanish Dialogues of 1524," *Alcheringa: Ethnopoetics* 4 (1980): 52–193 (transcription and trans. into English of the Nahuatl text of Sahagún's *Colloquios y doctrina christiana* [1564]).

15. Diego Muñoz Camargo, *Historia de Tlaxcala,* ed. Alfredo Chavero, facsimile of 1892 original (Guadalajara, Jalisco: Edmundo Aviña Levy, 1972), 174–175.

16. Sahagún, *Florentine Codex.*

17. Diego Muñoz Camargo, *Historia de Tlaxcala,* ed. Alfredo Chavero, facsimile of 1892 original (Guadalajara, Jalisco: Edmundo Aviña Levy, 1972), 174–175.

18. See John Leddy Phelan, *The Millennial Kingdom of the Franciscans in the New World,* 2d ed. (Berkeley and Los Angeles: University of California Press, 1970).

19. See, for example, Angel Ma. Garibay K., ed., *Teogonía e historia de los mexicanos: Tres opúsculos del siglo XVI,* 2d ed. (Mexico: Editorial Porrúa, 1973) (includes the *Histoire du Mechique*); and *Codice Chimalpopoca, Anales de Cuauhtitlan,* and *Leyenda de los soles,* trans. Primo Feliciano Velázquez (Mexico: Instituto de Investigaciones Históricas, UNAM, 1975).

20. See Alfredo López Austin, *Hombre-dios: Religión y política en el mundo náhuatl* (Mexico: Instituto de Investigaciones Históricas, UNAM, 1973).

21. Jacques Derrida, *Of Grammatology,* trans. Gayatri Chakravorty Spivak (Baltimore, Md.: Johns Hopkins University Press, 1976), 141–164.

22. Mircea Eliade, *Patterns in Comparative Religion* (New York: New American Library, 1974), 388–408.

23. Sahagún, *Florentine Codex* IX:9.

24. Sahagún, *Florentine Codex* IX:44; 1980: Klor de Alva, ed., "The Aztec-Spanish Dialogues," 58–59; and Miguel León-Portilla, "Quetzalcóatl-Cortés en la conquista de México," *Historia Mexicana* 24 (1974): 13–35.

25. On "local knowledge," see Clifford Geertz, *Local Knowledge: Further Essays in Interpretive Anthropology* (New York: Basic Books, 1983).

26. AGN, Inquisición, tomo 38, expediente 4 (my emphasis); see also Luis González Obregón, ed., *Procesos de indios idólatras y hechiceros* (Mexico: Publicaciones

del Archivo General de la Nación, 1912), 20; and J. Jorge Klor de Alva, "Martín Ocelotl: Clandestine Cult Leader," in *Struggle and Survival in Colonial America,* ed. David G. Sweet and Gary B. Nash (Berkeley and Los Angeles: University of California Press, 1981).

27. AGN, Inquisición, tomo 42, expediente 18; and González Obregón, ed., *Procesos de indios idolatras y hechiceros,* 181.

28. See Hernando Ruiz de Alarcón, *Aztec Sorcerers in Seventeenth-Century Mexico: The Treatise on Superstitions by Hernando Ruiz de Alarcón.*

29. Juan Bautista, *Diario,* ms in Archivo Capitular de la Basílica de Guadalupe, Colección Boturini (relevant text in Spanish in Miguel León-Portilla,"Testimonios nahuas sobre la conquista espiritual," *Estudios de Cultura Náhuatl* 11 [1945]: 155−169).

30. Alfredo López Austin, *Cuerpo humano e ideología: Las concepciones de los antigous nahuas,* 2 vols. (Mexico: Instituo de Investigaciones Antropologicas, UNAM, 1980), 55−98, 285−318.

31. See Charles Gibson, *The Aztecs Under Spanish Rule: A History of the Indians of the Valley of Mexico, 1519−1810* (Stanford, Calif.: Stanford University Press, 1964), 166−193; and James Lockhart, Frances Berdan, and Arthur J.O. Anderson, eds. and trans., *The Tlaxcalan Actas: A Compendium of Records of the Cabildo of Tlaxcala (1545−1627)* (Salt Lake City: University of Utah Press, 1986).

32. See Woodrow Borah, *Justice by Insurance: The General Indian Court of Colonial Mexico and the Legal Aides of the Half-Real* (Berkeley and Los Angeles: University of California Press, 1983).

33. The Sula document is found in the Tierras section of the Archivo General de la Nación in Mexico City.

34. James Lockhart, "Views of Corporate Self and History in Some Valleys of Mexico Towns: Late Seventeenth and Eighteenth Centuries," in *The Inca and Aztec States, 1400−1800: Anthropology and History,* ed. George A. Collier, Renato I. Rosaldo, and John D. Wirth (New York: Academic Press, 1982), 379−380.

35. Lockhart, "Views of Corporate Self and History in Some Valleys of Mexico Towns," 388.

36. Lockhart, "Views of Corporate Self," 382.

37. J. Jorge Klor de Alva, "Language, Politics, and Translation: Colonial Discourse and Classical Nahuatl in New Spain," in *Reincarnations: Lectures on Literary Translation,* ed. Rosanna Warren (Boston: Northeastern University Press, 1989).

38. See Lewis Hanke, *Aristotle and the American Indians: A Study in Race Prejudice in the Modern World* (Bloomington: Indiana University Press, 1970), 127 n 31.

39. See, for example, Arthur J.O. Anderson, Frances Berdan, and James Lockhart, eds. and trans., *Beyond the Codices: the Nahua View of Colonial Mexico,* Latin American Studies Series 27 (Berkeley and Los Angeles: University of California Press, 1976), 126−129.

40. See, for example, Anderson et al., *Beyond the Codices;* Karttunen and Lockhart, *The Art of Nahuatl Speech: The Bancroft Dialogues;* S. L. Cline and Miguel León-Portilla, *The Testaments of Culhuacan* (Los Angeles: UCLA Latin American Center, 1984); and Lockhart et al., *The Tlaxcalan Actas.*

41. See Lockhart et al., *The Tlaxcalan Actas,* 73−75; Gibson, *The Aztecs Under Spanish Rule,* 166−193; and Lockhart and Schwartz, *Early Latin America: A History of Colonial Spanish America and Brazil* (New York: Cambridge University Press, 1983), 113−116.

42. See, for example, Lockhart et al., *The Tlaxcalan Actas*, 72–73.
43. See, for example, Lockhart et al., *The Tlaxcalan Actas*, 75–77.
44. See, for example, Borah, *Justice by Insurance*.
45. Anderson et al., *Beyond the Codices*, 176–191.
46. See Georges Baudot, *Utopía e historia en México: Los primeros cronistas de la civilización mexicana (1520–1569)*, trans. Vicente González Loscertales (Madrid: Espasa-Calpe, 1983).
47. See, for example, Sahagún, *Florentine Codex;* and J. Jorge Klor de Alva et al., *The Work of Bernardino de Sahagún: Pioneer Ethnographer of Sixteenth-Century Aztec Mexico*, Studies on Culture and Society, Vol. 2 (Albany and Austin: Institute for Mesoamerican Studies [SUNY-Albany] and University of Texas, 1988).
48. See Luis Nicolau d'Olwer, *Fray Bernardino de Sahagún (1499–1590)*, trans. Mauricio J. Mixco (Salt Lake City: University of Utah Press, 1987), 78–86.
49. See, for example, Alonso de Molina, *Confesionario mayor en la lengua mexicana y castellana*, facsimile of 1569 original, ed. Roberto Moreno de los Arcos, Facsímiles de Lingüística y Filología Nahuas 3 (Mexico: UNAM, 1984).
50. See, for example, Bernardino de Sahagún, *Sermonario (Síguense unos sermones . . .)*, Ayer ms 1485 (Chicago: The Newberry Library, 1563).
51. *Doctrina cristiana, Doctrina cristiana en lengua española y mexicana por los religiosos de la orden de Santo Domingo*, facsimile of 1548 edition (Madrid: Ediciones Cultura Hispánica, 1944); and Sahagún, *Colloquios y doctrina christiana*. See Klor de Alva, ed., "The Aztec-Spanish Dialogues."
52. Garibay, *Teogonia e historia de los mexicanos*.
53. *Códice Chimalpopoca, Anales de Cuauhtitlán,* and *Leyenda de los soles.*
54. See, for example, Juan Bautista, *Diario*, ms in Archivo Capitular de la Basilica de Guadalupe, Colección Boturini, no date (relevant text in Spanish in Miguel León-Portilla, "Testimonios nahuas sobre la conquista espiritual," *Estudios de Cultura Náhuatl* 11 [1945]: 11–36); Domingo Chimalpahin Cuauhtlehuanitzin, *Sixième et Septième Relations (1258–1612)*, ed. and trans. Rémi Siméon (Paris: Maisonneuve et Ch. Leclerc ed., 1889); John Bierhorst, *Cantares Mexicanos: Songs of the Aztecs* (Stanford, Calif.: Stanford University Press, 1985).
55. See Alfredo Lopez Austin, ed. and trans., *Educación mexica: Antología de documentos sahaguntinos* (Mexico: Instituto de Investigaciones Antropológicas, UNAM, 1985); Miguel León-Portilla, *Los antiguos mexicanos a través de sus crónicas y cantares* (Mexico: Fondo de Cultura Económica, 1961).
56. See, for example, Diego Duran, *Book of the Gods and Rites and The Ancient Calendar*, trans. and ed. Fernando Horcasitas and Doris Heyden (Norman: University of Oklahoma Press, 1971), 299–300.
57. Sahagún, *Florentine Codex* II:172–173.

Part 4

Appropriation
in Popular Culture

Nell Jessup Newton

Memory and Misrepresentation: Representing Crazy Horse in Tribal Court

This essay focuses on a grievance widely shared by many Indian people in the United States, the commercial appropriation of Indian names, images, stories, and religious practices, and patterns. Seth Big Crow has invoked the Rosebud Sioux Tribal legal process to oppose one such practice, the marketing of a malt liquor named after his grandfather Tasunke Witko, or Crazy Horse. This lawsuit has multiple goals beyond winning the case. Seth Big Crow, acting as the representative of the family of Tasunke Witko, and his activist attorneys have deliberately constructed the legal case as part of a multiple strategy: as a vehicle to engender cohesion and community pride; to educate and to build opposition to the marketing of the malt liquor among Lakota people; as part of a broader effort to gain greater legitimacy for tribal courts within as well as outside tribes, in part by encouraging the use of tribal customary law in tribal courts; and to strengthen tribal court systems as centers of resistance to the jurispathic influence of state and federal laws.[1] More generally, this case is part of a multivocal, multi-local, struggle of Indian people in the late twentieth century to destabilize the stereotypes that make up the dominant society's image of Indianness and replace these historical, timeless, static, passive, decontextualized images[2] with the complex, multi-layered, multi-purposive, individual and collective identities shaped by internal and external forces, including law, claimed by Indian people and tribes in the late twentieth century.[3]

In re Tasunke Witko is unique among these efforts because it takes place within a tribal court, which will have the opportunity to characterize the legal issues and articulate a legal framework appropriate for their resolution, rather than in a state or federal court responsive to the values of the dominant culture. Whether or not the suit is ultimately successful, the case presents an opportunity to shift Tasunke Witko and the Sioux tribes from the background, as colorful relics of the old West, to the foreground, as separate, sovereign peoples with complex identities. If the Rosebud Sioux Tribal Court asserts jurisdiction over the non-Indian defendants, the entrepreneurs will be forced to defend their practices not only in the discourse of the dominant society, but also in the legal and moral discourse of the Rosebud Sioux Tribe and its related tribes, the Cheyenne River Sioux Tribe, and the Oglala Sioux Tribe, all with historic ties to Tasunke Witko.

To place this case study in its greater context, I will begin by presenting some of the arguments made by Indian people opposing the marketing of "Indianness," and then the justifications for the practices made by appropriators and those who support them. The rhetoric of each side demonstrates that each has very different visions of the place of American Indians in modern life. I then turn to the case study, beginning with the dispute phase. Identities are a major focus of the lawsuit: in the struggle over the meaning of the name Crazy Horse, and, more important, the interpretive community that has the strongest claim to be heard about the meaning, both sides make claims based on who they are as well as what Crazy Horse represents to various audiences, necessitating an examination of the parties who have come together in tribal court. Telling these stories and reporting on efforts to invoke federal and state laws to stop the marketing of Crazy Horse Malt Liquor provide an opportunity to consider the role of law in nourishing and countering the strong beliefs of each side. Since most Americans, including attorneys, are not familiar with tribal courts, I then digress to develop the tribal court context by introducing the tribal court system and the interplay between the federal legal system and tribal court systems in structuring choices of permissible defendants, available courts, and the law to be applied.[4] I then return to the case to focus on the litigation phase. Many of the appropriators' justifications are based on expectations nourished by American law that may (but do not necessarily) diverge from expectations grounded in tribal law. In the complaint filed in tribal court, Seth Big Crow and his attorneys sought to meld American and tribal law in ways that respected each. In the final section, I will report on the present status of the tribal court case and reflect on some of the intended and unintended consequences that may result from either success or failure of this legal strategy, to provide a basis to begin to think about the utility of using tribal court systems as part of the effort to contest the representation of tribes and tribal people by the dominant culture.

Marketing Native Images

Images of Indians have advertised and identified products and services too numerous to mention,[5] while demeaning images of African-Americans, Asian-Americans, and Mexican-Americans have largely disappeared from the commercial landscape, demonstrating the growing political and market power of these groups. Derogatory names such as Injun, Braves, Red Man, Squaw, and Redskins are used to sell everything from corn chips to football. Sports teams parade caricatured Indian mascots, such as Chief Wahoo (Cleveland Indians) or Illiniwek (Fighting Illini of Illinois).[6] Fans become "cultural cross-dressers," in the words of Michael Haney, a member of the Seminole Nation of Oklahoma, decked out in Day-Glo warpaint and turkey feathers.[7] The practices are so ingrained that Native people are met with public indifference when they complain about the most offensive examples of what Ted Jojola has called "image injustice."[8]

But Indian people are not only subject to degrading images that would be unacceptable if applied to other minority groups; their cultural and religious symbols and names are also mined by commerce for images to evoke emotions that will sell products and services. Purveyors of New Age religions,[9] non-Indian writers masquerading as Indian authors of "authentic" Indian books,[10] and filmmakers,[11] like sellers of automobiles and trucks, clothing, food, tools, and alcoholic beverages, have discovered that Indians are good business. In addition to generic racialized terms, such as "Indian," and familiar tribal names (Cherokee, Navajo), marketers have also adopted names of historical Indian people, including Crazy Horse, Geronimo, and Pontiac.

Native Objections

Native Americans object to having their images and symbols treated as goods lying about in the public domain ready to the hand of any entrepreneur with something to sell. They complain about this commodification in a number of public venues—letters to the editor, op/ed pieces, statements to reporters, demonstrations at the site of sports events, such as the opening of the new stadium in Cleveland in the fall of 1994, testimony to Congress, state legislatures, and in state administrative hearings, in panels at conferences, and even appeals on the Internet. These complaints express independent but related perceptions of the effect of these practices. They argue that the practice is dehumanizing. For example, Oren Lyons, the Haudenosaunee faithkeeper, noted: "Army had a mule, Navy had a goat, Georgia had a bulldog and Syracuse had an Indian"[12] They reject claims that these uses honor Indians: "Such honoring relegates Indians to the long-ago and thus makes them magically disappear from public consciousness and conscience," according to Michael Dorris, the Modoc writer.[13] Michael Haney complains: "I know they [Euro-Americans] are slow learners, but 500 years is an awful long time to understand that we are humans and that we have feelings."[14] Lynda Clause, a Native American writing in the *Cleveland Plain Dealer*, notes: "[I]f people can respect and accept my feelings on this so-called petty issue, that would let me know they accept me as a person, an equal. Then maybe we can work together to combat these other pressing issues and get things accomplished."[15] Suzann Shown Harjo, a native activist and plaintiff in a case challenging the right of the Washington football team to use the name "Redskins," states: "[W]e are not in the present tense or the future tense in the minds of the general population. If we were, policy would be better crafted for people who are not simply anomalies in the modern era."[16] She has also objected to being stereotyped: "[A] stereotype, whether it is the drunk in the gutter stereotype, which is inaccurate and undesirable, or a stereotype about bravery and nobility, which is unattainable for many people, is not useful."[17]

Some tribal people cast their objections in terms of erosion of scarce resources. Tribal people have already lost much land and natural resources; consequently their good names, their history, and cultural practices are all the more important to people who have so little. Tim Giago, the editor in chief of *Indian Country Today*, a national native newspaper, expresses the sense of loss when images and names are taken from tribal people: "You will see everything Indians hold sacred insulted. . . . The turkey feathers protruding from [sports fans'] heads insult another spiritual practice of most Plains Indians. The eagle feather is sacred. It is given to the recipient in a religious ceremony, usually to honor, to thank, or to bless."[18]

By using language describing these practices as dehumanizing, historical, decontextualized, essentializing, and appealing to the rights rhetoric of property rights, native peoples seek to articulate their felt sense of injustice in ways that members of the majority can understand. Native Americans and non-Indian supporters have also appealed to the empathic imagination of ordinarily nonreflective people by comparing the use of Native American names and symbols to similar uses of names and symbols demeaning to other racial groups,[19] as a way of asking, "How would you feel if this could be done to your people?" Such appeals have had some success in affecting the use of names and mascots by sports organizations, as measured by the college sports teams that have changed their names, colleges that have decided not to play teams with offensive names, and the news organizations that have adopted the policy not to use offensive team names.[20] Nevertheless, very little progress has been made in the effort to prevent the commercial use of Indian names.[21]

Appropriators' Justifications

Native Americans' protests against the appropriation of names and images are often met with indifference at best or lectures about Indians' overreacting. "And then you have Ph.D.'s telling you that it is harmless," complains Michael Haney.[22] Justifications often invoke the innocence of the appropriator and shift the blame by counterattacking those who complain. As an example of the innocence argument, an often-repeated justification dismisses felt insults based solely on the intent of the speaker. Since the speaker did not intend an insult, he must thereby be free from criticism. Another frequent invocation of innocence is the cynical argument that uses of Indian names and images are merely attempts to honor native peoples. Even the owners of the Washington football team maintain with a straight face that the term Redskins is also honorific, "represent[ing] the finest things in Indian culture."[23] The passage of time is frequently invoked: although the usage may have been offensive when it began, it is too late to do anything about the problem today. Objectors are portrayed as leading the populace down a slippery slope. Suzann Harjo has reported being asked if Indians can force Cleveland to stop using the name Indians, whether the next thing will be that the Society for the Preservation of the Bengal Tigers will demand the end of the name Bengals for the Cincinnati team. Harjo's characteristically pithy response was: "I thought, well, this is kind of a single species issue. That illustrated, to me, the problem is that we are still not considered human in the eyes of a whole lot of people."[24]

Counterattacks are also deployed with some effect. Tribal people are admonished to "get a life," and devote their time and efforts to far less trivial concerns.[25] Arguments are also directed at the lack of authority of those who speak out to truly represent the needs of tribal people, labeling them as publicity-hungry elites out of touch with real Indians. Presented as evidence of this fact is that the speaker has talked to Indians who do not see the problem. Certainly such people do exist. Recognizing the incredible difficulties inherent in the attempt to convey concerns of people as heterogeneous as native people,[26] one can still ask why the appropriators and those speaking for them can better represent native people's concerns than the so-called native elites as well as why the adducing of some contrary points of view must totally undercut the arguments of those who take offense. As Lynda Clause asked: "Why must my ethnic group be the only race of people required to agree on everything?"[27]

Another frequent, and related, counterattack is a table turning mechanism I call dueling essentialism. The appropriators accuse tribal people of presenting their own history as a collection of positive stereotypes, as if no other culture has ever presented itself in a favorable light. They follow this accusation with an exegesis on the "true" story, equally essentialized and romanticized in terms that preserve the appropriator's imagined past and present purposes.

The legal culture nourishes the appropriators' sense of these images, providing a rich source of metaphors associated with property rights and possessive individualism. The argument is frequently made, for example, that as the "creator" of property, the appropriator must be permitted to reap the fruits of his labor. The right to free speech provides a powerful talisman against infringements on commercial free speech rights. The First Amendment is also invoked as justifying the belittling of native complaints as "political correctness," a tactic often used against minority groups complaining about "words that wound."[28] The legal and political culture's recent discovery of the evils of "group rights," exemplified by the affirmative action debate, invokes the dangers of tribalism to privilege the autonomous rights holder over the claims of collectivities.[29] In short, liberal theory valorizes autonomous persons exercising the free will to choose from an array of possibilities unconstrained by the state, unless overriding state interests require limitation of individual choice. Tribal rights and complaints do not fit neatly into this framework, as the case study shows.

The Original Crazy Horse Malt Liquor

Malt liquor has a higher alcohol content than beer; so-called "up-strength" malt liquors have a still higher alcohol content.[30] "The Original Crazy Horse Malt Liquor," introduced in 1992, is 5.9 percent alcohol, high even for up-strength malt liquors. Although Tasunke Witko denounced the introduction of alcohol to Indian people and never permitted his image to be photographed or represented in any media, the forty-fluid-ounce whisky style bottle depicts an Indian chief in war bonnet and various Indian and pseudo-Indian designs, such as a medicine wheel. Styling the product as "handcrafted malt liquor," the label represents the importance of Crazy Horse in the following copy:

> The Black Hills of Dakota steeped in the History of the American West, home of Proud Indian Nations a land where imagination conjures up images of Blue Clad Pony Soldiers and magnificent Native American warriors. A land still rutted with wagon tracks of intrepid pioneers. A land where wailful winds whisper of Sitting Bull, Crazy Horse and Custer. A land of character, of bravery, of tradition. A land that truly speaks of the spirit that is America.

In an op/ed criticizing the introduction of the malt liquor, Michael Dorris asked, "Were these the same blue-clad lads who perpetrated the 1890 massacre of 200 captured, freezing Dakota at Wounded Knee?"[31]

Dorris described Crazy Horse as "a patriot . . . a mystic and a religious leader,"[32] and noted that Crazy Horse was murdered by pony soldiers after he gave himself up voluntarily at Fort Robinson, Nebraska. The company marketing the malt liquor has provided a counter-history, featuring a warrior named Curley who adopted a colorful nickname. The quite different meanings the parties attach to the name Crazy Horse are influenced by who they are as well as the cultures from which they come. Tasunke Witko is part of Lakota consciousness, and invocations of his name and story are part of the ongoing process of identity formation by Lakota people. The marketers of the malt liquor raise identity issues as well, about Crazy Horse as a historical person and about their own status as second-generation Italian-Americans fulfilling the American dream. A press release prepared by a beverage consultant puts the problem quite well. It is subtitled "Whose Attitudes Count?" If the legal system is going to privilege one group's attitudes, then it becomes necessary to examine the real people involved in the controversy.

The Dispute Arises

The introduction of "The Original Crazy Horse Malt Liquor" sparked a nationwide protest including op/ed articles, calls for boycotts, Tribal Council resolutions, and various other efforts to gain publicity about the importance of Crazy Horse's name to Indian people. President Bush's Surgeon General, Antonia Novello, and the Pine Ridge Tribe's Executive Director, Michael Her Many Horses, were among many who urged Congress to take action. These efforts resulted in federal legislation and state legislative and administrative decisions barring the use of Crazy Horse's name as a brand name for malt liquor.[33] Ferolito, Vultaggio, and Sons, the makers of the malt liquor, mounted a successful challenge to the federal law on the grounds the law violated free speech.[34] The same issue has also been raised in state administrative hearings regarding malt liquor labeling.

People on the Sioux reservations followed these developments with great interest. Relatives of Tasunke Witko live on the Pine Ridge, Cheyenne River, and Rosebud Reservations as well as in the large Rapid City, South Dakota, off-reservation Indian community.[35] One such relative is Seth Big Crow, a man who has spent fourteen years working in the tribal court system at Rosebud as a civil court lay advocate. Mr. Big Crow's office was next to the office of the tribe's public defender, Robert Gough, who had recently graduated from the University of Minnesota Law School and returned to the Rosebud

Sioux Reservation. Trained originally as a cultural anthropologist, Mr. Gough had worked on the Rosebud Reservation before law school as an archivist and anthropologist for the tribe, in the process becoming acquainted with many of the families on the reservation.[36] One of Gough's particular interests was tribal customary law. During his first year working for the tribe, he tried to raise grant money to work on a project considering how to incorporate customary law into tribal code provisions, frequently consulting with Leslie Fool Bull, a recognized authority on tribal customary law.

Although Gough and Big Crow had offices next to each other and became friends, Gough knew nothing about Big Crow's family history, because Big Crow, along with the other relatives of Crazy Horse, had been raised in a tradition of silence that prevented any discussion of the family's relationships to Tasunke Witko. Crazy Horse himself was believed to have instituted this silence, telling his relatives that they must never speak about their relationship to him. The two men often discussed the malt liquor after it was introduced in 1992, however. When the federal law was published in the local newspaper, Big Crow asked Gough whether he thought the producers of the product would respect the federal law. Gough expressed concern that the law was vulnerable to a constitutional free speech claim. At this point Big Crow revealed to an astonished Gough that he was a grandson in Crazy Horse's *tiyospaye*. Family members had met and decided that Big Crow should make the contact, perhaps because he had experience in the tribal court system.[37] In an interview in 1994, Big Crow explained why he decided to break his promise after forty-two years:

"I'd been listening to people seated right next to me saying: 'Where are Crazy Horse's descendants? Why won't they stand up for him?' And I couldn't acknowledge who I really was. Finally, after efforts by others failed, I knew I had to stand up."[38]

Once the silence was broken, Big Crow asked Gough to help plan a strategy for legal action against the marketers of the malt liquor. Gough, who had recently taken the bar examination, found himself puzzling over the problem in the way a law student might tackle a moot court problem, mentally reviewing the legal categories that might apply. He discovered a case in which Martin Luther King's estate had gone to court to prevent an unauthorized use of his name after death and thought that some of the principles in this case might translate into the tribal court context.[39] Gough and Big Crow decided to consider having the family seek a remedy on behalf of Crazy Horse's estate. A remedy for the estate would permit a request for injunctive relief to go forward immediately; moreover, if money damages were sought, the award would become part of the estate corpus. Consequently, difficult questions regarding how to distribute any potential compensation could thus be postponed until necessary.

Big Crow and Gough met with family members on the Rosebud Reservation and explained that if the estate brought a lawsuit, only an administrator would have to be named. That person alone would suffer the burden of the resulting publicity and the need to justify his relationship to the defendants and the public. Ann Fool Bull, the oldest member of the family (and the wife of Leslie Fool Bull, mentioned above), gave her permission at the meeting and authorized Mr. Big Crow to represent the estate, by filing a probate petition in Rosebud Sioux Tribal Court.

Representing a group that has a tradition of keeping membership silent poses problems for even the most experienced attorney. Big Crow talked to family members on Pine Ridge and Cheyenne River, but many people have not been forthcoming about their relationship. To Gough, it seemed that the more closely someone is related to Crazy Horse, the less likely that person is to make claims or talk about it. Big Crow put a notice in the Lakota Times, a widely read national Indian newspaper, and both Gough and Big Crow cooperated with reporters writing stories about the upcoming hearing in the Times and in local papers. Although the Pine Ridge Council objected to appointment of Mr. Big Crow as the sole administrator,[40] family members from Pine Ridge and Rosebud who attended the hearing did not object to the appointment; family members at Cheyenne River did not attend, but had communicated with Big Crow (the Cheyenne River Sioux Tribe has subsequently entered the case as an amicus).

Gough enlisted the help of two law school friends, Jonny Bearcub Stiffarm, an Assiniboine Sioux from the Fort Peck Reservation in Montana who is now serving as a senior court management consultant with the National Center for State Courts in Denver, Colorado, and Stuart Kaler, now practicing intellectual property law at Morrison, Foerster, in San Francisco, California. The three had become friends during law school, often studying together. Stiffarm and Gough frequently talked about the importance of tribal courts, and the role of both customary and common law in tribal court adjudication. In particular, the study partners discussed methods by which the mainstream courts could be induced to recognize tribal customary and common law as legitimate sources of law. The three co-counsels have a contigent fee arrangement with Big Crow and will thus be paid, if at all, out of any money damages or settlement. Mr. Big Crow has contributed to expenses of the lawsuit; family members have had fund-raising taco sales as well.[41] The attorneys and their client often share hotel rooms and in other ways pool their time and effort to work on the case within a shoestring budget.

Gough and Big Crow, joined at times by the other two attorneys, have held meetings at Rosebud, Pine Ridge, Cheyenne River, and in the off-reservation Indian community in Rapid City, South Dakota. These meetings have served both to ensure continuing support for the legal case, by informing interested tribal members about the progress in the case, and to persuade tribal members of the importance of taking a stand on the larger issue of commodification of tribal traditions. At a meeting attended by Jonny Bearcub Stiffarm, for example, Bob Gough brought examples of the malt liquor, but also labels and examples of other products. The attorneys told those attending about the strategy for the case, explained why the case was being brought on behalf of the estate, fielded questions, and asked for guidance.

These meetings have had an important educational mission as well, in building community consensus against the marketing of the malt liquor. According to Ms. Stiffarm, there were invariably two responses to the malt liquor bottle: the first, usually by younger Native Americans, was "That's cool." The second, primarily from those who were older, was an expression of pain. Gough reported that many of the older people would not touch the bottle when it circulated through the room. Making room for the groups to react to each other, Gough and Stiffarm would then relate the marketing strategy behind the malt liquor and discuss its high alcohol content, explaining that one bottle has as much alcohol as a six-pack of beer. During the lively group discussions that followed, the group that had initially responded favorably to the malt liquor joined the rest in making suggestions, including the names of persons who could be expert witnesses and family members and others who could be helpful in the social context as well as in the legal arena.[42]

During this period of community education, the attorneys began to fashion a lawsuit to be brought in tribal court. Gough had telephoned the firms producing and distributing the product after the federal law had been enacted to ask whether they planned to honor the law. He received in return a press package presenting the marketers' opposition to any changes in their business practices. The attorneys had also sent formal letters on behalf of the family asking the firms to stop distributing the product. After Mr. Big Crow was appointed administrator in April 1993, the attorneys and Big Crow filed the lawsuit against the Heileman Brewing Company, the Hornell Brewing Co., and Ferolito, Vultaggio, and Sons, the entities responsible for Crazy Horse malt liquor.

Since the litigation is a contest over identity, it is necessary to examine the identity claimed by the defendants and revealed in the public record. Dominic Ferolito and John Vultaggio, two self-styled "beer guys" from Brooklyn, are described in a press release as "second-generation Italian-Americans from Brooklyn; natives who had never travelled into America's heartland" before conceiving of an idea to market beer and soda as part of a " 'Family of American Originals' beverages, each package with a Golden American West motif."[43] Originally beer truck drivers in Brooklyn, the two men began to market their own products, which they sold to retailers by renting a limousine and visiting liquor store retailers night after night. They now co-own the Hornell Brewing Co., and have produced at least two beers, Midnight Dragon and the Original Crazy Horse Malt Liquor. In a 1992 memorandum Hornell's lobbyist described the business: "Their fledgling small business is their only way of finding a release from the confines of driving beer trucks on Brooklyn streets for the rest of their lives and achieving their vision of a better, more independent and secure life."[44]

The public record paints a somewhat different picture of the two partners, however, revealing that the appropriate context for the Crazy Horse malt liquor is not the American West theme mentioned in the press releases, but the much criticized practice of target marketing of malt liquors to African-American and Hispanic men, the groups which purchase nearly all the malt liquor produced in the United States.[45] Target marketing deliberately employs package designs, images, and phrases the advertisers believe will appeal to racial minorities by playing into "fantasies of potency and conquest."[46] These ads promise increased sexual success[47] and a powerful, even drug-like high.[48] The partners and the G. Heileman Beer Co., which is licensed to brew the beer (the partners merely design and market the products), have specialized in this practice. For example, Heileman created the short-lived "PowerMaster," a potent malt liquor marketed in inner-city black neighborhoods which caused a public outcry, threatened boycotts in six states, and a refusal by the Bureau of Alcohol, Tobacco, and Firearms (BATF) to permit the company to use the name.[49]

Ferolito and Vultaggio created their business by target marketing their malt liquors.[50] They also have a record of deliberately seeking controversy to increase sales. In 1986, the partners introduced their first malt liquor, Midnight Dragon,[51] another up-strength malt liquor produced by Heileman, which was advertised by a sexy woman model dressed all in red sipping the beverage through a straw and stating: "I could suck on this all night." The partners apparently relished this controversy. When women's groups complained, Ferolito was quoted by the *Wall Street Journal* in 1989 as saying: "Women don't drink malt liquor, so I came out with a poster to appeal to blue-collar, macho, chauvinistic men. Real men like sex and sex sells beer. I'm not interested in wimps and achievers who want to suck on a lime and drink Corona."[52] The ad campaign was subsequently suspended, however.[53] Their second product was originally to be named "Black Sunday." The proposed label for Black Sunday contained many of the motifs later incorporated in the Crazy Horse malt liquor label. Similar phrases on the front of the label are "The Original Black Sunday," "Dakota Hills Ltd.," "Handcrafted Malt Liquor," and "Forty Ounces." The back label depicts an Indian male with a headdress and contains the copy regarding the Black Hills of South Dakota quoted at the beginning of this essay, with the same references to Sitting Bull, Crazy Horse, and Custer. Although the partners denied the name Black Sunday had anything to do with target marketing to African-Americans, the news reports of the time drew that conclusion and, no doubt, contributed to the decision to withdraw the Black Sunday label and substitute "The Original Crazy Horse Malt Liquor."[54]

During the national campaign against their new product, the firm availed itself of all the justifications mentioned above. Their CEO suggested the protesters "get a life." At different times, the marketers maintained both that the name was deliberately chosen as a tribute[55] to Crazy Horse, and that the name was chosen without any knowledge of his place in history.[56] They even argued that they felt compelled to use the name to avoid offending Native Americans: "Well, if you celebrated the great American West and if you did not include Indians in that West, you most certainly would be slandering Indians, from that perspective."[57] In a particularly innovative use of dueling essentialism, they have downplayed Tasunke Witko's place in history: "The acceptance of Crazy Horse's role, whatever his role may have been, among Native Americans, was not, and is not, universal."[58] In their counterhistory Crazy Horse was an ordinary guy named Curley who became a brilliant warrior: "Although he was religious, in that he was devout, he was not a spiritual leader in the Pope Paul or Martin Luther King concept."[59]

As have others who have profited by using Indian names, symbols, and images, Ferolito and Vultaggio have argued they have proprietary and property rights in the names as well as rights to commercial speech protected by the First Amendment. Their company has applied for a trademark in the name Crazy Horse used in connection with a malt liquor. Although the standard statement is that trademarks do not create property rights,[60] they certainly create proprietary rights protecting holders' rights to use the name.[61] In August 1995, the patent and trademark examiner refused to grant the trademark, however, on the ground that it violates § 2(a) of the Federal Trademark Act (the Lanham Act), which bars trademarks that are "immoral . . . or scandalous matter; or matter which may disparage . . . persons, living or dead, institutions, beliefs, or national symbols, or bring them into contempt or disrepute."[62] (This provision has also been invoked to seek the cancellation of the trademark of the Washington football team.) Ferolito, Vultaggio, and Sons can be expected to challenge the trademark office's ruling on First Amendment grounds. As noted above, a federal court invalidated the federal law barring the use of the name Crazy Horse on liquor products. A generally worded law like the Trademark Act provision might well pass the heightened First Amendment scrutiny the federal courts apply to protect commercial free speech, for example.[63] But tribal courts are not required to give the same weight to commercial free speech as does the Supreme Court, or so it has been argued.

Indian Tribal Courts

Tribal courts originated as social control mechanisms imposed by the BIA to force tribal people to assimilate as part of the policy of detribalization of the late nineteenth and early twentieth centuries. During this period all branches of the federal government and the public at large united to rend Indians from their tribes and the cultures that elevated the tribe above the individual.[64] The creation of Indian courts was an important part of this detribalization policy. Forced allotment in severalty of tribal land was designed to strike at what was perceived as the heart of native cultural beliefs, that property is held in common. Forcing tribal people to become individual property owners would, it was thought, lead inevitably to the development of respect for property rights, which would in turn influence tribal people to embrace individual rights instead of communal values.[65] Education of children was also seen as a sure way to create a generation of assimilated Indians. At first, Congress entrusted various Christian denominations with control over education on specific reservations; conversion of Indian children to Christianity was seen as a first step to assimilation.[66] Toward the end of the nineteenth century, Indian boarding schools were preferred. Youngsters would be taken by force, if necessary, and sent away to schools, such as the Carlisle Indian School in Pennsylvania, founded in 1879, whose headmaster, Richard Pratt, promised to "kill the Indian in him, and save the man."[67]

It is in this context that one must place the creation of an Indian police force in 1878 and the Courts of Indian Offenses in 1883. The police and courts were creatures of the Interior Department employed for the task of assimilation. Offenses covered included participating in dances or feasts; entering into plural or polygamous marriages; engaging in practices of medicine men; destroying property of other Indians; engaging in immorality; intoxication; and misdemeanors as defined by the state or territory within which the reservation was located. A further offense of slacking off or simple vagrancy was added in 1892.[68] The Indian agents selected judges who would be suitable agents of this process; i.e., the more assimilated or "better" Indians on the reservation who were willing to adopt Euro-American practices such as cutting their hair, wearing western attire, practicing monogamy, and taking land allotments in individual ownership.[69] In 1888, a district judge described these courts in a famous phrase: "[T]he reservation itself is in the nature of a school, and the Indians are gathered there, under the charge of an agent, for the purpose of acquiring the habits, ideas, and aspirations which distinguish the civilized from the uncivilized man."[70]

Despite the immense pressures of the detribalization movement, Indian tribes continued to exist and maintain many traditional practices, including methods of dispute resolution. Federal policymakers began to back away from forced assimilation. The Indian Reorganization Act of 1934 (IRA)[71] reversed the assimilation policy by permitting tribes to organize modern governments, including courts.[72] At the beginning IRA governments were still very much under the thumb of the Bureau of Indian Affairs, which initially drafted "boilerplate" constitutions and codes for the tribes, usually requiring the approval of the Secretary of the Interior for any changes.[73] Not all tribes organized under the IRA; moreover, tribes that did organize often continued to operate traditional mechanisms of dispute resolution alongside the newer court systems. Some tribes, most notably the traditional Pueblos, do not have judicial dispute mechanisms; disputes are settled by the Governor and the Council.[74] The confluence of many forces has contributed to the current flowering of tribal institutions. The pan-Indian movement;[75] the struggles of other racial minorities in changing the boundaries of the acceptable; the increasing number of Native-American attorneys;[76] and the critical legal jurisprudence which has questioned the givens of Federal Indian law have encouraged tribal people to turn to their own court systems for resolution of disputes. As a result, many tribal courts have become vibrant institutions representing changing community values and brokering relationships among tribal communities and between tribes and outsiders. What is most notable about tribes as well as tribal courts is their incredible heterogeneity after centuries of attempts to first make them all become like "us," and second to flatten all tribes and tribal people into a homogeneous other.

To the extent that tribal courts apply tribal norms that do not deviate too much from the dominant legal system's norms, they are left alone and even protected. In recent years, they have flourished. Tribal courts have begun to exercise authority over non-Indians as well. Although criminal jurisdiction over non-Indians has been denied tribes since 1978,[77] the Supreme Court has recognized that tribal courts retain a measure of authority in civil cases.[78] To synthesize some complex rules of Indian law, a non-Indian defendant wishing to challenge the tribal court's jurisdiction must first bring this challenge in tribal court, including the tribe's appellate system. Only after the tribal case has been completed, the non-Indian may challenge the tribe's authority in federal court.[79] Even at this point, the federal court may not retry the case on the merits, but can only take up the issue of the tribe's authority over the person of the defendant or over the particular kind of lawsuit.[80]

Tribal Law

Tribal court systems are complex and multi-layered, combining Euro-American and traditional elements.[81] Using procedures more informal than adversarial, tribal courts have begun to tackle difficult questions of civil and political law in addition to ordinary misdemeanors and small civil disputes. Frank Pommersheim has described the evolution of tribal courts and the methods by which tribal courts creatively work to establish legitimacy in the eyes of tribal people as well as those outside the tribe, from non-Indian defendants, to the federal courts, and ultimately the general public.[82] As in all court systems, tribal judges must first apply the law of the tribe. Nevertheless, the BIA-drafted codes of many tribes instructed tribal judges to apply federal and state law to fill the many gaps in the early codes. Many tribal codes still permit reference to state laws, but only as persuasive authority. Nevertheless, tribal judges who need law to apply will often apply state law without questioning whether that law is suitable for the tribal context or resonates with tribal values. A Supreme Court jurisprudence that pushes tribal courts toward conformity with the U.S. legal system is certainly one cause of this cautiousness.[83] Lack of resources may be the main cause of overuse of state law, however. Courts are underfunded and operate without the aid of staff and law clerks, or libraries that hold anything more than a tribal code and state reports.

Recently tribal courts have begun to apply customary law that deviates in important respects from the patterns in American legal culture. Where authorized by tribal law, judges have also begun making common law responsive to tribal needs, instead of resorting to *Restatements* or other sources of common law applied in the states. This exciting development in tribal courts has been well-documented.[84] The Rosebud Sioux Tribal Code encourages innovation by instructing courts to apply United States law when that law is mandatory, then the tribe's constitution, its statutory law, and traditional laws. If none of these laws provides an answer, the judge is instructed to apply the law of any other tribe, and finally, the law of any other state.[85] Tribal courts applying tribal customary and common law courts can become loci for strategies of resistance and redefinition, giving voice and effect to tribal traditions in cases involving non-Indians who violate tribal norms.

Civil Rights in Tribal Courts

There are limits on tribal courts' ability to apply tribal law, however. As noted above, non-Indian defendants can challenge tribal court authority in federal court after the tribal court process has come to an end. In addition, tribal courts must apply relevant federal law. Although the Bill of Rights and the Fourteenth Amendment of the U.S. Constitution do not apply to tribal actions, the Indian Civil Rights Act of 1968[86] (ICRA) imposes upon tribes some of the constitutional guarantees of the federal Bill of Rights.[87] Nevertheless, the ICRA was tailored to preserve tribal cultural differences. For example, the ICRA does not contain an establishment clause out of deference to tribal religious differences; it also provides for a right to an attorney, but not one appointed by the tribe. I have argued that the ICRA's language and legislative history and the sovereign status of tribes permit tribes some leeway in interpreting the majestic generalities of constitutional phrases used in the ICRA, like due process, in culturally appropriate ways. But this is only as long as tribal court interpretations of these statutory phrases do not differ so radically from their constitutional counterparts as to undercut what the Supreme Court may label the core meaning of these phrases. In other words, respect for free speech need not compel a tribal court to grant heightened judicial scrutiny to commercial speech, or buy into every category in a category-laden (and extremely manipulatable) jurisprudence.[88] A tribal court might well conclude, for example, that commercial speech, which the courts have only recently moved from the nonspeech to the speech category, need not be weighed more heavily than "words that wound."[89] "Due process" is a similarly freighted concept. A tribe need not comply with every jot and tittle of the Supreme Court's interpretation of the Constitution's guarantee of fair procedures in criminal or civil trials. As long as the judges and prosecutors, themselves often not attorneys, conduct proceedings in accordance with tribal law and with norms of fundamental fairness developed and developing in international human rights law, in a manner respecting the dignity of the people within the court, the procedures should satisfy the ICRA's guarantee of due process. This point has been recognized by the Supreme Court of the Oglala Sioux Tribe in a recent case:

> It should not have to be for the Congress of the United States . . . to tell us when to give due process. Due process is a concept that has always been with us [and] means nothing more than being fair and honest in our dealings with each other.[90]

As noted above, Seth Big Crow, Robert Gough, and Jonny Bearcub Stiff-arm were quite familiar with tribal courts: Gough and Stiffarm had discussed their shared belief that tribal advocates and judges should consult customary law in tribal court cases; they had also debated the wisdom of encouraging judges to treat custom as not static but changing, in the way of common law adjudication. Gough had worked on the tribal customary law project with Leslie Fool Bull; Seth Big Crow had spent fourteen years as a lay advocate in the tribal courts. They were thus well aware of the lack of resources and the constant threat of federal intervention endemic to tribal court litigation; nevertheless they concluded that the tribal court system is the appropriate interpretive community to assess the importance of Tasunke Witko to those who live on the various Sioux reservations today and the availability of his image and memory as articles of commerce. They thus decided to fashion a lawsuit to be brought in tribal court invoking elements of tribal custom and Euro-American values. By so doing, they are urging the tribal court to give credence to present-day tribal values as they must develop to meet changing circumstances.

The Litigation

The attorneys and Big Crow began to work together to fashion legal claims that would resonate with the dominant society's vision of law and yet be consistent with the traditions of Lakota people. Gough had combed through federal[91] and state law, rounding up the usual suspects of tort and property claims. The problem of Crazy Horse Malt Liquor did not fit neatly within any of these existing categories. For example, tort principles associated with property and proprietary interests, such as unfair competition, dilution, and passing off, focus on protection of entrepreneurial choices by preventing mislabeling and other methods of consumer deception, not the kind of pain expressed by traditional people (recall that some refused to touch the bottle). They thus consulted general tort law principles and chose the label "intentional infliction of mental distress" as a possible claim. Making such a claim would be problematic under Anglo tort law, however, because the damages must be proven with some specificity, courts often require physical injury, and the tort protects individual interests and not group interests.

Gough consulted the Lakota archives at Sinta Gleska University, a tribally operated institution, and talked to members of the Lakota Studies Department at the University. Gough discussed these possibilities with Big Crow and considered which could be adapted for the tribal setting. Two Anglo remedies had seemed particularly promising: defamation and the right of publicity. Defamation actions permit local courts to have jurisdiction over far-away defendants, yet American law does not generally permit an action for defamation of the dead. Although there may be no shared belief about where people go when they die, there seems to be a shared belief in Euro-American culture that nothing that happens afterward will harm any of their interests. As Gough put it: "When you are dead, your feelings can't be hurt and your job possibilities are limited."[92] Yet in Lakota beliefs, spirits are more present: participants appeal to them in ceremonies; care is taken to avoid upsetting them. Thus the decision was made to invoke the generous jurisdictional base of defamation actions and to express the pain suffered by the spirit of Crazy Horse, by making a claim for defamation of the spirit under tribal customary law. This label invokes the concept of defamation, which has resonance because it is a claim traditionally available to individuals harmed by false statements; on the other hand the focus on harm to the spirit signals that this claim is outside Anglo tort law.

The right of publicity protects a person's right to exploit her name for commercial purposes. Whether classified as tort or property, this right protects names, images, and even nicknames of celebrities whether or not they have done any work to create their image and survives the death of the rightholder descending to her estate. A football player nicknamed Crazylegs Hirsch, for example, prevented the use of the name Crazylegs for a hair removal product.[93] To invoke such a legal concept to protect the name of Crazy Horse seems perverse; a man who never permitted his likeness to be made hardly qualifies for *People* magazine. But in one case, the estate of Martin Luther King invoked the publicity right to prevent Dr. King's name from being used for commercial purposes.[94] Names remain very important in Lakota tradition; Crazy Horse's naming story has been recorded,[95] and naming ceremonies are still used. Thus the decision was made to invoke the right of publicity as a way to protect the name from use without the consent of the family. As James Boyle has pointed out, the Anglo legal culture recognizes that some kind of property, including kinds of knowledge like insider information, cannot be sold just as livers, babies, and spleens cannot be sold.[96] Obviously, what kind of property should be taken out of the market is culturally contingent, and the right to publicity claim would permit the tribal court to make this important determination either under the rubric of publicity or under a more accurate name.

Remedies

The request for relief in the petition contains similarly mixed Anglo and traditional remedies. Mr. Big Crow seeks an injunction against the misuse. He also seeks a written public apology from the companies to be published in major papers. Finally, the Estate requests compensation "in a culturally appropriate manner" for damages suffered by the misuse of the Crazy Horse name, including traditional damages of one braid of tobacco, and a racehorse and a four-point Pendleton blanket for each state and month in which products were sold. Having a former tribal archivist as an attorney in the case was quite useful at this point. Gough recalled that when Crow Dog killed Spotted Tail, his family accepted reparations in cash, blankets, and ponies. It was this traditional settlement, designed to restore harmony between the families, that was regarded as so barbarous that Congress enacted a law to make murder of an Indian by an Indian a federal crime punishable in federal court.[97] Tobacco was added at the family's suggestion, because the burning of tobacco is used as an offering to spirits and thus seemed a particularly appropriate way to show respect for Crazy Horse. The estate also requested punitive damages, however, a quintessentially Anglo remedy, but one that has been found to be very effective in shaping behavior.

Tribal Court Decision

The tribal judge, Stanley Whiting, issued an opinion holding that the court had no jurisdiction over the defendants. Jurisdictional issues are issues of sovereignty and thus of power.[98] From the beginning, the attorneys expected the issue of personal jurisdiction, the power to force a defendant to come to a particular court, to be a difficult one. Jurisdiction over the defendant is treated as a question of due process requiring an assessment of the defendant's contacts with the forum, the plaintiff, and the litigation to determine whether it is fair to require her to appear in the plaintiff's chosen court. The Rosebud Sioux Tribal Code permits jurisdiction "to the greatest extent consistent with due process of law," and the tribal court often refers to the Supreme Court's precedents in resolving questions of jurisdiction. The attorneys noted that the tribal court was not required to follow these decisions slavishly, but argued that even if the tribal court did apply Supreme Court precedent, the precedents in defamation cases supported them. In concluding that the defendants' contacts with the reservation community were insufficient, Judge Whiting adopted a fairly strict interpretation of the Supreme Court precedents.[99] The opinion appears to have bought into the defendant's characterization of the case as more like a products liability case, in which a product bought in one state ends up in another and injures a plaintiff. Once the trial judge accepted this framing of the issue, the conclusion must have seemed inevitable, since the defendants deliberately avoided marketing the product in South Dakota. Judge Whiting's decision thus represents a victory for this marketing strategy.

Nevertheless, Judge Whiting did borrow a leaf from Chief Justice John Marshall's book, by expounding on the merits while dismissing the case for lack of jurisdiction. The court stated for the first time that the tribe does recognize the right to publicity. Unfortunately, the court did not address the claims based on traditional Lakota customs and laws, because the court had not afforded the petitioner the opportunity for fact-finding to determine the nature of these beliefs. Mr. Big Crow commented on the opinion by saying: "We have made history. This ruling upholds our traditional right to protect the names of our ancestors. For this we are grateful." The attorneys have appealed Judge Whiting's decision to the Rosebud Sioux Supreme Court. The appeal was argued in April 1996.

Conclusion

The estate is not guaranteed to win the case in tribal court; the jurisdictional issues are difficult, and the Rosebud Sioux courts are well aware of the dangers of federal court interference with tribal court authority in cases involving non-Indians. Having chosen the tribal court system, Seth Big Crow and his attorneys are prepared to accept the decision of this interpretive community, whether the court ultimately agrees or disagrees with them. An interpretive community is not a community which shares a point of view, but a set of assumptions.[100] In other words, in the tribal context different tribal members may disagree about the result in a given case, but their very disagreements will be grounded in shared webs of belief. There are considerable benefits to bringing challenges to commodification of tribal culture in tribal courts whether or not an individual case succeeds. The lawsuit and the community meetings attendant to it have raised a great deal of interest among Lakota people and coalesced community opposition to the misuse of tribal names and symbols. Even if the estate loses the case, the threat of a similar lawsuit may deter other entrepreneurs from treating Indian names and symbols as part of the public domain.

Nevertheless, the drawbacks to the lawsuit are also considerable, even if the estate is successful in tribal court. Native Americans have no reason to be confident that the federal courts (and the Supreme Court in particular) will respect their differences.[101] In the light of this jurisprudence, it may seem foolhardy to expect the federal court system to uphold a decision that could have a major impact off the reservation. Just as the Supreme Court used one case from the Suquamish Indian Tribal Court in the state of Washington to deny all tribes criminal jurisdiction over non-Indians, a decision against the estate in federal court may become a decision against *all* tribal judicial systems. This is a question that the attorneys and their client must consider at every stage of the litigation. The case may also result in a settlement, which will be a victory not requiring the risk posed by federal court intervention. Nevertheless, settlements of group claims pose another set of questions. As the administrator of the estate, Mr. Big Crow will have to make the decision whether to accept any settlement offers. The pressures to accept an offer short of stopping the production of the malt liquor may be intense. Even if the defendants agree to stop production, the acceptance of a money settlement could open Mr. Big Crow to criticism from tribal people and his relations for accepting too much, or too little. Distributing a money judgment or a settlement fund could also pose significant problems. At that time it will become necessary to decide whether to distribute the money to the heirs or use it for some other purpose, such as setting up a community organization. The tribal court will have to determine how such decisions can be made and which claimants are legitimate heirs of Crazy Horse. Attention can be expected to focus on the attorneys' contingency fee arrangement at that time as well. Even though these attorneys have worked closely with the tribal community, they may not escape the kind of anger directed in the past toward attorneys seeking to collect substantial fees. Finally, the impact on Seth Big Crow is incalculable. Having drawn attention to himself in a very public way in order to attempt to end the marketing of the malt liquor, Mr. Big Crow has done something that is counter to the tradition of silence imposed by Crazy Horse as well as the traditional ways of his people. In an interview in the *Boston Globe* he said: "In a spiritual sense, I can never go home again. I'm a changed man."[102]

Using the tribal courts permits actors familiar with the culture a chance to characterize the facts and argue for a legal theory that is culturally appropriate. In these cases, litigants may contest visions and categories of Anglo law and seek innovative remedies. The story *In re Tasunke Witko* is far from over. If the appeal is successful, the case will go to trial on the merits, permitting the attorneys to present the substantial testimony they have gathered regarding Lakota traditions. As mentioned above, it is only after the defendants have exhausted all their remedies in tribal court that they can challenge the jurisdiction of the court in federal district court. If Seth Big Crow is successful in tribal court, the tribal court opinions will then speak to the dominant culture from a position of authority, the principles of Lakota custom and law having been thoroughly debated and defended in the tribal forum.

Notes

This essay is a shortened version of an article in the *University of Connecticut Law Review Symposium on Indian Law Connecticut Law Review* 27 (1995):1003. Many thanks to Rosemary Coombe, Peter Jaszi, Howard DeNike, Robert Gough, Jonny Bearcub Stiffarm, Stuart Kaler, the participants in the Working Conference on Appropriation of Tradition held at American University, especially Philip S. Deloria, Vernon Bellecourt, Suzann Shown Harjo, Michael Haney, Chad Smith, Tad Jojola, Joseph William Singer, and Tom Greaves. Acting Dean Claudio Grossman generously supported the working conference and my research in this project. Versions of this essay have been presented at the Law and Society Association, the American Anthropological Association, and at works-in-progress presentations at Santa Clara University and Hastings College of Law.

1. Robert Cover argued that courts are jurispathic, because they destroy law generated by interpretative communities. Robert Cover, "The Supreme Court, 1982 Term—Foreword: Nomos and Narrative," *Harvard Law Review* 97 (1983): 4, 40. In the sense that tribal customary law is capable of reflecting the law created by the relatively small tribal communities, I believe that tribal courts have more potential to be jurisgenerative than federal and state courts.

2. See Edward W. Said, *Orientalism* (New York: Vintage Books, 1979); and Rosemary J. Coombe, "The Properties of Culture and the Politics of Possessing Identity: Native Claims in the Cultural Appropriation Controversy." *Canadian Journal of Law and Jurisprudence* 6 (1993): 249–285.

3. See Wendy Espeland, "Legally Mediated Identity: The National Environmental Policy Act and the Bureaucratic Construction of Interests," *Law and Society Review* 28 (1994): 1149; and Susan Staiger Gooding, "Place, Race, and Names: Layered Identities in *United States* v. *Oregon,* Confederated Tribes of the Colville Reservation, Plaintiff-Intervenor," *Law and Society Review* 28 (1994): 1181.

4. See Judith Resnik, "Dependent Sovereigns: Indian Tribes, States, and the Federal Courts," *University of Chicago Law Review* 56 (1989): 671 (arguing that federal court jurisprudence should take note of Indian legal questions).

5. Hal Morgan, *Symbols of America* (New York: Viking, 1986).

6. Raymond William Stedman, *Shadows of the Indian* (Norman: University of Oklahoma Press, 1982); Ward Churchill, *Indians Are Us? Culture and Genocide in Native North America* (Toronto: Between the Lines Press, 1994).

7. Michael Haney, "Overview," at the Working Conference on Appropriation of Traditions (American University, Washington College of Law, Washington, D.C., April 15–17, 1994) (transcript of remarks on file with author). Michael Haney has been active in the National Coalition Against Racism in Sports and the Media.

8. Ted Jojola, "Negative Image Exploited to Undercut Indian Self-Government," *Albuquerque Journal,* June 27, 1993, sec. B, Op-Ed page. Dr. Jojola is a member of the Isleta Pueblo, the director of the Native American Studies Program at the University of New Mexico.

9. Lisa Aldred, "The Right to Religious Freedom in Light of the Commodification, Fetishization, and Legal Construction of Native American Spirituality in the Navajo-Hopi Dispute" (unpublished work in progress, presented at the American Anthropological Association annual meeting, 1994) (decrying appropriation of native spirituality by new age religious practitioners over the protests of many Native Americans as reinforcing Anglo rhetoric of individual religious rights and undercutting the Navajo peoples' claims to land based on religious freedom.); Michael F. Brown, "Who Owns What Spirits Share?: Reflections on Commodification and Intellectual Property in New Age America," *POLAR* 17 (1994): 7 (relating disputes among channelers about appropriate invocations of particular "sources," phrased in the language of ownership); Wendy Rose, "The Great Pretenders: Further Reflections on White Shamanism," in *The State of Native America: Genocide, Colonization, and Resistance,* ed. M. Annette Jaimes (Boston: South End Press, 1992), 639 (criticizing the adoption by whites of an Indian shaman's persona in writing poetry and fiction).

10. See, e.g., Coombe, "The Properties of Culture and the Politics of Possessing Identity," 249 (relating the debate over appropriation of voice in Canada).

11. Stedman, *Shadows of the Indian* (collecting stereotypes of Native people from film, cartoons, novels, and popular art).

12. Oren Lyons, discussing his participation in the successful campaign to persuade his *alma mater,* Syracuse University, to change their team name from the Saltine Warriors, reported by Robert Lipsyte, "How Can Jane Fonda Be a Part of the Chop?" *New York Times,* October 18, 1991, B10.

13. Michael Dorris, "Noble Savages? We'll Drink to That," *New York Times,* April 21, 1992, A23, col. 2.

14. Michael Haney, "Overview," in Working Conference on Appropriation of Tradition (American University, Washington College of the Law, Washington, D.C., April 15–17, 1994) (transcript of remarks on file with the author).

15. Lynda Clause, "Not an Honor, but an Insult," *Plain Dealer,* June 20, 1993, C3 (available in LEXIS NEWS library).

16. Suzann Shown Harjo, interviewed by Catherine Crier, *Crier and Company,* CNN Transcript #62, May 27, 1992.

17. Suzann Shown Harjo, ibid., May 27, 1992.

18. Tim Giago, "Drop the Chop! Indian Nicknames Just Aren't Right," *New York Times,* March 13, 1994, § 8, page 9, col. 2.

19. Richard Cohen, "Redskin Reservations," *Washington Post,* April 17, 1988, W7 (imagining teams named after other groups, such as the New York WASPs, the Detroit Ay-rabs, the L.A. Hispanics, the Chicago Blackskins, the Miami Hymies, the Boston Harps, and the Cincinnati Krauts). Honor, a non-Indian organization in Minnesota, has published a very effective cartoon depicting three products side-by-side: Dr. Martin Luther Dark Beer; Rabbi Rabinowitz's Nacho Flavored Pork Rinds, and Crazy Horse Malt Liquor, and asking, "Which one of these is legal to sell?" Although two of the products may in fact be legal to sell, the point of the ad is to raise awareness about the impact of public opinion.

20. See Bruce C. Kelber, " 'Scalping the Redskins': Can Trademark Law Start Athletic Teams Bearing Native American Nicknames and Images on the Road to Racial Reform?" *Hamline Law Review* 17 (1994): 533, 544.

21. The plaintiffs' effort to cancel the trademark of the Washington football organization as scandalous and derogatory has met with success before a patent commissioner, however. If the trademark is canceled, the team will still be able to use it, but not prevent others from using the name. *Harjo v. Pro Football,* 30 U.S.P.Q.2d 1828 (1994) (striking the Washington football organization's affirmative defenses of lack of standing, laches, and estoppel; at trial the challengers need only establish that the term "Redskins" does fit within the statutory wording).

22. Haney, "Overview," 9.

23. John Cooke, vice-president, quoted in Leonard Shapiro, "Offensive Penalty Is Called on "Redskins": Native Americans Protest the Name," *Washington Post,* November 3, 1992, D1. Mr. Cooke lists the best of Indian culture as "bravery, organization, the whole works. The name Redskins means football in Washington."

24. Harjo, CNN transcript, 16.

25. "I would suggest these people need to get a life." Mike Schott, Chief Operating Officer of Ferolito and Vultaggio, quoted in Greg W. Prince, "Tall Order: The Making and Marketing of Arizona Iced Tea," *Beverage World* (June 1994): cover story

(celebrating the business acumen of Ferolito and Vultaggio in a long profile written after the company introduced AriZona Iced Tea).

26. See, e.g., Gayatri Chakravorty Spivak, "Can the Subaltern Speak?" in *Marxism and the Interpretation of Culture*, ed. Cary Nelson and Lawrence Grossberg (Urbana and Chicago: University of Chicago Press, 1988), 271–313.

27. Clause, "Not an Honor, but an Insult," sec. 3C (Ms. Clause described herself as an American Indian citizen of Cleveland).

28. Mari Matsuda et al., *Words That Wound: Critical Race Theory, Assaultive Speech, and the First Amendment* (Boulder, Colo.: Westview Press, 1993); Stanley Fish, *There's No Such Thing as Free Speech, and It's a Good Thing, Too!* (New York: Oxford University Press, 1994).

29. The equal protection clause states a non-subordination principle that has been applied to protect rights of minority groups. See, e.g., Owen Fiss, "Groups and the Equal Protection Clause," *Philosophy and Public Affairs* 5 (1976): 107 (arguing in favor of such a principle). The Rehnquist Court has used equal protection theory to invalidate efforts to benefit minority groups, constructing modern equal protection doctrine as solely aimed at protecting individual rights. See, e.g., *Adarand Constructors, Inc. v. Pena*, 115 S. Ct. 2097, 2112 (1995) (stating "the basic principle that the Fifth and Fourteenth Amendments to the Constitution protect persons not groups" as justification for strict scrutiny of all racial classifications). The term "tribalism" has been invoked frequently by California Governor Pete Wilson to decry the effect of affirmative action policies. See, e.g., John Marelius, "The Fight over Affirmative Action: Wilson Eager to Tackle Issue in the Spotlight," *San Diego Union-Tribune*, July 19, 1995, A1 (quoting the governor as stating, "We must not allow Americans to be infected by the deadly virus of tribalism" in a speech to a group of employers).

30. George Lazarus, "A Ready-to-Brew Malt Controversy," *Chicago Tribune*, November 27, 1991, C2.

31. Dorris, "Noble Savages?"

32. Ibid.

33. Jessica R. Herrera, "Not Even His Name: Is the Denigration of Crazy Horse Custer's Final Revenge?" *Harvard Civil Rights–Civil Liberties Law Review* 29 (1994): 175, 179–180.

34. *Hornell Brewing Co. v. Brady*, 819 F. Supp. 1227, 1236 (E.D.N.Y. 1993) (holding using name is commercial speech and that although purpose of preventing alcohol abuse among Native Americans is sufficiently important, the means used, barring the use of the name on a product, is not directly related as required by the heightened scrutiny applicable to commercial speech).

35. Interview with Robert Gough, attorney for Seth Big Crow, December 1, 1994.

36. Robert Gough, "Presentation," at the Conference on Commercial Appropriation of Tradition (American University, Washington College of Law, Washington, D.C., April 15–17, 1994) (transcript on file with the author.)

37. Interview with Jonny Bearcub Stiffarm, July 20, 1995.

38. Seth Big Crow, quoted in Meg Vaillancourt, "Big Crow's First Stand: Descendant of Crazy Horse Goes Public to Keep Legendary Warrior's Name Off High-Octane Beer," *Boston Globe*, December 4, 1994, Sunday city edition (reporting on the competing claims of Seth Big Crow on behalf of the estate and the attorney for Ferolito and Vultaggio).

39. *Martin Luther King, Jr. Center for Social Change, Inc.* v. *American Heritage Products,* 694 F.2d 674 (11th Cir. 1983) (even though King was a public figure who did not exploit his name for economic purposes during life, Alabama's right to publicity encompasses a protectable interest in the estate to protect his name from such exploitation after death).

40. The court dismissed the Pine Ridge Council's objections on the grounds that only family members could contest the appointment of an administrator. Interview with Robert Gough, attorney for Seth Big Crow, December 1, 1994.

41. Interview with Jonny Bearcub Stiffarm, July 20, 1995.

42. Ibid.

43. Hank Shafran and Mark Rodman, "Backgrounder: Is Socially Acceptable Marketing in America Changing? Products and Marketing Considered Tasteful by Some, Are Decried as Offensive by Others. Whose Attitudes Should Count?" (undated press release on file with the author). Shafran and Rodman are associated with Beverage Distribution Consultants, of Swampscott, Massachusetts. Although Annie Oakley Lite and Jim Bowie Lager have been mentioned as part of the series, I could find no evidence that these products have been introduced.

44. Memorandum to Hon. Frank Wolf from Beverage Distribution Consultants, November 6, 1992, *Re: The Original Crazy Horse Malt Liquor—HR 5488* (memorandum inserted in information packet sent to Robert Gough by the Hornell Brewing Company on file with the author).

45. See, e.g., Alix M. Freedman, "Suggestive Malt-Liquor Ads Stir Critics," *Wall Street Journal,* May 31, 1989, available in Westlaw Database WSJ (noting malt liquor is almost exclusively consumed by men, mostly young blacks and Hispanics); David Inman, "Fighting for Black Dollars and Black Health," *Gannet News Service,* April 1, 1990, available in LEXIS, Nexis Library, Curnws File (quoting Pat Winters, a liquor industry reporter for *Advertising Age* magazine and describing the controversy over target marketing). See also Celeste J. Taylor, "Know When to Say When: An Examination of the Tax Deduction for Alcohol Advertising That Targets Minorities," *Law and Inequality* 12 (1994): 573. Target marketing has been very effective in selling liquor and cigarettes. For a description of R. J. Reynolds's plan to market a cigarette called Dakota targeted toward blue-collar "virile females," see Stuart Elliott and James Cox, "Target Marketers Now a Target," *Gannet News Service,* February 19, 1990, available in LEXIS, Nexis Library, Curnws File.

46. Rupert Cornwell, "Out of the West: Trouble Brews for a Popular Beer," *The Independent,* July 3, 1991, available in LEXIS, Nexis Library, Curnws File.

47. Examples abound, including a Colt 45 series of ads depicting Billy Dee Williams, a handsome African-American actor, using the product to seduce beautiful women. "It works every time" is the tag line for the ad series, promising equal success to purchasers of his product. See also David Inman, "Fighting for Black Dollars and Black Health," *Gannett News Service,* April 1, 1990, available in LEXIS, Nexis Library, Curnws File. An ad depicting Ice Cube, an African-American rap singer, holding a malt liquor and adjuring his audience to "grab a six-pack and get your girl in the mood quicker" is described in Celeste J. Taylor, "Know When to Say When: An Examination of the Tax Deduction for Alcohol Advertising That Targets Minorities," *Law and Inequality* 12 (1994): 573, 583.

48. While the name Olde English 800 does not invoke these images, the company advertised its malt liquor by showing three sexy women around a pool table with the

line "Eight Ball, anyone?" According to the *Wall Street Journal*, the term "eight ball" is street slang for an eighth of an ounce of cocaine. See, Freedman, "Suggestive Malt-Liquor Ads Stir Critics."

49. The BATF has authority to approve liquor labels, but its mandate is limited to jurisdiction over such issues as whether the label is misleading or impermissibly advertises the alcohol content of liquor. The BATF denied approval because the term "power" suggests a high alcohol content. See Bruce Horovitz, "Brewer Faces Boycott over Marketing of Potent Malt Liquor," *Los Angeles Times*, June 25, 1991, D1 (quoting a BATF official).

50. Jon Newberry, "New York Beverage Firm Opens Area Office," *Greater Cincinnati Business Record*, May 30, 1994, vol. 6, no. 47, sec. 1, p. 4 (Midnight Dragon and Crazy Horse malt liquor to "urban blacks and Hispanics."); Greg W. Prince, "The Other Side of Arizona," *Beverage World* (June 1994): 28 (relating Ferolito and Vultaggio's history of using offensive ads).

51. See, e.g., Jon Newberry, "New York Beverage Firm Opens Area Office," *Greater Cincinnati Business Record*, May 30, 1994, available in LEXIS, Nexis Library, Curnws file; Emily DeNitto, "Arizona Iced Tea Is in Steep Ascent," *Advertising Age*, July 4, 1994, 31.

52. John Ferolito, reported in Freedman, "Suggestive Malt-Liquor Ads Stir Critics."

53. See Vincent McCraw, "Black, Latino Health Groups Fight Macho Malt-Liquor Ads," *Washington Times*, August 24, 1989, C10 (reporting that although the Midnight Dragon advertisement did not come within the Bureau of Alcohol, Tobacco, and Firearms' jurisdiction, the ad campaign was suspended after the Bureau wrote the company a letter expressing concern about the ad).

54. See George Lazarus, "A Ready-to-Brew Malt Controversy," *Chicago Tribune*, November 27, 1991, C2 (asserting the African-American market as the largest for malt liquors and speculating that the same Black leaders who had labeled Heileman, the brewer of PowerMaster, socially irresponsible might be expected to do the same if the new brand is perceived in the same way, despite the statement of Hornell that the brew was not targeted at Blacks); Greg W. Prince, "Tall Order: The Making and Marketing of AriZona Iced Tea," *Beverage World* (June 1994), cover story (reporting that Mike Schott, CEO of Ferolito and Vultaggio, asserted the label "got shot down in the post-PowerMaster 'malt-liquor-is-bad' atmosphere of 1991").

55. See Press Release dated May 19, 1992, prepared by Beverage Distribution Consultants on behalf of Hornell Brewing Company (stating, "Hornell never intended to insult or offend Native Americans; in fact, they meant to celebrate a man who has been described as 'the greatest leader of his people in modern times,' a man respected for his leadership, pride, discipline, self reliance and independence").

56. Doug Grow, "Relative of Crazy Horse Questions Brewer's 'Honor,'" *Minneapolis Star Tribune*, April 21, 1995, 3B (noting Mr. Vultaggio admitted in a deposition and testimony in a hearing protesting state ban on malt liquor that he was not aware that Crazy Horse was an honored Dakota chief).

57. Jim Mattox, consultant to Hornel Brewing Company, interviewed by Catherine Crier, *Crier & Company*, CNN Transcript 62 (May 27, 1992).

58. "Backgrounder: Is Socially Acceptable Marketing in America Changing?" (undated press release on file with the author).

59. Memorandum to Senator Alfonse D'Amato, from John Ferolito and Don Vultaggio, dated September 24, 1992 (addendum to Press Release, prepared by Beverage Distribution Consultants, dated September 26, 1992).

60. See Rosemary J. Coombe, "Objects of Property and Subjects of Politics: Intellectual Property Laws and Democratic Dialogue," *Texas Law Review* 69 (1991): 1853.

61. By proprietary rights, I mean the kind of interest recognized in *International News Service* v. *Associated Press Service*, 248 U.S. 215 (1918) (recognizing a "quasi-property" right in intangible business assets; namely, news collected by Associated Press).

62. 15 U.S.C. § 1052(a)(1988). The Trademark Act of 1946, ch. 540, 60 Stat. 427 (codified as amended at 15 U.S.C. §§ 1051–1127 (1988 & Supp. V, 1993), provides for registration of certain kinds of marks, words, or symbols associated with goods, services, or entities, 15 U.S.C. § 1127 (defining trademarks, service marks, and certification marks) and confers advantages on the holder, including access to federal court for enforcement actions. See J. Thomas McCarthy, *Trademarks and Unfair Competition*, 3d ed. (Rochester, N.Y.: Lawyers Co-operative, 1995), §19.05 (listing advantages of registration in principal register over state common law of trademark).

63. Constitutional challenges have been dismissed as not raising free speech issues on the theory that cancellation of a mark, for example, ends protections accorded under federal law but does not prevent use of the mark. See *In re McGinely*, 66. F.2d 481 (C.C.P.A. 1981). For criticisms, see Rosemary J. Coombe, *Object of Property and Subjects of Politics: Intellectual Property Laws and Democratic Dialogue*, 69 *Tex. L. Rev.* 1853, 1873–1877 (1991); Robert C. Denicola, *Trademarks as Speech: Constitutional Implications for the Emerging Rationales for the Protection of Trade Symbols*, *Wis. L. Rev.* 158, 190–206 (1982).

64. Nell Jessup Newton, "Federal Power over Indians: Its Sources, Scope, and Limitations," *University of Pennsylvania Law Review* 132 (1984): 219–222 (describing the cooperation of Congress and the Supreme Court in domesticating Indian law).

65. Frederick E. Hoxie, *A Final Promise: The Campaign to Assimilate the Indians, 1880–1920* (Lincoln: University of Nebraska Press, 1984); Francis Paul Prucha, *The Great Father II* (Lincoln: University of Nebraska Press, 1984), 609–657; Robert F. Berkhofer Jr., *The White Man's Indian: Images of the American Indian from Columbus to the Present* (New York: Knopf, 1978) 166–176.

66. Berkhofer, *The White Man's Indian: Images of the American Indian from Columbus to the Present*, 149–151; William T. Hagan, *American Indians*, 3d. ed. (Chicago: University of Chicago Press, 1993), 139–141.

67. Richard H. Pratt, "The Advantages of Mingling Indians with Whites," extract, *Official Report of the Nineteenth Annual Conference of Charities and Correction*, 1892, excerpted in *Americanizing the American Indians: Writings by the "Friends of the Indian," 1880–1990*, ed. Francis Paul Prucha (Cambridge, Mass.: Harvard University Press, 1973), 260, 261.

68. See Thomas J. Morgan, "Rules for Indian Courts," Report of August 27, 1892, in House Executive Document No. 1, part 5, vol. II, 52 Congress, 2 session, serial 3088, 28–31, excerpted in *Americanizing the American Indians: Writings by the "Friends of the Indian," 1880–1990*, ed. Francis Paul Prucha (Cambridge, Mass.: Harvard University Press, 1973), 300. Although the dances and rites barred were supposedly those that glorified war, in fact, most native religious rites were swept within

the prohibition. See Vine Deloria Jr. and Clifford M. Lytle, *American Indians, American Justice* (Austin: University of Texas Press, 1983), 115 (noting that the ban of rites included banning such peaceful and sacred rites as that of "keeping the soul," a condolence rite).

69. William T. Hagan, *American Indians*, 3d. ed., 155–157.

70. *United States* v. *Clapox*, 35 F. 575, 577 (D.C. Or. 1888).

71. *Reorganization Act of 1934*, ch. 576, 48 Stat. 984, codified as amended at 25 U.S.C. §§ 461–479.

72. Robert N. Clinton, Nell Jessup Newton, and Monroe E. Price, *American Indian Law: Cases and Materials*, 3d ed. (Charlottesville, Va.: Michie Co., 1991), 152–155.

73. Vine Deloria Jr. and Clifford M. Lytle, *American Indians, American Justice* (Austin: University of Texas Press, 1983) 116–119; Frank Pommersheim, *Braid of Feathers: American Indian Law and Contemporary Tribal Life* (Berkeley and Los Angeles: University of California Press, 1995), 64–66.

74. Many of the Pueblos do have court systems, however. See Christine Zuni, "The Southwest Intertribal Court of Appeals," *University of New Mexico Law Review* 24 (1994): 309 (explaining the cooperative intertribal arrangements that sustain the Southwest Intertribal Court of Appeals).

75. See, generally, Stephen Cornell, *The Return of the Native: American Indian Political Resurgence* (New York: Oxford University Press, 1988) (treating the factors culminating in the modern pan-Indian movement in Indian-white relations).

76. Interview with P. S. Deloria, Director, American Indian Law Center, Inc., July 21, 1995 (giving examples of positions held by graduates).

77. *Oliphant* v. *Suquamish Indian Tribe*, 435 U.S. 191, 208 (1978) (holding that the implicit understanding of the three branches of the federal government establishes that tribes' inherent sovereignty does not permit exercise of criminal jurisdiction over non-Indians).

78. *National Farmers Union Ins. Cos.* v. *Crow Tribe*, 471 U.S. 845 (1985); *Mut. Ins. Co.* v. *LaPlante*, 480 U.S. 9 (1987).

79. Pommersheim, *Braid of Feathers*, 81–98; Kevin Gover and Robert Laurence, "Avoiding *Santa Clara Pueblo* v. *Martinez*: The Litigation in Federal Court of Civil Actions Under the Indian Civil Rights Act," *Hamline Law Review* 8 (1985): 497.

80. For a comprehensive treatment of lower court cases applying the exhaustion principle, see Timothy W. Joranko, "Exhaustion of Tribal Remedies in the Lower Courts After National Farmers Union and Iowa Mutual: Toward a Consistent Treatment of Tribal Courts by the Federal Judicial System," *Minnesota Law Review* 78 (1993): 259.

81. Deloria and Lytle, *American Indians, American Justice*, 110–136.

82. Pommersheim, *Braid of Feathers*, 61–79.

83. Robert A. Williams Jr., "The Algebra of Federal Indian Law: The Hard Trail of Decolonizing and Americanizing the White Man's Indian Jurisprudence," *Wisconsin Law Review* (1986): 219.

84. Pommersheim, *Braid of Feathers*, 99–135; Gloria Valencia-Weber, "Tribal Courts: Custom and Innovative Law," *New Mexico Law Review* 24 (1994): 225, 236–244.

85. Rosebud Sioux Tribal Law and Order Code, §4-2-8 (copy in author's possession).

86. 25 U.S.C. §§ 1301–1303.

87. For an excellent history of the legislative process leading to the ICRA, see Donald L. Burnett Jr., "An Historical Analysis of the 1968 'Indian Civil Rights' Act," *Harvard Journal on Legislation* 9 (1972): 557.

88. Stanley Fish, *There's No Such Thing as Free Speech, and It's a Good Thing, Too!* 102–109.

89. Mari Matsuda et al., *Words That Wound: Critical Race Theory, Assaultive Speech, and the First Amendment.*

90. *Bloomberg v. Dreamer,* Oglala Sioux Civ. Ap. 90-348, at 5–6 (1991), quoted in Frank Pommersheim, *Braid of Feathers: American Indian Law and Contemporary Tribal Life* (Berkeley and Los Angeles: University of California Press, 1995), 135.

91. Although the complaint contains several counts based on federal statutory law, this article focuses on the state law–inspired claims as they provide more room for tribal court innovation. One aspect of federal law deserves some reference, however. Since many of these commercial images are trademarks, intellectual property laws, both federal and state, could be invoked to contest some misuses of tribal signs and symbols. A full discussion of trademark law and unfair competition law is beyond the scope of this essay and the skills of its author. But not, fortunately, beyond the skills of J. Thomas McCarthy; see, generally, J. Thomas McCarthy, *Trademarks and Unfair Competition,* 3d ed., vols. 1–5 (1995). Tribes might consider registering symbols, images, and names, or to oppose the granting of trademark status to such names for economic reasons. Because the Lanham Act expresses the values of the dominant culture, which is a culture of consumerism, attempts by Indian nations to fit their concerns into the framework of the Lanham Act require the conscious deployment of legal arguments and strategies that may not only be counterintuitive—an argument that a trademark might cause confusion in purchasers thinking the tribe endorsed a product, when the real issue is the sense of outrage at the use of an tribal name or symbol, for example— or violative of deeply held tribal religious or cultural beliefs—such as revealing tribal secrets to the outside world.

92. Interview with Robert Gough, attorney for Seth Big Crow, December 1, 1994.

93. *Hirsch v. S.C. Johnson and Son, Inc.,* 280 N.W.2d 129 (Wis. 1979).

94. *Luther King, Jr. Center for Social Change, Inc. v. American Heritage Products,* 694 F.2d 674 (11th Cir. 1983).

95. Mari Sandoz, *Crazy Horse: The Strange Man of the Oglalas* (New York: Knopf, 1942), 118.

96. See James Boyle, "A Theory of Law and Information: Copyright, Spleens, Blackmail, and Insider Trading," *California Law Review* 90 (1992): 1413. Boyle argues that a categorical process of characterizing the type of information into public or private creates anomalies which are then resolved by awarding the right to the information to whoever can fulfill the image of the romantic author, creating something of value out of nothing.

97. Robert N. Clinton et al., *American Indian Law,* 3d ed., 148; Deloria and Lytle, *American Indians, American Justice,* 168–170.

98. Judith Resnik, "Dependent Sovereigns: Indian Tribes, States, and the Federal Courts," *University of Chicago Law Review* 56 (1989): 671.

99. *In re Tasunke Witko,* civ. no. 93-204 (memorandum decision, October 25, 1994).

100. Stanley Fish, *Doing What Comes Naturally: Change, Rhetoric, and the Practice of Theory in Literary and Legal Studies* (Durham, N.C.: Duke University Press, 1989), 141 (characterizing an interpretive community as "a point of view or way of organizing experience that individuals shared in the sense that its assumed distinctions, categories of understanding, and stipulations of relevance and irrelevance were the content of the consciousness of community members who were therefore no longer individuals, but insofar as they were embedded in the community's enterprise, community property")

101. I have argued that the structure and processes of the Indian land claims systems elevated the needs of the majority society over tribal needs in a number of ways—by foreclosing remedies seeking return of land in favor of money damages, thus equating land with money in a way that native peoples have not; by foreclosing arguments based on loss of tribal identity and community; and by rigid application of time bars. For a full discussion of the claims system, see Nell Jessup Newton, "Indian Claims in the Courts of the Conquerors," *American University Law Review* 41 (1992): 753. The Supreme Court has adjudicated Indian cases without any historical context, or worse, the kinds of complete misstatements of history illustrated by Justice Rehnquist's statement in *Oliphant v. Suquamish Indian Tribe,* 435 U.S. 1991, 208 (1978) that "Indian tribes do retain elements of quasi-sovereign" authority after "ceding their lands to the United States and announcing their dependence on the Federal Government," as if Indian tribes freely choose the relationship of subservience to the dominant legal system. For critical treatments of this process, see Vine Deloria Jr., "Laws Founded in Justice and Humanity: Reflections on the Content and Character of American Indian Law," *Arizona Law Review* 31 (1989): 202 (noting that the history in Indian law as mostly fictional); Milner S. Ball, "Constitution, Court, Indian Tribes," *American Bar Foundation Research Journal* (1987): 1 (criticizing the misuse of history in general and the *Oliphant* language in particular). On the abuse of history in recent Indian law jurisprudence, see Aviam Soifer, "Objects in the Mirror Are Closer Than They Appear," *Georgia Law Review* 28 (1994): 533, 534 (arguing that recent cases illustrate "how commonplace it is for judges to make claims from history, while blithely remaining blind to the crucial understandings at the confluence of memory, moaning, and historical accuracy"). Joseph Singer has criticized the Court's manipulation of legal categories to produce the same result—tribes lose—based on opposite categorical imperatives. For example, he argues that courts label the legal issue one of sovereignty or one of property as an expedient to reject Indian claims. Joseph William Singer, "Sovereignty and Property," *Northwestern University Law Review* 86 (1991): 1.

102. Seth Big Crow, quoted in Vaillancourt, "Big Crow's First Stand: Descendant of Crazy Horse Goes Public to Keep Legendary Warrior's Name Off High-Octane Beer."

Deborah Root

"White Indians": Appropriation and the Politics of Display

The West Coast can be a weird place to come back to: the 1960s are alive out here, the past seems to collapse into the present, and it all flows back, all too horribly at times. Soon after my arrival on a small island in British Columbia, I stopped to pick up a hitchhiker, a man about my age dressed in full counter-cultural regalia. He got into the car and noticed the medicine wheel hanging from the mirror. "Far out," he said, "is that Indian?" I answered yes, and after introducing himself as Karma, he proceeded to announce that he did not consider himself to be white because his spirit was Native; he was, he said, a "white-skinned Indian." "Oh, yeah?" I answered uneasily, while examining him covertly. Karma was dressed in the usual hippie mishmash of Native, Afghani, and South American styles, and he wore a headband on his center-parted blond hair. Although he took pains to appear appropriately mellow, I could sense a certain tension and challenge in his manner.

I found my encounter with Karma extremely disturbing, and it was difficult to put my finger on precisely why. I had known plenty of guys like that back in the old days, but I assumed they had all cut their hair and gone to work for insurance companies and changed their names back to John or Stanley.[1] Over the following weeks, I gave rides to similar white men who made similar statements about being Native on the inside, with the medicine wheel on the mirror again functioning as the point of conversational departure.

225

I jettisoned my hippie mannerisms long ago and find it embarrassing to be reminded of the way we so blithely appropriated bits and pieces of what appeared to us to be floating cultural exotica. The contemporary version of this is also embarrassing, if in a more distanced way. A white guy used to show up at the Mohawk support vigil at Queens' Park in Toronto during the Oka summer of 1990, eagle feather in hand, hair carefully braided, and speaking ponderously as if he had just finished a chapter of *Black Elk Speaks*. We would all roll our eyes and refer to him as "one of those," which meant, of course, one of those white people trying too hard to be Native: a wanna-be. I ridiculed this man along with everyone else, but the fact remains: I am white, I used to wear headbands, and I have a medicine wheel in my car. It is easy to reassure myself that I have absolutely no kinship with Karma or the guy at Queens' Park, but there is a relation between my own practice as a white woman who does Native solidarity work and the West Coast hippies or contemporary wanna-bes. For many of us who focus on the politics of race, this relation may in fact be fairly tenuous after years of activism, but it exists and deserves some inspection, if only because we grew up in the same racist climate as other white people. Our hidden affinities with wanna-bes and their ilk have implications for the possibilities of solidarity and antiracist work and for our role as white people in this work. And even though we go to great lengths to distinguish ourselves from "those other white people," the embarrassment generated by their presence is, I think, symptomatic of a recognition that we may be too quick to deny.

Hippies and Westerns

I think most of us of a certain age can remember when a fantasy of Native people functioned as a metaphor for the rejection of mainstream, bourgeois, white society. Native culture, or, more properly, the bogus version of Native culture that existed in the white imagination, came to stand for authenticity and redemption. Many of us appropriated the most superficial and hackneyed marks of this romance—beads, feathers, fringe—as a means of displaying our opposition to our own cultural background and the flatness and hideous pastels of suburbia.

It is almost impossible to look back and imagine what we supposed Native culture to be or, indeed, if we imagined anything beyond the beads and feathers. Our concerns at the time for the most part had to do with political and social tensions within middle-class white society rather than with Native people. It seems obvious now that the images of Native people we mined for our countercultural costumes came directly from television and the movies, hardly sources outside the mainstream bourgeois culture we set ourselves against. And despite the flurry of shows in the early 1970s that seemed at first glance to represent Native people in a "positive" light (*Little Big Man, Soldier Blue,* the *Star Trek* episode where Captain Kirk marries an alien "Native" woman), the images themselves drew upon and remained in the same narrow range as those in traditional westerns, albeit differently valorized.

How was our supposed rejection of the "straight" world mirrored in these movie images of Indians? In white films and literature, Native people usually appear as those who are by definition victims of an inevitable historical fate, executed and enforced by the American government, the army, and the swarms of settlers. It was the movies' racist subtext—that Native people are destined to vanish in the face of "progress"—that made them seem heroic to us and made us want to affirm headbands and fringe as a way of marking our dislike of our parents' commodity culture. There is very little attention paid in these narratives to resistance, to the real issues that came up during the colonial invasions of Native territories, or to what continues to be at stake in struggles over land rights. Of course, this oversight is not accidental. We were exposed to colonial tales that reinforced the notion of Native people as heroic victims or, perhaps more accurately, as people who are heroic precisely because they have been victimized. At the same time, we were presented with the old stereotypes of cruelty, savagery, and, more equivocally, closeness to nature, which in traditional Christian thinking is always an ambivalent quality.

In westerns and similar narratives that claim to describe encounters between Natives and non-Natives, the white people also tend to have limited roles. The soldiers and cowboys and, to a lesser extent, the dance-hall girls all have an agenda of nation-building and acquisition of wealth, which is the reason for outlaw activities. The cowboy loner appears from time to time, enigmatic and often cruel, but always looking out for himself. The movies assume that the white people are the ones who are going to win, despite internal squabbles over fencing the range or robbing the bank or doing whatever. There are no real victim roles for white people in these narratives, except in the most individualized way (which is also no accident). In this way, white histories are also emptied of meaning, and it becomes almost impossible to imagine an alternative to the colonizer role, which seems to be part of Karma's problem.

As Pierre Clastres has reminded us, the ethnocidal tendency in Western culture, the fear and horror of difference that resulted in attempts to suppress aboriginal traditions, has a long history.[2] The West was ethnocidal inside itself first: margins were suppressed, people were thrown off their land, order was imposed. Given these histories, the category "white people" is as much a construction as "the Other." The narratives of popular culture make it extremely difficult to call into question the monolithic nature of the historical representation of the conquest and settlement of the Americas. Indentured laborers, miners, people who challenged the conceits of Manifest Destiny, are forgotten in the grand fictions of the colonial stories.

Why would Karma and his countercultural predecessors identify with people who, time and time again, are presented as victims? First Nations writer Deborah Doxtator makes the point that it is precisely the image of Indians as doomed victims that some white people identify with: she calls this the "I'm a victim too" complex.[3] Indeed, Friedrich Nietzsche conceived something like this complex as the very core of Christian culture, underlining the link between pity and contempt. Thinking of someone else as a victim is a way of displacing one's own pain: in reactive Christian thinking, I am less of a victim than you because you are more of a victim than me. White hippies do tend to recognize some of the oppressive aspects of industrial, consumerist society but manifest this by focusing on and identifying with people who seem to be even more oppressed, thus reproducing the 1970s movie version of Natives as defeated victims who exist only in the past.

Western culture is permeated with the duplicitous, Christian notion of victimization, which on the one hand implies a moral or spiritual superiority and on the other a kind of weakness that is to be overcome. Martyred saints are represented as suffering physical torment with a heroic steadfastness of faith. Yet the body, whether sinful or suffering, is thought to be inherently abject. Thus, to be a victim is to be both heroic and abject. White representations (both "sympathetic" and explicitly racist) of colonial wars tend to maintain this definition and underline the view that Native heroism derives from and is the consequence of defeat.[4] The white fascination with the romantic, abstract heroism of Native people is thus able to function as another means of colonial pacification because it presupposes the inevitable defeat and disappearance of the nations. Colonialism adds a new twist to the Christian view that people are victims by their very nature or essence, and here the relation between aggressor and victim becomes wholly static and cannot shift. Everyone is frozen into his or her position and role. And, of course, conceiving of an enemy nation as heroic also makes the oppressors look good because they have defeated a truly worthy and valiant enemy. This, too, is nothing new in Western culture. Recall the famous Roman sculpture of the dying Gaul, an image of a heroic, yet defeated enemy.

Here we approach what it was we all forgot in our eagerness to embrace the representation of Indians as heroic victims: if Native nations are portrayed as inherently abject and doomed to defeat, white viewers will not feel any connection to colonialism, either in the past or in the present. This is why the phony Native culture of movies, Edward Curtis photographs, and television is so appealing to white people: if, as Hollywood and capitalism would have it, the nations are foreordained to assimilate and vanish, then white viewers need not question racism or face the discomfort of interrogating our continuing position as members of a colonizing nation. We will not feel connected to ongoing struggles in James Bay, Chiapas, Kanesatake, and elsewhere and to the different relation to the land that these struggles express. Any sense of connection to events occurring on the ground is lost, and "Native" becomes another empty category that can be mined for its trappings and images. And the "love" of Indians professed by counterculture old and new continues to have nothing to do with Native people and certainly nothing to do with supporting contemporary Native struggles. Westerns and other colonial narratives are in the business of producing binarisms, which have had effects on all of us. As white people, we need to rethink and recover the histories erased by popular culture and school textbooks. There were always alternatives to John Wayne. We also need to think through the nature of power and its relation to culture. John Trudell said somewhere that there is a difference between being oppressed and being powerless: Native people may be oppressed, but the traditions have power; white people may be "in charge" within a colonial context, but our culture has lost its heart, soul, and life—its power. It is up to us to look into how our traditions were taken over and distorted by a destructive, soulless ethos and find ways to heal our cultural diseases.[5] This is where Karma's approach breaks down: he thinks he has to turn himself into a "white-skinned Indian" because he cannot find a way to transform and locate power in his own tradition. Because of the elided histories, he is unable to identify with the white people who have resisted oppression over the centuries. He, too, is rendered passive by the romantic discourse of inevitable defeat and disappearance. And because Karma thinks white culture is one thing—the dead, shopping-mall culture of our time—appropriation becomes his only escape, and it becomes impossible for him to imagine standing side by side with Native people as equals.

The Politics of Display

Despite the current incarnation in the New Age of the old hippie culture, it has all but died out, except for a few pockets here and there. Why dwell on what was, after all, a brief cultural phenomenon? For one thing, the countercultural imaginary has a long genealogy. Since the advent of modernism, a particular stream of Western thought has located the solutions to the disasters of Western culture *someplace else:* in "exotic" tribal cultures, in places like Mexico and India, in an aristocratic past. European romanticism attempts to generate a space of possibility in the construction of a fictional, yet redemptive, Other. Like Antonin Artaud and so many others before him, Karma thinks that Native culture will save him from alienation and despair.

Although the appropriation of Native culture has been an ongoing problem, I am surprised that the countercultural version of this has persisted virtually unchanged for so long. I had always assumed that appropriation was about stealing other peoples' traditions in order to make money, and the hippie wanna-bes claim to be uninterested in capitalizing on their appropriations (although this is not entirely true, if what I see at West Coast crafts fairs is any indication). I understand that a fanciful image of Native people, conveniently located in the past, is less demanding than the reality, but what is truly troubling is how the image continues to be affirmed in a way that is removed from contemporary Native struggles around land rights and sovereignty issues. So many white people—hippies, New Agers, some environmentalists—continue to talk about Native people rather than to them and to affirm an idea of Native culture as a source of redemptive spirituality that can be taken up at will.

I do not want to unfairly reproach the "white Indians" of British Columbia. Although their wide-eyed declarations are intensely irritating, their naïveté makes them a little too easy to target, and in some ways they are saying aloud what other, supposedly more sophisticated white people think but are too cunning to say outright. I think the hippie wanna-bes are reasonably sincere in their desire to find a language to describe their disaffection with modern culture, as, more dangerously and duplicitously, are the New Agers. But good intentions can occlude the persistence of extremely problematic assumptions about culture and history. Sincerity is not enough and can be damaging in its own right, in part because it can be used as a pretext to gain discursive terrain, while evading the question of who controls, or is trying to control, the discourse. This brings me to another facet of the wanna-be problem; the commodification and display of style.

I do want to say that there are more important issues than style. The land is dying, attempts at genocide continue, racism breaks out everywhere. It can be difficult to sustain our commitment in the face of all this and to balance this commitment with economic survival. Worrying about whether white people wear fringe or beaded earrings is, in some respects, beside the point. At the same time, how we choose to present ourselves in the public arena has to do with questions of identity and, as such, is political.[6] We utilize specific codes to display our politics, which link up to and have implications for the larger issues, including the problem of guilt and fear that paralyzes so many white people and allows racism to continue.

I think that when many non-Natives begin to get involved in solidarity work, or even when we consider ourselves in a vague kind of way to support

Native issues, we sometimes assume that it is a compliment or mark of respect to Natives to dress in Native-style regalia. It seems to us to be a way (and, indeed, one of the most superficial and easiest ways) to announce our identification with Native people, both to Natives and to other whites. We think it will operate as a kind of social lubricant, making it easier for "them" to accept "us" and to recognize that we are indeed good people. At one level, there does not seem to be anything terribly wrong with this, except, again, a certain naïveté.[7]

Part of the problem lies in how the display of affiliation enables white people to insist on being the center of attention. The proclaiming of our alliance in a visible, emphatic manner has a performative quality that demands instant recognition and approval. It manifests a certain impatience; rather than demonstrating our affiliation over time with actions, some of us want immediate recognition of our good intentions (this insistence on recognition is, I think, one reason for Karma's tense manner). Displaying the fringe and jewelry can become a way of attempting to seize discursive space from Native people, and to the extent that it functions as a demand, this display constitutes an endeavor to extend and underline the authority of the white person. The dressed-up white man at Queens' Park seemed (or certainly tried) to do a lot of the talking. We are reminded here of Frantz Fanon's observation that the colonist is an exhibitionist, who seeks constantly to "remind the Native out loud that he [or she] alone is master."[8]

This issue can cut very close, especially on those days when everything seems charged with political significance. Whenever we go to powwows or Native solidarity functions, we see white people dressed in fringed jackets, beaded and turquoise jewelry, sometimes feathers. This display can produce twinges of embarrassment in some of us reminiscent of that provoked by Karma as well as a particular form of shopping anxiety. The jewelry and clothing are both beautiful and available because people set up booths at these events to sell their own work and the work of other Native artists. They obviously want to sell the stuff and make some money. But what about the problem of consumption? They are selling, and sometimes we buy, but should we? What about the wanna-be factor? Sometimes people give us gifts of traditional jewelry. But when should we wear it? There is a very fine line between appreciation and appropriation, respect and self-aggrandizement, a line that is always shifting and impossible to decide in advance.[9]

Appropriation always goes hand in hand with colonialism and the display of authority. Wanna-bes have rendered the old colonial "We want it, so we'll take it" mentality into something rather more complex in that appropriation can seem to be a mark of "sensitivity" to another culture. What has caused this turn? Or is it a turn at all or simply a reiteration of the colonial moment utilizing a different grammar? Many white people seem "genuinely" to feel "sensitive" to Native issues (which I suppose is a start), but they may be unwilling to take their sensitivity further by relinquishing authority, which begins by putting everything into question, including our right to do as we please.

One comment I hear a lot is that white people think everything is for sale. If we refuse to interrogate the extent to which politics, like style, can become a commodity to be advertised by the gesture of display, then we reinforce the notion that how we present ourselves is more important than what we do. Thinking of identity or tradition or jewelry as a commodity that can be bought and sold makes it too easy to forget that if we are going to ask for something from another community, we have be willing to give something back.

I espied Karma again at the grocery store and hid from him in the frozen food section, as if the wanna-be disease were contagious. Although I tend to become nervous around people who ostentatiously pretend to be something they are not, I have always had a certain furtive sympathy for the white wanna-bes because I understand their desperation: Western culture seems so bankrupt and uninteresting; of course they are going to grab onto something else. But this does not work, even though we can probably wear our beaded earrings from time to time. Rather than seeking authenticity elsewhere, we need to transform how we look at our histories and traditions and find ways to unravel these from all the racist versions to which we have been subjected. We need to confront the painful histories as a way to begin abandoning the essentialist notions of "white" identity as well as positions that construct Native culture as the imaginary space that can save us from ourselves. This, too, is part of solidarity politics.

Notes

This project received financial support from the Ontario Arts Council. A different version of this essay appears in chapter 3 of *Cannibal Culture: Art, Appropriation, and the Politics of Display* (Boulder: Westview Press, 1995).

1. During my stay in British Columbia I came across Aura, Coyote, Antelope, and Phoenix, among others. These, like Karma, are all white people of various ages who identify with the West Coast version of the counterculture.

2. Pierre Clastres, "Of Ethnocide," in *Archaeology of Violence*, ed. Pierre Clastres, trans. Jeanine Herman (New York: Semiotext[e], 1994), 43–54.

3. Deborah Doxtator, *Fluffs and Feathers: An Exhibit on the Symbols of Indianness* (Brantford, Ont.: Woodland Cultural Centre, 1992), 34.

4. Think of the continuing popularity of the Curtis photographs of Chief Joseph and other defeated Native leaders.

5. For an analysis of the cannibal disease and its effect on Western culture, see Jack Forbes, *Columbus and Other Cannibals: The Wetiko Disease of Exploitation, Imperialism, and Terrorism* (Brooklyn, N.Y.: Autonomedia, 1992).

6. The link between clothes and colonialism goes back a long way. During the French conquest of Algeria, it was fashionable in Paris to wear Arab clothing. El Al flight attendants in the 1960s wore Palestinian-style uniforms. We see this kind of thing over and over again.

7. This can also link up to the problem of white guilt. A lot of white people seem to be having problems with this issue, and some handle it by focusing on real or possible Native ancestors at distant points on the family tree, the so-called Indian grandma syndrome. On the one hand, many of us are not as white as our families would have us believe; secret relatives no one talks about because they are the wrong ethnicity, people of color passing as white as a way to survive, and the climate of racism all make for hidden family histories of this nature. But what do these claims really mean? Is deciding you are not "really" white a naive way to get out of the painful and difficult problem of white guilt? Is it another form of display? There seem to be no easy answers to these questions.

8. Frantz Fanon, *The Wretched of the Earth* (New York: Grove Press, 1963), 53.

9. Sometimes appropriation can come down to something very simple, like economics. I recall an older Native friend telling me that it hurts her to see whites wearing the beautiful Native jewelry she cannot afford.

Part 5

The Appropriation
of Scientific Knowledge

James D. Nason

Native American Intellectual Property Rights: Issues in the Control of Esoteric Knowledge

Conflict, loss, and cultural domination have been dominant themes in most of the history of Indian-white relations in the United States, yet recent chapters in this history speak to the renewed strength and resurgence of Native American communities and the reassertion of fundamental Native American sovereign rights. Most accounts of this general history have focused on such obvious issues as military actions, struggles for political and economic control over land and natural resources, and an array of concerns that might collectively be lumped under the rubric of cultural life and welfare. These events and processes are fundamentally important in our understanding of contemporary Native American concerns in the United States.

The same is true in this essay, which deals with a less-well-known but significant topic of emerging concern and conflict: the control of Native American intellectual property. And since intellectual property is by its very nature a kind of cultural property, it is essential that any discussion of it first begin with a recapitulation of recent changes in the concepts, policies, and legislation of cultural property. This recapitulation will clarify the degree to which the specific range of problems that surrounds intellectual property rights is related to but distinct from the kinds of concerns and actions that have heretofore fallen within the cultural property realm. I hope that it will be equally clear that Native American intellectual property rights issues not only are significant but should also be the subject of efforts for their timely remediation, efforts similar to those directed at other kinds of cultural property. For both cultural property and intellectual property, the fundamental areas of conflict and compromise are essentially the same: What types of property can be appropriately controlled? Who has the legitimate authority to control it?

Modern Controversies over Cultural Property Rights

Nineteenth-century scientific work in Native American communities was increasingly dominated by the belief that Native Americans were disappearing as people and as distinct cultures. By the end of the century, this belief had motivated extensive efforts to create large-scale collections of contemporary material culture, human remains, and antiquities as well as related oral history, linguistic, and cultural information. It was the legacy of the creation of these massive collections, housed in museums, that led to discord between the scholarly community and Native Americans, who did not, as we know, disappear either physically or culturally.

The contemporary battle over the control of this significant heritage of cultural property began in earnest in the 1960s within an international context of massive looting of archaeological sites, widespread museum and heritage center thefts, and associated smuggling and other illicit transfers of cultural property from their places of origin.[1] Scholarly outrage and general public concern with these matters grew as information about the sheer magnitude of these abuses became more and more apparent. The rampant destruction each year of thousands of archaeological sites, with the inevitable permanent loss of data; the onslaught of embarrassing public revelations about blatant acts of illicit acquisition of smuggled art and artifacts, often involving major museums; and growing nationalistic sensitivities about this general loss of cultural heritage through what amounted to organized international piracy all contributed to new levels of awareness about the nature of significant cultural property.

The situation had become sufficiently alarming by the end of the decade that it became the focus of an international convention, the 1970 UNESCO Convention on the Means of Prohibiting and Preventing the Illicit Import, Export, and Transfer of Ownership of Cultural Property.[2] Even though one fundamental purpose behind the 1970 Convention was to ensure the open exchange of "the fullest possible information regarding [the] origin, history, and traditional setting . . . of cultural property," the convention did more centrally establish for the first time international guidelines that cultural property of all kinds should be protected by all nations and should be the subject of repatriation when illicitly removed. In other words, the 1970 Convention was a watershed moment in both national and international concerns in what has been a protracted, decades-long struggle to establish fundamental elements of cultural property rights between peoples.

One element that made the 1970 Convention remarkable was what it included in its purview as relevant cultural property. Most so-called Third World nations had by 1970 already created their own laws to protect cultural property deemed vital to the heritage and patrimony of the nation, including provisions for the identification, ownership, and export control over such property. But few of these national cultural property laws had the range of generic property coverage to be found in the 1970 UNESCO Convention, which encompassed all possible objects of importance for archaeology, anthropology, history, literature, art, or science, including fauna, flora, minerals, palaeontology, monuments or parts of archaeological sites, antiquities, all types of artworks, incunabula, documents, stamps of all sorts, furniture and musical instruments, and all archival materials. Of special interest here is the inclusion in the last category of documents, books, and photographic, cinematographic, and sound recordings, all key forms of what has become known as intellectual property. In other words, the 1970 Convention extended the definition of patrimony and the proposal that it be protected and repatriated to the more usual forms of cultural property and to intellectual property as well.

For the government of the United States, the furor over cultural property was perhaps somewhat unexpected, as Americans had only rarely undertaken any legislative action to protect anything that might be thought of as American national cultural property. Indeed, it was believed by some cynics that the United States essentially did not have a national cultural policy, except in the laissez-faire sense of allowing the purchase, sale, and import or export of almost everything to anyone anywhere. Although the United States did not adopt one form of the basic tenets of the 1970 Convention until 1983, and then only after considerable debate, the national government did begin in the 1970s to take steps to recognize these issues at both national and international levels.[3] At the international level, this recognition came with the 1970 treaty on pre-Columbian artifacts with the Republic of Mexico and subsequent regulatory actions of the U.S. Customs Service over the importation of pre-Columbian materials from other nations.[4]

At the national level, U.S. government agencies and museums were confronted with increasing demands from the Native American community on a number of issues involving political and cultural sovereignty, including control over cultural property. One area of immediate interest was the issue of religious freedom, including access to, if not control over, sacred sites and objects. This issue was raised in response to two situations that Native Americans found objectionable. First, many museum collections contained sacred materials important to ongoing religious practice and believed to have been inalienable in the first instance. Second, many sacred sites traditionally used for religious purposes were on federal lands and under the control of agencies that barred Native American access. These matters became the focus of the 1978 American Indian Religious Freedom Act (AIRFA), which theoretically sought to give Native Americans access to sites on federal land and which established as a general principle that Native Americans should have the "use and possession of sacred objects."[5] But no mandatory repatriation was required by AIRFA, and few federal agencies actually changed the way in which they dealt with Native American concerns.[6] In the end, AIRFA was of limited value in addressing Native American needs and at best gave some tribal leaders greater bargaining power on a moral level in their discussions with museums about the return of sacred objects.

All throughout the late 1970s and 1980s, concerns and demands for action on continuing cultural property issues escalated both here and abroad. These ranged from renewed Greek demands for the repatriation of the Elgin Marbles from the British Museum, to concentrated efforts in the United States to secure the repatriation of Native American human remains and associated cultural materials. Native American concerns were for the most part directed toward the collections and practices of museums and especially the maintenance of human remains and sacred objects in those collections.[7] By the end of the 1980s, thirty state governments had responded to these concerns with the passage of legislation that established protection for Native American burials and that in some cases also required state museums to repatriate Native American human remains to tribes.

This movement culminated in 1990 with the passage of a new national law, the Native American Graves Protection and Repatriation Act (NAGPRA).[8] This is in many respects the single most important piece of national cultural property legislation ever adopted by the United States because it recognizes the special relationship of patrimonial, sacred, and funerary objects and remains to a particular set of communities and adopts mandatory requirements for notification as well as procedures for repatriation and protection of human remains and key categories of cultural property. The passage of this legislation, despite concerted lobbying against it by leaders of both museum and scholarly organizations, was a stunning victory for Native American communities in the United States.

Cultural Property Implications in NAGPRA

Although the final verdict on NAGPRA's success is yet to be written, the law does have two key elements that are significant in any discussion of cultural property. First, NAGPRA and all earlier legislative efforts have been largely, if not solely, directed toward cultural property in the form of material culture, things that are tangible (let us leave aside for the moment its equally significant provisions for human remains). Second, NAGPRA has prompted many tribal governments and museums as well as nontribal institutions and scholars to consider more broadly the implications of cultural property and its control. Both of these elements deserve close attention.

The focus on tangible heritage properties in NAGPRA is contained in its identification and definition of four specific categories of objects that are subject to repatriation: (1) sacred objects, (2) objects of patrimony, (3) unassociated funerary objects, and (4) funerary objects. Furthermore, NAGPRA recognizes the existence of a special relationship between Native American communities and their traditional lands, both with regard to how cultural affiliation can be territorially defined with respect to objects and in regard to new protections for Native American graves, including ancient burials. In other words, NAGPRA deals with four particular kinds of "personal property" (chattels) and with "real property" (land). Within NAGPRA's defined categories of personal property are funerary objects, which are presumed to be "private" property formerly controlled by individuals as well as "public" property as represented by both sacred and patrimonial objects. The sovereign federally recognized tribal community as a corporate body has the authority both to seek repatriation and subsequently to decide on the disposition of repatriated materials (NAGPRA also provides that lineal descendants can make claims). In some instances a tribal community may present repatriation claims on behalf of a primary owner and decision-maker in the form of an intratribal society or other corporate group, such as a clan. This fact is of special importance when we consider how NAGPRA has defined objects as "sacred" or as "patrimony."

NAGPRA defines sacred objects as those "specific ceremonial objects which are needed by traditional Native American religious leaders for the practice of traditional Native American religions by their present day adherents."[9] Cultural patrimony is defined as an "object having ongoing historical, traditional, or cultural importance central to the Native American group or culture itself, rather than property owned by an individual Native American, and which, therefore, cannot be alienated, appropriated, or conveyed by any individual regardless of whether or not the individual is a member of the Indian tribe or Native Hawaiian organization and such object shall have been considered inalienable by such Native American group at the time the object was separated from such group."[10]

These definitions have been widely assumed to refer strictly to tangible objects, as tangible sacred and patrimonial objects which were the focus of attention in the first instance. For example, a sacred object might refer to a mask or rattle or pipe but not, from this perspective, to a song or chant. Similarly, cultural patrimony would also be objects but not oral literature. In other words, our usual understanding of the provisions contained in NAGPRA would not lead us to believe that it also encompasses intellectual property in the form of songs, chants, visual arts and motifs, oral literature of all kinds, or the recorded versions of any of these in drawings, paintings, photographs, film, or sound recordings.

We might well ask, then, what value NAGPRA has in the consideration of intellectual property issues. There are, on the face of it, three key points in NAGPRA that relate to intellectual property. First, NAGPRA generally establishes protections for cultural property and affiliations between tribal communities and traditional lands. Second, NAGPRA establishes tribal governments as sovereign entities with special powers of ownership and control over key types of cultural property. And, third, NAGPRA defines patrimony as being that which is inalienable and corporate in character, a concept of importance when we consider much that falls within the rubric of intellectual property in Native America.

Esoteric Knowledge

As we have seen, most of the attention paid in the United States to Native American cultural property rights has focused on NAGPRA. Yet it is equally true, although perhaps not as well appreciated, that many tribal governments have also been actively concerned about their intangible cultural heritage and have taken steps to develop means of controlling access, use, and "export" of that intangible cultural heritage as well as ensuring its perpetuation. Attention to this intangible cultural heritage is broadly based and ranges from concerns about the maintenance of traditional languages, to concerns about traditional religious lore and practice, traditional and detailed knowledge of the natural world, and all types of oral history, oral literature, and other knowledge that could generically be referred to as "lore." Of particular interest are the esoteric knowledge that has been the subject of attention by outside scholars and concomitant Native American concerns with sharing that esoteric knowledge. By esoteric knowledge I refer specifically to traditional, valued knowledge that is intended for and is to be used by the specially initiated or trained and that is most often owned or held in trust and treated as private or secret by an individual, by a group within the community (such as a clan or society), or by the community as a whole. This knowledge may in some cases be sacred and in others cases be patrimonial in nature. In whatever form it takes, such specialized knowledge is characteristically regarded as property within tribal legal systems and therefore constitutes a key form of traditionally defined intellectual property.

Although the historical acquisition of large quantities of material culture to form museum collections lay at the heart of contemporary disputes between Native American communities and scholars, it was not just the scale of such collecting that was the problem, although the fact that nearly all of the traditional material culture heritage of most Native American communities was alienated from them has certainly been a disconcerting fact. Nor was the often inaccurate and stereotypic interpretation of these materials to the public in museum exhibits or popular media a singular issue. Beyond these concerns lay two points of major importance. The first was the belief that many collections contained materials that had been illicitly obtained through acts of direct theft or grave-robbing as well as through legal but unethical means in contexts of great duress, such as desperate reservation conditions. The second was the belief that such illicit or unethical collection holdings included sacred and patrimonial objects that by traditional practice, belief, and law could never have been alienated from the tribal community. When issues such as these arose in this century, they were often countered with cases in which materials had been willingly transferred to trusted outsiders because there had been no one else left in the community to care for them or in which owners did willingly sell their property for various reasons beyond those of desperate need. Yet some acquisitions were made in ways that cannot be defended today and that did not involve the knowing or willing agreement of community members. Similar concerns about the history of the acquisition of esoteric knowledge have also been raised.

Scholars and scholarly institutions such as museums did acquire, from the 1800s onward, huge collections of Native material heritage as well as substantial records of specialized knowledge, much of it accompanying associated sacred and other culturally sensitive objects. Indeed, Native Americans are among the most, if not the most, studied peoples in the history of the modern world. There have been countless studies, reports, articles, and books on Native Americans done by anthropologists, archaeologists, economists, historians, medical specialists, political scientists, and sociologists, for example, of every possible theoretical and methodological stripe on virtually every conceivable topic. These intense studies have subjected Native American communities to detailed scrutiny and certainly not least so with respect to cultural esoterica. The details of how and why these multitudinous transfers took place are well beyond the scope of this discussion, although it is clear that Native Americans were considered to be important, appropriate, and fair targets for in-depth research; were not always in a position to refuse cooperation with such research; and, in at least some instances, did see transfer as a potentially better option than loss for both some objects and some knowledge.

There is one other point that should be made. Whereas some cultural objects may well have been stolen outright, it seems unlikely that a similar claim could be made with regard to the acquisition of esoteric knowledge, although coercion could have been a factor for both knowledge and objects. In any event, the legal and ethical activities of well-intentioned and dedicated scholars as well as the unscrupulous and illegal work of others did result in the transfer of considerable knowledge, including esoteric knowledge, as well as objects, including culturally sensitive materials. And both knowledge and objects have through scholarly and commercial means been disseminated widely throughout our society, which in some respects is perhaps the most significant end result of this process.

Just as this process may have preserved from absolute loss some aspects of cultural heritage, it has also revealed for all and sundry much that Native Americans may now regret finding in the public domain. Examples of the latter range from that body of sacred knowledge that has, much to the dismay, if not disgust, of many in the community, made possible some aspects of pseudo-Indian religiosity in so-called New Age beliefs, to the stereotypic trivialization of Native American beliefs and principles found in American popular media.[11]

The sheer volume of ongoing research activity has increasingly driven tribal community concerns about the nature, impact, and potential control of such work by scholars who seek to conduct work in tribal communities, especially in areas that involve esoteric knowledge. Such knowledge may, as we know, constitute the essential core of the intellectual property of a community. The full range of such knowledge will probably never become entirely known, but it certainly includes detailed traditional knowledge about the uses of plants and animals; songs, chants, and related music of various kinds; oral histories from the creation of the world to more recent historical events; ritual knowledge and other forms of religious knowledge; certain types of technological knowledge; and knowledge related to graphic and plastic arts, including knowledge that involves motifs and symbols. Much of this esoteric knowledge, even that which is regarded as culturally sensitive, has already been collected, recorded, and put into the general public realm by virtue of publications. Other esoteric knowledge has been collected but remains "hidden" in archival and museum collections in the form of field journals, notebooks, aging photo and early sound record collections, and the like. Still more and "undiscovered" types of this esoteric knowledge remain entirely in the possession of Native American specialists and are the object of attention by new researchers who seek to acquire it for both scholarly and commercial purposes.

The difference between scholarly and commercial collection and use of traditional knowledge is often not clear to many Native Americans. From their perspective, even scholarly use may well be a kind of commercial application since books may earn royalties and enhanced scholarly reputations may lead to higher earnings. From the traditional Western scientific perspective, knowledge is and should be essentially "free" and open; this notion remains a cornerstone of many of the professional attitudes, training, and ethics maintained by scholarly societies. Indeed, with some exceptions, research that results in classified or restricted access to data is usually abjured, if not condemned. At the same time, professional ethics may call for service payments to informants (i.e., the data may be "free" but not the process of its acquisition) and for the protection of the interests of those in the community. Some of the difficulties inherent in this matter can be found, for example, in the code of ethics for archivists adopted by the Society of American Archivists. It states that archivists "make available records and papers that have lasting value to the organization or public that the archivist serves," while also declaring that "archivists respect the privacy of individuals who created or are the subjects of records and papers, especially those who had no voice in the disposition of the materials."[12] The problem with such ethical codes from the Native American point of view is that, even though the privacy of the informants or subjects may be important, the privacy of the information itself may be even more paramount.

What informants know about the intentions and implications of research work has been a consideration as well. Human subject rights legislation, which arose from medical research, also applies to work with informants and has in recent decades required that informed consent be obtained, with appropriate forewarning of potential risks. Even with such safeguards in place, however, it is not difficult to see how deliberate or inadvertent problems with culturally sensitive data could arise, including violations of confidentiality, secrecy, and traditional legal principles of ownership of such data.[13] And prior to the 1960s, there were no requirements for informed consent or the discussion of potential risks. Some of the consequences of this lack come to light every year in universities and colleges in the form of phone calls from individuals who want to know whatever happened to the film or sound recording or notes taken years ago by some researcher of important information held by the caller or a relative of the caller. Largely unheard are the complaints from tribal community members about privileged information that was published in the past and can now be found in libraries.

Native American Control of Esoteric Knowledge

Contemporary efforts by Native Americans and other indigenous peoples in the world to control their esoteric knowledge and other forms of important intellectual property have focused primarily on the control of research, artistic and related cultural heritage, and knowledge related to plants and animals. By the early 1970s, for example, a number of tribal governments in the Pacific Northwest were seeking to control research activity and its potential for alienation of information by establishing their own research approval processes for anyone proposing to work within the community. In the United States, tribal authority to restrict research within the community comes from the exclusion powers possessed by tribes as sovereign entities and is explicitly outlined in some tribal constitutions. The Cheyenne River Sioux constitution, for example, as well as Lummi tribal ordinances, provides for the exclusion of non-members if they present a criminal or moral hazard to the community.[14] For some Northwest tribes this approach required outside researchers to submit research permit applications for the review of the tribal government. Such permits required detailed information not only on how the research work was supported but also on intended methods and anticipated results. In at least one case the permit required guarantees that the researcher (1) would turn over all recordings and notes to the tribe; (2) would not publish any personal stories or information without tribal permission; (3) would not publish anything without tribal opportunity to review and comment, with comments as a part of the publication; and (4) would turn over to the tribe all royalties from the results of the work (see, for example, Hesquiat Indian Band Agreement 1972, Masset Band Agreement, n.d.). Other tribal research permit policies—for example, those of the Northern Cheyenne—give the tribe power to retain ownership of data as a part of its research approval process.

This effort on the part of many tribes to control contemporary research has not, apparently, become widely known. For example, Lynne Goldstein, an American archaeologist, recently commented on the future import of NAGPRA by saying, "They'll ask next for field notes, tapes, photographs, and they'll insist that you have their permission before you publish."[15] The fact is, of course, that many tribes have already done exactly this and seek to do more. That such permit requirements were and are viewed with alarm by scholars seems in some respects at least a little odd, given the ethical codes that have been and are in effect. For example, the American Anthropological Association Principles of Professional Responsibility, adopted in 1971, states, among other things, that (1) "every effort should be exerted to cooperate with members of the host society in the planning and execution of research projects"; (2) that "the rights, interests, and sensitivities of those studied must be safeguarded"; (3) that "there should be no exploitation of individual informants for personal gain"; and, (4) that "there is an obligation to reflect on the foreseeable repercussions of research and publication on the general population being studied."[16] By this standard, the so-called "host society" does have every right to impose research permit restrictions if it believes such restrictions to be in the community's best interests. The fundamental premise behind such an approach has also recently been expressed in new cultural policies in Australia. Although these largely concern museum collections, they deal with intellectual property as well, recognizing "the inherent interests of Aboriginal and Torres Straits peoples in the care and control, spiritual and practical, of their cultural property," especially with regard to "rights of control and ownership of their own cultural property both tangible and intangible."[17]

Another important contemporary example of the interest of indigenous peoples in controlling research and maintaining rights over intellectual property can be found in the growing discord over the patenting of life forms. This is of interest to us because so much of what is under scrutiny for patents stems from traditional knowledge of plant uses, especially for medicinal purposes. Not only did a substantial portion of the papers in a recent publication on indigenous intellectual property rights deal with this issue,[18] but it has also appeared in a variety of other forums as well. These issues are at the heart of a number of recent developments in other countries. In June 1993, for example, the First International Conference on the Cultural and Intellectual Property Rights of Indigenous Peoples, held at Whakatane, New Zealand, resulted in the Mataatua Declaration."[19] This declaration asks U.N. member states to recognize the rights of indigenous peoples to control in all respects their cultural and intellectual property and to be the inherent beneficiaries, in the first instance, of such property.[20] The Mataatua Declaration is founded on the premise that existing national laws have failed to protect these property interests and to recognize that (1) such property rights are multigenerational, (2) there needs to be retroactive action taken to protect "historical as well as contemporary works," and (3) biological and botanical knowledge requires specialized treatment. The latter stipulation of the Mataatua Declaration is further specified in a number of key points:

- Indigenous flora and fauna are inextricably found in the territories of indigenous communities, and any property right claims must recognize their traditional guardianship.
- Commercialization of any traditional plants and medicines of indigenous peoples must be managed by the indigenous peoples who have inherited such knowledge.

- A moratorium on any further commercialization of indigenous medicinal plants and human genetic materials must be declared until indigenous communities have developed appropriate protection mechanisms.
- Companies and institutions both governmental and private must not undertake experiments or commercialization of any biogenetic resources without the consent of the appropriate indigenous peoples.

The debate over whether life forms can or should be patented, and how corporations or researchers should gain access to such data, remains a contentious issue involving corporate interests, government interests, religious and scientific leaders, and indigenous peoples.[21]

Issues of cultural sovereignty and the control of artistic designations, manufactures, and commercial applications have also become more commonplace in recent years. The Hopi Tribe, for example, has publicly complained about non-Hopi (especially Navajo) artists creating what is otherwise traditionally Hopi art as well as such commercial ventures as a liquor company decanter in the form of a kachina and a comic book featuring kachina characters.[22] The commercialization and resulting trivialization of other traditional arts, especially those that originally had a religious character, such as Navajo sand paintings, Zuni fetish carvings, or so-called rock art in the form of petroglyphs and pictographs, have been a matter of concern. And the misrepresentation of art as being Native American has also been the subject of controversy and, more recently, legislation.[23] The Indian Arts and Crafts Act passed by Congress in 1990, for example, attempts to establish guidelines that will guarantee to buyers in the commercial marketplace the "authenticity" of Indian manufacture. This otherwise worthwhile intention has met with Native American opposition since some Native American artists who are not members of federally recognized tribes cannot be considered "authentic" in this context.[24]

Earlier and continuing efforts to control issues of misrepresentation have also led to the creation of Indian arts organizations whose logos identify the work of members and to the passage of fair trade regulations authorizing applicable art to be sold with a genuine-Indian-made label. And even though contemporary individual artistic creations by Native Americans can be and are copyrighted, the issue of whether a community can hold a copyright to older "art" is not entirely clear. Similarly, no satisfactory solution has yet been found to deal with ongoing issues that surround the commercial or other usage of ancient traditional symbols and motifs, such as those found in petroglyphs or pictographs, since current copyright laws obviously do not apply to such designs. This is a matter that extends to oral literature and other elements of traditional heritage knowledge commonly found in archival collections as well.

Archives, Ancient Knowledge, and Copyright

The legal reality of repatriation under NAGPRA has led, at least in part, to renewed expressions of concern about how to control Native American traditional knowledge. One aspect of this issue emerged in a recent survey of tribal museum and center personnel in the United States and Canada.[25] They were asked about "culturally sensitive materials," referring not to NAGPRA-defined categories but to the large body of tape recordings, records, film, and documents found in archival collections, libraries, and museums. Nearly all tribal museum and center personnel who were contacted in the survey stated that tribes should have veto power over access to and use of such materials, whether by members of their own communities or by others, and most especially so for any commercial access. Another example of this concern has recently come from the Hopi Tribe. In its own reply to museum summaries generated by NAGPRA, the tribe requested a temporary halt to all ongoing or new research on materials that had been archived. As Leigh Jenkins, director of the Hopi Tribal Office of Cultural Preservation, noted: "We feel very strongly that here is a connection between the intellectual knowledge and the sacred objects that were collected from our religious altars. The knowledge and the object are one."[26]

The issue of how to deal with archived materials is not at present subject to easy resolution. For most public museums, for example, the Hopi tribal request could not be honored if only because of existing laws regarding the public trust obligations that museums have with respect to collections and the impact of federal and state freedom-of-information acts on public access to collections. The Hopi request does, however, extend the object-based intentions and definitions in NAGPRA to include intellectual property and also raises the question of what to do about such property when it has already been collected and disseminated. It may not be useful for Native Americans to expend great effort in trying to regain absolute rights of ownership over the vast body of knowledge that has already become a part of the public domain through scholarly and other writings, films, and so on. Aside from existing copyrights to such materials and the application of freedom-of-information laws to their access, the mere fact that so much already exists in publicly accessible forms makes the notion of repatriation of ownership or restriction of access daunting in the extreme. In the absence of some new national law that avoids the constitutional issues of the taking of property, free speech, and other legal entanglements, the damage that has been done probably cannot be undone, although Paul Steidlmeier has argued that third parties (such as tribes) can have a legitimate stake in another's private property rights if they are affected by the consequences of the owner's property decisions.[27] This argument suggests, for example, that commercial or other usages of such materials, including symbols, in a manner that causes harm or damage could be subject to tribal intervention and thus some degree of control.

Whether anything can be done about the unpublished materials in the public domain as the property of public museums, libraries, and archives, unless such materials were access restricted from the start, is also at issue.[28] A great deal depends on whether such organizations gained the rights of copyright to unpublished materials when those materials were acquired. If so, then an extension of the arguments concerning repatriation could be made to such materials that came within a culturally sensitive category. For example, at least one Native American community has always considered any image portraying a sacred object to be sacred itself, thus making photographs of sacred objects sacred. And since so much of the knowledge that is culturally sensitive is associated with intratribal entities, such as clans or societies, the fact that NAGPRA permits repatriations to such groups is also of critical importance. An extended issue is whether courts would today recognize copyrights on behalf of such corporate groups within a tribe or by a tribe for that matter. This may be most significant with respect to oral literature, which is usually held by individuals but is otherwise the collective representative knowledge and heritage of a group or of the community as a whole. That such knowledge has economic value has already been well demonstrated, but this alone would not seem to qualify it for protection under a patent or trade secret application.

The key issues for copyright protection for this form of intellectual knowledge are quite different. Copyright, for example, is commonly used to protect various rights of creative authorship in intellectual property, including works of music, drama, literature, art, film, and architecture. Although the role of economic interests in such works is inherent in the range of protections provided by copyright, the doctrine of fair use does also exist and would still provide for access and certain types of use in ways potentially contrary to Native American interests. The consideration of traditional Native American art and oral literature in this connection quickly draws us to the issues of creative authorship and common public familiarity. It is not possible, for example, to copyright symbols or designs or names that are already well established in the common public arena. Neither has the applicability of ancient knowledge held corporately as a copyright form of valid authorship been fully explored.[29]

Attempts to exercise tribal rights over traditional knowledge may lead to other problems. It may not be reasonable for a tribe to seek means to exert tribal community authority over the full range of either older or modern intellectual cultural property per se since to do so would potentially conflict with other legal protections for creative works, such as an artist's rights. Could a tribal community legally exercise control over the wishes of an individual if the latter wanted to convey information in opposition to community desires? In what form might this occur? Would it be akin to a national security act? Or could a group within a tribal community wishing to copyright specific bodies of knowledge do so without divulging what that knowledge was? For example, could a clan seek to protect clan-held spiritual knowledge without specifying publicly the nature of that knowledge?

And these questions bring us to the nub of the issue: (1) What is the cultural property that tribes might seek to control and safeguard? (2) What cultural property can tribes actually expect to control and safeguard? (3) In what manner can such control be exercised? The fundamental answer to the first question, in very general terms, is that it is likely to be all forms of intellectual property. As to the second question, the United Nations Subcommittee on Prevention of Discrimination and Protection of Minorities draft Declaration on the Rights of Indigenous Peoples has stated, "Indigenous peoples are entitled to the recognition of the full ownership, control, and protection of their cultural and intellectual property."[30] It is not clear that U.N. members will take any action on this declaration or on the Mataatua Declaration or similar documents, but then it was not clear just a few years ago that any law such as NAGPRA would ever be passed.

What should concern us most at this juncture, I believe, are the third question and its implications. Of first importance is to find out if there is, in fact, any general agreement within Native American communities that the control and safeguarding of esoteric knowledge are desirable goals. If this is not so, then the issues are moot and the problems associated with such knowledge are very different ones. If there are common goals, then the question becomes whether there is any general agreement about what kinds of knowledge should be protected, either within given communities or across the country. I believe that such agreements are possible, despite the broad range of esoteric and culturally sensitive information that will be the focus of tribal attention. Within this large corpus, it is perhaps effectively too late to deal with the bulk of published and otherwise disseminated and copyrighted materials. In this context, restitution in some form might be feasible, but probably not repatriation in any literal and exclusive sense.

With regard to issues of control, do we know if research permits or similar procedures are really working as controls over the loss of relevant knowledge, and if not, what steps can be taken to ensure that they do work? Are other mechanisms available through memoranda of understanding and contractual agreements between tribal governments and institutions and government agencies to control access and use to existing knowledge outside of tribal possession? Some agreements of this kind already exist, although changes in freedom-of-information laws are essential if such arrangements are to be broadly considered. Also, have tribal governments fully considered the passage of tribal laws, including specialized forms of copyright law, that can protect and govern the use, where appropriate, of such knowledge? And are tribal leaders and communities prepared to consider the possibility of moving what has thus far been a largely moral dilemma into the world of general legislation, as was done with repatriation?

Conclusion

What may be accomplished in the protection of Native American esoteric knowledge remains to be seen. What is obvious is that we need to firmly establish the desirable parameters for tribal collective interests in the access, use, and transfer of such knowledge. This does not mean that knowledge would not or could not be shared, only that the sharing not be to the ongoing detriment of Native American communities or exclusive of tribal rights of control. This is a complex issue but one so important that we cannot fail to find, as we confront the issues, practicable solutions. Some of the essential ideological and legislative underpinnings for those solutions are already in place:

- The 1970 UNESCO Convention's identification of archival materials for protection as patrimony
- The 1993 U.N. declaration that the intellectual property of indigenous peoples is theirs to own and control
- The 1990 NAGPRA designation of sacred and patrimony objects as re-patriable and specification that tribal governments have sovereign powers that can be exercised over special categories of inalienable property

What is required at this moment is a fundamental acceptance that intellec-tual property and most especially esoteric knowledge are vital components of the living cultural heritage of Native American communities. As such these properties have been and are today held in tribal communities under different but equally valid and sensible legal precepts. The continuing critical impor-tance of esoteric knowledge and other forms of intellectual property means that a way must be found to acknowledge and implement appropriate Native American controls over such knowledge.

Notes

1. See, for example, Karl E. Meyer, *The Plundered Past* (New York: Atheneum, 1977).
2. Bonnie Burnham, *The Protection of Cultural Property: A Handbook of National Legislations* (Paris: ICOM, 1974).
3. See Public Law (PL) 97-446, Title III, Implementation of the Convention on Cultural Property.
4. United States of America, *Recovery and Return of Stolen Archaeological, Historical, and Cultural Properties: Treaty Between the United States of America and Mexico*, Treaties and Other International Acts, Series 7088, 1970; PL 92-587, Title II, Regulation of Importation of Pre-Columbian Monumental or Architectural Sculpture or Murals.
5. PL 95-341; 42 USC 1996.
6. See, for example, Anon, "American Indian Religious Freedom Act, P.L. 95-341," *Council for Museum Anthropology Newsletter* 3(3) (1979): 5–6; Bowen Blair, "American Indians vs. American Museums—a Matter of Religious Freedom," *American Indian Journal* 5 (May 1979): 13–21, and 5 (June 1979): 2–6; Charlotte J. Frisbie, "Navajo Jish, or Medicine Bundles and Museums," *Council for Museum Anthropology Newsletter* 1(4) (1977): 6–23; T. J. Ferguson, "The Repatriation of Ahayu: Da Zuni War Gods: An Interview with the Zuni Tribal Council on April 25, 1990," *Museum Anthropology* 14(2) (1990): 7–14; Kathryn Harris, "The American Indian Religious Freedom Act and Its Promise," *American Indian Journal* 5 (June 1979): 7–10; and C. Patrick Morris, "The Spirit and the Law: Indian Policy and Indian Religious Freedom," in *The Concept of Sacred Materials and Their Place in the World*, ed. George Horse Capture (Cody, Wyo.: Buffalo Bill Historical Center, 1989).
7. See, for example, Richard Hill, "Indians and Museums: A Plea for Cooperation." *Council for Museum Anthropology Newsletter* 4(2) (1980): 22–25; and James D. Nason, "Finders Keepers?" *Museum News* 51(7) (1973): 20–22.
8. PL 101–601.
9. Ibid., sec. 2(C).
10. Ibid., sec. 2(D).
11. Sherman Alexie, "White Men Can't Drum," *New York Times Magazine*, October 4, 1992, 30–31.
12. National Park Service, *Museum Handbook, Part I* (Washington, D.C.: National Park Service, 1990).
13. See, John Red Horse, "The Utility of Scholarship: An Interview with John Red Horse," *Tribal College* 4(3) (1993): 18–19; and Paul Boyer, "The Model Scholar," *Tribal College* 4(3) (1993): 20–21.
14. Sharon O'Brien, *American Indian Tribal Governments* (Norman: University of Oklahoma Press, 1993).
15. Virginia Morell, "An Anthropological Culture Shift," *Science* 264 (1994): 20–22.
16. American Anthropological Association, *Principles of Professional Responsibility* (Washington, D.C.: American Anthropological Association, 1971), 1.
17. Council of Australian Museum Associations, *Previous Possessions, New Obligations: Policies for Museums in Australia and Aboriginal and Torres Strait Islander Peoples* (Melbourne: Council of Australian Museum Associations, 1993), 3, 5.
18. Tom Greaves, ed., *Intellectual Property Rights for Indigenous Peoples* (Oklahoma City: Society for Applied Anthropology, 1994).

19. United Nations, *The Mataatua Declaration on Cultural and Intellectual Property Rights of Indigenous Peoples, June 1993* (New York: Commission on Human Rights, Subcommission on Prevention of Discrimination and Protection of Minorities, Working Group on Indigenous Populations, 1993), GE 93-14346; H. M. Mead, "The Mataatua Declaration and the Case of the Carved Meeting House Mataatua," *University of British Columbia Law Review* (special issue) (1995): 69–75.

20. United Nations, *The Mataatua Declaration.*

21. Ronald Cole-Turner, "Religion and Gene Patenting," *Science* 270 (1995): 52; Stanley Meisler, "Report: Drug Makers Don't Pay for World's Traditional Plant Cures," *Seattle Times*, September 17, 1995, A24; Darrell Addison Posey, "Intellectual Property Rights: What Is the Position of Ethnobiology?" *Journal of Ethnobiology* 10(1) (1995): 93–98; and Lori Wolfgang, "Patents on Native Technology Challenged," *Science* 269 (1995): 1506.

22. "Controversy Hits '95 Gallup Ceremonial," *Indian Trader* 26(9) (1995): 5–6.

23. "Student Challenges Sales of Fake Indian-Style Art in Bozeman," *Indian Trader* 26(9) (1995): 6.

24. Kay Walking Stick, "Kay Walking Stick on Indian Law," *Art Forum* 30 (1991): 20–21.

25. James Nason, "Native American Tribal Museum and Center Survey on Storage, Care, and Access" (Washington, D.C.: National Museum of the American Indian, Smithsonian Institution, 1992, unpublished report).

26. Morell, "An Anthropological Culture Shift," 20–22.

27. Paul Steidlmeier, "The Moral Legitimacy of Intellectual Property Claims: American Business and Developing Country Perspectives," *Journal of Business Ethics* 12 (1993): 157–164.

28. On collection access issues, see Marie C. Malaro, *A Legal Primer on Managing Museum Collections* (Washington, D.C.: Smithsonian Institution Press, 1985). On a possible approach to this legal issue, see David J. Stephenson, "A Legal Paradigm for Protecting Traditional Knowledge," in *Intellectual Property Rights*, ed. Greaves, 179–189.

29. For another perspective on oral history copyrights, see John A. Neuenschwander, "Oral History and Copyright: An Uncertain Relationship," *Journal of College and University Law* 10(2) (1984): 147–165.

30. Cited in Audrey R. Chapman, "Human Rights Implications of Indigenous Peoples' Intellectual Property Rights," in *Intellectual Property Rights*, ed. Greaves, 219.

Naomi Roht-Arriaza

Of Seeds and Shamans: The Appropriation of the Scientific and Technical Knowledge of Indigenous and Local Communities

Indigenous, tribal, and traditional resource-based peoples and communities have long used intimate knowledge of their surroundings and resources to shape ecosystems; provide food, medicines, and other useful products; and breed better crops and livestock.[1] This knowledge has not been recognized as being either scientific or valuable to the dominant culture and so has been freely appropriated. The appropriation of the scientific and technical knowledge of traditional and resource-based peoples, of the products of that knowledge, and even of the genetic characteristics of the people themselves has become both notorious and contested.

This essay first describes the appropriation of local communities' knowledge by global biotechnology, pharmaceutical, and agribusiness corporations and their allies in Northern universities, seed banks, and research centers. Second, this essay exposes the mechanisms of appropriation. I focus on the limited and culturally determined definitions of what is "wild" versus "cultivated," what is "knowledge" and who can possess it, and what is "innovation" and "invention." I also look at the role of the concept of "common heritage" in fostering appropriation and at its application in seed banks, gene banks, and other ex situ forms of conservation of genetic material.

Third, I look briefly at possible frameworks for ending appropriation. These include broadened and redefined intellectual property regimes, private contracts between communities or states and "bioprospectors," and expansion of the concept of farmers' rights to provide both compensation and control to indigenous and local communities. All these possibilities raise the essential problem of defining the holders of the right to patent, sell, or protect the technical and scientific knowledge at issue. Possible right-holders include individual inventors or breeders, the state where the resource is located, and the local community that has protected, developed, and used it through the years. Any solution to the issues of cultural appropriation in this area will require profound rethinking of how we define, empower, and protect communities and their historical knowledge base.

The Scientific and Technical Knowledge of Indigenous and Local Communities

Traditional groups have a long history of using plants for almost all needs, including food, shelter, clothing, and medicine. Common remedies used today were originally developed by healers prior to contact with industrial societies. Twenty-five percent of the prescription drugs in the United States originated from plants, with a total retail value in 1990 of approximately $8 billion; and many species still have not been assessed for their pharmacological capabilities.[2]

Although many drugs and cosmetics originated from the stewardship and knowledge of indigenous and local communities, that knowledge remains unrecognized and uncompensated until it is removed from the communities and appropriated by Western corporations or institutions. To cite a few examples:

- Quinine, used as a cure for malaria, is made from the bark of the Peruvian cinchona tree. Andean indigenous groups used it as a cure for fevers, supposedly learning of the bark's powers while observing feverish jaguars eating it.[3]
- The rosy periwinkle, unique to Madagascar, has been found to contain properties valuable in the treatment of leukemia and other cancers.[4] The drugs vincristine and vinblastine have been developed from the periwinkle, resulting in $100 million in sales annually for Bristol-Myers Squibb and virtually nothing for Madagascar.[5]
- For thousands of years, indigenous farmers in India have used the leaves and seeds of the neem tree as a natural insecticide. Juice from the tree has been used for centuries to prevent scabies and other skin disorders, villagers use neem twigs as toothbrushes, and Gandhi chewed neem leaves.[6] Over a dozen patents have now been granted in the United States and

other industrialized countries for products based on the neem plant. W. R. Grace, which received a patent for an insecticide based on the active ingredient in neem, has said it has no plans to compensate anyone in India for providing the knowledge that underlies the neem-based product.[7]

- The endod berry, a member of the soapwort family, had been used for centuries in Ethiopia as a laundry soap and fish intoxicant. A patent for its crustacean-killing properties has been filed by the University of Toledo after a scant few weeks of testing. The endod derivative may help stop the zebra mussel invasion in the Great Lakes, an environmental disaster that has crippled water supplies and threatened marine ecosystems.[8] Neither Ethiopia nor the local people who recognized the worth of the endod and protected it through the years will receive any of the expected financial rewards.

- The University of California and Lucky Biotech, a Japanese corporation, recently submitted a patent application for the sweetening proteins naturally derived from two African plants, katempfe and the serendipity berry. Thaumatin, the substance that makes katempfe sweet, is two thousand times sweeter than sugar, yet is calorie free. Although any transgenic plant containing these proteins would be covered by the patent, no arrangements have been made to return part of the benefits to the local communities, which have long used the plants as sweeteners.[9]

- In 1990 scientist Sally Fox of California received a U.S. patent for colored cotton based on the 1970 Plant Variety Protection Act. This patent was especially significant to corporations such as Levi Strauss and Esprit, which want environmentally friendly materials for their clothes. The seed for Sally Fox's patented cotton came from a U.S. Department of Agriculture collection obtained by Gus Hyer during his travels to Latin America. Colored cotton is the result of long periods of development and cultivation by indigenous groups of Latin America. Fox's patent directs any profits to her, not the indigenous developers.[10]

- The U.S. government in 1993 applied for U.S. and world patents on the cell line of a twenty-six-year-old Guaymi Indian woman from Panama.[11] After international protests from the Guaymi General Congress and others, the government withdrew its claim. Nonetheless, U.S. agencies have patented the T-cell line of a Papua New Guinean and have applications pending on two people from the Solomon Islands; the patent applications indicate that the cell lines may be useful for understanding or combating a virus associated with adult leukemia and chronic neurological disease. It is unclear to what degree the people whose DNA has been sampled are aware of the potentially lucrative nature of the research or the intention to patent their cell lines.

In these examples, scientific knowledge, resources developed using that knowledge, and even the bodies of the people themselves are appropriated from indigenous and local communities by Western scientists and corporations. Historically, access to the biological resources and local knowledge of these communities has been free and uncompensated, and they have been considered part of anthropological studies and the public domain. Industrial users, however, have been able to profit from the technological uses made of these same materials and knowledge.

The increasing interest in the use and preservation of the knowledge and resources of indigenous and local communities stems from the development of a lucrative biotechnology/genetic resources industry dependent on Southern genetic resources and knowledge. This development coincides with an increasing sense of urgency surrounding the need to preserve genetic and biological resources, a recognition of the importance of involving local people in conservation efforts, and the new visibility of indigenous peoples' fight for survival, land rights, and self-determination.

The growth of the biotechnology industry and the use of genetically engineered materials in pharmaceuticals, agricultural supplies, and many other industries vastly increase the commercial value of genetic resources in plants, animals, and microorganisms. Changes in the nature of basic science have made it possible to apply research on life forms to a number of different commercial activities, leading to an emerging "genetics supply" or "life" industry that depends on raw genetic material from fields, forests, and communities.[12]

That material is fast disappearing. Species and varieties are becoming extinct or eroding at unprecedented rates as a result of the use of ever-fewer high-yield commercial varieties in agricultural production as well as habitat loss and other factors.[13] Much of the world's genetic diversity has been lost: 97 percent of the vegetable varieties sold by commercial seed houses in the United States at the beginning of the century are now extinct, as are 87 percent of the pear and 86 percent of the apple varieties.[14] Fifty percent of Europe's domesticated animals have become extinct in this century.[15] Most of the world's remaining biodiversity is concentrated in "gene-rich" Southern countries, where most indigenous and traditional communities are also located. For agricultural crops, the genes necessary to combat new diseases and maintain yields come to a large extent from the South.

The alarming loss of ecosystem, species, and genetic diversity led to negotiation of the 1992 Convention on Biological Diversity, which brought concerns over use and appropriation of indigenous and local scientific knowledge of natural resources and systems squarely within an international ecological perspective. Among the convention's stated objectives is "the fair and equitable sharing of the benefits arising out of the utilization of genetic resources, including by appropriate access to genetic resources and by appropriate transfer of relevant technologies, taking into account all rights over those resources and to technologies, and by appropriate funding."[16] In other words, conservation of and access to Southern biodiversity, including genetic diversity, are given in exchange for access to Northern biotechnology and funding. The convention vests sovereign rights to biological resources, including genetic resources, with the state.[17]

Concern over biodiversity loss has led to increasing recognition that indigenous and local communities preserve much of the remaining biodiversity and are necessary partners in conservation efforts. These communities have long known how to use much more of the biodiversity to be found in their lands than Western scientists. For example, by consulting indigenous peoples, bioprospectors can increase the success ratio in trials for useful substances from one in ten thousand samples to one in two.[18] Coupled with this rediscovery of the positive role of local communities in sustainable development is a more general appreciation of the special contributions and needs of indigenous peoples and of the value of cultural as well as biological diversity in an increasingly homogeneous and threatened world.

What Counts as Knowledge? Mechanisms of Appropriation

Perhaps the most prevalent, and insidious, form of appropriation of indigenous knowledge and its products has been the construction of conceptual and legal categories of valuable knowledge and resources that systematically exclude the knowledge and resources of local communities, farmers, and indigenous peoples. This construction of exclusion takes several forms. Western science characterizes certain natural materials that local peoples and communities have cared for, preserved, improved, and developed as mere wild species or, at the most, as "primitive species" or "landraces." Formal, scientific systems of innovation and research have, at least until recently, denigrated and denied the value of farmers' and communities' informal systems of knowledge transmission and innovation.[19]

In addition, whereas the products of formal knowledge systems have been protected as "property," those of informal, traditional systems have been tagged the freely available "common heritage of humanity." In particular, patentability under current intellectual property law is systematically biased against the innovations and knowledge of indigenous and farmers' communities. And the products of this knowledge have been delinked from their ecological and sociocultural base through removal and preservation in

Northern-dominated seed banks, gene banks, and research projects, with the knowledge attaining merely anthropological interest. Thus, the living knowledge of existing communities is treated as either "quaint, quackery or quits."[20]

Although law generally distinguishes between tangible and intangible property, in this case the two are so closely linked that the distinction is unhelpful. The tangible resources at issue are commercially valuable mostly because of their (intangible) genetic information, and the purpose of appropriation is to gain access to this information so that it can then be synthesized in a laboratory. More important, to a large extent the resources exist in their current form thanks to the applied knowledge of indigenous and traditional communities in conserving and often improving them for specific purposes.[21] And for these communities themselves, the difference among intellectual, cultural, and material property is artificial. All are part of the heritage of these communities:

> "Heritage" is everything that belongs to the distinct identity of a people and which is theirs to share, if they wish, with other peoples. It includes all of those things which international law regards as the creative production of human thought and craftsmanship, such as songs, stories, scientific knowledge and artworks. It also includes inheritances from the past and from nature, such as human remains, the natural features of the landscape, and naturally-occurring species of plants and animals with which a people has long been connected.[22]

Furthermore, for indigenous communities, their heritage does not consist of mere economic rights over things but of a bundle of relationships with the animals, plants, and places involved. One of the mechanisms of appropriation has been precisely the separation of what is considered knowledge from what is considered physical resources; an end to appropriation means viewing them together.

Wildness Landraces, and the Construction of Agricultural Value

Indigenous and local farming communities have contributed significantly to the quality and diversity of the germ plasm that forms the basis of crop production. Genes from the fields of developing countries for fifteen major crops contribute more than $50 million in annual sales just in the United States.[23] This genetic diversity is developed and maintained by community-based innovation systems through which farmers breed varieties suited to their specific local needs and microenvironments.

Western science has been largely unable to recognize or value the role of indigenous and traditional farming communities because the innovators themselves have been invisible, the forms of transmission of knowledge incomprehensible, and the purpose of the work different from that of much formal science. The work of testing, comparing, and breeding "folk" varieties of seed is usually unrecognized as "plant breeding" by Western scientists.[24] It is done in fields rather than laboratories and is highly specific to the local micro-environment.[25] That landraces or farmers' varieties are also known as "primitive cultivars" is perhaps the clearest expression of the cultural biases inherent in these distinctions.

Often formal scientists fail to appreciate innovative practices because the plant breeders are peasant women. Women in many parts of the world play key roles in seed selection, vegetative propagation, and livestock management, all of which are central to the preservation and encouragement of diversity. This work may or may not be recognized within the local communities, where women often lack visibility and power, but it is clearly unrecognized by Western-style farmers, extension agents, and researchers.[26]

In addition, much knowledge about the qualities and uses of plants, animals, and microorganisms is transmitted orally, often through stories and songs. Descriptions of uses of plants, animals, or soils for medicinal purposes may be dismissed because the corresponding maladies or diseases are described in ways that integrate the physical, mental, and spiritual and so are alien to Western researchers. Such knowledge is easily dismissed as folklore, superstition, old wives' tales, or quaint remnants of dying cultures.

Many of the useful genetic characteristics of plants are found not in "domesticated" varieties but in those related varieties that are not cultivated. They can be found in the environs of traditional farm and indigenous communities. These species, because they were not cultivated in ways obvious to Western researchers, were called wild or semiwild and were considered to have ended up in undeveloped areas by luck or natural bounty. It is now becoming clear, however, that almost all the different types of species to be found in and around traditional rural communities have been nurtured or developed by local people.[27] Far from being wild, these partner or associated species are often an integrated part of farming or forest/farming systems.[28]

Many local communities draw a significant share of their resources from these partner species and make little distinction between wild and cultivated foods. Similarly, many rural communities have conserved and protected wild plants known to have medicinal qualities without formally cultivating them. Such communities have also recognized the value of other wild plants and microorganisms and protected them indirectly through preservation and improvement of the local ecosystems of which they form a part.[29] Yet because these plants are not cultivated in ways that are obvious to visiting Western scientists or researchers, they are deemed to exist fortuitously, independently of human intervention. As such, they are free for the taking.

The plant breeding and selection undertaken by farmers and traditional communities also escape notice because they are not necessarily aimed at producing the highest possible yield for sale. Rather, traditional farmers, who produce at least in part for their own consumption, may choose lower-yielding varieties for traits including hardiness, flavor, diversity as an insurance strategy, and even religious associations.[30] These varieties are then dismissed as nonproductive, low-yielding cultivars that evidence farmers' lack of initiative and ability. Moreover, these varieties tend to be adapted to particular ecological conditions and socioecological practices that cannot be easily replicated. Studies show that traditional farmers aim to increase the diversity of their crop base, encouraging diversity both within each crop and in the mixture of food, forage, medicinal, shelter-related, and other useful plants grown in order to achieve maximum complementarity and synergy among crops, animals, and people.[31] Commercial breeders, in contrast, seek both uniformity and applicability to a wide variety of conditions. Thus, what has little commercial applicability is relegated to the category of landrace, worthwhile only in its potential for future incorporation into scientifically engineered varieties, which can then be sold at market rates to a wide variety of farmers. That local communities might innovate for a different purpose is rarely recognized.

Nonrecognition of Informal Innovation Systems

Much of the recent debate about appropriation of the scientific and technical knowledge of traditional and indigenous peoples has centered on the role of intellectual property rights in the recognition of formal (but not informal) innovation. Such rights, generally expressed through patents, have historically served to provide financial rewards to those appropriating indigenous knowledge and its products, while denying such rewards to the communities whose knowledge is appropriated.[32] The aim of the patent system is to encourage innovation by providing an inventor with a time-limited monopoly (usually from fifteen to twenty years) over the invention in exchange for fully describing it and making it available to others.[33] Patents may be granted for products or processes. Patents are generally granted on a national level, and each state may decide what to exclude from patenting. Nonetheless, under the recently concluded General Agreement on Tariffs and Trade (GATT) (1994) all members of the World Trade Organization (WTO) must provide "effective" protection of intellectual property rights, including those in living matter.[34] Several of the provisions of national laws governing patentability systematically exclude indigenous and traditional communities' knowledge.

Possessing Novelty or Newness

Patentable inventions must be new or novel. In U.S. law, this means that a patent cannot be issued if the invention was known or used by others in the United States, if it was described in a printed publication, or if the putative patent-holder did not invent the subject matter sought to be patented.[35] Thus, patents reward the kind of individual, secretive effort epitomized by the lone scientist in his basement laboratory. In contrast, most traditional and indigenous knowledge is collective and is passed down from generation to generation. It builds on prior knowledge in an organic, accretional way that makes it difficult to single out a certain individual or point of time. Even in those cases where it is not widely held (as in the case of medicinal knowledge held by shamans or healers), the accretion and transmission of knowledge from generation to generation would still invalidate it on novelty grounds. Moreover, the individual nature of patent law is reinforced in the trade-related intellectual property rights (TRIPs) agreement, incorporated into the new GATT/WTO agreement, which recognizes intellectual property rights only as private rights.[36] Rights belonging to the public, or a sector of it, do not fit easily.

The novelty requirement means that investors must seek a patent at the earliest possible moment; if they do not, they cannot "catch up" later. Those whose inventions are now known cannot retroactively apply for patent protection. Indigenous and traditional communities that are only now beginning to debate and demand a place in world intellectual property systems (albeit with much disagreement about that place), and that had no practical opportunity to participate in the system's development, are frozen out.

Requiring an Inventive Step

The TRIPs agreement requires that patentable items "involve an inventive step." U.S. law expresses the same requirement through the term *nonobvious*. One corollary of both the novelty and nonobviousness requirements is that "products of nature" cannot be patented.[37] The substance of a patent may not be the discovery of some natural phenomenon. Thus, medicinal plants in their natural state, or even diluted or otherwise processed, are not patentable. However, if a Western scientist isolates the active substance in a plant in a way that does not occur in nature, it becomes patentable.[38] The knowledge gained outside a chemical laboratory is downgraded to a substance "which nature has intended for the use of all men," even though there may be no reason or need for traditional or indigenous peoples to isolate or extract the exact chemical compounds that give a substance its utility.[39] Conversely, once a substance has been isolated in a chemically pure or non–naturally occurring state, it becomes patentable even though the knowledge of the substance's qualities may have been widely known in traditional or indigenous communities.[40] Similarly, the inventiveness involved in isolating and identifying a specific gene makes genetically engineered plants and animals patentable, whereas the labor involved in selecting for and preserving the same genetic qualities in the field merely potentiates further development.[41]

Being Capable of Industrial Application

A third requirement is that, according to TRIPs, inventions must be "capable of industrial application." According to some commentators, this excludes anyone who produces and innovates outside the industrial or agro-industrial sector, although the assimilation of the term to the U.S. requirement of "useful" may allow for broader interpretation.[42] But the underlying theory of the TRIPs accord is that the invention is being created in order to be sold and obtain economic benefits; the less monetized the society is, the less validity this assumption has. Indeed, the very name of the TRIPs initiative limits its application to goods potentially involved in international trade, excluding those created for local or national consumption. To the extent that patent systems privilege the protection of commodities, they reflect a limited, Western view of the purposes of intellectual inquiry and knowledge seeking, one that attributes a profit motive to peoples who may base their scientific inquiry on different foundations. Only the inventions of the profit oriented will be protected.

Displaying Reproducibility

Utility patents require that the inventor describe the product or process so that others skilled in the industry can reproduce it. In the case of biological materials not easily described in words, U.S. patent applicants may deposit a sample of the biological material with a recognized depositary.[43] Again, this requirement works against the more site-specific, less stable, and less uniform products of the informal innovation system. By their nature and objectives, many inventions of indigenous and traditional communities can be reproduced only in the specific ecological, social, and cultural conditions that gave rise to them. For example, the greater genetic variability of farmers' seeds may mean that they will produce the desired traits only under a certain combination of soils, rainfall, nearby crops, cultivation practices, or the like particular to a place or culture, and that even then they are less reliable than high-tech hybrid varieties. This characteristic does not make them any less innovative than laboratory applications aimed at wider applicability. But to the extent it becomes more difficult for others to reproduce the desired traits because they do not share the necessary ecological, social, and cultural conditions, the utility of the patent system for such innovations is reduced.

The case of the neem seed is illustrative.[44] The seeds themselves would be a "product of nature," and the traditional method of scattering seeds as a pesticide would not be patentable because as a traditional method, it was not "invented" by the applicant. Nonetheless, patents have been granted for a process of pretreating the neem bark that results in extracts with a greater degree of purity.[45] Patents have also been issued for the active ingredient in the seed, azadirachtin, and for insecticides derived from it. The derivatives, because they are the product of a laboratory and are slightly modified versions of the original, are no longer considered products of nature.[46] No recognition, or compensation, is due to the people who discovered the beneficial uses of the seed and nurtured it through the centuries.

Ensuring Plant Breeders' Rights

Additional criteria apply to intellectual property over plant genetic resources. Under TRIPs, these resources need not be patented but must be protected "either by patents or by an effective sui generis system or by any combination thereof."[47] The most well-known existing sui generis system for plants is the Union for Protection of Varieties (UPOV convention).[48] UPOV sets minimum plant breeders' standards and mandates plant breeders' rights for the discovery as well as breeding of new species. Plant breeders' rights differ from patents mostly because they allow the free use of a protected variety to breed and commercialize other new varieties and because they historically have allowed farmers to save their own seed for the next production cycle without paying royalties.[49] Over time, the UPOV convention has been amended to provide greater protection for breeders and less for farmers. For example, farmers' rights to save seed are no longer guaranteed, rights can be granted for "discovery" as well as breeding of new varieties, and breeders' rights to compensation now extend to "essentially derived varieties" tracing their heritage to protected varieties.[50] All these changes favor large research and agribusiness concerns over farmers, especially smaller or traditional farming communities where seed saving and sharing are a way of life.

As with patents, traditional farmers find it difficult to obtain protection for their own innovative breeding work under UPOV. To be protectable, plant varieties must be uniform, stable (salient traits must be passed from one generation to the next), and distinct (from other varieties).[51] Uniformity and stability are traits usually sought by large agribusiness seed companies interested in selling seed in many different climactic and soil conditions and for large-scale harvesting. Traditional farmers, in contrast, may be more interested in fomenting adaptability to many different conditions and may select seeds tailored to many different microenvironments. Landraces and farmers' varieties may thus be less uniform and stable than those of commercial varieties. As a result, although UPOV works to traditional farmers' disadvantage when it comes to using the protected varieties of others, these requirements would make it difficult for such farmers to use UPOV to protect their own innovations. Even though the requirements admittedly have a technical rationale, they also reflect a bias in favor of large-scale commercial agriculture.[52]

Seed Banks, Gene Banks and the Common Heritage

Intellectual property laws appropriate indigenous and traditional scientific knowledge by denying it legitimacy as a protectable interest while allowing it to be freely used by others. The products of this knowledge are also subject to appropriation. The fruits of indigenous and traditional knowledge are tagged the common heritage of humanity rather than the evolving product of defined living communities. Whereas such common heritage resources can be freely collected, those same resources brought into mostly Northern-controlled seed banks, gene banks, and laboratories can be "improved" and then given or sold to private interests, which treat the results as private property.

Of course, the uncompensated removal and transport of plants from one area to another go back to the beginnings of exploration. The world's great botanical gardens, Italian cuisine and Irish potatoes, among others, are a product of the plant resource movements that accompanied the colonizations of the sixteenth through nineteenth centuries. The unrestricted movement and sharing of plant genetic resources have improved diets and increased sources of food and useful materials throughout the world.[53] Indeed, farming communities often exchange seed with other communities.[54] The problem is not with the free use and exchange of resources per se but with the designation of only some resources as common, while others are protected as private.

The fight over the status of plant genetic resources illustrates the selective use of the common heritage concept. Under the auspices of the U.N. Food and Agriculture Organization (FAO), the nonbinding International Undertaking on Plant Genetic Resources was negotiated in 1983.[55] The original version of the undertaking, supported by gene-rich developing countries, declared that *all* plant germ plasm, both raw and elite breeders' lines, was equally part of the common heritage of mankind and therefore available to all.[56] The undertaking thus represented an attempt by Southern countries to place laboratory-bred varieties on the same plane as their undeveloped plant genetic resources.

Predictably, most developed countries rejected this premise of the undertaking, and by 1989 FAO members, arguing that the text conflicted with the

UPOV convention, had effectively added protection for breeders' rights.[57] By 1991 the undertaking had been amended to practically abandon the common heritage concept for improved varieties, while retaining it for farmers' varieties.[58] The inequality inherent in the use of the common heritage concept led to its rejection in the 1992 Convention on Biological Diversity, which affirms sovereign state rights over genetic resources along with other biological resources.[59]

The common heritage principle has long been applied to the collection and storage of plant germ plasm in seed banks. These are giant ice boxes where seeds are held under cold, dry conditions and periodically grown out. Many states and national agricultural institutions maintain extensive seed collections; altogether gene banks hold some 4.35 million crop accessions.[60] Sixteen International Agricultural Research Centers (IARCs) collect crop and wild germ plasm, including varieties of wheat, corn, rice, potatoes, millet, sorghum, barley, and livestock.[61] The Consultative Group on International Agricultural Research (CGIAR), an informal grouping of mostly Northern donor governments, universities, research centers, and individuals, manages the centers.

Gene banks collect southern germ plasm and distribute it to gene-poor northern countries. A large proportion of commercially used genetic material moves to the developed countries via the IARCs. The Rural Advantage Foundation International (RAFI), based on a 1982 Organization of Economic Cooperation and Development report, estimates that the Third World has contributed $500 million annually worth of germ plasm to the United States. Other studies estimate that, for example, 21 percent of the U.S. wheat crop was derived from material stored at the International Maize and Wheat Improvement Center, the IARC for wheat.[62] Seed companies are dependent on this germ plasm for sustenance of their genetically engineered and hybrid varieties.

Furthermore, the IARCs, although their stated purpose is to protect and develop plant genetic resources for all of humanity, have sometimes served as donors of raw materials then incorporated into protected varieties by multinational seed companies. Again, the germ plasm in the banks is free, considered common heritage, but the products engineered in laboratories on the basis of this germ plasm are protected and must be bought. As a result, farmers from the areas where the germ plasm was originally protected and selected may end up paying for the "end product of their own genius."[63]

The storage of genetic materials in seed and gene banks, moreover, makes them practically inaccessible to traditional and indigenous communities. Most genetic materials collected in southern countries—68 percent of all crop seed, 85 percent of all livestock breeds, and 86 percent of microbial culture collections—are held at the IARCs or in industrialized countries.[64] Northern governments hold by far the largest number of seed accessions. Even though theoretically these are available upon request to researchers and farmers, practical knowledge, distance, and cost obstacles mean that the material is inaccessible to informal innovators in local farming and indigenous communities; it becomes functionally extinct for those communities. Moreover, there is no reason to think that the improved breeding stock produced from IARC research will make its way back to farming communities. According to one study, so far only 15 percent of samples from research centers connected to the international system, which includes CGIAR and the IARCs, have gone to developing nations.[65] Finally, the Convention on Biological Diversity, by excluding any material now held in seed banks from its provisions on national sovereignty, may legitimize the current ability of northern governments and corporations now holding some of the most valuable germ plasm to own and control it.[66]

Although seed banks contribute to preserving those genetic resources that cannot otherwise be saved, a concentration on ex situ collections has served to establish Northern formal scientific control over large genetic stocks as well as to undervalue and ignore the role of living communities in preservation of local biodiversity. The underlying assumption is that the living communities that have sustained and developed biological resources in the past are unable or unqualified to do so or are doomed to disappear. All that remains for the international community is to safeguard as much as possible of the resources formerly under these communities' control without any active role for them in either conservation or development. Similarly, since indigenous communities are disappearing, the response is not to attack the conditions that threaten such communities but to create knowledge banks that will save their wisdom for future generations.[67] There is a role for such strategies, especially if designed and implemented by communities themselves, but these strategies can also reflect a view of indigenous and traditional communities as dead or dying, unable to live and participate in history and to use and develop their knowledge and traditions rather than simply preserve them in a mummified state.[68]

These limitations on the seed bank idea are most explicit in the collection and attempted patenting of the human cell lines of indigenous peoples themselves. The Human Genome Diversity Project, an informal consortium of universities and scientists in Europe and North America, plans to collect samples of the DNA of some four hundred indigenous communities.[69] The project's purpose is to preserve the genetic map of disappearing ethnic groups because the peculiar genetic characteristics of such groups could some day prove invaluable to medicine. The underlying assumption is that these indigenous groups will inevitably disappear; they are referred to as "Isolates of Historic Interest" "that should be sampled before they disappear as integral units so that their role in human history can be preserved."[70] The project aims to spend five years and $23–35 million to collect blood samples, which will be stored at the American Type Culture Collection in Rockville, Maryland. To date, little effort has been made to consult with or include indigenous people themselves in the design of the project.[71] Under this type of project, the very being of indigenous peoples becomes part of the common heritage, to be collected and stored outside their control.

Answers to Appropriation

The last several years have witnessed a lively and complex debate on the mechanisms needed to reverse the appropriation of indigenous and local community scientific knowledge. Running through this debate is a difference in the scope of the goals pursued: some schemes stress compensation for past and future contributions while assuming unrestricted access; others focus on control over access and stress the right of communities as well as states to decide when and whether their knowledge and resources are to be used.

Another issue permeating the debate is whether the rights to knowledge and resources should be vested in individuals, communities, and/or states. Industrial intellectual property schemes reward individual effort (or that of corporate or institutional employees), whereas the Convention on Biological Diversity vests sovereign rights over resources in the state. Thus, the state is free to legislate the appropriate property regime within the limits previously described.

The vesting of rights only in individuals marginalizes the interests and contributions of indigenous and traditional communities. The vesting of rights only in the state as representative of its communities also has several drawbacks.[72] First, states have not generally been protective of the rights or interests of indigenous and traditional communities; indeed, they have often been among the primary forces facilitating the destruction of these communities. Second, there is no reason to assume that resources obtained on behalf of communities will actually be used for their benefit, as a history of misguided "development" projects demonstrates. Third, state ownership of resources often results in centralized bureaucracy, which is inimical to both continuing innovation and appropriate preservation of natural resources.[73] Fourth, from a resource conservation point of view resources are more likely to be effectively protected if local communities are invested and involved in their use and stewardship.[74]

Several international instruments recognize to some extent the special role of indigenous and local communities. The link between community resources and conservation is explicit in the Convention on Biological Diversity. The convention commits states to take measures, "as far as possible and as appropriate," to establish in situ conservation measures. As part of that effort, each state party shall

> 8(j) subject to its national legislation, respect, preserve and maintain knowledge, innovation and practices of indigenous and local communities embodying traditional lifestyles relevant for the conservation and sustainable use of biological diversity and promote their wider application with the approval and involvement of the holders of such knowledge, innovations and practices and encourage the equitable sharing of the benefits arising from the utilization of such knowledge, innovations and practices.[75]

The provision recognizes for the first time in a global treaty the special role of both indigenous and local communities in innovation and knowledge. Other declarations arising from the 1992 U.N. Conference on Environment and Development make the same point.[76] Nonetheless, the reference to national legislation and the lack of concrete obligations weaken the provision, while other articles of the convention committing states to guaranteed access to genetic resources may reduce the ability of indigenous and local communities to control their knowledge and resources.

The FAO's International Undertaking on Plant Genetic Resources balances recognition of elite variety plant breeders' rights with the concept of farmers' rights. The latter rights are defined as "rights arising from the past, present and future contributions of farmers in conserving, improving and making available plant genetic resources, particularly those in the centres of origin/diversity."[77] Although the current language recognizes the collective nature of farmers' contribution, farmers' rights are not vested in farmers or farming communities directly but in "the International Community, as trustee for present and future generations of farmers."[78] The FAO simultaneously set up a fund to support future research by farmers, but contributions to the fund (unlike intellectual property royalty payments) are voluntary and have so far been meager. Thus, the undertaking recognizes the contributions of farmers but provides for neither ownership of the products of these contributions nor direct compensation.

Human rights instruments recognize the interests of indigenous peoples in traditional knowledge and its fruits.[79] The draft Declaration on the Rights of Indigenous Peoples, approved by the U.N. Human Rights Subcommission on Prevention of Discrimination and Protection of Minorities in 1994, calls for a right to restitution of cultural, intellectual, religious, and spiritual property taken without the free and informed consent of indigenous peoples or in violation of their laws, traditions, and customs.[80] More specifically, Article 29 states: "Indigenous peoples are entitled to the recognition of the full ownership, control and protection of their cultural and intellectual property. They have the right to special measures to control, develop and protect their sciences, technologies and cultural manifestations, including human and other genetic resources, seeds, medicines, knowledge of the properties of fauna and flora, oral traditions, literatures, designs and visual and performing arts."[81]

The draft declaration raises squarely the question of what kinds of "special measures" will best serve this goal. Indigenous peoples themselves, in conjunction with others, have begun to discuss ways to structure regimes to protect their knowledge and resources and reflect their priorities, interests, and concerns. The schemes can be grouped into three types: (1) expand the definition of intellectual property rights in national and international law to include collective innovators and informal innovations; (2) encourage, and impose standards on, private contracts between communities and corporate or government bioprospectors; or (3) focus more broadly on mechanisms to promote rights to use, manage and control community livelihood systems, including tangible and intangible resources. This last, most ambitious option, would include elements of resource control and management and of compensation.

Expanding Intellectual Property Rights

One obvious response to the appropriation of indigenous and traditional knowledge and its fruits is to modify existing systems of national and international intellectual property protection to encompass the informal innovations of indigenous and local communities. In general, such changes would allow for patenting by collective entities, protect cumulative or accretional knowledge, and extend protection to those innovations involving traditional or nonlaboratory technologies.

Changes in patent law would require national legislation. However, the completion of the Uruguay Round of the GATT as well as the Convention on Biological Diversity has introduced international constraints. The TRIPs provisions of the Uruguay Round require states to implement patent systems that utilize the traditional criteria of novelty, nonobviousness, and utility and that extend some form of intellectual property protection to plants.[82] The nature of such sui generis systems is one of the most controversial facing many national legislatures.

The Convention on Biological Diversity deals with intellectual property protection in a vague and contradictory manner.[83] The convention states that, first, in case of technology subject to patents and other intellectual property rights, such access and transfer (to/of technology) shall be provided on terms that recognize and are consistent with the adequate and effective protection of intellectual property rights.[84] Parties then agree to ensure (through appropriate legislation affecting both public and private researchers) that those developing countries providing access to genetic resources will in turn have access to the biotechnology that uses those resources, "on mutually agreed" terms and "in accordance with international law"—presumably including trade laws. However, at the same time, the contracting parties are to ensure that intellectual property rights are supportive of and do not run counter to the convention's objectives.[85] Taken in toto, the provisions leave the protection of industrial intellectual property rights intact and impose few substantive obligations beyond a commitment not to completely restrict access to either raw materials or technology.

Within this context, most proposals contain both an affirmative aspect that modifies industrial patent rights to cover collective, accretional, and informal invention and a negative aspect that aims at preventing others from profiting from indigenous and local knowledge without the consent of those communities. Proposals originating with indigenous peoples' organizations and nongovernmental groups stress control over mere compensation. The goal is not simply to receive money in exchange for access to knowledge and resources but to control whether, and how, such knowledge is commercialized, while leaving it available for noncommercial uses. Thus, several international gatherings of indigenous peoples have demanded control over their own intellectual property rights.[86] Indigenous peoples especially demand the ability, through modified intellectual property schemes or otherwise, to deny others the ability to commodify their knowledge. As one recent report put it, "The first concern of indigenous peoples is their right NOT to sell, commoditize, or have expropriated from them certain domains of knowledge and certain sacred places, plants, animals, and objects."[87]

The emphasis on control raises a fundamental question about adoption of modified or expanded intellectual property rights: should indigenous people (or other traditional or local communities) try to modify existing systems to suit their needs, or are such systems irredeemably inappropriate? Both philosophical and practical concerns arise.

On a philosophical level, the concept of private intellectual property rights is foreign to indigenous peoples. Even though some indigenous knowledge may be restricted or secret, the reasons for the restrictions are usually not commercial in nature. For some indigenous groups the privatization and commodification of knowledge and of living resources are both incomprehensible and reprehensible. Indeed, according to Darrell Posey, indigenous people "are more concerned about the misuse or misinterpretation of their knowledge, culture and cultural expressions."[88] By attempting to manipulate the prevailing Western paradigm to suit their needs, will indigenous peoples accelerate the very commodification of knowledge and of living things that many find so objectionable? Worse, will they be forced to adopt foreign categories as their own, to shoehorn their worldviews and values into an alien set of concepts and laws? After all, indigenous peoples have long experience in the disastrous effects on their communities of imposed Western-style individual property rights in land. But is to refrain from pressing demands for indigenous intellectual property rights merely to maintain the status quo or reify a museumlike vision of unchanging, ahistorical, "noble savages"? Some have argued that it is utopian to expect Northern countries to retreat on imposing ever-broader intellectual property protections and that indigenous and local communities have no choice but to make a foreign system work for them.

Even if an emphasis on control over access and noncommercialization, rather than on mere compensation, resolves some of these philosophical issues, practical problems remain. In numerous cases, more than one community makes similar use of the same resources, sometimes using the same processes. In these cases, which community is to receive the intellectual property rights: the first to invent, the first to file, or the first to show a long use of the process or product at issue? Often, resources taken from local communities find a slightly different use in developed countries than the traditional use. How are these cases to be resolved?

Furthermore, the current intellectual property system is heavily stacked against indigenous and local communities, which are overwhelmingly poor and far from the centers of Northern legal power. An expansion of intellectual property systems to cover indigenous and local innovation could require communities to challenge patent applications or to sue for patent infringement, in many countries simultaneously, against some of the world's most sophisticated corporations and governments. Indigenous and local communities may end up spending scarce resources on investigators and attorneys to protect their newly won intellectual property rights. Even if nongovernmental organizations representing or aligned with these groups will do the work, is this the best use of their time and resources? And does the choice of forum necessarily mean that communities will be beholden to others, or even to a few of their own, to protect their interests? Expansion of intellectual property rights under such unfavorable conditions may disempower communities rather than empowering them. Suggestions for special ombudsmen, tribunals, and financial support for community legal work might alleviate, but will not eliminate, some of these problems.[89]

The Contracts Option

Interest in biological resources from biotechnology, pharmaceutical, and other corporations has opened the possibility of direct contractual relationships between purveyors and buyers of indigenous and traditional knowledge. Under the typical terms of exchange, a company or research institute obtains a temporary monopoly of indigenous knowledge or resources from a delimited area in return for initial and/or royalty payments.[90]

One of the first such contracts was negotiated between Merck Pharmaceuticals and INBio, a private nonprofit biodiversity institute in Costa Rica. According to the terms of the contract, Merck provides $1.135 million up front, plus a share of any royalties on commercial products developed from the accessions, in exchange for ten thousand extracts from Costa Rica's plants, insects, and microorganisms.[91] INBio contributes a portion of the funds to the government for park conservation, and Merck provides technical assistance and training of Costa Ricans.

In December 1993 the U.S. National Institutes of Health (NIH), Conservation International, Bristol-Myers Squibb, Virginia Polytechnic Institute and State University, and the Missouri Botanical Garden teamed up with the country of Suriname to study medicinal plants. Bristol-Myers will pay royalties to the indigenous people of Suriname for any drugs derived from plants gathered there. Shamans and other traditional healers will be eligible to share patent rights to these compounds.[92]

Other NIH-sponsored initiatives include an agreement between Monsanto and the Cayetano Peruvian University to study medicinal plants from Andean rain forests; one among Walter Reed Army Institute of Research, the University of Yaounde in Cameroon, and several U.S.-based conservation groups and pharmaceuticals companies to look for parasitic drugs in the African rain forest; and another involving American Cyanamid and various universities of Argentina, Chile, Mexico, and the United States to study medicinal properties of plants from arid regions.[93] One U.S.-based company, Shaman Pharmaceuticals, uses ethnobotanical science as a drug discovery technique. It has several patent claims already pending and has pledged to return a portion of its sales from drugs derived from community-based knowledge to the communities involved through its nonprofit arm, the Healing Forest Conservancy.[94]

Scholars, activists, and indigenous peoples' representatives disagree on the potential of such private contracts. On the one hand, contracts have the advantage of allowing indigenous and local communities to bypass the state—albeit within a state regulatory framework—and negotiate on their own behalf. The benefits of any such arrangements may go directly to the local community, not the state treasury. Contracts decentralize controls over use of resources and offer flexibility in the designation of individual or collective owners of different kinds of knowledge and in the tailoring of provisions to a given situation. Moreover, parties to a contract may stipulate protective conditions.[95]

On the other hand, private contracts, even those regulated by codes of conduct or including protective provisions, pose potential problems. First, the two parties to the deal have vastly different resources and abilities to enforce its provisions. One proposed answer is to stipulate an initial escrow fund, paid by the corporation/researcher, to pay legal fees of the community in any case of dispute. But the question is not simply of money but of access to information (about the potential commercial value of a certain product, for example). A network of advisers and the training of indigenous and local people would ameliorate the problem, but in any case the community will lose direct control over part of its resource base. Of the possible options, bilateral contracts provide, in practice, the least opportunity for control; the whole point is to facilitate access in exchange for compensation, and any controls on access limit the attractiveness of the deal.

Second, contracts may exacerbate divisions among indigenous and local communities as parts of the community, to the exclusion of others, seek to capitalize on lucrative opportunities.[96] Often the same plant or microorganism is found in several different communities spanning national borders. Corporations and scientists could play one place off against another for the most favorable terms.

Third, contracts may limit community control over the amount and distribution of whatever benefits accrue. For example, Shaman Pharmaceutical does not plan to return royalties directly to source communities but to a northern-run nongovernmental organization that will distribute the proceeds as it sees fit. In a recent consortium deal, Searle Pharmaceutical (Monsanto) agreed to pay $15,000 per year in up-front payments for the benefit of local inhabitants of the collection area, but the money will be paid to, and distributed by, Washington University in the United States. Any royalty payments, ranging from 0.2 percent to 1 percent of any licensed product, will also be distributed through Washington University after costs for research, development, and management by the Northern-based scientific institutions involved have been deducted. The amount of money that actually reaches local communities under these terms may be much less than expected, amounting to little more than the employment of local people as cheap labor in the collection process. And Northern environmental nongovernmental organizations and research institutes, not local communities, may control the use of any funds that do materialize.

Multilateral Agreements and Funds

Given the drawbacks of private frameworks, the best option may be a public multilateral set of agreements among states and communities governing access to indigenous and local knowledge and its products. Such agreements could cover at least the majority of cases where it is impossible to associate a certain material or technique with a unique ethnic or geographic group as well as those resources already collected and held in gene banks where the exact provenance is unknown.[97]

The most frequently discussed multilateral framework would incorporate a revised FAO undertaking either as a separate binding treaty or as a protocol to the Convention on Biological Diversity.[98] The most promising part of the current undertaking is its reference to farmers' rights, which could be redefined to provide for participation of indigenous and traditional communities in the control and compensation of genetic knowledge. Direct participation of indigenous and local communities is not now part of the undertaking: farmers' rights are vested in the international community as trustee. FAO officials, moreover, have tended to equate farmers' rights with the rights of developing countries.[99] Similarly, as of now the fund set up to compensate farmers for their past, present, and future contributions is both inoperative and functionally state centered. Any replacement fund would have to be mandatory and to include participatory mechanisms for funds to directly reach communities.

Conclusion

Any of these three options presents drawbacks as well as advantages, and the emerging regime may combine a number of modalities. Under any regime, three issues will be key: defining and ensuring the participation of different kinds of local communities, recognizing the multiple roles such communities play, and framing solutions that link the issues of appropriation of knowledge and resources to the larger agenda of community protection and development.

Some communities are easier to define than others. Indigenous peoples, although often divided along gender, power, or philosophical lines, are relatively well defined internationally, and their existence as distinct groups, if not as peoples, is finally becoming accepted.[100] Their demand for intellectual property rights is part of a larger fight for control over their land and resources and for self-determination. Moreover, indigenous peoples have an effective and growing network of local, national, regional, and global organizations able to represent them.

Not so "local" or "traditional" communities. These overlap somewhat with indigenous peoples but may also include subsistence farmers or those who produce for regional markets, inshore fisherpeople, nomadic herders or hunter/gatherers, forest peoples, artisan communities, and others who derive a large part of their livelihood from the natural world. These communities, long the stewards of local biodiversity, often exist precariously on the edge of, and are threatened by, industrialized, high-input systems of agribusiness; long-distance trawler fishing; and large-scale cattle ranching as well as by industrial systems and mass tourism. Although many such communities have local organizations of one sort or another—peasant or farmers' leagues, development associations, and the like—few have an effective political voice at the international (and even the national) level. Whereas some are closely bound by ties of ancestry, language, or other cultural characteristics, others share no bond other than their use of and dependence on natural resources for a livelihood, relative remove from the centers of power, and sense of themselves as a community.

How are these communities to be adequately defined and represented for purposes of control, and receipt of the benefits, of their knowledge and resources, within either a multilateral or communal framework? Some general characteristics of such communities—a natural resource base, a form of social organization, and a sense of membership—may serve as guideposts.[101] Beyond that, some system of self-declaration or registration of communities wishing to protect their innovations, combined with a mechanism for resolving conflicts both within communities and among different communities claiming ownership of the same knowledge, might be useful.[102] Effective mechanisms to allow for community participation and control over decision-making will be key.

An end to appropriation requires recognition of the role of indigenous and traditional or local communities as stewards of scientific and ecological knowledge and resources, as innovators, and as practitioners of sustainable production and life systems.[103] For these communities, the right to control their scientific knowledge and its associated resources is inseparable from rights to the communities' communal heritage—including its tangible and intangible elements. Heritage rights may encompass land and resource rights, secure land tenure, measures to defend local artisanry and agriculture from the destructive effects of global commerce, and, in the case of indigenous peoples, more broadly defined rights to self-determination. In the long run, the ability of indigenous and traditional peoples to obtain a say in the use of their knowledge and the products of that knowledge will depend on the vibrancy, visibility, and agency of those communities. Ending the discriminatory appropriation of these resources is only part of this larger agenda.

Notes

Maria Montes and Kathleen Yurchak did extensive research and wrote drafts for this essay, and I deeply appreciate their help in doing research and in discussing the issues with me. I also profoundly thank Monica Moore at Pesticide Action Network North America and everyone at Genetic Resources Action International (GRAIN) in Barcelona for help and support.

1. Throughout this essay, I use the terms *indigenous, traditional, resource-based,* and *local* communities interchangeably, although the definitions of these terms are quite problematic. Indigenous or tribal peoples, according to one definition, are "those who share customs and local knowledge of specific geographic territory and are relatively independent of, or have little contact with, the dominant national society of the country in which they live." Traditional peoples "encompass many of the rural and peasant communities that inhabit the countryside . . . and live on marginal lands relatively removed from many of the accoutrements of modern life." See Edith Brown Weiss, *In Fairness to Future Generations: International Law, Common Patrimony, and Intergenerational Equity* New York: United Nations University Press, 1990), 264–265. Many traditional peoples are also indigenous. Although there are numerous differences, for my purposes both types of communities have suffered the appropriation of their knowledge and resources, and both are stewards of much knowledge of ecosystems, genetic resources, and the natural world.

2. Desiree McGraw, "The Politics of Plants: Should Countries like Canada Pay Royalties for Using Plant Species from the Amazon Jungle?" *Montreal Gazette,* December 19, 1994, B3 (citing U.N. Environment Program figures).

3. Catherine Farley and Daphne Field, "Healing Plants' Alternative Therapies— Many of Which Are Based on the Wisdom of Ancient Practices—Are Becoming Increasingly Popular: A Canadian Health Monitor Survey Found That More Then 20% of Canadians consult Alternative Health Practioners," *Toronto Star,* January 8, 1995, B1.

4. Rick Weiss, "Scientists Try to Turn Weeds into Wonder Drugs," *Washington Post,* May 10, 1994, Z12.

5. William Boly, Valerie Fahey et al., "Wishing on a Falling Star: The Drug Taxol," *Health* (September 1993): 62.

6. Sandy Tolan, "Against the Grain: Multinational Corporations Peddling Patented Seeds and Chemical Pesticides Are Poised to Revolutionize India's Ancient Agricultural System. But at What Cost?" *L.A. Times Magazine,* July 10, 1994, 18. See also Vandana Shiva, *Monocultures of the Mind: Perspectives on Biodiversity and Biotechnology* (Atlantic Highlands, N.J.; Zed Books, 1993).

7. Ibid.

8. Chakravarthi Raghaven, "Patent Application Highlights 'Stealing' of South's Genetic Resources," *Third World Network Features* (1993): 5.

9. RAFI, "Conserving Indigenous Knowledge: Integrating Two Systems of Innovation," *United Nations Development Programme,* September 1, 1994, 8; Genetic Resources Action International, "Intellectual Property Rights for Whom?" *Seedling,* no. 4, pt. 2 (June 1994): 1.

10. Martin Teitel, "Selling Cells: The Thriving Business of Patenting Life," *Dollars and Sense* (September–October 1994): 38. See also RAFI, "Conserving Indigenous Knowledge," 9.

11. RAFI, "The Patenting of Human Genetic Material," *RAFI Communique* (January-February 1994).

12. RAFI, "Conserving Indigenous Knowledge," 6.

13. Jack Kloppenberg and Doug Kleiman, "The Plant Germ-Plasm Controversy," *BioScience* 37(3) (1987): 190; Cary Fowler and Pat Mooney, *Shattering: Food, Politics, and the Loss of Genetic Diversity* (Tucson: University of Arizona Press, 1990), 130; Calestous Juma, *The Gene Hunters: Biotechnology and the Scramble for Seeds* (Princeton, New Jersey: Princeton University Press, 1989), 100; Rebecca L. Margulies, "Protecting Biodiversity: Recognizing International Intellectual Property Rights in Plant Genetic Resources," *Michigan Journal of International Law* 14 (1993): 322, 327.

14. Fowler and Mooney, *Shattering*, 62–63.

15. RAFI, "Conserving Indigenous Knowledge," 14. The loss of genetic variation within species leaves the species vulnerable to attack by pests and diseases. Access to new and unknown strains and varieties of useful plants is essential to creating resistance to such plagues. At the same time, of course, countless species are going extinct in their entirety, leading to the loss of potential medicines, industrial products, and unknown potential applications, many of them also nurtured and preserved by local and indigenous communities that are themselves under extraordinary survival pressures. Cultural diversity and biological diversity are inextricably linked.

16. Convention on Biological Diversity, opened for signature, June 5, 1992, *International Legal Materials* 31 (1992): 822.

17. Preamble, Article 3, and Article 15 all reaffirm the sovereignty of states over their natural resources. Article 15 specifically recognizes that access to genetic resources is subject to each state's national legislation. This marks a change from the prior status of genetic resources as part of the common heritage of humanity. States agree to facilitate access to genetic resources and to share the results of research and development and the benefits arising from the commercial and other utilization of genetic resources with the contracting party providing them, upon mutually agreed terms. States also agree, according to Article 16, to facilitate access to and transfer of biotechnology to developing countries "under fair and most favorable terms." *See*, generally, Steven M. Rubin and Standwood C. Fish, "Biodiversity Prospecting: Using Innovative Contractual Provisions to Foster Ethnobotanical Knowledge, Technology, and Conservation," *Colorado Journal of International Environmental Law and Policy* 5 (1994): 23, 31–36. There is a huge literature on the convention and its implications.

18. RAFI, "Conserving Indigenous Knowledge," 22. *See*, generally, Walter V. Reid et al., eds., *Biodiversity Prospecting: Using Genetic Resources for Sustainable Development* (Baltimore, Md.: World Resource Institute, 1993).

19. RAFI, "Conserving Indigenous Knowledge," 1.

20. Ibid. Even the designation as "formal" and informal" reflects the privileging of the former type of innovation over the latter.

21. They could as easily be considered part of the cultural property of these groups, intimately connected to their definition and survival. Cultural property is understood here as those objects of historical, archaeological, artistic, or ethnographic interest that are bound up in a peoples' identity, history, and future sense of self. See, e.g., James Nafziger, "Protection of Cultural Property," *California Western International Law Journal* 17 (1987): 283–289; Peter H. Welsh, "Repatriation and Cultural Preser-

vation: Potent Objects, Potent Pasts," *University of Michigan Journal Law Reform* 25 (1992): 837.

22. Erica-Irene Daes, "Study on the Protection of the Cultural and Intellectual Property of Indigenous Peoples," U.N. Subcommission on Prevention of Discrimination and Protection of Minorities, U.N. Doc. E/CN.4/Sub.2/1993/28, July 28, 1993, para. 24.

23. RAFI, "Conserving Indigenous Knowledge," 19; see also FAO, *Harvesting Nature's Diversity* (Rome: FAO, October 1993), 8–9. (Between 1976 and 1980, wild species of crops contributed some $340 million per year in yield and disease resistance to the U.S. farm economy.)

24. RAFI cites several examples of informal innovation, including Kayapo women in Brazil who preserve representative crop samples in hillside gene banks, the Mende farmers of Sierra Leone who conduct field trials by testing new seeds against different soil types and comparing notes, and Ethiopian farmers who document the performance of different varieties on doorposts. RAFI, *"Hungoo,* Arrogance, and the 'Gene' Revolution," *RAFI Special Report* (1989): 2.

25. See, generally, Bertus Haverkort, Johan van der Kamp, and Ann Waters-Bayer, eds., *Joining Farmers' Experiments: Experiences in Participatory Technology Development* (London: Intermediate Technology Publications, 1991): Walter de Boef, Kojo Amanor, Kate Wellard, and Anthony Bebbington, *Cultivating Knowledge: Genetic Diversity, Farmer Experimentation, and Crop Research* (London: Intermediate Technology Publications, 1993), for numerous examples of the experimentation done by and in traditional and local rural communities.

26. See Consuelo Quiroz, "Biodiversity, Indigenous Knowledge, Gender, and Intellectual Property Rights," and Maria E. Fernandez, "Gender and Indigenous Knowledge," *Indigenous Knowledge and Development Monitor* 2(3) (1994): 12 and 6, respectively.

27. "Landraces are the outcome of a continuous and dynamic development process. They are not stable products which have existed for time immemorial or which have remained static after coming into being . . . [but reflect] adaptation to local agroecological production conditions, local sub-optimal production conditions, and to the specific production preferences of different socio-economic, gender and ethnic groupings within farming communities." De Boef et al., eds., "Introduction," *Cultivating Knowledge,* 2.

28. Crucible Group, "People, Plants, and Patents: The Impact of Intellectual Property on Biodiversity, Conservation, Trade, and Rural Society," *International Development Research Centre* (1994): 44. Partner or associated species have played a key role in maintaining food production and improving resistance to diseases. For example, a kind of rice grown by traditional farmers near Gonda in Utter Pradesh, India, provided the single gene that gave resistance to a grassy-stunt virus that decimated Asian rice fields during the 1970s. FAO, *Harvesting Nature's Diversity,* 9. Partner and associated species can also serve to supplement diets, especially in times of scarcity or famine, and may eventually provide keys to new food sources.

29. Michel Pimbert, "The Making of Agricultural Biodiversity in Europe," *Rebuilding Communities: Experiences and Experiments in Europe,* ed. Vithal Rajan (Darlington, England: Green Books, 1993), 59, 61.

30. See Bertus Haverkort and David Millar, "Constructing Diversity: The Active Role of Rural People in Maintaining and Enhancing Biodiversity," *Etnoecologica* 2(3)

(1994): 51. Ecological and genetic diversity allows small farmers some security against pests, diseases, and climactic changes, even at the cost of lower yields. See also Keystone Center, "Global Initiative for the Security and Sustainable Use of Plant Genetic Resources" (Final consensus report of the Keystone International Dialogue Series on Plant Genetic Resources, Oslo, Norway, and Keystone Center, Colo., May 31–June 4, 1991.

31. Haverkort and Millar, "Constructing Diversity," 51, 53.

32. The basic requirements for patentability were established in the Paris Convention for the Protection of Industrial Property, *B.D.I.E.L* 1 (March 20, 1883): 681.

33. As patent protection has expanded to cover new categories including drugs, living matter, and plant and animal varieties, debate as to whether the system actually does encourage innovation has grown. For a summary discussion, see Crucible Group, "People, Plants, and Patents," 55–59 (for the view that patents serve the interests of the large and powerful, deter innovation, and reward those with largest legal staffs versus the view that patents are necessary to protect small, new inventors from predatory business practices and allow for companies to invest in research, knowing they can recoup their investment).

34. The European Patent Convention, for example, prohibits the patenting of plant and animal varieties (Article 53[b]), although not of genetically engineered plants and animals themselves. Nonetheless, several individual European countries have granted patents for genetically engineered animals and plant varieties. See, e.g., *Rote Taube* Decision of March 27, 1969, Federal Supreme Court, Fed. Rep. of Germany, 1 IIC 136 (1970). Under TRIPs, states members of the World Trade Organization must mandate patent protection for inventions, including microorganisms (viruses, fungi), similar to that now provided in Northern countries. Plants and animals need not be patented, nor must diagnostic, therapeutic, and surgical methods of treatment. However, plants must be covered by either patents or an effective sui generis system. General Agreement on Tariffs and Trade, Final Text of the GATT Uruguay Round Agreements, Annex IC—Agreement on Trade-Related Aspects of Intellectual Property Rights, GATT Doc. MTN/FA, December 15, 1993, reprinted in *International Legal Materials* 33 (1993) 1: See, generally, Carlos Alberto Prima Braga, "The Economics of Intellectual Property Rights and the GATT: A View from the South," *Vanderbilt Journal of Transnational Law* 22 (1989): 243.

35. Conditions for Patentability; novelty and loss of right to patent, 35 U.S.C. 102 (West 1992).

36. General Agreement on Tariffs and Trade, TRIPs Preamble. See Vandana Shiva, "Farmers' Rights and the Convention on Biological Diversity," in *Biodiplomacy: Genetic Resources and International Relations*, ed. Vicente Sanchez and Calestous Juma (Nairobi: ACTS Press, African Centre for Technology Studies, 1994), 107, 115.

37. *Funk Bros. Seed Co. v. Kalo Inoculant Co.*, 333 U.S. 127, 130 (1948). See, generally, Michael D. Davis, "The Patenting of Products of Nature," *Rutgers Computer and Technology Law Journal* 21 (1995): 293.

38. In some cases, the purification or isolation of the substance must be accompanied by proof that the transformed product demonstrates "unexpected properties." Shayana Kadidal, "Plants, Poverty, and Pharmaceutical Patents," *Yale Law Journal* 103 (1993): 223, 238, citing *Ex parte Gray*, 10 U.S.P.Q. 2d (BNA) 1922, 1924 (Bd. Pat. App. and Int. 1989).

39. *Ex parte Latimer, Dec. Commercial Patents* (1889) 123, 126 (denying patent for fiber from *Pinus australis* tree). For a more detailed discussion, see Yano, "Protection of the Ethnobotanical Knowledge," 452; Davis, "The Patenting of Products of Nature," 323.

40. See Kadidal, "Plants, Poverty, and Pharmaceutical Patents," 223. Kadidal frames the issue as the way in which pharmaceutical companies have evaded the "product of nature" doctrine through the use of "semisynthetic" copycat methods. Kadidal then suggests several mechanisms within patent law to protect natural substances from such copying of genetic materials (244). But as other commentators put it: "The issue is not whether to lower the threshold for patentability to include products of nature, but whether there is a need to reconceptualize the entire idea of "inventiveness.'" Edgar J. Asebey and Jill D. Kempenaar, "Biodiversity Prospecting: Fulfilling the Mandate of the Biodiversity Convention,'" *Vanderbilt Journal of Transnational Law* 28 (1995): 703, 711.

41. *Diamond v. Chakrabarty,* 447 U.S. 303, 309 (1980); James O. Odek, "Bio-Piracy: Creating Proprietary Rights in Plant Genetic Resources," *Journal of Intellectual Property Law* 2 (1994): 141, 153–56, criticizes developed country arguments that plant genetic resources are of unknown value until they have been evaluated and their traits identified, that they cannot be priced, and that collection of germ plasm does not result in deprivation to the source country because only a few seeds are taken. On this last point, Odek points out that the value of the whole lies in its genetic material, which is present even in minimal amounts of material.

42. See Shiva, "Farmers' Rights," 107, 115, see TRIPs, Art. 27, n 1. Under U.S. Supreme Court precedent, the test of usefulness requires only a present beneficial application, which may encompass inventions created for noncommercial purposes so long as they are not merely a prelude to further research or testing. See *Brenner v. Manson,* 383 U.S. 519 (1966).

43. 35 U.S.C. sec. 112. The requirement that biological materials that cannot adequately be described in words be placed in a public depository was recently challenged by a biotechnology firm that refused to place a patented gene-altered mammalian cell in such a depository. The Federal Circuit has held that such "artificial" biological materials need not be deposited. *Amgen, Inc. v. Chugai Pharm. Co.,* 927 F2d 1200 (Fed. Cir. 1991). See also Diana Brahams, "Sharing the Fruits of Research," *The Lancet* 338 (September 28, 1991).

44. Gurdial Singh Nijar, "A Conceptual Framework and Essential Elements of a Rights Regime for the Protection of Indigenous Rights and Biodiversity," *Third World Network, Biodiversity Convention Briefings* (1994): 4.

45. U.S. Pat. no. 4,537,774.

46. Kadidal, "Plants, Poverty, and Pharmaceutical Patents," describes the manner in which pharmaceutical companies routinely evade the product of nature doctrine through duplicating a natural compound's chemical structure and then introducing slight modifications that create a "new" substance while retaining the beneficial effects of the original (238–241).

47. TRIPs, Article 27.3(b) reads: "Members may exclude from patentability . . . plants and animals other than microorganisms, and essentially biological processes for the production of plants or animals other than non-biological and micro-biological processes. However, Members shall provide for the protection of plant varieties either by patents or by an effective sui generis system or by any combination thereof."

48. "International Union for the Protection of New Varieties of Plants," December 2, 1961, 33 U.S.T. 2703. Almost all the developed states, and almost no developing ones, are parties.

49. John H. Barton and Eric Christensen, "Diversity Compensation Systems: Ways to Compensate Developing Nations for Providing Genetic Materials," in *Seeds and Sovereignty: The Use and Control of Plant Genetic Resources,* (Durham, ed. Jack R. Kloppenburg Jr. Duke University Press, 1988) 338, 342; Carlos M. Correa, "Biological Resources and Intellectual Property Rights, *E.I.P.R.* 14 (1992): 15, 155. UPOV also allows for compulsory licensing for "reasons of public interest."

50. See Friends of the Earth, IPRs and Biodiversity: The Impact of Trade Laws (unpublished ms available in ECONET: Biodiversity conference).

51. Pimbert, "The Making of Agricultural Biodiversity," 78.

52. The UPOV requirements go to the need for adequate definition and reproducibility of the new variety.

53. Of course, such movement has also led to huge economic dislocations and commercial dominance of some states over others: witness the catastrophic effect, for example, of the theft of a few Brazilian rubber plants and their export to Singapore during the 1800s. From the world's major rubber producer, the Brazilians within a few years found their industry destroyed by the British.

54. See, e.g., Mario e. Tapia and Alcides Rosas, "Seed Fairs in the Andes: A Strategy for Local Conservation of Plant Genetic Resources," in *Cultivating Knowledge,* ed. de Boef et al., 111.

55. Report of the Conference, Food and Agriculture Organization of the U.N., 22nd sess., p. 285, U.N. Doc. 83/Rep (1983); FAO Conference Resolution 8/83, supplemented by Conference Resolutions 4/89, 5/89, and 3/91.

56. See Margulies, "Protecting Biodiversity," 322, 329–330. The common heritage concept has been used to describe areas where no one state has jurisdiction, such as the moon or the high seas. Developing countries have recently objected strenuously to extending the concept to resources, such as forests or genetic diversity, that exist within the sovereign territory of states.

57. UPOV implicitly recognizes free access to the original varieties (Article 6). Breeders' rights accrue whether the initial variation from which the protected variety comes is artificial or natural. Odek, "Bio-Piracy," 148. See also FAO, *Harvesting Nature's Diversity,* 11.

58. The amended undertaking states that "the concept of mankind's heritage, as applied in the [undertaking] is subject to the sovereignty of the states over their plant genetic resources." FAO, *Report of the Conference of FAO, Genetic Resources and Biological Diversity,* Annex 3, U.N. Doc. C91/REP (1991), 1. In exchange for recognition of plant breeders' rights, developed states agreed to the concept of "farmers' rights" arising from farmers' contributions to conserving and improving plant genetic resources. States agreed to revision of the undertaking in July 1993, with many suggestions that the revised text be made legally binding, perhaps as a protocol to the 1992 Convention on Biological Diversity. In addition, a June 1996 Fourth International Technical Conference on Plant Genetic Resources will consider issues of appropriation of plant genetic resources.

59. See Article 15 of the convention. The Preamble affirms that "conservation of biological diversity is a common concern of humankind," but the clear sovereign

rights to negotiate access to such resources "on mutually agreed terms" makes clear that "common concern" is not the same as "common heritage."

60. GRAIN, "In-Situ, Ex-Situ: Forgetting the Farmers?" *GRAIN Biobriefing* 4(3) (June 1994): 2.

61. For a full description, see Fowler and Mooney, *Shattering*, 130.

62. Pat R. Mooney, "Exploiting Local Knowledge: International Policy Implications," in *Cultivating Knowledge*, ed. de Boef et al., 175.

63. Ibid., 178.

64. RAFI, "Conserving Indigenous Knowledge," 15.

65. Fowler and Mooney, *Shattering*, 189.

66. Article 15.3 defines the genetic resources that states may control access over to exclude those now held in ex situ collections. Resolution 3 appended to the convention recognizes that this problem will have to be resolved as soon as possible. "Interrelationship Between the Convention on Biodiversity and the Promotion of Sustainable Agriculture," Resolution 3, Convention on Biological Diversity, June 1992.

67. See, e.g., Weiss, *In Fairness to Future Generations*, 271–278.

68. Rosemary J. Coombe, "The Properties of Culture and the Politics of Possessing Identity: Native Claims in the Cultural Appropriation Controversy," *Canadian Journal of Law and Jurisprudence* 6 (1993): 249, 258. Many nongovernmental organizations and associations of indigenous peoples have stressed the need to incorporate and consult with indigenous and traditional communities in on-farm or territorially based conservation efforts. See, e.g., World Resources Institute et al., *Global Biodiversity Strategy: Guidelines for Actions to Save, Study, and Use Earth's Biotic Wealth Sustainably and Equitably* (Washington, D.C.: World Resources Institute, 1992).

69. RAFI, "Indigenous Peoples and Human Genetic Diversity," *RAFI Communique* (May 1993): 1.

70. Ibid., citing Draft Proceedings of the Second Human Genome Diversity Workshop, Pennsylvania State University, State College, Penn., October, 29–31, 1991.

71. Guaymi Indians protested that blood samples were taken from them under false pretenses. However, researchers who patented the human T-lymphotropic virus of a member of the Hagahai tribe of Papua New Guinea insist that they discussed the possible patenting of the cell line and stated that half of any resulting royalties would be given to the tribe. Reginal Rhein, "Canadian Group Is 'Mouse That Roared' on Gene Patents," *Biotechnology Newswatch,* December 4, 1995. In the wake of considerable controversy, the Human Diversity Genome Project researchers have begun talking to representatives of indigenous peoples' groups about their concerns. However, even if "informed consent" for research was to be granted, it is unclear what truly informed consent would mean in a vastly different cultural context where the consent of entire groups and communities, not individuals, is at stake.

72. Vesting rights in the state could take several forms: direct ownership of resources, residual ownership of only those resources or knowledge that cannot be clearly traced to particular communities or individuals, or a trust on behalf of groups or communities. Even though I believe that a trust relationship is the most viable option, a trust without effective input and participation by beneficiaries would be just another form of appropriation.

73. See Odek, "Bio-Piracy," 176.

74. See, e.g., Fulai Sheng, "Integrating Economic Development with Conservation," in *Rebuilding Communities,* ed. Rajan, 35.

75. Convention on Biological Diversity, June 5, 1992, *International Legal Materials* 31 (1992): 822, Art. 8(j).

76. The Rio Declaration in Principle 23 recommends that states "recognize and duly support the . . . identity, culture and interests [of indigenous people and their communities, and other local communities]." The Non–Legally Binding Authoritative Statement of Principles for a Global Consensus on the Management, Conservation, and Sustainable Development of All Types of Forests (Forest Principles), U.N. Doc. A/CONF.151/6/Rev.1 (1992), para. 5(a) states that "national forest policies should recognize and duly support the identity, culture and rights of indigenous people, their communities and other communities and forest dwellers." Agenda 21, the conference's action plan, calls for "participation of indigenous communities in the economic and commercial benefits derived from the use of . . . traditional methods and knowledge" (para. 15.4[g]). See, generally, Lee P. Breckenridge, "Protection of Biological and Cultural Diversity: Emerging Recognition of Local Community Rights in Ecosystems Under International Environmental Law," *Tennessee Law Review* 59 (1992): 735.

77. FAO Resolution 5/89 (Annex 2 to the undertaking), sec. 4.

78. Ibid.

79. General human rights instruments protect intellectual property rights, albeit in a limited way. For example, Article 27(2) of the Universal Declaration of Human Rights provides that "everyone has the right to the protection of the moral and material interests resulting from any scientific, literary or artistic production of which he is the author." U.N.G.A. Res. 217 (III), U.N. Doc. A/810 (1948). The singular pronoun, if strictly interpreted, would limit the usefulness of this article to informal innovation. The same right appears in the International Covenant on Economic, Social, and Cultural Rights, December 19, 1966, 993 U.N.T.S. 3, 6 I.L.M. 360, Art. 15(1)(c). The International Labour Organization's Convention Concerning Indigenous and Tribal Peoples in Independent Countries, No. 169 (1992), Art. 4, requires special measures to safeguard the property, labor, and cultures of indigenous peoples.

80. Draft Declaration on the Rights of Indigenous Peoples, U.N. Subcommission for the Prevention of Discrimination and Protection of Minorities, 46th sess., U.N. Doc. E/CN.4.Sub.2/1994/56, October 28, 1994, Art. 12. The draft declaration was received by the U.N. Human Rights Commission in February 1995 and referred to a working group to prepare a draft for submission to the General Assembly. Resolution 1995/32 of the U.N. Commission on Human Rights, 53d meeting, U.N. Doc. E/CN.4/1995/L.11/Add. 2, March 3, 1995. Negotiations over the draft declaration in the Human Rights Commission, where governments, rather than independent experts, are represented, are likely to be difficult and protracted.

81. Ibid., Art. 29.

82. Art. 27.3, TRIPs. Several such sui generis systems for plant breeders' rights exist on a national level; UPOV is one international example of such a system. Even though the drafters of TRIPs clearly intended plant breeders' rights as defined by UPOV to qualify as the sui generis system adopted, there is no reason states cannot develop their own sui generis systems, which could be more friendly to the claims of indigenous and traditional communities. The limit to how far such sui generis systems can depart from traditional plant breeders' rights is a function both of the interpreta-

tion of the word *effective* in the TRIPs agreement and the dispute resolution system of the World Trade Organization.

83. See, e.g., Abdulqawi Yusuf, "Technology and Genetic Resources: Is Mutually Beneficial Access Still Possible?", in *Biodiplomacy,* ed. Juma and Sanchez, 233, 237 (provisions of Article 16 are ambiguous, confusing, and sometimes contradictory). See also Margulies, "Protecting Biodiversity," 334–335.

84. Art. 16.2. The words *adequate and effective protection* are generally held to mean "up to U.S. standards."

85. Article 16(5) reads: "The Contracting Parties, recognizing that patents and other intellectual property rights may have an influence on the implementation of this Convention, shall cooperate in this regard subject to national legislation and international law in order to ensure that such rights are supportive of and do not run counter to its objectives." The phrase may be self-canceling: the international law embodied in TRIPs, for example, like U.S. patent law, does not allow a state to deny patent protection to otherwise patentable materials when a state alleges that a patent would hurt global or local biodiversity.

86. The Charter of the Indigenous-Tribal Peoples of the Tropical Forests, for example, postulates that "since we highly value our traditional technologies and believe that our biotechnologies can make important contributions to humanity, including 'developed' countries, we demand guaranteed rights to our intellectual property, and control over the development and manipulation of this knowledge." Art. 44, Malaysia, 1992, quoted in Marcus Colchester, "Some Dilemmas in Asserting Indigenous Intellectual Property Rights" (October 1994) (unpublished document on file with author). Similarly the Mataatua Declaration on Cultural and Intellectual Property Rights of Indigenous Peoples, the result of a 1993 conference convened by indigenous groups in New Zealand, demands that the fundamental right of indigenous peoples to define and control traditional knowledge be protected by the international community. Darrell Posey et al., "Traditional Resource Rights: Protection, Compensation, and Conservation," A Project of WWF-I (July 1994): 6.

87. Posey, "Traditional Resource Rights," 7.

112. Darrell Posey et al., "A Handbook for Indigenous, Traditional, and Local Communities," A Project of WWF-I (July 1994) 5 (unpublished draft on file with author).

89. See RAFI, "Conserving Indigenous Knowledge," 30–31; Crucible Group, "*People, Plants, and Patents,*" 67–68.

90. Materials transfer agreements conform a variant, a bilateral arrangement that treats genetic material as a commodity rather than as knowledge per se. Some authors have suggested these could be used to cover material from gene banks.

91. Walter V. Reid, "Biodiversity Prospecting: Strategies for Sharing Benefits," in *Biodiplomacy,* ed. Juma and Sanchez, 241.

92. Ibid.

93. Weiss, "Scientists Try to Turn Weeds into Wonder Drugs."

94. Rubin and Fish, "Biodiversity Prospecting," 30, citing David Riggle, "Pharmaceuticals from the Rainforest," *Business* (February 1992); 26.

95. Such provisions might include patent protection of indigenous knowledge, adequate documentation of the origin of the knowledge, creation of a legal fund and/ or an ombudsman to assist indigenous or local communities in the necessary legal arrangements, training of local people in collection and processing of specimens, joint

planning, and corporate responsibility to prosecute infringements of the patent. Ibid., 23, 47–48. The Traditional Resource Rights Group has developed the model Covenant on Intellectual, Cultural, and Scientific Property Rights Between a Corporation, Scientist, or Scientific Institution and the Indigenous Group embodying provisions for responsible research and equitable trade. The covenant includes the ability of the indigenous group to decline commercialization of some knowledge, to enter into agreements with other parties, to keep information confidential, to ensure ecological and cultural sensitivity by research partners, and to independent monitoring of agreements. Third World Network has also developed model provisions for such contracts. See Singh Nijar, "A Conceptual Framework and Essential Elements of a Rights Regime for the Protection of Indigenous Rights and Biodiversity.

96. Jack R. Kloppenburg, Jr., "Whither Farmers' Rights?" (October 7, 1994: unpublished ms): 4, for a discussion of the drawbacks of bilateral approaches. See also RAFI, "Bioprospecting/Biopiracy and Indigenous Peoples," *RAFI Communique* (November 1994).

97. In most cases, it is impossible to trace the provenance of a given gene-bank accession to a specific area or community. FAO, Revision of the International Undertaking on Plant Genetic Resources, Doc. No. CPGR-6/95/8 Supp. (CPGR—Ex 1/94/5/supp.). 7.

98. Kloppenburg, "Whither Farmers' Rights?" Another central element of many proposals for protocols is the elaboration of the prior informed consent (PIC) procedure envisioned in Article 15.5 of the Convention on Biological Diversity, whereby communities and/or governments would have to consent to the removal of genetic resources from their territory and could therefore impose conditions on any removal. For a discussion of a PIC model applied to genetic resources, see Frederic Hendrickx, Veit Koester, and Christian Prip, "Access to Genetic Resources: A Legal Analysis," in *Biodiplomacy,* ed. Juma and Sanchez, 139 . Proposals to improve the undertaking will be discussed both at the next meeting of the Conference of the Parties to the Convention on Biological Diversity in November 1996 and at the June 1996 FAO International Technical Conference on Plant Genetic Resources.

99. Kloppenburg, "Whither Farmers' Rights?"

100. A common definition includes elements of shared control of territory and/or resources, self-definition as a member of the group, nondominant status within the larger society, continuous governing structures, and, perhaps, continuity with precolonial societies. See J. Martinez Cobo, *Study of the Problem of Discrimination Against Indigenous Populations,* U.N. Subcommission on Prevention of Discrimination and Protection of Minorities, reissued as U.N. Doc. E/CN.4/Sub.2/1986–87 and Adds. 1–4.

101. Singh Nijar of Third World Network suggests as a working definition "a group of people having a longstanding social organization that binds them together whether in a defined area or howsoever otherwise," to include both indigenous peoples and local farming communities. Nijar, "A Conceptual Framework," 6.

102. I am indebted to Kathleen Yurchak for this idea.

103. See GRAIN, "Framework for Full Articulation of Farmers' Rights" (Barcelona: GRAIN, June 1995).

Part 6

Appropriation and Tangible Cultural Property

James D. Nason

Beyond Repatriation: Cultural Policy and Practice for the Twenty-first Century

Some museum professionals have tended to regard the recently passed repatriation legislation in the United States as an end point in what was a lengthy and often rancorous debate about a major cultural policy issue. It is my intention here to briefly outline the background to the passage of this legislation, characterize what the law has accomplished, and then set forth what I believe will arise as the future cultural policy consequences of the law. It is my contention that American repatriation legislation represents only the initial first step in dealing with a number of related concerns that will confront museums and legislative bodies. At the center of these concerns will be discordant ethical and legal perspectives about who can legitimately control what kinds of material culture and, beyond that, what rights of access, use, care, and disposition can be conveyed or retained. The ultimate outcome(s) of these matters will result in a far more dynamic and relational construct for the creation of new and important cultural policies in our society.

The Road to Repatriation

The passage of the Native American Graves Protection and Repatriation Act by the U.S. Congress on November 16, 1990, was the culmination of decades of protest, private negotiations, and legal action by Native American communities across the country.[1] These conflicts revolved primarily around the relationships between Native American communities and non-Native museums. Community concerns focused then, as now, on four major issues:

1. The perceived lack of interest and accountability of museums in providing accurate and appropriate representations of Native American culture and history in exhibits
2. The presence of sacred and other culturally sensitive objects in museum collections
3. The belief that many of the collection materials in museums had been illicitly obtained in the first instance and were therefore held without sound legal titles
4. The maintenance in collections and even exhibition of Native American humans remains.[2]

Incidents through the 1960s and beyond that were characteristic of these community concerns ranged from protests in museum galleries over the content of displays, to concerted efforts by community leaders to negotiate with museums for the return of sacred materials. Although the Zunis' now-famous quest for the return of their war gods from museums did ultimately meet with considerable success, it would not be until the 1980s that any significant number of museum staff began to think about consulting community representatives over exhibit content or other sensitive issues.[3]

These actions by Native Americans were not isolated phenomena. From the perspective of the international museum community, they were only one element within a much larger arena of ethical and legal questioning that had arisen over how objects were acquired for museum collections. Persistent expressions of outrage over plundered and looted artifacts and other noxious illicit dealings in art filled the pages of the museological literature from the late 1960s onward.[4] Professional attention to these issues was especially pronounced following the November 1970 Convention on the Means of Prohibiting and Preventing the Illicit Import, Export, and Transfer of Ownership of Cultural Property adopted by the UNESCO General Conference in its sixteenth session in Paris. The UNESCO Convention, which classified virtually all categories of objects as "cultural property," called on states to ensure, among other things, that the illicit trade in materials was halted, that illicitly acquired materials were restored to their country of origin, and that efforts be made to protect and preserve in situ materials, create or improve museums and other facilities, and educate the public about the importance of cultural heritage.

The convention was a trigger event that came at a time when a number of other important cultural policy developments were occurring, including,

- The 1970 creation by UNESCO of an ethics of acquisition policy with a request that all museums adopt it
- The 1970 treaty between the United States and Mexico on the Recovery and Return of Stolen Archaeological, Historical, and Cultural Properties
- The 1970 adoption of resolutions on illicit antiquities and collecting by a number of professional societies, such as the Archaeological Institute of America, the American Association of Museums, and the American Anthropological Association
- The adoption of new collection policies by museums, often accompanied by new deeds of gift with statements for donor or seller signature containing clauses of indemnification for the museum should the material later be proved illicit
- The beginning of efforts to seek passage of legislation in the United States adopting the 1970 UNESCO Convention (efforts that would not succeed until 1982 with Public Law 97-446, Title III, Implemention of Convention on Cultural Property)

These varied actions at different levels of national government and institutional concern all sought to establish new ways of handling the collection and acquisition of cultural property. The goal of forcing museum acquisition procedures not only to conform with existing national cultural policy laws but also to be beyond any hint of reproach was to be achieved either directly through the imposition of new laws and regulations, such as the treaty between the United States and Mexico and the broader customs regulations that ensued, or indirectly through new ethical and professional guidelines, which were being rewritten throughout the 1970s.[5]

It was quite clear that American professional societies and museum organizations did not favor the imposition of binding national legislation but sought instead to rely on self-regulated ethical and operational policies. On the one hand, there was obvious concern with the ongoing destruction of archaeological sites as a primary mechanism for feeding materials into the illicit artifact market. On the other hand, there was equal concern that the sweeping language of the UNESCO Convention, were it to become law, would deleteriously affect, if not effectively end, even legitimate international traffic in materials and thus impact ongoing scientific work and museum public programs.

At the same time, the more cynical within the museum world did not believe that it would be possible to either revise or create new national laws, policies, and practices to protect cultural heritage in many of the poor countries that were "suppliers" of artifacts. From this perspective, laws that might require reparations or repatriations of artifacts later shown to have been illicitly obtained by American institutions would reward only corruption and benign indifference in many of the countries of origin for those artifacts. In the 1973 *Resolution on Acquisition of Cultural Properties,* for example, seven U.S. scholarly societies stated that "museums can henceforth . . . [refuse] to acquire . . . cultural property exported in violation of the laws obtaining in the countries of origin" and that all nations should "establish effective export laws and develop proper controls over export." At the same time, the resolution called on nations "whenever possible, [to consider] legitimate and honorable means for the acquisition of cultural property . . . for the advancement of knowledge and for the benefit of all peoples."[6] These sentiments were echoed by matching resolutions passed by the Society for American Archaeology, the American Association of Museums, the College Art Association, the Association of Art Museum Directors, the Archaeological Institute of America, and the U.S. National Committee of the International Council of Museums.

Disbelief in the potential effectiveness of national laws and policies protecting cultural heritage may have been partly based on the reputedly dismal history of such legislation in actual practice in some countries. An examination of Bonnie Burnham's compendium of national heritage laws shows that relatively few nations outside of Europe had created such laws prior to 1940, whereas in the period from 1940 to 1970 there had been an explosion of heritage protection laws in nations in Africa, Asia, Southeast Asia, the Pacific, South America, and the Middle East, a phenomenon clearly related to the postcolonial independence of many nations.[7] That many of the more stringent laws were already in place in nations that were now facing the greatest illicit trade problems was a sign to some in American museum and art circles that such laws could not alone be useful.[8]

The dilemma in the United States over what might appropriately be done in this situation was made worse by the conflation of American attitudes about cultural heritage, attitudes within the museum community about the profession, and growing concerns over Native American issues closer to home. American attitudes about cultural heritage issues were considered by some in the museum and art field to be centered on a kind of cultural laissez-faire notion that everything could and perhaps should be available for purchase. And in fact, prior to 1970 relevant U.S. cultural law consisted primarily of the 1906 Antiquities Act, the 1935 Historic Sites Act, and the 1966 National Historic Preservation Act. In other words, there were those who felt that it was almost un-American to place limits on an otherwise freewheeling marketplace for art and culture. The museum community had also created, by the 1970s, its own new attitudes about museum work. A growing sense of professionalism within the field was combined with a belief that museums did occupy the moral high ground and that any potential abuses involving the illicit trafficking of art or artifacts were isolated and unusual events well beyond the ordinary and acceptable. From this perspective, the idea that new legislation might be required to enforce standards of conduct was thought by some to be as insulting as it was needless. There is also no question that the reaction to the passage of the American Indian Religious Freedom Act (AIRFA) by the U.S. Congress in 1978 fueled concerns over the evils of ill-thought-out legislation.

The American Indian Religious Freedom Act represented a victory for Native Americans in their ongoing fight for cultural and civil rights.[9] AIRFA recognized that federal agencies had both by policy and by ignorance taken actions that had abridged the religious freedom of Native Americans. In attempting to remedy this situation, AIRFA resolved: "That henceforth it shall be the policy of the United States to protect and preserve for American Indians their inherent right of freedom to believe, express, and exercise the traditional religions of the American Indian, Eskimo, Aleut, and Native Hawaiians, including but not limited to access to sites, use and possession of sacred objects, and the freedom to worship through ceremonials and traditional rites."

The passage of AIRFA sent shock waves through the American museum community. What did "use and possession" actually mean? The initial fear was that this somehow gave tribes federal authority to reclaim sacred materials in museum collections. But, as Philip Deloria has noted, Congress took no actions to establish means for implementation of the legislation, and although federal agencies were required to review their operations to ensure compliance, relatively few changes were made.[10] In some ways the situation became worse when government agencies sought to obtain sacred site information from Native American communities, a process seen by many in the community as only another avenue that would lead to the destruction or abuse of such sites. For museums, AIRFA resulted only in providing Native American communities with greater moral authority in one-on-one negotiations with museums, but the act did not result in any significant movement of objects from museums to tribal communities. In other words, AIRFA was a warning shot across the collective museum bow, an indication of ongoing federal government interest in Native American rights issues.[11]

New calls for changes in museum relationships with Native American communities became more frequent in the 1980s.[12] In 1981 a very concrete proposal came when the newly created North American Indian Museums Association (NAIMA) issued its "Suggested Guidelines for Museums in Dealing with Requests for Return of Native American Materials," which out-lined who had the authority to make requests, what kinds of objects might be claimed, and how to approach the issue of transfers of ownership.[13] These guidelines were significant for two reasons. First, they came for the first time from Native American museum professionals working in established tribal community museums. This meant that it was no longer possible for some museums to claim that repatriation or other forms of transfer to Indian com-munities was impossible because those communities lacked relevant cultural institutions.[14] Second, the guidelines did prominently focus on the issues of sacred objects and archaeological materials, especially human skeletal remains and grave goods, while maintaining that identification and repatriation deci-sions on these materials should be the sole prerogative of appropriate tribal community authorities. Although NAIMA did not persist as an active organi-zation, its 1981 guidelines unequivocally identified what would be, through-out the 1980s, the major points of contention between museums and tribal communities.

The continued efforts by organizations such as the Native American Rights Fund and American Indians Against Desecration as well as by tribal governments to seek mandatory repatriation of both sacred materials and hu-man remains in museum collections occasioned considerable rethinking about the rationale behind museums and their collections. It also alarmed scholars whose work dealt primarily with human remains and associated materials and brought into the professional literature an increasing poundage of opinions on all sides of the issue.[15]

In the midst of the national debate over repatriation, there was also in-creased lobbying at the state government level to enact new laws to protect Indian burial sites and, in some cases, to require the repatriation of human remains and grave goods in state museum collections to tribes. By 1989 such laws had been passed in some thirty states, including Washington, Kansas, Nebraska, Kentucky, Indiana, Texas, Minnesota, and New Mexico. Both the formal and published and informal and unpublished positions in support of and against repatriation were essentially in place by 1985. And, as with the UNESCO Convention in 1970, professional societies issued position papers that basically said that museums and scholars knew what they were doing, could do it with respect toward Native American materials and concerns, could involve Native Americans in appropriate ways, but had to retain sole discretion over the materials because of their research importance and because museums and scholars had legitimate ownership and use of collections on behalf of the general public. The American Anthropological Association statement, for example, declared that "individuals and communities have valid concerns . . . about the treatment and disposition of human remains that may conflict with valid research and educational interests. A balance must be struck between [these] interests in each situation and the concerns of different cultures. . . . Human remains are to be treated with respect. Respect can include careful curation and a recognition that valuable anthropological, historical, and medical information can be obtained through analysis."[16] These sentiments were echoed by the policy issued by the American Association of Museums in 1987, which called on museums to repatriate illegally acquired materials "if requested to do so" and declared that "museums should also weigh the value of such objects to their public mission with the interests of the requesting party."[17]

At another level, action such as the Native American Skeletal Remains bill introduced in the California Assembly in 1989 (Assembly Bill 2577) was seen by affected institutions, in this case the administration of the University of California, as a costly and inappropriate attack on research activity and prompted vigorous reactions. The opposition to the California bill, for example, was founded on the by-now-familiar grounds that collections were needed for important research, that such collections represented an important market value public asset, that it would not be feasible to establish Native American affiliations with the collections, and that any implementation or fixed-date implementation of the legislation would be unreasonably costly.

Additional public awareness of the controversy over Native American human remains and grave goods came through major public exposés in publications such as *Science* and *National Geographic,* which graphically illustrated the results of grave-robbing and site despoilation in the United States.[18] By the end of 1989, Congress had passed, in the National Museum of the American Indian [NMAI] Act, the first piece of legislation to deal with repatriation. This act, which established the authorization for this new museum within the Smithsonian family, also required that an inventory and repatriation procedure be enacted for NIMAI collections. In the meantime, Congress deliberated over other far more sweeping repatriation bills introduced into the House by Representative Morris Udall and into the Senate by Senators Daniel Inouye and John McCain.

By the end of 1990, it had become clear to national museum community leaders that repatriation legislation in some form would be passed by Congress, despite their intense lobbying in opposition. In characterizing this outcome at a special session of the Western Museums Conference meeting in October 1990, Dan Monroe, special American Association of Museums representative on repatriation, noted that ultimately Congress considered the museum community's perspective on repatriation to be retrogressive and lacking in both moral leadership and moral standing, which also left the scientific arguments lacking.[19] In this situation the thinking of the museum establishment shifted toward efforts to find grounds for compromise and consensus with the Native American position and to negotiate specifically on various key areas of concern in the proposed legislation, including timetables, standards of ownership proof, and definitions of repatriable categories.

Up to this point, the opposition to any repatriation legislation had centered on a number of major arguments, starting with the premise that no legislation was required since museums could resolve any really serious issues through informal case-by-case negotiations. Beyond this "We are ethical professionals and know what is best" approach lay a series of other arguments. Most notable was that scientific rights of inquiry would be intolerably infringed by such legislation, a perspective founded on the premise that true scientific investigation was inherently a good and valuable service to humankind. Unspoken most of the time was the correlative belief that science should not be shackled by the religious beliefs of a minority. A more purely museological argument was that museums existed to preserve objects for study and education for as long as possible, thus making a possible repatriation outcome of reburial seemingly contradictory, if not nonsensical. Other less central arguments were also made: that museums were always willing to discuss issues with Native American communities; that it was inappropriate for members of one part of our society (or race) to dictate the terms for scientific inquiry to members of all others; that modern-day Indians were not truly religious in any traditional sense; that Indians sought materials only to sell them; and that it would not be possible to establish cultural affiliation with many collections in any event. Particularly compelling for many scholars was the prospect that repatriation and subsequent reburials would eliminate forever the possibility of new and yet-unthought-of research.

The Native American call for repatriation legislation turned several of the scholarly and museum arguments on their heads. For example, Native Americans argued that attitudes about the sacrosanct nature of scientific inquiry amounted to the imposition of a supposedly superior Western cultural value on Native American life. Similarly, the idea that members of one part of society ought not to be allowed to dictate on such matters of belief to members of another part was echoed, but from the opposite perspective. Less central arguments pointed to included the lack of appropriate care for many museum holdings, including human remains; the lack of significant research results of any benefit to Native American communities; the possibility that museums had inappropriately or illegally obtained materials for their collections; and the lack of prior meaningful discussions by a majority of museum personnel with Native Americans on these issues. Nor were Native Americans at all swayed by arguments that the antiquity of some materials, including burial remains, eliminated the possibility of proving cultural affiliation or that future research opportunities might be lost. As Walter Echo Hawk, an attorney for the Native American Rights Fund working on repatriation, said: "We don't accept any artificial cut-off date set by scientists to separate us from our ancestors. . . . What Europeans want to do with their dead is their business. We have different values."[20] Indeed, these arguments as well as the perspectives of museum scholars were aired in the public controversy that took place in 1989 when Stanford University decided to return for reburial some 550 human remains thought to be ancestral to the Ohlone-Costanoan people of California.[21]

In the end, the reality was that American museum collections contained many thousands of Native American human remains (one estimate gives this as many hundreds of thousands) and sacred objects and that the presence of these was then, and remains today, deeply offensive to Native American communities across the land. And in the end, Congress agreed that such holdings by museums were not appropriate and that repatriation should be the law of the land. On November 23, 1990, the Native American Grave Protection and Repatriation Act (NAGPRA) was signed into law.[22]

The Basic Elements of NAGPRA

There are only four primary areas of legislative concern outlined in NAGPRA. First, it establishes legal protections for Native American burials on tribal and federal lands, with associated mechanisms that automatically involve tribes as the central agents in making decisions about burials that are found. Second, NAGPRA makes it illegal to deal in Native American human remains and designated cultural items (such as sacred objects) in the marketplace. Third, museums and federal agencies are required to summarize their cultural property holdings, inventory their human remains and associated grave goods, and provide potentially affiliated tribes with this information, with open access to all museum records relating to such materials. Fourth, museums and federal agencies are required to actively seek consultations with Native American tribal community representatives and repatriate human remains and relevant cultural materials when the conditions outlined in the law are met. NAGPRA is, in other words, legislation that mandates the necessity, with calendar deadlines, for museums and federal agencies to undertake very specific actions to ensure that tribes can gain possession to human remains and cultural materials through repatriation.

The approach to repatriation taken in NAGPRA made it necessary for the federal government to make some crucial decisions. Among the most significant of these were the sole focus on federally recognized tribes, the exclusion of museums that had not received federal funding support and what support meant in this case, the nature of acceptable data that could support repatriation claims, and the definitions of what could be subject to repatriation. All of these decisions have lasting import for museums, scholars, government agencies, and Native American communities. For example, given the often peculiar history of federal recognition (and derecognition) of tribal communities, it was inevitable that there would be debates over the federal list of recognized tribes. This inevitability was heightened by three factors: (1) the ongoing attempts by a number of tribes to obtain recognition and cases such as the recent ruling, that the Samish Tribe in Washington had been improperly denied recognition by the Bureau of Indian Affairs, (2) the inclusion of all Alaskan Native villages as separate entities under the law, and (3) the very vague wording that surrounds how Native Hawaiian groups might be defined under the law (especially by comparison with the far stricter definitions applicable to Indian tribes).

Potentially more serious for museums were those NAGPRA provisions that gave to tribal communities wide discretion in both the kinds of data that could be presented and the identification of the kinds of materials that might be subject to repatriation. The data issue revolves around the matter of cultural affiliation. Beyond all else, a successful repatriation claim under NAGPRA must prove that there is cultural affiliation between the claimant (individual or group) and the material in question. This had been one of the points of contention in earlier debates about repatriation, with some scholars claiming that it could not be possible, for example, to realistically establish affiliation with acceptable data between contemporary tribal communities and ancient materials. NAGPRA's wording on this point is "a relationship of shared group identity which can reasonably be traced historically or prehistorically between members of a present-day Indian tribe or Native Hawaiian organization and an identifiable earlier group."[23] Appropriate evidence in support of cultural affiliation claims can include geographical, kinship, biological, archaeological, anthropological, linguistic, folklore, oral tradition, historical, and other relevant information or expert opinion.[24] In other words, an extraordinary range of data, some of which is rarely used in association with museum specimen documentation, could be submitted to museums in support of repatriation claims. Similarly, museums would be responding to what tribes might identify as being either sacred or patrimonial, within NAGPRA's definitions, thus placing the onus of any further verification for concurrence on museum staff.

Adding to these uncertainties for museums were the deadlines for summaries and inventories in November 1993 and 1995 and the lack of any final regulations implementing NAGPRA. Even though draft regulations were finally issued by the Department of the Interior in 1993, final regulations had not yet been issued as of October 1995.[25] NAGPRA thus requires museums to create new data sets for summaries and inventories of their relevant holdings, to share this with potentially more than 750 Native American communities, to actively seek consultations, and to react in a timely way to tribally identified materials for repatriation in a number of different categories, with supporting data of a potentially wide array. Not unexpectedly, many museums were not really prepared for these tasks and often could not generate new resources sufficient to fulfill the deadline expectations effectively, much less to begin generating the new kinds of data and data reviews that might be required in reaction to repatriation claims. What museums also did not anticipate was the degree to which tribal governments would also find themselves hard-pressed to undertake their part in the repatriation process.[26] Indeed, the relative pace of tribal repatriation actions has apparently been much slower than originally expected.

The View Beyond NAGPRA

In the end, the sentiment from many Native American community leaders and national museum leaders after the passage of NAGPRA was that the law should herald a new era of cooperative engagement between museums and tribes.[27] And, as Raymond Thompson has so accurately pointed out, the key point now is not the mechanics of repatriation per se but the far more important and broader issue of who ultimately has the right to control a group's heritage.[28] Nevertheless, the most significant feature of NAGPRA in the long run may be its function as key civil rights legislation that empowers tribes in their dealings with the government, especially as tribes move forward on other issues involving sovereignty, such as gambling and natural resources development. Alhtough NAGPRA did resolve at the national level, at least on the face of it, some of the most pressing and noxious cultural policy issues vis-à-vis Native American communities, other concerns remain. These include the issue of culturally sensitive materials in museum collections, intellectual property rights, and issues related to how research in Native American communities is conducted and is presented in publications. Three major areas of concern are (1) associated museum operational issues, (2) further tribal issues beyond repatriation, and (3) the broader national and international issues that will affect museums and tribes alike.

Museum Operations Issues

The implications of NAGPRA for museum operations are extensive and serious for a number of reasons. First, museums must adopt new mission and operational policy statements that incorporate internal procedures for and perspectives about repatriation or adapt existing documents that reflect the tenets of this new legislation. This may mean a change as simple as establishing new designated staff mechanisms to handle repatriation claims, or it might extend to more far-reaching and significant actions such as the creation and empowering of community advisory groups for collection practices as well as for repatriation or the refusal to accept new materials that might fall within a repatriable category.

Second, because there is no time limit feature to NAGPRA legislation and to the application of its requirement that museums must notify tribes about cultural holdings, museums now must begin to determine how often and in what manner they will alert tribes to newly acquired materials. If, for example, by 1996 a museum has accepted one hundred new Native American objects into its collections, then those new materials should be reported to culturally affiliated tribal communities. This presumes, of course, that museums will continue to acquire through various means new materials, which seems a safe, if not certain, presumption to make.

Of greater potential interest is whether museums could or should acquire objects that potentially fall into repatriation categories at all and what mechanism could be developed in cooperation with tribes to deal with the preacquisition identification of such materials. This may be important for several reasons: (1) a museum's acquisition of a sacred object, for example, might indicate to a concerned tribe a lack of willingness (or educability) on the part of the museum staff to follow the intent established by NAGPRA; (2) the formal acquisition of materials that must then be repatriated entails considerable extra work for museum staff; and (3) existing Internal Revenue Service policies require that a museum maintain a newly donated collection for a minimum of one year in order for the donor to qualify for an appropriate tax deduction, an obvious problem if a museum is repatriating material in less time. The key feature here is NAGPRA's assumption that museums cannot and should not arbitrarily decide what objects might or might not fall into which repatriable categories, as this authority is vested solely with tribal governments and their representatives.

Third, museums need to address the issue of interpretation policies and practices with respect to Native American materials. NAGPRA has provided to tribal communities an important role in defining at the outset what is sacred or patrimonial and even affiliated (or not) with a given community. But questions remain. What mechanisms should now be put into place to secure community review or oversight on exhibit plans? Will community representatives be given veto power over curatorial exhibition plans in general, the proposed use of specific objects, or the characterization of materials and their meanings in labels? How will a museum react appropriately when Native

American community representatives and curators fundamentally disagree about what can and should be said about objects on display or about what kinds of objects are relevant and appropriate for display in the first instance?

Fourth, it is now in the best interests of museums to begin creating new and more effective ways of generating contextual and other data about collection holdings and of coordinating and accessing such data. We have, in the past, seen far too limited documentation work done on the majority of objects in museum collections. Even though many objects come to museums with virtually no data, the very breadth of information applicable under NAGPRA suggests that museums can and should significantly extend their collection research activity whenever possible. The continuing needs of communities to adequately and effectively access museum collection records, combined with legislative demands for reporting, also strongly suggest the need for creative, simple, and secure database management programs, especially for larger and more complex collection data sets.

Fifth, museums will probably have to consider how best they can accommodate new pressures for access to collections as well as to collection records. NAGPRA has, in part, given carte blanche rights to Native Americans to access museum records and collections. For many museums, this is a new level of access demand. As an ongoing process this may force some museums to rethink the ways in which they can most effectively provide supervised access to materials, particularly for the kind of research that some community representatives may wish to carry out. Access in these terms implies not only set-aside physical space but also the availability and time of both personnel and equipment (such as computers and copiers for records access). In addition, museums must begin to consider Native American unhappiness with the kinds of conservation treatment given to materials, with the ways in which certain materials are stored, and certainly with the kinds of commercial and other access given to culturally sensitive portions of collections. And these needs all escalate with every extension of repatriation policy in either de facto or de jure terms to other communities with which museums wish to maintain amicable relations in the future.

Sixth, museums should begin to explore other ways in which they can creatively engage Native American communities for mutual benefit. This might mean providing assistance to tribes in the planning of tribal museums or cultural centers, in the training of tribal personnel, or in some form of museum in-trust holding agreements for repatriated collections. Mutual cooperative agreements on collecting and research of all kinds would clearly be to everyone's benefit, along with special loan or outreach arrangements that can strengthen and extend a museum's educational mission within Native American communities.

There are a number of reasons that actions such as these are desirable. First, it is inherently better for the museum community at large to have within it a strong and viable tribal museum element. This would, at the very least, eliminate a part of the paranoia based on ignorance that some museum staff originally felt when confronted with the need to consult "unknown" Indians. Second, because some of the organic specimens now in many museum collections simply will not last all that much longer as a result of environmental deterioration, it is wiser to share existing resources that can then inspire the production of new cultural objects for our general benefit. Third, museums should explore new types of cooperative cultural agreements with tribes for research and collecting, especially of new arts and technologies that illustrate contemporary Indian life. Fourth, collaboration with tribal colleagues, who inevitably have information that in-house museum staff do not, will allow museums to improve and refine their educational role within the general community, especially in the presentation through exhibits of the many perspectives about what objects are and what they mean.

Tribal Concerns

Museum personnel have largely overlooked the impact that NAGPRA has had on tribal communities and tribal museums and centers. Logistically, many tribal museums and governments have been very hard-pressed to respond to data summaries issued by museums, much less to actively pursue repatriation actions with a majority of museums. In some communities, tribal personnel are already so engaged with other ongoing concerns that taking on the new and often complex burdens associated with NAGPRA represents a real stretch for their resources. Repatriation is also a costly exercise for tribes since ideally it involves sending tribal representatives directly to museums to conduct in-depth reviews of records and collections.

That NAGPRA also requires tribes to select representatives who will act on behalf of the tribal government and community in repatriation negotiations has its own consequences, notably the need for tribal governments to consider who and what is being represented. This issue is particularly acute in tribal communities that are reservation-created confederations of many formerly autonomous tribes, many of which are distinct from one another in language, history, traditions, and various aspects of culture. Concerns on the part of any single confederated tribe or band that its interests are not being properly pursued or that its materials or human remains be assigned directly cannot be accommodated under NAGPRA but must be addressed internally by the confederated tribal community government. The opposite condition is also found in those cases where there are separate reservation communities of the same original tribal community, thereby calling into question another facet of the representation issue. Groups such as the Southern Paiute are an example of this, with ten distinct tribes or bands organized in Utah, Arizona, and Nevada. Of these, five groups in Utah have separately banded together to form the Paiute Tribe of Utah, while the three groups in Nevada (the Moapa, Las Vegas, and Pahrump) are not at this time recognized by the federal government at all. For the latter, this means that any materials relating to them or to their portion of the traditional territory of the Southern Paiute could be repatriated only to their federally recognized brethren.

This matter focuses attention as well on the more general issue of how the U.S. government has chosen to define an Indian tribe. NAGPRA qualifies confederated communities but not their individual tribal or band elements, while at the same time identifying each discrete Alaskan native village as a tribe but ignoring the existing tribal communities not currently recognized by the federal government. In the Native Hawaiian case, there are community and state-based organizations as well as groups seeking the restoration of a sovereign Hawaiian monarchy, with all that implies.

Tribes have in many cases had to carefully consider the creation of their own new cultural policies that reflect the contemporary communities' beliefs and attitudes about singularly important traditional issues. One recent example of this can be seen in the actions recently taken by the Zuni to clarify their position on issues of cultural affiliation and to essentially create new approaches to dealing with human remains in museums.[29] Tribes that face the repatriation of large volumes of materials have also had to develop plans for their own effective handling or storage of such collections.

Other post-NAGPRA concerns were identified in a survey of U.S. and Canadian tribal museums and cultural centers carried out by the author in 1992 for the National Museum of the American Indian.[30] Among other things, these survey data indicated that nearly one-third of tribal personnel interviewed thought that non-Indian museums would continue to retain culturally sensitive materials and that such materials would ideally require specialized storage and conservation treatment by tribal specialists. The issue of access was even more definitive, with 94 percent stating that prior tribal review should be required before museums gave access to culturally sensitive materials.

These attitudes follow long-established community principles about the traditional ownership and use of certain properties and the application of these principles to new materials, such as songs and the recordings of songs, photographs or other graphic images of sacred objects, so-called rock art, and ceremonial activities. Of special concern to tribes are the commercial requests that museums often receive for access to and use of such materials, which again raises the issue of tribal community–museum collaborations.

The prospect that nontribal museums and tribal personnel may work collaboratively on projects requires that thought be given in advance to the ownership of resulting information. In some current cases of government-tribal conjoint projects, agreements have been worked out that provide the tribes with full discretionary powers over the disposition of certain types of jointly collected data. Similar agreements concerning in-trust holding arrangements and other forms of cooperative work will also need to be developed. For some scholars in nontribal museums, this is a touchy issue since the ethical principles of some professional scholarly organizations proscribe any arrangement that does not make possible the open and free exchange of information resulting from research. Similarly, questions of access to nontribal collections are constrained at present by the various freedom-of-information acts passed by states and by the federal government, which apply to many museums. Under these laws, museums cannot automatically deny access or defer access requests to third parties. If museums and tribes agree that tribes should have oversight on such access, then freedom-of-information laws must be modified.

Finally, tribes must search for ways to deal with the sales of sacred and other culturally sensitive materials in the open marketplace. For all of the benefits of NAGPRA, it did not put an end to such sales. In 1991, for example, Sotheby's auction house in New York sold three rare and sacred Hopi and Navajo ceremonial masks, which may have been part of a theft of such materials from Oraibi Village in 1978. Despite tribal protests, the sale continued.[31] In this, as in other important areas, tribes must also create their own heritage codes and policies that clearly outline what actions, procedures, and bases are significant to the tribe in managing its own cultural resources.[32] In some cases, this may take the form of proactive efforts to prevent harm to cultural and natural resources located on traditional lands under federal control.

Expanding National and International Concerns

Just as the passage of NAGPRA was not an isolated cultural and legal event in the United States, so, too, it is not an isolated element within the international framework of cultural policy concerns. The protests and sense of outrage over looting and other illicit cultural activities from the 1960s and 1970s have not abated in the interim, and illicit acquisition and marketing of cultural materials continue.[33] One of many reactions to these activities is represented by the ongoing work of UNESCO, including its efforts to convince states to adopt or ratify the 1970 UNESCO Convention (which had seventy-one national signatories as of 1993, with only the United States, Canada, and Australia being major art-importing nations), the creation of the Intergovernmental Committee for Promoting the Return of Cultural Property to Its

Countries of Origin or Its Restitution in Case of Illicit Appropriation, and cooperative work with other agencies concerned with the illicit market in cultural materials. One example of the latter is the cooperative effort between the International Council of Museums (ICOM) and UNESCO with Interpol to develop standardized forms for recording the details of stolen objects.[34] UNESCO has also encouraged bilateral discussions and agreements for the restitution of cultural property, such as the late-1980s agreement between the Jordanian Department of Antiquities and the Cincinnati Art Museum or a similar agreement between the J. Paul Getty Museum and the Museum of Archaeology of Antalya (Turkey).

The impact of directed bilateral agreements on American museums is obvious. On a more general level, museums should begin to think of legislation such as NAGPRA, or the American version of the 1970 UNESCO convention, as likely first steps in an ongoing evolution of concern on the part of many nations and ethnic groups within nations over their cultural heritage. As Alexandra Peers has noted in an article in the *Wall Street Journal,* between 1991 and 1994 Croatia, Cyprus, Ecuador, Guatemala, Hungary, Lebanon, Peru, and Turkey all engaged in lawsuits to recover materials held in American and European collections.[35] During the same period, the Institute for the Unification of Private Law (UNIDROIT) hosted a series of major international conferences negotiating a new convention on stolen cultural materials. The draft UNIDROIT Convention on the International Return of Stolen or Illegally Exported Cultural Objects, which emerged from a meeting of international governmental experts in Rome in late 1993, concerns itself with stolen cultural property, unlawfully excavated and retained property, and property that was illegally exported. Unlike the 1970 UNESCO Convention, this effort aims specifically at dealing with the differences between common and civil law systems in various countries in order to create a unified code allowing claimants easy access to courts in the country of a signatory state. Thus, whereas the 1970 UNESCO Convention required government ratification followed by government action in each case, the UNIDROIT Convention would eliminate the need for government agency involvement and place matters directly in courts of law. In the UNIDROIT Convention meeting held in June 1995, a final treaty document was agreed upon and has now been circulated to member states for further action. Whether this document meets the same dismal fate as the 1970 UNESCO Convention in major art-importing nations remains to be seen, although it is clear that without their involvement, the convention lacks substantive meaning except on a moral plane.

Other actions, however, may prove to be of greater interest and import, including the emergence of new policies for museums in other nations. The Council of Australian Museum Associations, for example, has developed its own new repatriation and general cultural policy statement for Australian museums with respect to Aboriginal and Torres Strait Islander peoples.[36] This policy outlines new understandings for the repatriation of historic period human remains and sacred materials and provides for new interactions on displays and collection management. Such policies are of direct interest to museums outside of Australia whenever loaned materials are sought for exhibition or research, as the new policies would require more than simply the involvement of Australian museum personnel.

Finally, Native peoples in many countries are increasingly concerned about their control over traditional knowledge that is often directly related to the collections and collecting important to museums. In 1993, for example, the First International Conference on the Cultural and Intellectual Property Rights of Indigenous Peoples was held in Whakatane, New Zealand, hosted by the nine Maori tribes of Mataatua. After six days of discussions involving some 150 delegates, the convention produced the Mataatua Declaration on Cultural and Intellectual Property Rights of Indigenous Peoples, which was forwarded to the Commission on Human Rights in the United Nations. Fundamentally, the Mataatua Declaration seeks to establish legal protections and controls for indigenous groups over the full range of their cultural and intellectual property. In some respects this has been accomplished by some Native American groups in both the United States and Canada through the imposition of research permit requirements that sharply delimit the future use of research data, a form of action that may become more commonplace in the future.

Within the United States, NAGPRA may also generate changing attitudes about even broader national cultural policies. Unlike most nations, the United States does not have cultural policy legislation that either generally identifies or restricts the export of materials of essential interest to the American people or to any set of such materials of more particular interest. Examples such as the Canadian Cultural Property Export and Import Act of 1977, despite some of their potential problems, may be of future interest in this connection.[37] Other elements of a national cultural and heritage policy that depend on governmental financial support are also of increasing interest, including the various funding programs that support Native American language programs, historic preservation programs, and conservation efforts to preserve everything from holdings in the National Archives to important systematic collections in museums. In these and many other respects, the United States has at best only started to create a coordinated and rational approach to a significant cultural policy for the nation and its diverse heritage.

Conclusion

The explosion of legal and extralegal attention on issues of cultural property and heritage over the last thirty years was born of the frustration and anger of indigenous peoples whose rights and perspectives about cultural property and heritage issues had been largely absent and essentially unwanted by the museum community. At the heart of this conflict is, on the one hand, a fundamental difference in basic worldviews about what is appropriate in scientific research and in museum collecting and on the other hand, a battle over whose rights would be recognized as superior by virtue of assigned legal powers. It is undeniably true that many within the professional museum and scholarly community remained unconvinced by the arguments and viewpoints held by Native Americans. It is equally true that this lack of conviction no longer means much in the face of NAGPRA's passage. As perhaps the most important single example of cultural policy legislation in the history of the United States, NAGPRA has permanently changed the ways in which museums can operate.

What has been less obvious and certainly less discussed are the long-term implications that NAGPRA has for both museums and Native American communities. As this essay has tried to show, some of these implications and consequences are very pragmatic whereas others may entail far-reaching considerations of new approaches to museum affairs by virtue of new cultural policies and laws on the international scene. Here, as elsewhere, these new approaches have also been accompanied by calls for new kinds and levels of museum-community collaboration, cooperation, and interaction. The range of concerns that we must now all confront in this human rights and cultural rights arena suggests that such cooperative engagement will be to our clear advantage.[38] It is not possible to accurately predict the full extent and nature of the issues that will emerge in future years, but what we already see on the near horizon is sufficiently complex that only through increased interactions between museums and communities can relevant and satisfactory outcomes of lasting importance for us all be realized.

Notes

A part of the data referring to tribal museum and cultural center views on museum operations was originally collected for and with the support of the National Museum of the American Indian in 1992 and augmented by additional data collection in 1993, with the support of the American Indian Studies Center at the University of Washington and with the assistance of William Seaburg. This support and assistance are very gratefully acknowledged.

1. Public Law (PL) 101-601, 43 CFR Part 10.

2. See, for example, Bowen Blair, "Indian Rights: American Indians vs. American Museums," *American Indian Law Review* 7(1) (1979): 125–154; Richard Hill, "Reclaiming Cultural Artifacts," *Museum News* 55(5) (1977): 43–45; James Nason, "Finders Keepers?" *Museum News* 51(7) (1973): 20–26.

3. See, for example, Michael Ames, "Free Indians from Their Ethnological Fate: The Emergence of the Indian Point of View in Exhibitions of Indians," *Muse* 6(3) (1987); James Nason and Robin K. Wright, "Sharing Heritage: Native American Exhibits," *Museum News* 73(3) (1994): 43, 57–60.

4. See, for example, Robert M. Adams, "Illicit International Traffic in Antiquities," *American Antiquity* (January 1971); C. P. Bracken, *Antiquities Acquired: The Spoilation of Greece* (London: David and Charles, 1975); Bennet Bronson, "The Campaign Against the Antiquities Trade," *Field Museum of Natural History Bulletin* 43(8) (1972); Hector Cardenas, "Paradise Lost: Recovering Mexico's Heritage," *Museum News* 50(7) (1972): 32–33; Trevor L. Christie, *Antiquities in Peril* (New York: Lippincott, 1967); Clemency Coggins et al., "Illicit Traffic of Pre-Columbian Antiquities," *Art Journal* 29 (1969): 94–98; Roy C. Craven Jr., "The Looting Continues—a New Solution?" *Museum News* 52 (1974): 14; Hester A. Davis, "Is There a Future for the Past?" *Archaeology* (October 1971): 300–306; Milton Esterow, *The Art Stealers* (New York: Macmillan, 1966).

5. See, for example, American Association of Museums (AAM), *Museum Ethics* (Washington, D.C.: AAM, 1978); ICOM, *Code of Professional Ethics* (Paris: ICOM, 1987); Martin Mayer, "New Code of Ethics for Art Historians," *Art News* 73(6) (1974): 34–36.

6. American Anthropological Association, *Resolution on Acquisition of Cultural Properties* (Washington, D.C.: American Anthropological Association, 1973), 1.

7. Bonnie Burnham, *The Protection of Cultural Property: A Handbook of National Legislations* (Paris: ICOM, 1974).

8. For a contrasting view, see Hansegeorg Dickmann and Jurgen Wilke, "The Art of the Poor Nations in the Museums of the Rich," *Council for Museum Anthropology Newsletter* 3(3) (1979): 14–18.

9. 95-341.

10. Philip J. Deloria, "The Twentieth Century and Beyond: Sovereignty," in *The Native Americans,* ed. Betty Ballantine and Ian Ballatine (Atlanta: Turner Publishing, 1993), 431–457.

11. The 1978 *American Indian Religious Freedom Act* had already been preceded by the Indian Civil Rights Act of 1968, the Alaska Native Claims Settlement Act of 1971, the Indian Education Act and Indian Financing Act of 1972, the Indian Self-Determination and Educational Assistance Act of 1975, and the Indian Child Welfare Act earlier in 1978.

12. See, for example, Grand Council of Chiefs (of the Houdenosaunee), "Policy Statement on Medicine Masks. Turtle," *Native American Center for Living Arts Quarterly* 2(3) (Fall 1980): 8; Richard Hill, "Indians and Museums: A Plea for Cooperation," *Council for Museum Anthropology Newsletter* 4(2) (1980): 22–25.

13. NAIMA, "Suggested Guidelines for Museums in Dealing with Requests for Return of Native American Materials," in *Directory of North American Indian Museums and Cultural Centers* (Niagara Falls, N.Y.: NAIMA, 1981).

14. After the passage of NAGPRA, there were still staff in some museums who believed that they would not have to deal with repatriation requests from tribes if the tribes had no museums or cultural centers for the "comparable" handling of materials.

15. See, for example, Charles Baker, "In My Opinion: Indian Artifacts and Museums, a Question of Ownership," *History News* 49(4) (1985): 14–16; Jane E. Buikstra, "Reburial: How We All Lose, an Archaeologist's Opinion," *Council for Museum Anthropology Newsletter* 7(2) (1983): 2–5; Walter Echo Hawk, "Sacred Material and the Law," in *The Concept of Sacred Materials and Their Place in the World*, ed. George Horse Capture (Cody, Wyo.: Buffalo Bill Historical Center, 1989), 67–81; Thomas P. Myers, "In Defense of Principles: Indian Skeletal Remains in Museums," *Council for Museum Anthropology Newsletter* 8(4) (1984): 5–6; Frank A. Norick, "The Reburial Controversy in California," *Council for Museum Anthropology Newsletter* 6(3) (1982); Michael Tymchuk, "Skeletal Remains: In Defense of Sensitivity and Compromise," *Council for Museum Anthropology Newsletter* 8(3) (1984): 2–8; Deward E. Walker Jr., "Anthropologists Must Allow American Indians to Bury Their Dead," *Chronicle of Higher Education*, September 12, 1990: B2.

16. American Anthropological Association, *Statement of the American Anthropological Association Commission on the Treatment of Human Remains* (Washington, D.C.: American Anthropological Association, n.d.).

17. American Association of Museums, *Policy Regarding the Repatriation of Native American Ceremonial Objects and Human Remains* (Washington, D.C.: AAM, 1987).

18. Harvey Arden, "Who Owns Our Past?" *National Geographic* (March 1989): 376–393; Carol Ann Bassett, "The Culture Thieves," *Science* 7(6) (1986): 86.

19. Dan Monroe, "Special Repatriation Session Address" (Address presented at the Annual Meeting of the Western Museums Conference, San Jose, Calif., 1990).

20. Virginia Morell, "An Anthropological Culture Shift," *Science* 264 (1994): 20.

21. Chris Raymond, "Some Scholars Upset by Stanford's Decision to Return American Indian Remains for Re-Burial by Tribe," *Chronicle of Higher Education*, July 5, 1989, A4–A5.

22. 25 USC 3001.

23. 43 CFR Part 10, Subpart A, 10.2(c).

24. 43 CFR Part 10, Subpart A, 10.14(d).

25. Department of Interior, "Native American Graves Protection and Repatriation Act Regulations (Notice of Proposed Rulemaking)," *Federal Register* 58(102) (May 28, 1993): 31122–32234.

26. Some tribes—for example, the Navajo or Hopi—could anticipate receiving hundreds of communications from museums with culturally affiliated materials. How to respond in any rapid way to all of these, much less in a detailed way following the analysis of the museum data, was obviously going to be a daunting matter. In some communities, there were no specific tribal government staff charged with cultural heritage responsibilities, much less with well established cultural policies on how to approach this matter. By 1993 some tribes had not yet had the opportunity to review the legislation and react to it. Moreover, many of the smaller tribes did not have the financial resources to send tribal representatives to review museum collections—a key step in many cases if successful repatriation claims were to be made.

27. See, for example, Dan Monroe and Walter Echo Hawk, "Deft Deliberations," *Museum News* (July-August 1991): 55–58.

28. Raymond H. Thompson, "Dealing with the Past and Looking at the Future," *Museum News* 70(1) (1991): 36–40.

29. Pueblo of Zuni, *Pueblo of Zuni Statement Regarding the Treatment and Protection of Human Remains and Associated Funerary Objects* (Zuni, N.M.: Pueblo of Zuni, November 1992); Pueblo of Zuni, *Statement of Cultural Affiliation with Prehistoric and Historic Cultures* (Zuni, N.M.: Pueblo of Zuni, July 1995).

30. James Nason, *Native American Tribal Museum and Center Survey: Storage, Care, and Access Policies for Museum Collections* (Washington, D. C.: National Museum of the American Indian, 1992).

31. Navajo Times, "Masks Auction Sparks Protest from Tribes," *Navajo Times* 31(21) (May 23, 1991): A1.

32. See, for example, Hopi Tribe, "Protecting Heritage of Paramount Importance in Code Creation," *Hopi Tutuveni* 4(5) (September 23, 1994): 6–7.

33. See, for example, Andrew Decker, "Lost Heritage: The Destruction of African Art," *Art News* 89(7) (1990): 108–119.

34. ICOM, "Return or Restitution," *ICOM News* 40(2) (1987): 17.

35. Alexandra Peers, "Art World Shaken by Nations Seeking to Reclaim Items," *Wall Street Journal*, June 21, 1994.

36. Council of Australian Museum Associations (CAMA), *Previous Possessions, New Obligations: Policies for Museums in Australia and Aboriginal and Torres Strait Islander Peoples* (Melbourne: CAMA, 1993).

37. Marie C. Malaro, *Legal Primer on Managing Museum Collections* (Washington, D.C.: Smithsonian Institution Press, 1985).

38. See, for example, Evan Roth, "Success Stories," *Museum News* (January-February 1991): 41–45.

Lynn S. Teague, Joseph T. Joaquin, and Hartman H. Lomawaima

A Coming Together: The Norton Allen Collection, the Tohono O'odham Nation, and the Arizona State Museum

Museum exhibits and collections very often generate more questions than answers. A recent exhibition at the Arizona State Museum in Tucson is a case in point. The special exhibition of a newly acquired collection of ancient Hohokam pottery and shellwork attracted scores of people, from the region's Tohono O'odham Indian Nation. Visitors, young and old alike, looked upon the collection in awe and asked questions such as "Where did these pieces come from?" "Why were they created, and by whom?" "Who were the persons that excavated or recovered the materials?" "Where have they been kept, and how did they get here?" Some Tohono O'odham parents and elders offered their children an important clue to the answers by saying, "These were made by the Hohokam, your ancient ancestors." This essay chronicles the story of this special collection, known as the Norton Allen Collection. It is also a case study that may provide the reader with some useful insights into the process that will ultimately result in the return of the collection to the Tohono O'odham Nation for exhibits and educational programs.

Tohono O'odham Nation

The Tohono O'odham Nation consists of four reservations in south-central Arizona that have a combined area of nearly three million acres, comparable to the state of Connecticut. According to a 1993 Indian Health Service Survey, the nation has a population of twenty-thousand people. This figure does not include members living off reservation or kin who occupy lands just across the international boundary in northern Mexico. The land base is part of the larger Sonoran Desert. It is the desert environment that gives the Tohono O'odham, or "Desert People," their unique identity among Native Americans. Since Spanish colonial times, the Tohono O'odham have most often been called Papago or some version thereof by outsiders. Today the people are recognized by their Native name in public records ranging from government documents to newspaper accounts. Federal, state, and tribal agencies are the largest contributors to the nation's economy, followed by gaming, agriculture, cattle raising, mining, and tourism.

In 1989 the tribal legislature created the Cultural Preservation Committee to deal with matters of intellectual property rights, repatriation, protection of historic and sacred sites, reburial of human remains recovered from archaeological sites, and the wake of land development activities. The committee and its chairman have taken their charge to new levels and are held in high regard by government agencies, museum professionals, and other Native Americans. Some of the committee's activities are highlighted in the discussion that follows.

The Arizona State Museum

The museum was founded in 1893 by territorial legislation. Its primary mission over the years has been to collect, research, interpret, and preserve material culture of indigenous peoples of the greater Southwest. Its holdings range from material produced by contemporary southwestern Native American hands to those that date from twelve thousand years ago. As an official state agency, the museum enforces and monitors state antiquities laws and other mandated acts. Located on the University of Arizona campus, it is also an important resource for students, scholars, and the public at large.

For more than a century, the museum has had many ties to southwestern tribes. However, a recent agreement between the museum and the Tohono O'odham Nation represents a new era in these relationships, one that moves beyond legally mandated repatriation activities to a cooperative long-term undertaking. The donation of the Norton Allen Collection was the impetus for the agreement, which intends to preserve an important collection and ensure that this collection is available to the descendants of its makers, the members of the Tohono O'odham Nation, for their use in exhibits and educational programs. At the same time, the agreement creates a permanent tie between the museum and the nation, working together to preserve this collection and to develop greater autonomy for the nation in curating and interpreting its past.

The Norton Allen Collection

The Norton Allen Collection has long been known among professional archaeologists and museum professionals as the most significant collection of prehistoric Hohokam artifacts in private ownership. The collection is the consequence of decades of dedicated work by Norton Allen, a native of San Diego, California. The collection is distinguished by its remarkable quality, and quantity, including some of the finest pottery and shellwork ever recovered from the sites of southern and central Arizona. The scientific value of the collection is established by the excellent records associated with these objects.

Allen became concerned about the destruction of important archaeological sites in the Gila Bend, Arizona, area during the Depression era and over more than forty winters worked to salvage archaeological sites endangered by agricultural development. He was aided first by his father, Ernest G. Allen, and later by his wife, Ethel Allen. Unlike those who vandalize sites for personal gain, his goal was the preservation of this significant aspect of Arizona's cultural and historic heritage. Working with the encouragement of Emil Haury, at that time director of the museum, Allen saved and meticulously documented materials from sites along a lengthy portion of the Gila River, from Painted Rocks Dam to Gillespie Dam. At the end of each winter's investigations, he returned to his California home, where he painstakingly restored the vessels excavated during that season.

Hohokam sites in the Gila Bend area that were investigated by Allen date principally to the Santa Cruz and Sacaton phases, although at least one—the Rock Ball Court Site—is earlier. The most intense prehistoric occupation of the area fell between about A.D. 700 and 1150, when Gila Bend seems to have been a critical link in the very active Hohokam trade in shell from the Gulf and from the Pacific coast. Extensive canal systems testify to active agriculture, including the cultivation of such basic foods as corn and beans. It is also likely that the Hohokam grew a great deal of cotton, a crop that would have done as well there in A.D. 900 as it does now, more than one thousand years later. The Gatlin Site, near the modern village of San Lucy, was one of the earliest in Arizona where a platform mound was built for religious ceremonies. Ball courts, also evidence of close contact with areas far south in Mexico, are found at almost all villages in the area.

The material from the Norton Allen Collection reflects the richness of this area. It includes almost five-hundred vessels, principally red-on-buff pots showing the artistry of the Hohokam in depicting birds, lizards, and other desert inhabitants as well as curvilinear geometric designs. Allen also found carved animal figures incorporated into stone vessels and stone palettes and exceptionally skillful shell carvings of human figures, birds, snakes, and lizards.

His excavations included human burials, which were in immediate danger of destruction. Today a state law (ARS 41–865) protects burials on private lands, but at the time of Allen's excavations there was no prohibition against simply grading them away to make room for modern fields. Because of his sensitivity to the respect due to the remains of these prehistoric people, Allen reburied human remains in nearby locations where they would not be in immediate danger of destruction. He also collected for reburial many human bones that he found on the surface of sites, where they had been left by diggers concerned only with the acquisition of burial objects.

During the many years of his studies, and even after he ceased active field-work, Allen was a familiar figure at the museum, where he established a close working relationship with Emil Haury and with other archaeologists who were actively involved in Hohokam archaeology. The Allens welcomed numerous students and professionals into their home, where they studied the unique materials stored there and shared information freely with others who shared their interest in the prehistory of the western Gila. Major projects, like that conducted by the museum and the U.S. Army Corps of Engineers in association with the construction of Painted Rocks Dam, profited enormously from Allen's knowledge and insights.

Early Plans for the Collection

Allen believed from the beginning that this collection and its supporting documentation belonged in a public institution in Arizona, where they would be accessible to the public and especially to the Tohono O'odham people. Living in Gila Bend during the winters, the Allens formed lasting friendships with families in villages throughout the reservation. Elders of the area recall that even though the Allens were not O'odham, their persistence in trying to identify the best solution for disposition of the collection was consistent with O'odham feelings. Elders further observed that, even though the material was removed "in not the right way," the Allens' resistance to selling portions or all of the collection was refreshing and praiseworthy. It was realized by all parties that these processes are important. Joseph Joaquin, chairman of the Cultural

Preservation Committee, has observed that we should not feel that we are in the business of punishing past deeds; rather, we must respond and work with all parties in finding solutions to cultural resources matters.

As repatriation laws became a reality, however, new factors entered into these plans. One was potentially negative. Allen was deeply concerned that after donation to the museum, the collection would be fragmented by claims from the various tribes claiming descent from the prehistoric Hohokam people. The collection was obtained from private lands and so long as it remained in Allen's possession was not subject to either federal or state repatriation laws. However, once donated to a public institution, it would become subject to these statutes.

Although Allen did not collect human remains, there are many unassociated funerary objects and also possible sacred objects in this collection. The other factor was very positive. Sentiment was building among the Tohono O'odham for the development of their own museum, a place where collections could be cared for and could be interpreted by the descendants of those who had made them.

During the late 1980s and early 1990s, Allen discussed his concerns with archaeologists and museum curators. It became clear that a way had to be found to resolve the potentially negative impact of new legal initiatives, preferably by resorting to the positive effects of those same laws. Alternatively, Allen might choose some other disposition altogether for the collection. It was legally his private property, and he could sell it to institutions abroad or to private collectors. This would be a very unsatisfactory outcome not only for the museum and the nation but also for the Allens, who still wished to see the materials accessible to the O'odham and to the other people of Arizona.

Negotiating an Agreement

In 1992 the museum arranged a meeting at Gila Bend to bring together the parties with the greatest stake in plans for disposition of the Allen Collection. Norton and Ethel Allen were there. The Tohono O'odham Nation's Cultural Preservation Committee was represented by Joseph Joaquin and other members. A number of individuals from San Lucy village, including John Reno, a member of the Tohono O'odham Legislative Council from the Gila Bend reservation, also attended. The museum was represented by Mike Jacobs, archaeological curator, and Lynn Teague, curator of archaeology and repatriation coordinator.

The first suggestion made by the museum was very straightforward: the collection should be donated to the Tohono O'odham Nation, with the museum serving as the nation's repository until a suitable museum could be built by the nation. The museum already curates several important collections belonging to the nation and serves as the nation's repository pending construction of a Tohono O'odham museum. This would keep the collection intact and would provide the nation with the maximum legal control of its own heritage. Other tribes, of course, would still retain the right to make repatriation claims against the collection but would have little cause to do so with the material in the ownership of other descendants of the Hohokam, with whom they are in close cooperation on repatriation issues. The four O'odham-speaking tribes—Tohono O'odham Nation, Gila River Indian Community, Ak-Chin Indian Community, and Salt River Pima-Maricopa Indian Community—are united by common repatriation goals and officially by a joint resolution of their respective tribal governments stating their common claims of Hohokam ancestry and their intention to work cooperatively in repatriation matters. The Hopi Tribe of Arizona, claiming Hohokam ancestry on behalf of a number of Hopi clans with migration traditions describing Hohokam origins, had already cooperated with the four southern tribes in a number of repatriation cases, and a formal cooperative agreement has been under discussion for several years.

However, Allen rejected the proposal that the collection be donated directly to the Tohono O'odham Nation. Although he believed the availability of the collection to the Tohono O'odham was an important objective of his donation, there was still no Tohono O'odham museum capable of curating the material, and there was no certainty that there would be one in the future. Allen was therefore uncomfortable with the long-term security of the collection should the nation choose not to build a museum.

Joint ownership by the museum and the nation was the next option explored by the group. At this point, it became clear that everyone involved required legal advice in order to come up with a workable plan. Over a period of many months, the museum's attorneys, Nancy Laney and later Michael Proctor, both of the University of Arizona Attorney's Office; Fred Lomayesva, assistant director of the University's Office of Indian Programs and an attorney; and the nation's attorney, Dean Suagee, researched this possibility. It became apparent that tribal sovereignty presented a formidable obstacle to this path. Should there be disagreements between the parties, there would be no common legal path to resolution. Nonjudicial mediation processes were considered but provided no adequate answer to the legal issues raised by sovereignty.

Finally, it was proposed that the collection be donated to the museum but that prior to the donation the museum and the nation enter into an intergovernmental agreement providing that the highest priority for use of the collection would always be for exhibits and educational programs of the

Tohono O'odham Nation, once a suitable facility was established. The agreement also provided for negotiation by the museum and the nation of guidelines for treatment of the collection while it remained at the museum and for museum technical assistance to the nation in developing a curatorial facility meeting current standards.

Meetings were again held between the museum and the nation, and a document embodying the concerns of both was drafted and then sent to the lawyers. This proved to be by far the most time-consuming part of the process. It was easier to find ways to resolve issues raised by a century of museum-tribal relationships, and to address the concerns of a donor who had devoted his entire adult life to the preservation of the collection, than to elicit a final document from the University of Arizona Attorney's Office and the Office of the Attorney General of the Nation.

Finally, in August 1994 the Legislative Council of the Tohono O'odham Nation voted unanimously to approve the agreement, and it was sent to the University of Arizona for signature. There, it was referred to the Arizona Secretary of State's Office, where it languished for several months. Eventually, inquiries established that the copy sent to the state capital had been lost. It was replaced and signed for the State of Arizona in December 1994.

The final agreement satisfied the concerns of all of the parties involved in negotiations for the disposition of the Norton Allen Collection and set the stage for bringing an exceedingly important body of material evidence of Arizona's past back home to the state and to the O'odham people. At the same time, the agreement set the stage for a close permanent partnership in cultural preservation and education between the Arizona State Museum and the Tohono O'odham Nation.

Future Plans

One of the highest priorities of the Tohono O'odham Nation is the design and construction of a secure place for the nation's current and future holding of cultural materials. There is also an identified need to educate nation members about local ordinances and about state and federal laws on repatriation and reburial. The Cultural Preservation Committee, in its discussions with outside agencies, developers, and the archaeological community, has observed that we are all talking about being compliant with the laws, but all too often compliance is defined on different levels. The truth of the matter is that we are coming from different worlds and are trying very hard to converge and converse on topics of mutual interest. Significant progress has been made. The committee chairman notes that today the committee is notified or included in discussions that affect land outside the Tohono O'odham Nation's boundaries because these lands are also ancestral areas. From the nation's perspective, one of the best strategies in working within the laws is to have one voice. Whether it is the Tohono O'odham Nation or the consortium of O'odham people, it is essential to have one voice and come together as one.

Cultural Appropriation: A Selected Bibliography

Pratima V. Rao

The Appropriation of Music and Musical Forms

Manuel, Peter. "Puerto Rican Music and Cultural Identity: Creative Appropriation of Cuban Sources from Danza to Salsa." *Ethnomusicology* 38 (1994): 249–280.

Regis, Humphrey A. "American Appropriation of Reggae." *Caribbean Review* 16 (Summer 1990): 7.

Seeger, Anthony. "Singing Other Peoples' Songs." *Cultural Survival Quarterly* 15–16 (Summer 1991): 36–39.

Stephens, Gregory. "Rap Music's Double-Voiced Discourse: A Crossroads for Interracial Communication." *Journal of Communication Inquiry* 15 (1991): 70–91.

Wallis, Roger, and Krister Malm. *Big Sounds from Small People: The Music Industry in Small Countries.* New York: Pendragon Press, 1984.

Appropriation in Art and Narrative

Alcoff, Linda. "The Problem of Speaking for Others." *Cultural Critique* 19–20 (Winter 1991–1992): 5–32.

Ellinson, Dean A. "Unauthorised Reproduction of Traditional Aboriginal Art." *University of New South Wales Law Journal* 17(2) (1994): 327–344.

Flood, John-Michael. "As if Other/as if Indian: Reader Response to Appropriation of the Native Voice in Contemporary Fiction of Northern Ontario." Ph.D. diss., University of Toronto, 1993. Abstract in *Dissertation Abstracts International* 53 (1993): 4326A–4327A.

Goddard, Barbara. "The Politics of Representation: Some Native Canadian Women Writers." *Canadian Literature* 124–125 (1990): 183–225.

Hill, Richard. "One Part per Million: White Appropriation and Native Voices." *Fuse* 15 (Winter 1992): 12–22.

Hladki, Janice. "Problematizing the Issue of Cultural Appropriation." *Alternate Routes* 11 (1994): 95–119.

Lutz, Hartmut. "Cultural Appropriation as a Process of Displacing Peoples and History." *Canadian Journal of Native Studies* 10 (1990): 167–182.

Maracle, Lee. "Moving Over." *Trivia: A Journal of Ideas* 14 (Spring 1989): 9–12.

Monture, Joel. "Native Americans and the Appropriation of Cultures." *Ariel* 25 (1994): 114–121.

Morrison, Ann Katherine. "Canadian Art and Cultural Appropriation: Emily Carr and the 1927 Exhibition of Canadian West Coast Art—Native and Modern." Master's thesis, University of British Columbia, 1991.

Pask, Amanda. "Cultural Appropriation and the Law: An Analysis of the Legal Regime Concerning Culture." *Intellectual Property Journal* 8 (1993): 57–86.

Price, Sally. "Provenances and Pedigrees: The Western Appropriation of Non-Western Art." In *Imagery and Creativity: Ethnoaesthetics and Art Worlds in the Americas*, ed. Dorothea S. Whitten and Norman E. Whitten Jr. Tucson: University of Arizona Press, 1993, 45–65.

Puri, Kamal. "Cultural Ownership and Intellectual Property Rights Post *Mabo*: Putting Ideas into Action." *Intellectual Property Journal* 9 (1995): 293–347.

Reynolds, Annette E. "Of Symposiums and Doorkeepers: Theorizing Cultural Appropriation and Authenticity." Master's thesis, University of British Columbia, 1993.

Richard, Neil. "The Latin American Problematic of Theoretical-Cultural Transference: Postmodern Appropriations and Counterappropriations." *South Atlantic Quarterly* 92 (Summer 1993): 453–459.

Rowell, John. "The Politics of Cultural Appropriation." *Journal of Value Inquiry* 29 (1995): 137–142.

Todd, Loretta. "Notes on Appropriation." *Parallelogramme* 16 (Summer 1990): 24–32.

Tyler, Stephen. "On 'Writing up/off' as 'Speaking For.'" *Journal of Anthropological Research* 43 (1987): 338–342.

Young, James O. "Should White Men Play the Blues?" *Journal of Value Inquiry* 28 (1994): 415–424.

Appropriation in Colonial and Postcolonial Discourse

Adam, Ian, and Helen Tiffin, eds. *Past the Last Post: Theorizing Colonialism and Post-Modernism.* Calgary: University of Calgary Press, 1990.

Bhabha, Homi. *The Location of Culture.* London: Routledge, 1994.

Chanady, Amaryll. "Latin American Discourses of Identity and Appropriation of the Amerindian Other." *Sociocriticism* 6 (1990): 33–48.

Coombes, Annie E. "The Recalcitrant Object: Culture Contact and the Question of Hybridity." In *Colonial Discourse/Postcolonial Theory*, ed. Francis Barker, Peter Hulme, and Margaret Iversen. Manchester: Manchester University Press, 1994, 89–114.

Gelder, Ken, and Jane M. Jacobs. "Talking Out of Place: Authorizing the Aboriginal Sacred in Postcolonial Australia." *Cultural Studies* 9 (1995): 150–160.

Griffiths, Gareth. "Imitation, Abrogation, and Appropriation: The Production of the Post-colonial Text." *Kunapipi* 9 (1987): 13–20.

Gupta, Anjuli. "English Writing in India: Fear of Experimentation, Fear of Appropriation—Death of Creativity?" In *Crisis and Creativity in the New Literatures in English,* ed. Geoffrey Davis and Hena Maes Jelinek. Amsterdam: Redopi, 1990, 151–168.

Hutcheon, Linda. "Circling the Downspout of Empire: Post-colonialism and Post-modernism." *ARIEL* 20 (1989): 149–175.

Indyk, Ivor. "Assimilation or Appropriation: Uses of European Literary Forms in Black Australian Writing." *Australian Literary Studies* 15 (October 1992): 249–260.

Said, Edward W. *Orientalism.* New York: Vintage Books, 1979.

———. "Representing the Colonized: Anthropology's Interlocutors." *Critical Inquiry* 15 (Winter 1989): 205–225.

Spivak, Gayatri C. "Can the Subaltern Speak?" In *Marxism and the Interpretation of Culture,* ed. Cary Nelson and Lawrence Grossberg. Urbana: University of Illinois Press, 1988, 271–313.

Appropriation in Popular Culture

Churchill, Ward. *Indians Are Us? Culture and Genocide in Native North America.* Toronto: Between the Lines, 1994.

Francis, Daniel. *The Imaginary Indian: The Image of the Indian in Canadian Culture.* Vancouver: Arsenal Pulp Press, 1992.

Phillips, Brian. "Cross-cultural Appropriation: Seven Wolves and Its American Sources (Levels of Imitation in Popular Chinese Cinema)." *Journal of Popular Culture* 27 (1994): 195–209.

Root, Deborah. *Cannibal Culture: Art, Appropriation, and the Politics of Attire.* Boulder: Westview Press, 1995.

The Appropriation of Scientific Knowledge

Breckenridge, Lee P. "Protection of Biological and Cultural Diversity: Emerging Recognition of Local Community Rights in Ecosystems Under International Environmental Law." *Tennessee Law Review* 59 (1992): 735–785.

Daes, Erica-Irene. *Discrimination Against Indigenous Peoples: Study on the Protection of the Cultural and Intellectual Property of Indigenous Peoples.* New York: Subcommission on Prevention of Discrimination and Protection of Minorities, Economic and Social Council, United Nations, July 28, 1993.

Elisabetsky, Elaine. "Folklore, Tradition, or Know how?" *Cultural Survival Quarterly* 15 (Summer 1991): 9–13.

King, Steven R. "The Source of Our Cures." *Cultural Survival Quarterly* 15 (Summer 1991): 19–22.

Kloppenburg, Jack R. Jr., ed. *Seeds and Sovereignty: The Use and Control of Plant Genetic Resources.* Durham, N.C.: Duke University Press, 1988.

Yano, Lester I. "Protection of the Ethnobiological Knowledge of Indigenous Peoples." *UCLA Law Review* 41 (1993): 443–486.

Appropriation and Tangible Cultural Property

Assembly of First Nations and Canadian Museums Association. *Turning the Page: Forging New Partnerships Between Museums and First Peoples.* 3d ed. Ottawa: Task Force on Museums and First Peoples, 1994.

Bell, Catherine. "Aboriginal Claims to Cultural Property in Canada: A Comparative Legal Analysis of the Repatriation Debate." *American Indian Law Review* 17 (1992): 457–521.

DeVallance, Brian, and Pace Julie A., eds. "Symposium on Cultural Property." *Arizona State Law Journal* 24 (1992): 1–562.

Gerstenblith, Patty. "Identity and Cultural Property: The Protection of Cultural Property in the United States." *Boston University Law Review* 75 (1995): 559–688.

Handler, Richard. "Who Owns the Past?" In *The Politics of Culture*, ed. Brett Williams. Washington, D.C.: Smithsonian Institution Press, 1991, 63–74.

Herz, Richard. "Legal Protection for Indigenous Cultures: Sacred Sites and Communal Rights." *Valapraiso Law Review* 79 (1993): 691–716.

Mastalir, Roger W. "A Proposal for Protecting the 'Cultural' and 'Property' Aspects of Cultural Property Under International Law." *Fordham International Law Journal* 16 (1992–1993): 1033–1093.

"Material Culture in Flux: Law and Policy of Repatriation of Material Culture." *University of British Columbia Law Review* (Special issue) 29 (1995): 1–345.

Merenstein, Adele. "The Zuni Quest for Repatriation of the War Gods: An Alternative Basis for Claim." *American Indian Law Review* 17 (1992): 589–637.

Merryman, John H. "Two Ways of Thinking About Cultural Property." *American Journal of International Law* 80 (1986): 831–853.

Messenger, Phyllis Mauch, ed. *The Ethics of Collecting Cultural Property: Whose Culture? Whose Property?* Albuquerque: University of New Mexico Press, 1989.

Pearce, Susan, ed. *Museums and the Appropriation of Culture.* London: Athlone Press, 1994.

Contributors

Joane Cardinal-Schubert is an artist and essayist presently living in Calgary, Alberta. She received her B.F.A. (in printmaking and painting) from the University of Calgary in 1977, although her first public exhibition had been held in 1967. Since that time, her work has been exhibited extensively throughout Canada and the United States (and, in 1993, in the Czech Republic). She has lectured and written extensively on matters relating to art, art history, and aboriginal issues in the arts. In 1986 Cardinal-Schubert was nominated to the Royal Canadian Academy of Arts.

Rosemary J. Coombe is an associate professor of law at the University of Toronto. She received her doctorate in law, with a minor in anthropology, from Stanford University. Her research addresses implications of intellectual property laws in the cultural politics of subaltern struggle. Her articles, published in anthropology, cultural studies, political theory, and law and society journals, are being revised for her book *Cultural Appropriations: Authorship, Alterity, and the Law,* which is forthcoming from Routledge. In 1994 she organized the conference Commercial Appropriations of Native Cultural Tradition: Legal Challenges for Indigenous Activists, in Washington, D.C. Her current projects include an ethnographic study of West African traders in Harlem and their involvement in global circulations of commodities and commodified meanings. She is also working on a book on copyright and early English colonialism in the context of industrialization and evangelism and on a collection of essays that addresses the socially constitutive functions of the trademark in the context of nineteenth-century American imperialism.

Kwame Dawes, poet, playwright, storyteller, essayist, musician, actor, and fiction writer, was born in Ghana in 1962. He moved to Jamaica in 1971, where, at the University of the West Indies, he received an honors degree in English. He completed his Ph.D. at the University of New Brunswick, Canada. Dawes has published three collections of poems, numerous critical essays, and reviews on race, film, literary theory, arts and culture, and theater in prominent journals in North America, the Caribbean, Europe, and Africa. Dawes is an assistant professor of English at the University of South Carolina at Columbia.

Perry A. Hall hold degrees from the University of Michigan (B.A., psychology) and Harvard University (Ph.D., education and social policy). His professional life has been devoted to the project of establishing and building African-American studies as a field of study. For eight years he served as director of the Center for Black Studies at Wayne State University, Detroit, Michigan; during that period he also served in various official capacities with the fledgling National Council for Black Studies. Presently, he works in the Curriculum in African and Afro-American Studies at the University of North Carolina at Chapel Hill. His recent publications include "Beyond Afrocentrism: Alternatives for African American Studies," *Western Journal of Black Studies* (Winter 1991); "Toward a Dramaturgical Analysis of Historical Transformation in African-American Musical Culture," *Word: A Black Culture Journal* (Spring 1991); and "Introducing African American Studies: Systematic and Thematic Principles" *Journal of Black Studies* (July 1996).

Jonathan Hart, professor of English and adjunct professor of comparative literature, has been a visiting scholar at Harvard, a visiting fellow at Cambridge, and a senior fellow at Toronto. He has edited several special issues of journals and collections of essays: *Explorations in Difference* (with Richard Bauman) (University of Toronto Press, 1995), *Reading the Renaissance* (Garland, 1996), and *Imagining Culture* (Garland, 1996). He is also the author of *Theater and World* (Northeastern University Press, 1992) and *Northrop Frye* (Routledge, 1994).

Joseph T. Joaquin is chairman of the Tohono O'odham Nation Cultural Preservation Committee and is council representative of the Sells District to the nation's legislative branch. He is a well-known figure in the national dialogue on Native American cultural resources.

Lenore Keeshig-Tobias is an author, poet, playwright, essayist, activist, and traditional storyteller. She was born on the Neyaashiinigmiing (Cape Crocker) reserve on the Bruce Peninsula in Ontario, Canada, where she now lives. In 1993 Lenore and her daughter Polly won the Living a Dream Book Award for their book *Bird Talk* (Sister Vision Press, 1991), which Lenore wrote and Polly illustrated. Keeshig-Tobias has been involved in curriculum development for use in First Nations' schools and currently serves as a school trustee for the Chippewas of Nawash First Nations Board of Education and as the chair of the Nawash Curriculum Development Committee. Her most recent works include *Emma and the Trees* (Sister Vision Press, 1996) and *Into the Moon* (Seventh Generation Books, forthcoming), an anthology of aboriginal women's writing.

J. Jorge Klor de Alva, professor of comparative ethnic studies and anthropology at the University of California, Berkeley, earned his degrees from the University of California, Berkeley (B.A., J.D.) and University of California, Santa Cruz (Ph.D.) Before moving to Berkeley, he was professor of anthropology at Princeton University. His research interests, focused primarily in the United States, Mexico, Latin America, Europe, and South Africa, include the comparative study of interethnic/interracial relations, critical cultural studies, historical ethnography, colonialism and post-colonialism, the development and uses of nationalism, and educational reform. He has published over seventy scholarly articles, is coauthor of eight social studies textbooks, and is author/coauthor or editor/coeditor of fifteen books on related subjects. His forthcoming or in-progress publications include *The Norton Anthology of Indigenous Mesoamerican Literature,* (Norton, forthcoming); *American Identities: Traditional, Contested, and Imagined* (Smithsonian Institution Press, forthcoming); and (with Cornel West) *Together Forever Tonite: Black-Brown Relations in the U.S.* (tentative title).

Hartman H. Lomawaima is associate director of the Arizona State Museum. He has worked in the field of museum curation and administration for the past sixteen years. Hartman is from the Hopi village of Sipaulovi in northern Arizona.

James D. Nason, a member of the Comanche Nation, is currently director of the American Indian Studies Center and professor of anthropology. He is also chairman of the Graduate School Interdisciplinary Program in Museology, curator of Native American ethnology in the Burke Museum at the University of Washington, and member of the Canadian Studies faculty in the Jackson School of International Studies. His research in Micronesia, Canada, and the United States has resulted in publications on technology and social change, social organization and political development, cultural policy, conservation, museum law, and various other museological topics. His recent research includes consultation work for the Smithsonian Institution on the design of the new National Museum of the American Indian, a comparative study of intellectual property rights, and ongoing work on ethnohistoriographic methodology.

Nell Jessup Newton is a professor of law at American University, Washington College of Law, where she teaches property, constitutional, and American Indian law. She has written on American Indian issues since 1980. With Robert N. Clinton and Monroe Price, she is the coauthor of *American Indian Law* (Michie, 1991, supp. 1994). She is presently serving as editor in chief, with Robert Clinton, of a project to revise the *Handbook of Federal Indian Law.*

M. Nourbese Philip is a poet and writer who lives in the City of Toronto. Her short stories, essays, reviews, and articles have appeared in magazines and journals in Canada, the U.K., and the U.S.A., and her poetry and prose have been extensively anthologized. She has published four books of poetry, *Thorns; Salmon Courage; She Tries Her Tongue, Her Silence Softly Breaks;* and *Looking for Livingstone: An Odyssey of Silence,* a poem in prose and poetry. Her first novel, *Harriet's Daughter,* was published in 1988 by Heinemann (England) and the Women's Press (Canada). Her manuscript collection of poetry, *She Tries Her Tongue,* was awarded the 1988 Casa de las Americas prize for poetry. Philip has held a Guggenheim Fellowship (1990) in poetry, and a Macdowell Fellowship (1991). Among her recent works is *Frontiers: Essays and Writings in Racism and Culture* (Mercury Press, 1992), an essay from which appears in this volume. In April 1994, Philip's short story "Stop Frame" was awarded the Lawrence Foundation Award by the American journal *Prairie Schooner.* In September 1995 she was awarded the Arts Foundation of Toronto award in writing and publishing.

Pratima V. Rao was formerly a researcher at the Faculty of Law, University of Alberta. She holds degrees in sociology and law. Her forthcoming publications include a monograph on Canadian health law in *Kluwer Encyclopaedia of Laws* (with Patricia James) (Kluwer Law and Taxation) and an article on the intersection of Marxism, postcolonialism, and social theory. Currently, she is doing graduate work in international relations and is a foreign service officer with the Department of Foreign Affairs and International Trade, Canada.

Naomi Roht-Arriaza received both a J.D. and an M.P.P. from the University of California, Berkeley. She teaches in the areas of global environmental law and international human rights at Hastings College of Law in San Francisco. She was a fellow in international law and organization at Boalt Hall, University of California, Berkeley, during 1991–1992, and in 1995 she was a Fulbright scholar in Spain. Her publications include "Precaution, Participation, and the 'Greening' of International Trade Law," *Journal of Environmental Law and Litigation* 57 (1992) as well as studies on the relationship between trade and conservation of tropical forests. She is on the board of directors of Pesticide Action Network and Human Rights Advocates.

Deborah Root teaches art history at the Ontario College of Art and critical theory in the Faculty of Architecture at the University of Toronto. She received her Ph.D. in social and political thought from York University in 1990. She is the author of *Cannibal Culture: Art, Appropriation, and the Commodification of Difference* (Westview Press, 1995) and numerous articles on the politics and epistemology of cultural difference in colonial contexts. She is currently working on a project on the iconography of imperial terror.

Anthony Seeger is an anthropologist, ethnomusicologist, archivist, and recording company executive. He received his B.A. from Harvard University and his M.A. and Ph.D. from the University of Chicago. A specialist in the music, cosmology, and social organization of lowland South American Indians, he is the author of four books and over fifty articles on these topics. He served as director of the Indiana University Archives of Traditional Music and since 1988 has been curator and director of Smithsonian/ Folkways Recordings.

Lynn S. Teague is curator of archaeology at the Arizona State Museum, University of Tucson. She is a specialist in cultural resource management and serves as Arizona's repatriation coordinator.

Bruce Ziff is a professor of law at the University of Alberta in Edmonton. He has written extensively in the fields of family law and property law. He is the author of

The Matrimonial Home (Alberta Law Reform Institute, 1995) and *Principles of Property Law*, 2d ed. (Carswell, 1996), the leading text on the Canadian law of property. Currently, he is engaged in a project to develop land law reforms in Ukraine. He is also the founder and editor in chief of *The Electronic Easement: A Property Law Web Site*.

Index

aboriginal, *see* Native
aesthetics, 19, 24
affirmative action, 115, 116, 200
African Americans: attitude of white America toward, 32–33, 34–35, 37–39, 44; culture of, 33, 37, 87–88; material advantage, deprivation of, 39, 49; music (*see* African-American music); racism against (*see* racism); segregation of, 36; social position of, 99–100; sociostructural isolation of, 33; voice of, 100; writers, 100, 102, 104–105
African-American music, 2, 31–51; appropriation of, 21, 31–51; be-boppers, 42; blues, 36, 37; boogie-woogie, 42–43; call-response rhythmicity in, 44; and "chitlin circuit," 42; contribution to American musical culture of, 32, 34–35; Creole tradition of, 36; diffusion of, 37–39, 47; dilution of, 38–39; disproportionate rewards to white musicians in, 39, 44, 49; dissociation from Black culture of, 37–39, 41–43, 44, 49; evolution of, 32, 34, 35–37; gospel, 44;

hip-hop, 46; improvisation and, 42; influence of Euro-American culture on, 32, 37; influence on European and American music of, 35, 36–37, 38, 48; instruments, use of, 36–37; and innovation, 35–37; jazz, 34, 35, 36–37, 38, 39, 40–41, 42, 47, 48, 51n50, 114; jump-blues, 42; Motown, 44; oral tradition of, 36–37; ragtime, 34–35, 36, 38; rap, 46, 138, 140; record companies and, 43; rhythm and blues, 43–44, 45, 47; rhythms of, 34, 35, 36–37, 42, 43; separation of aesthetic and experiential dimensions in, 38; soul music, 44, 45; symphonic jazz, 38, 44. *See also* African musical tradition
African musical tradition, 36–37, 41, 42
agricultural value, 260–262
AIDS, 10–11
American Anthropological Association Principles of Professional Responsibility, 246–247
American Indian Religious Freedom Act (AIRFA), 295

identity politics, 10–11, 87
imagination, 97, 102–103
imperialism, 12, 137, 148
Indian agents, 123, 207
indigenous: definition of, 278n1; knowledge, 19, 23; music, 21. *See also* Native
intellectual property, 4, 14, 19, 90, 93,
142, 255, 276, 285n79, 286n85; and
contracts, 274–275; control over, 272–
273, 276; expansion of, 271–273; law
of, 14, 77, 82, 86, 223n91, 266; multilateral agreements on, 276; protection
of, 262–263
International Council for Traditional
Music, 53–54
interpretation, 153–154
intertextuality, 4
Ives, Charles, 35

James, Harry, 41, 47
Janvier, Alex, 124, 125, 128
jazz, *see* African-American music: jazz
Jenkins, Henry, 3
Jim Crow, 36, 41
Jones, Leroi, 42
Joplin, Scott, 48

kandé, 54–55, 59. *See also* Suyá Indians
King, Martin Luther, 202, 212, 219n39
Kinsella, W. P., 2
Knight, Gladys, and the Pips, 45
knowledge, rights to, 269
Krupa, Gene, 47
Kushner, Tony, 10

Laine, "Papa" Jack, 35
Lakota, 201, 211, 214, 215
land claims, *see* Native Canadians: and land
claims
law, 143, 144; colonial, 143; common, 16,
203; customary (*see* Native: customary
law); entertainment, 52–53. *See also*
copyright; intellectual property: law of;
patent; tribal courts
Lawrence, Margaret, 107
Lennon, John, 40
Little Richard, 43, 44
Lomax, John A., 61
Long, Shorty, 45
Lunceford, Jimmy, 40

Mataatua Declaration, 247–248, 308
material advantage, deprivation of, 14–15,
24, 39, 49, 62, 64–65, 117, 122, 262
mediation and mediators, 152–153, 155,
156, 159, 160, 161, 162
Meech Lake, 116
Métis, 81, 89, 162–164
Mexica, 178–179, 180, 182
Miller, Glenn, 40, 47
Montecuhzoma, 172, 174
Moore, George W., 34
Morrisseau, Norval, 124
Morton, Ferdinand "Jelly Roll," 38, 47,
48
Moten, Bennie, 42, 47
MTV, 45
multiculturalism, 77, 80, 138, 139, 140,
144
museums: collection of Native artifacts,
238–243; obligations of (*see* Native
American Graves Protection and Repatriation Act [NAGPRA]: and museums); relations with Native communities, 292–296, 298–299, 301, 303,
306, 311n14
music, 52–67; appropriation of, 52–65 (*see
also* African-American music: appropriation of); copyright (*see* copyright);
ethics of intercultural use of, 64–65;
ownership of, 53–56, 57, 63–65; postwar popular, 43–46; recording of, 56–
61; sampling, 61. *See also* ethnomusicology; Suyá Indians

Nahua, 2, 22, 152, 153, 169–189; appropriation of Spanish culture, 170–173,
181, 182; appropriation of Spanish-style
administration, 184; appropriation of
voice of Other, 187; historical consciousness of, 173–174; image of the
Other, 172–173, 186; language
(Nahuatl), 183–189; limited perspective
of, 172–173; literacy of, 181–189;
moral and political discourses of, 170–
173; notaries, 183–184; religion, 171;
underestimation of Spanish threat, 172–
173
national culture as property, 84
National Gallery of Canada, 129
national heritage, 3

Parker, Charlie, 42
Parthenon Marbles, 1, 4, 13, 18, 240
patent, 14, 19, 263–266, 281n32, 281n33,
   281n34, 282n40, 282n47, 286n85
Perkins, Pinetop, 13
"people of color," 109, 112, 120
Plato, 155
Poitras, Jane Ash, 125, 129
political correctness, 200
possession, nonrivalrous, 4
possessive individualism, 88–89, 91, 92,
   142
postcolonialism, 80, 93, 137, 139, 141,
   161; and appropriation, 155–157; and
   postmodernism, 158–161
postcolonial law, 143
postmodernism, 141
Presley, Elvis, 40, 43
Primitivism, 85
privilege, 100–101, 105–106, 119
property rights, 18, 20, 86, 198, 206, 296–
   297; law of, 15, 18, 76, 142–143 (see
   also law). See also cultural property; intellectual property
Pueblos, 208

Quebec, 84. See also francophone, Canadian
Quetzalcoatl, 174, 175, 180

racism, 22, 34, 86, 87, 91, 97–107, 110–
   111, 113–116, 128, 129, 132, 164, 227,
   228, 230; institutionalized, 115; privileging of, 98; in writing/publishing,
   104–107
ragtime, see African-American music: ragtime
Rainey, Ma, 45
realism, 104; magic, 97, 103–104
Red River, 162
Redmon, Don, 40, 47
repatriation legislation, 291
Riel, Louis, 162–164
riffing, 47
right of publicity, 211–212
rights, 3, 53, 57, 58, 65, 92
rock and roll, 43–44, 46
Romanticism, 22, 75–78, 82, 86, 87, 91,
   142

royalty fee, 20, 59, 60, 62–63, 85, 86, 88,
   95n42, 126, 274–275, 284n71

sacred practices, 23
Said, Edward, 12, 17, 159–161
Saturday Night Fever, 45
scientific and technical knowledge of indigenous and local communities, 256–
   259; appropriation of, 259–269; and biological diversity, 259; and biological
   resources, 258; and conservation of
   plants, 261; contracts for, 274–275; and
   genetic resources, 258; and landraces,
   260, 261, 262, 280n27; patentability of,
   263–266; and use of plants, 256–257;
   women's role in, 261
seed banks, 255, 260, 266–269
Shakespeare, William, 139–140, 157
Shaw, Artie, 40, 47
Sioux, 196, 201, 203
Smith, Bessie, 45
Socrates, 155
solidarity politics, 232
sovereign claims, 24; failure to recognize,
   15–16
Spanish: colonization, 169–189; influence
   on Nahua (see Nahua); moral and political discourses, 171, 186
stereotypes, 106, 125, 198, 227
stewardship, 12–14, 19, 24
stories, 71–72, 112–113, 120, 261
Stravinsky, Igor, 35
Sula, 177–179, 181
Suyá Indians, 54–59, 62–65; "Big Turtle
   Song," 60–61, 62; collective songs, 55–
   56; curing invocations, 56; individual
   songs, 55; owner/controller, 54–56, 58,
   59, 66n8, 66n9; person-without-spirit,
   55, 59, 66n9; shout-songs, 55
swastika, 12
sweat-lodge ceremony, see Native Canadians: and sweat-lodge ceremony
swing bands, 40, 42, 47

target marketing, 205
Taylor, Charles, 11–12
Teton, Juan, 175, 176
textual poaching, 3
"This Land Is Your Land," 60

Tohono O'odham Indian Nation (Papago), 313–320; and Arizona State Museum, Norton Allen Collection, 313, 314, 315–320; Cultural Preservation Committee, 314, 317; Hohokan artifacts of, 313, 315–316; and repatriation of property, 313, 314
tolerance, 119, 121n4
Tomorrow Tamer, The (Lawrence), 107
Trade-Related Intellectual Property Rights (TRIPs) Agreement, 263–265, 271
trademark, 14–15, 19, 75, 207, 223n91
traditional community: characteristics of, 277; definition of, 278n1; lack of political voice of, 277; role of, 277
translatio imperii, 145
Travolta, John, 45

UNESCO Convention on the Means of Prohibiting and Preventing the Illicit Import, Export, and Transfer of Ownership of Cultural Property (1970), 18, 238–239, 252, 292–293, 296, 306
United Nations Subcommittee on Prevention of Discrimination and Protection of Minorities Draft Declaration on the

Rights of Indigenous Peoples, 251, 252, 270–271

values, *see* culture

Waldron, Jeremy, 9
Walker, Junior, and the All-Stars, 45
whites, 227; artists, 128; counterculture, 229; guilt of, 233n7; "Indians," 225–233; society, 109–110; writers, 97, 98, 101, 102, 103, 105–106
Whiteman, Paul, 38–39, 44, 45
Western democracies, 99
Williams, Patricia, 20
Wolverines, 39
women, 99, 100, 103, 105, 106, 261; role in innovation, 261; voice of, 99
World Intellectual Property Organisation (WIPO), 19
World Trade Organization (WTO), 262, 263
writer, 76–77, 82, 85, 97–107. *See also* Orientalism; Romanticism
Writers' Union of Canada, 17–18, 79, 97, 104–105

Young, Lester, 42
YoungMan, Alfred, 125